Trees and Shrubs for the Southwest

Trees and Shrubs for the
SOUTHWEST

Woody Plants for Arid Gardens

MARY IRISH
with photographs by Gary Irish

TIMBER PRESS
Portland · London

Frontispiece: *Acacia farnesiana* (sweet acacia)

Photographs by Gary Irish unless otherwise noted.

Published in 2008 by Timber Press, Inc.

The Haseltine Building
133 S.W. Second Avenue, Suite 450
Portland, Oregon 97204-3527
www.timberpress.com

2 The Quadrant
135 Salusbury Road
London NW6 6RJ
www.timberpress.co.uk

Library of Congress
Cataloging-in-Publication Data

Irish, Mary, 1949–
    Trees and shrubs for the Southwest: woody plants for arid gardens/Mary Irish.
        p. cm.
    Includes bibliographical references and index.
    ISBN-13: 978-0-88192-905-8 (alk. paper)
    1. Ornamental trees—Southwestern States.
2. Ornamental shrubs—Southwestern States.
3. Arid regions plants—Southwestern States.
I. Title.
    SB435.52.S69I75 2008
    635.9′770979—dc22   2008009643

A catalog record for this book is also available from the British Library.

Printed in China
Designed by Susan Applegate

This book is dedicated to Ed Kutac,

who labored long and hard on the plants of Austin, Texas,
and by extension the western Hill Country and the southern plains.
He published about birds, but he found another great love in plants.

During the course of writing this book,
I was the happy recipient of most of his formidable botanical library.
I have consulted and used these books,
read his notes and notations,
and absorbed the records he made.

We came to plants in separate ways,
but the root of it all for both of us was in the farms of central Texas,
where we both grew up around people who grew what they ate
and noticed what grew around them.

Tecoma stans (yellowbells)

Contents

Prosopis chilensis (Chilean mesquite)

Acknowledgments

It always takes the help of a fleet of friends, associates, and colleagues to bring a book like this to life. Some of them don't even know how much they helped over the years; others are undoubtedly clearer about their contribution. But they all made me look at woody plants and palms with interest and excitement, and I thank them all. Specifically I want to make note of the invaluable contributions of John Eisenhower, Matt Johnson, Judy Mielke, Terry Mikel, Jeff Novakovich, Steve Nuzzo, and Dennis Swartzell, as well as the staffs of AridZone Trees, Desert Tree Farm, Desert Trees, and Mountain States Wholesale Nursery. And no one contributes more for less public recognition than Gary Irish, who is the mainstay of our shared life, garden, and projects like this.

9

Caesalpinia mexicana (Mexican bird of paradise)

Introduction

The American Southwest is new territory for many of its residents, and those who begin a garden or search for plants for their gardens often find it a daunting experience. I subscribe to the view that the key to successful gardening, regardless of location, is to understand the conditions under which you garden and to find species that accommodate those conditions with ease. These guidelines are crucial in a harsh and exacting climate like the dry, hot parts of the American Southwest.

Choosing Species for the Southwest

This book offers a selection of species that will satisfy the needs of gardeners in the arid and semiarid areas of the Southwest who are seeking attractive woody plants that can withstand the region's intense heat, alkaline soils, and meager rainfall. You will find descriptions and photographs of the species in Chapter 3, Plant Profiles. These species thrive without lots of supplemental water and extra care. It sounds like the dream of all gardeners—perfect plants with minimal effort—but these species do indeed have long-lasting beauty and high tolerance for local conditions, and they require only modest investments in water and care.

Many of the species in this book are native to the region. Native species come ably equipped to deal with the particular growing conditions of the area and are relatively immune to anything an arid or semiarid climate offers. In addition, many of these species grow well in dry but less severely hot areas where they need even less watering than they do in the deserts.

I have also included species from other arid parts of the world, particularly arid parts of central and western Australia and the Chihuahuan Desert areas of Mexico. And I have included species from semiarid shrub lands, the dry hills of the Mediterranean, and the arid grasslands of the interior of southern Africa. The particulars of their care are found in the species accounts of Chapter 3. These species were included because they have proven themselves to be well adapted to the rigors of the low-elevation, arid regions of the Southwest with its alkaline soils, high heat, and sparse and erratic rainfall.

The term *drought tolerant*, often used in the Southwest, can be misleading. The drought tolerance of any species is dependent on the particular place where it is grown. This is because the rate of evapotranspiration in any given area varies widely depending on the temperature and relative humidity of that area. The dry air of Phoenix or of the Palm Springs area, for example, sucks water away from plants considerably more rapidly than the conditions of higher humidity found in southern Arizona or central Texas. So the same species requires more water to stay fit in the former areas than it does in the latter.

For this book I discuss drought tolerance in several ways. Species that are *moderately drought tolerant* are those that need weekly watering in the summer in the hottest deserts but much less watering when the temperatures are less severe or the humidity is increased. Species are described as being *highly drought tolerant* when they live on either natural rainfall or on supplemental watering no more than two times a month in the summer regardless of where they are planted. For those species that are able to live on natural rainfall in the hottest deserts, or with irrigation once a month or less, I used the term *extremely drought tolerant*.

To grow a garden entirely on natural rainfall, particularly in the deserts, requires a shift in expectations. Woody plants, like creosote (*Larrea tridentata*) or palo verdes (*Parkinsonia* spp.), survive on natural rainfall even in the hottest desert, but their growth rates are much slower and they often lose a significant proportion of their leaves for much of year. Although natural, this denuded appearance is not the look most gardeners want to achieve, so some supplemental watering is usually desirable. The trick is to make watering as minimal and infrequent as possible and still have a luscious-looking plant. More details for watering particular species are provided in the plant profiles in Chapter 3.

When you consider the twin perils of continuous population growth in this rapidly developing region—the potential for a protracted regional drought and the increasing reliance on diminishing water supplies—it makes great sense to choose woody plants, especially trees, that use as little water as possible. With water becoming an increasingly precious commodity, it is incumbent on all of us who live and garden in the arid Southwest to use species that do not place an unbearable strain on our environment. And we can do this without giving up the glorious gardens we all want.

In addition, using species that are native to the region in your garden enhances the close connection that I believe all gardens ought to have with the natural landscape that surrounds them. Generous use of native species offers a strong sense of place, even in a dense urban area, while still being able to maintain flair and originality.

What Is a Tree or a Shrub?

For the purpose of this book I subscribe to the classic definitions of tree and shrub. A tree is a woody plant with a strong, persistent central leader or stem from which secondary branches arise; a shrub is a woody plant with no significant central leader and with secondary branches that arise from a number of different stems.

In some desert species, however, these distinctions may fall apart. Just what is a foothills palo verde (*Parkinsonia microphylla*) or an ironwood (*Olneya tesota*)? Are they trees or the biggest shrubs in the neighborhood? Palms, also included in the book, are not woody at all but are monocots and therefore are more closely related to bulbs, grasses, and agaves. Palms have a single growing point rather than the numerous growing points in both shrubs and trees. So tree and shrub must be flexible gardening terms when referring to species of the desert Southwest.

The Region

The American Southwest is a large and variable region that extends roughly from central and western Texas through all or part of New Mexico, Arizona, Utah, Nevada, and California. This book covers the warmer parts of the Southwest, those areas below 4000 ft. (1219 m) in elevation. These areas have mild to warm winters and long, hot summers; they are arid to semiarid with low annual rainfall that comes in seasons rather than uniformly throughout the year.

I have divided the region into the same three zones established in my book *Perennials for the Southwest*: the hottest (or low-elevation) deserts, the mid-elevation deserts, and the milder areas. While the geography and climates of the region do not fall neatly into these categories, some distinctions, particularly regarding the area's heat and cold extremes, are helpful when assessing plant performance. Temperatures are given in degrees Fahrenheit, with centigrade equivalents rounded to the nearest whole number.

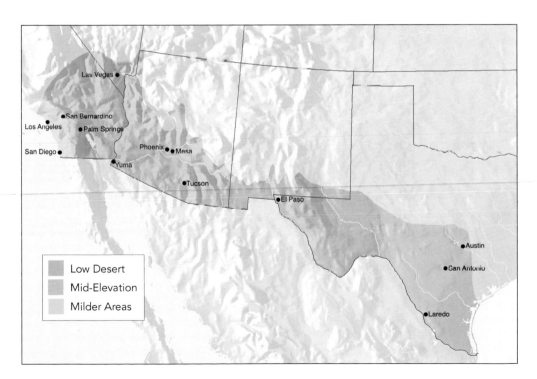

The Hottest Deserts

The hottest deserts occur in a long band from the Coachella Valley of California east to the Phoenix metropolitan area. This zone includes the cities of Palm Springs and Palm Desert, California, and their associated cities; Yuma, Arizona; the smaller cities along the Colorado River; and the Phoenix metropolitan area. The entire area is below 2500 ft. (762 m) and some of it is at or near sea level.

In the California parts of the zone, the soils are sandy and without significant amounts of nitrogen. Wind may be continuous and in some areas moves sand around to form impressive dunes. Winters are mild, often frost free, averaging 57°F (14°C), and rarely below 35°F (2°C). Summers are long and ferocious: July's average temperature is 108°F (42°C), and days over 110°F (43°C) are common and numerous. Rainfall averages 5 in. (125 mm) per year and most of it falls in the winter.

The Phoenix metropolitan area is more complex, owing both to its complicated interplay of mountains and valleys as well as to the effect of the great urban mass. Soils are variable and may be clay, loam, or mineral and rocky, and the landscape is often punctuated by extensive caliche outcrops. Caliche is an impenetrable layer of calcium carbonate left over as water evaporated from these alkaline soils during the change from wetter to drier climates. Neither water nor roots penetrate it, and thick layers near the surface are a gardening problem where they occur. Winters are mild with the January temperature averaging 43°F (6°C). While freezing temperatures may occur in some locations, they are of short duration, rarely over three or four hours. Rainfall averages 8 in. (200 mm) a year, with about a third in the winter and the rest in the summer.

Mid-elevation Deserts

The hottest deserts are enclosed by a roughly U-shaped, mid-elevation area that is still extremely arid but is milder in the summer and colder in the winter. This arc extends through the Mojave Desert, the cities of Lancaster and Palmdale, California, and Las Vegas, Nevada, as well as most of the rest of southern Nevada and a tiny corner of southwestern Utah. This desert zone lines the southern boundary of the hottest deserts in and around the city of Tucson, Arizona, and continues east in an interrupted pattern to include the cities of Las Cruces, New Mexico, and El Paso, Texas.

Elevation is important in understanding these deserts because rainfall patterns and temperature ranges are greatly affected by the interruption of higher hills and mountains that define this area. This zone, the mid-elevation deserts, includes those areas at 2000 to 4000 ft. (610 to 1219 m) in elevation and with 12 to 15 in. (305 to 381 mm) or less of average annual rainfall. As in the hottest deserts, soils vary widely from place to place from tight clays to gravelly mineral soils with caliche outcrops.

In the California and Nevada parts of the mid-elevation deserts, the winters are considerably colder than in the hottest deserts, with January highs averaging 33°F (1°C), and at least a few overnight freezes are common every year. But summers are hot, with July averaging 106°F (41°C) in Las Vegas and a bit less in the California areas, but high summer temperatures prevail for a month less than in the hottest deserts. Rainfall averages a mere 5 to 6 in. (127 to 152 mm) per year, with wide variations from year to year and most of the rain falling in the winter.

The mid-elevation deserts of Tucson and the northernmost suburbs of Phoenix have somewhat cooler winters and milder summers than the hottest deserts. The January average for Tucson is 39°F (4°C). A few freezing nights are expected every year, but periods of temperatures below freezing are of short duration. The July average temperature for Tucson is 104°F (40°C), and days over 108°F (42°C) are rare, with the summer also lasting up to a month shorter than in the hottest deserts. Rainfall is both more abundant and more reliable in southern Arizona than in the hottest deserts. Annual rainfall averages 12 in. (305 mm), with up to 60 percent of the rainfall occurring during the summer thunderstorm season and the remainder between November and March.

The desert in and around Las Cruces and El Paso as well as the Trans-Pecos region of west Texas is still markedly arid but much colder than all the other deserts of the region. While the soils have much of the same variability as the deserts to the west, they also have pockets of deep sand. Winter lows average around 25°F (−4°C) and almost half of the nights in December and January may be below freezing. Summer highs average in the high 90s°F (approximately 37°C) and are rarely up to or exceeding 105°F (41°C). Rainfall averages a scant 9 in. (229 mm) a year. Summer and winter rainy seasons are divided by long periods without rain.

Bauhinia divaricata (Mexican orchid tree)

Milder Areas

On the edges of the desert core of the region, there are areas that are distinctly different from the deserts. The western edge is just as arid but has vastly milder temperatures. The eastern edge has significantly more rainfall, but its thin, rocky soils and high summer heat create semiarid growing conditions in most years. From the perspective of most of the species in this book, the two edges are extremely congenial locations, and many of the region's best arid- and heat-adapted choices come from these areas.

The western end of the zone lies over the mountains that surround the Coachella Valley of California and includes the huge sprawl of southern California cities around Los Angeles, as well as most of Orange, San Diego, and Ventura Counties, especially the parts that are not adjacent to the Pacific Ocean. Winters are mild, with daytime highs similar to those of the hottest deserts. Freezing temperatures are uncommon in most areas, and when they occur they are of short duration, rarely lasting more than a few hours. Summer temperatures are the mildest within the region: only

the most inland areas experience temperatures at or near 100°F (38°C) for more than a day or two at a time. Rainfall averages 8 to 10 in. (203 to 254 mm) annually and almost all occurs during the winter.

The eastern edge of the milder zone includes the parts of central and southwestern Texas known as the Edwards Plateau (also called the Hill Country), the South Texas Plains, and the Rio Grande Valley. It includes the cities of Austin and San Antonio, among many others. Here soils are alkaline, and while many are thin and rocky, deep clays as well as loamy soils are scattered throughout the area. Rainfall is much more abundant than in the rest of the region, up to 35 in. (889 mm) a year, but it is far from even, both from year to year and within a year. Long dry periods lasting months may be followed by torrential rains, and extremely dry years may be followed by incredibly wet ones. Winters are similar to those around El Paso, with freezing nights common in December and January. But again, sudden and unexpected extremes are the rule. A balmy week may be followed by a spectacularly cold week. Summers are hot and frequently more humid than in the rest of the region, but temperatures rarely exceed 100°F (38°C) and then only for a day or two.

Leucophyllum frutescens (Texas ranger)

Taxonomic Note

The naming of species has baffled gardeners and horticulturists since the entire effort began. Plant scientists tend to arrange and order species according to perceived or known relationships and the names are shifted as new work emerges and suggests new relationships. It is wise to remember that botanists and systematists are well-informed people who believe they are clarifying matters, and occasionally this is so. Regardless of the nimbleness it requires, I firmly subscribe to the belief that knowing the scientific name of the species you grow and using that name fluently not only makes you more knowledgeable but also minimizes confusion. And it does help you to know that anything in the genus *Quercus*, for example, is an oak, which gives you a sense of whether it is suitable for your needs.

To establish the right and proper names for the many species in this book, I relied on a number of sources. My primary source was the *Flora of North America*, if the species was listed there. I also relied heavily on the work of the Biota of North America Program (BONAP), which is also the principal reference for the United States Department of Agriculture (USDA). In addition, for the gargantuan legume family, I doubled-checked each species with the International Legume Database (ILDIS).

Mexican, Central American, or South American species were often a bit more difficult to verify. These regions have few up-to-date floras, so I relied on the published floras of Texas, New Mexico, Arizona, California, and the Sonoran Desert, all of which are cited in the bibliography. In addition, I found invaluable Hendrickson and Johnston's unpublished manuscript "Flora of the Chihuahuan Desert" as well as regional publications from an array of Mexican botanists.

For the species native to Australia, I relied on a wide array of databases that originate out of the Australian National Botanic Garden and its partners. Those sources are also cited in the bibliography.

Cultivars and selections presented another challenge. In most cases I relied on the most widely accepted and commonly used names in the region. Readers need to be aware that in species that have been in horticulture for a long time and are used on both sides of the Atlantic and Pacific Oceans, the names of identical forms, selections, and even cultivars may be different. This situation exists usually because the plants were independently reinvented or found and a distinct local name became common.

Regarding common names, I relied on my own common sense and what I am familiar with or find in local publications and local gardening sources, as well as what I have gleaned from gardeners in the region. Most species have far too many common names and many are confusing or even ridiculous. In most cases where there was a Spanish common name, I used it only if it is widely used in the region. Some authors include a number of Indian language names for species in Mexico and countries to its south, but I resisted. Although these names are fascinating and often lovely, they didn't pass the test of common usage. The same held true for many Australian common names: they aren't all that common on this side of the ocean, so I picked the name that I thought was in common usage.

Cordia boissieri (Texas olive)

1 Using Trees and Shrubs in the Garden

Gardens rarely come into their full glory without the determined work of the gardener who creates them. Despite these efforts, all gardens are subject to specific regional soil and climatic conditions. Wise gardeners listen to the gentle guidance of the natural world around them when choosing plant species and the style in which to arrange them. This principle is particularly applicable for large plants—such as woody trees and shrubs, and palms and conifers—that frame and shape most of our gardens. Such plants are usually the largest as well as the longest-lived plants in your garden, so it pays to give ample consideration to which ones suit the garden you are trying to create, not just from the viewpoint of adaptation to the soil or the climate, but also how well they fit into the space and style of the garden.

The happy union of the right plants in the right place is what makes a garden successful and deeply satisfying. Marrying the needs of the plants and the interests of the gardener is what garden design is all about. While the individual species descriptions found in Chapter 3 tell you about the various plants' needs, I'd like to offer a few general guidelines to help you discover and understand how woody plants or palms may satisfy your garden's needs.

Style

Style is a personal statement reflecting the look or attitude that you bring to your garden. Congenial style offers a nod to the peculiarities of the local area, the surrounding buildings, and perhaps even the neighborhood. Style is the union of function with aesthetics. Trees, for example, take up lots of space and vividly set the character of a garden, so it is important to choose trees that fit the style you want to convey. Tall, symmetrical trees like Arizona cypress (*Cupressus arizonica*) or some pines strongly complement a formal planting scheme. Open-branched, spreading trees like palo brea (*Parkinsonia praecox*) or honey mesquite (*Prosopis glandulosa*) fit well with an informal, outdoor-living type of garden, while the deep curtain of an ironwood (*Olneya tesota*) creates the perfect complement to a naturalistic planting. Densely crowned species like Texas ebony (*Ebenopsis ebano*) or plateau live oak (*Quercus fusiformis*) cool down an area subjected to the brilliant light of a desert summer.

Quercus fusiformis (plateau live oak)

For many of us, trees may already inhabit our property, making for some tough choices in planning our gardens. In large parts of the region, older neighborhoods are filled with large deciduous trees reminiscent of the midwestern regions from which earlier residents came. With the recent shift in gardening sensibilities toward more natural-istic gardens, some of these species don't fit well in the Southwest. Even more of an issue is that some of these old trees are beginning to die. When mature trees are healthy, it is easier and cheaper to just work around them. But if you decide to eliminate a few or some start to decline, taking out mature trees is a big decision and the work is best done by professionals. Also, the removal of a tree either by preference, or because of death, disease, or wind damage, will dramatically alter the appearance of the garden.

When I first moved into my current home, a large Mexican palo verde (*Parkinsonia aculeata*) grew on the east side of the main patio. It provided exquisite shade and its spreading crown protected more than one bed of peren-nials from the summer sun. But after work on the septic tank beneath it cut the root sys-tem in half, a spectacular thunderstorm blew the tree over onto the patio. It wasn't just the plants that were shocked; our entire scheme for that part of the garden had to undergo a radical shift. But over time this change was a gift. It gave us room for many more plants, and it opened up an entire area of the garden for some sun-loving species I wanted to plant. I don't know if I would have ever removed such a large tree, but with it gone, I have no interest in having it back.

In new gardens, I advise gardeners to choose trees and plant them first. The trees are the arbiters of the look and feel of the garden. They define and delimit the spaces for all activities and future plantings. They eventually dictate where and how much sun and shade fall in the garden. Take your time in finding just the right tree for each spot so you won't be faced with removing a tree in the future.

Shrubs are much the same, especially large

Olneya tesota (ironwood)

ones. These plants also define space, create areas and limits inside and outside the garden, form backgrounds or boundaries, and hide or enhance views. Removal of large, well-rooted shrubs is difficult. So it is important to put them in good places the first time around.

Shade

Woody species are the dominant type of plant in arid lands, including deserts, around the world. Trees cloak the rough, dry soils of deserts, filling up the hills and valleys. They shelter the smaller and more vulnerable spe-cies, offering living space and food for most of the wildlife in the desert. They serve as a nursery for an immense range of other spe-cies. Beneath their extended branches is shade, a rare and welcome commodity in arid regions. All manner of plant and ani-mal life cluster beneath these sheltering boughs. Below a tree, the duff of discarded leaves and flowers creates an enriched soil that holds more moisture, creating a perfect place for seeds to take hold. This phenom-enon of larger plants providing a nursery for smaller ones is widespread. In the Sonoran Desert, a mythology has developed about the long-lived saguaro (*Carnegiea gigantea*) that stands as a lone sentinel in the plains, having outlived the wolfberry (*Lycium* spp.) or the palo verde (*Parkinsonia* spp.) under which it germinated.

Trees

Trees play a similar and generous role in the overall comfort of the garden. The desert sun is intense and unrelenting, creating an astonishing amount of heat and glare, day after day more or less year-round. Coupled with low humidity, which offers minimal air moisture to soften the onslaught of sunlight, shade is a necessity in a desert climate not only for our general comfort but also to expand the range of species that live in our gardens.

Shade works in two important ways. The leaves of a tree take up solar radiation from the sun, absorbing it for photosynthetic use while giving everything beneath the tree relief from the terrific heat. In addition, plants transpire, and because trees are large and have countless leaves, they transpire a lot. You don't see it, but all those leaves are exuding tiny amounts of water vapor all the time, and that vapor, too, is making the zone under the tree's boughs just a bit cooler.

Shade comes in many different versions. Mesquites (*Prosopis* spp.), palo verdes, and many legumes provide what is known as high or light, filtered shade, which is formed by breaking up the light as it passes through the throngs of tiny leaflets that make up the canopy of trees. It is almost perfect shade, uniform in its array and not so dark as to cause plants to stretch out, etiolate, or deform. Everything grows well in this kind of shade, even succulents and cacti.

Dense or deep shade is found under the limbs of larger trees, often evergreen trees like oaks and pines or shrubs like oleander (*Nerium oleander*). This type of shade is perfect for shading walls, buildings, or roofs, but species that grow beneath these larger trees must be able to tolerate reduced light.

Useful shade is not always directly underneath a plant. It may be found on the east side of a large planting that blocks the afternoon sun, making the patio or pool more comfortable in the evening. This is one of the best ways to shade a pool area: if you plant away from the pool on the west or southern side, litter won't fall into the pool and cause problems with filters and screens.

This kind of sideways shade also plays an important role in the heating and cooling of our houses. When shrubs or trees are grown near or against a southern or western wall or window, they prevent most of the sun's rays from striking the surface and transferring all that heat into the house. A wall covered by lots of woody plants may be as much as 25 degrees Fahrenheit or 14 degrees Celsius cooler than an unprotected wall. Such a differential significantly reduces the demand for air-conditioned cooling in the house.

Trees that are large enough to shade a roof have the same effect on the overall heat load of the house. In the Southwest, the conflict is continuous between the approach to building newer housing divisions where views are considered vital and the feeling in established developments where the shade provided by large trees is considered so beneficial. But if you look at old housing areas, or old desert farmhouses and ranches, you often see that the house is smothered in trees, mainly on the west and south sides, wisely prohibiting

Acacia stenophylla (shoestring acacia)

the ferocious sun from beating down on all or part of the roof for the entire day.

Many cities in the Southwest find that they are becoming hotter and hotter, particularly at night, as they become larger and more densely settled. This phenomenon is called the urban heat effect or urban heat island. Urban heat islands result from the accumulation of heat from concrete, buildings, asphalt, and other hard, heat-holding surfaces. One of the surest ways to reduce some of that heat is to plant more trees and large shrubs, especially ones native or suited to the climate. This kind of simple change is clearly important, for the overall comfort of city dwellers and to achieve reduced energy use. While much discussed, however, this simple answer to a problem—planting more trees to get increased shade—still remains unimplemented. A city as hot as Phoenix seems to have a tough time promoting trees as a shade solution. But for individual homeowners, I encourage everyone to use woody plants near southern and western windows and walls. And I look forward to the day when all public spaces in our region are under a continuous canopy.

Planting deciduous trees or shrubs is also a strategy for managing cold in the winter. In the winter, when the plants are leafless, they permit the warming rays of the gentle winter sun into the window and onto the walls, warming the house when it needs it.

Palms

Palms are widely planted in the warm winter areas of the Southwest. While rarely considered shade plants, they can provide reliable shade. But using palms for shade requires

some thought and often a different approach to planting them.

A single, 40-ft. (12.2-m) California fan palm (*Washingtonia filifera*), or any palmate-leaved palm, won't offer much shade beneath it. But a small grove of these palms will provide shade that is delightfully lush and cool. Desert palms grow naturally in generous groves, providing respite from the sun and heat of the arid lands.

The spreading crowns of date palm (*Phoenix dactylifera*) and Canary Island date palm (*Phoenix canariensis*) are large enough to provide significant shade with just one plant. But here again, a grove is elegant and creates beautiful shade that is light, airy, and inviting. Large species like these are also useful when planted at the far western end of the garden where the shade from their spreading heads will settle over a large area.

Two or three neighborhoods in Phoenix and Palm Springs are built beneath old date palm groves. The large trees are revered by the neighborhood for their high, light shade that not only shelters plants and people but also provides cooling relief for their homes. I have to wonder why such good ideas in nature are not used more often in landscaping.

Shrubs

Shrubs offer shade in a somewhat different way. Rarely are they large enough to walk under, sit under, or shelter the roof, but a hedge of any type, especially of large species, provides excellent shade on the side away from the sun. In some gardens, shrubs may be used effectively to protect a patio or a pool as well as hot walls and windows. Once again,

Washingtonia robusta (Mexican fan palm)

Cordia parvifolia (little-leaf cordia)

the principal effect is that the leaves readily absorb the radiant heat of the sun, preventing it from striking and heating the walls of the house

Establishing Boundaries

When you are starting a new garden on a barren site or considering renovating one that has been neglected, it is hard to know where to start. After deciding where the trees should go, next consider shrubs as you shape the garden. Shrubs are the plants we use chiefly for privacy and to establish boundaries along the edge of and within a garden.

Nerium oleander hedge

In identifying what kinds of shrubs you want, look first at the boundaries of the entire garden. Do you need shrubs to hide unpleasant views, or a neighbor's boat, or to conceal the garden from the window down the alley? Do you feel that your garden is too wide open, and you want a bit more privacy? If so, then a boundary or border hedge may help.

A hedge is usually thought of as a long uninterrupted line of a single species with uniform height and density. In the Phoenix area, oleander is widely used for this purpose, regardless of the size of the lot. While such hedges are common and effective, they are also uniform and can be uninteresting.

There is an old tradition, not much seen today, of the tapestry hedge. That charming name refers to a hedge of mixed species, with plants of varying sizes and heights, both deciduous and evergreen, including some with extravagant bloom and others with more cryptic flowering. Such hedges may include big woody species like Chisos rosewood (*Vauquelinia corymbosa*) or desert hackberry (*Celtis ehrenbergiana*), which can't make up their minds whether they are trees or shrubs. A tapestry or mixed hedge is a wonderful way to prevent spying eyes from accessing your garden and for enclosing the outer perimeter of the garden with interest and diversity.

Blending a mix of shrubs and trees is also especially useful when the garden borders a natural feature like a wash, a park, or a natural area. Selecting an array of woody plants, particularly ones native to the region, makes the boundary between wild land and the tamed garden less abrupt and allows the garden to seem as if it was gradually formed out of the surrounding landscape.

Hedges also work to either hide or enhance a fence. There is nothing particularly attractive about chain-link fencing, but it is often the most practical choice because it is not terribly expensive, it is relatively easy to install, and it is strong and durable. You may have inherited such a fence and it would be difficult to remove it. Such a fence can be masked perfectly by placing shrubs in front of it or behind, depending on space. Vines are the common choice for such fences, but shrubs work just as well, and grow taller than the fence where that feature is desirable. Such a planting hides the fence and makes it attractive as well.

Shrubs do more than provide privacy when used to define the borders of the entire garden. They also are a bastion against dust, grit, and noise. For gardens located on busy streets or along unpaved or dusty areas, a hedge of shrubs will trap an incredible amount of dirt on the leaves and will absorb sounds like a baffle. Within the garden, shrubs are also used to define spaces such as on a corner, so that you cannot see what is around it, or for creating a living enclosure—a garden room—that can be used as a retreat within the garden itself.

It is popular to consider gardens, or portions of gardens, as rooms. This makes abundant sense in most of the Southwest, where temperatures are ideal for outdoor living during a large portion of year. The idea is that a garden may be broken up into discrete areas, either based on uses, such as a pool area, play area, vegetable garden, and for seating, or simply for drama and interest in displaying the plantings. Even the smallest garden benefits from this principle.

Placing furniture in an area makes it a garden room even though it may not have living walls. Select spots that offer views of surrounding features, or that make an excellent place to appreciate sunrise or sunset, or where you get the best vantage of a particularly handsome blooming plant. Set out a chair or two and you instantly have a small garden room.

The most memorable gardens maintain a place for repose—at least one place, and perhaps more if the garden is large enough—where you can stop, sit, and look at the entire garden or a portion of it and delight in what has been created. A tiny garden, even just a patio, can achieve this with a small screen of shrubs that keeps out the hubbub beyond. Such a tranquil space is a grace note for any garden.

Whether you are trying to make a defined garden room or not, it is usually best not to provide the whole view of the garden the moment you come out the door. Plants of varying scale, particularly shrubs, are extremely useful in preventing the garden from giving up all its treasures in one glance. Placing a shrub right in front of your view as you enter a garden is a highly effective device. Placing large, dense shrubs or low-growing trees behind a seating area prevents you from seeing what is beyond, thereby encouraging exploration.

Shrubs help to divide the garden into a more manageable or more intriguing place. Setting a large shrub in the middle of a wide planting bed divides the bed so that one end may be planted differently from the other. A well-placed shrub may provide the background for a patio or a seating area, and if it is on the west side it may make the area more comfortable in the evenings. If you have particular areas, like a pool, a vegetable bed, or a dog run, shrubs placed within the garden are as effective as fences to hide those things from immediate view or from the most well-used parts of the garden.

Shrubs also make great accents or focal points within a garden, especially ones that have stunning bloom or exceptional features. Tall shrubs, like the summer-blooming lucky nut (*Thevetia peruviana*) or oleander, rise up over a painted wall to create a lovely scene throughout the summer. One well-placed red bird of paradise (*Caesalpinia pulcherrima*) illuminates the view down a path when you sit to have coffee on the patio in the morning. Bright red fairyduster (*Calliandra californica*) provides a light background for a view out the window and also draws in a wide range of hummingbirds for viewing.

Despite these useful roles in the garden, large shrubs can also be inhibitors to useful access. In gardens of any size, you still have to get around and find the back gate if that is where you enter or deliver the trash. So when choosing shrubs, keep in mind just how big each plant will grow if you are going to put it near a walkway or an area where people gather.

Scale

Scale is where many urban gardeners lose their minds. With plants that will be ultimately tall and wide, it is vital to consider the relationship they will have to any building. A sweet little 5-ft. (1.5-m) pine that began as a Christmas tree now towers over a two-story house at maturity. The blue palo verde (*Parkinsonia florida*) that is a lean wand in a container will grow and spread to encompass the entire reach of a good-sized patio.

It is important to truly consider how big the tree, shrub, palm, or pine is going to grow, both in height and girth. I am deeply chagrined every time I see a Canary Island date palm nestled against the doorway of a house, filling the space nicely now but destined to burst through the eaves one day. There is a rubber tree (*Ficus elastica*) down the street that I am sure was an enchanting thing by the door when it was young but is now a tortured, twisted thug that is twice the size of the house. Considering how much plants really do grow, it is best to give them ample room when you plant them. And yet, you say, the hard part is that the 20 ft. (6.1 m) or more that you need to give large shade trees can make that area of the garden look empty at first.

I have never been a fan of overplanting and then getting rid of things later when they impinge on each other. It seems such a waste. So my advice is, plant as if the plants are old and space them for their maturity, not their present youth. There is a garden near my house that I call the arboretum. It was planted about eight years ago in a space that is roughly 30 by 40 ft. (9.1 by 12.2 m). The homeowner planted five Afghan pines (*Pinus eldarica*), five blue palo verdes, six California fan palms, two Italian cypress (*Cupressus sempervirens*), and at least two South American mesquites (*Prosopis* spp.). These plants grew so that you now cannot see the shape of any individual, and they have not attained their natural form because they are too tightly spaced. Already removals have begun, and it painful to witness such wonderful plants being yanked out simply because the gardener did not plan for the future. If you do not have the patience for the spacing big plants need, fill in with small perennials, succulents, or annuals, all of which are easily moved later when the trees or shrubs overtake them.

Acknowledging growth is even more vital for the vertical height of a tree or large shrub. Power companies do not practice pruning; they simply run along their right of way removing everything that's too high. This type of shearing is ruinous to trees, destroying not only their beauty but their health. It becomes an unlucky choice to plant a species that will be too large for its location.

Cold

Many cities in the Southwest are built in and around small hills and mountains. Therefore, gardens in these areas often have a lot of elevation change in a small area. Even if your particular garden does not have much relief, the neighborhood probably does. These small hills and valleys create an array of microclimates, often only feet from each other. As cold moves downhill, it collects and sinks into the recesses of the garden until stopped by walls, where it collects and remains. For species that barely tolerate cold weather, whether they are woody or not, these are lethal locations. Such species, often from tropical areas, need to be planted in the highest part of the garden to avoid the ravages of intermittent cold weather.

Large plants also form microclimates beneath and around them, offering a place with additional warmth in the garden. In much of the region, freezing nights are the result of radiant cooling. So the space under the limbs of a large, particularly evergreen, tree prevents the rapid rise of warm air, forcing it back down to the earth, and keeping the temperature under the tree slightly higher than in open ground. I saw this effect most vividly some years ago when I worked at the Desert Botanical Garden in Phoenix. I placed a number of potted aloes that would be sold at a plant sale under a huge mesquite. These plants were pups lifted from plants growing in an open, exposed location in the garden. One morning after a hard freeze, I looked with concern at the potted plants, but they had no damage at all. However, the ones in the open were almost destroyed by the same cold weather.

Attracting Wildlife

Rich is the garden that provides a home to a wide array of life beyond our own. The singing and merry antics of birds, the delicate attentions of butterflies, the rapid-fire hunting of lizards, and the endless parade of nearly invisible insects that make your garden their home add not only to our enjoyment but also succor the health of the garden.

Lycium (wolfberry) with butterfly

These are the pollinators and the pest controllers, all working hard to eat and raise their young. Watching a hunting lizard is more than just a lesson in lizard tactics; it is witness to the fragile balance that changes a garden from being a static, beautiful environment to a bustling center of life.

While woody plants support and encourage a great abundance of wildlife, it is the birds that are the most visible and usually the easiest to welcome. Birds are looking for three things in our gardens: shelter, including nest sites, food, and water. They are alert to the presence of potential predators, and I count on them to raise the alarm when the gopher snake is out and about. Birds are satisfied when they have a suitable place to preen, forage, and raise their young and a handy place to hide when necessary. They pollinate countless species while foraging for food and consume an abundance of insects, some of which the garden is best off without.

Shrubs and trees offer excellent shelter for birds. Using woody plants of varying heights and density in your garden provides suitable spots for a wide range of species. Doves prefer an overnight roost that is high, well over our heads. The sturdy limbs of mesquite, palo verde, or desert fern (*Lysiloma watsonii*) are ideal. Quail look to the same sort of trees to sleep in, especially large mesquite, but demand big shrubs, ideally with limbs to the ground, for both nesting and daytime resting. Cardinals, mockingbirds, and towhees prefer to nest at about head height, deep inside a dense, tangled shrub. Cactus wrens, thrashers, and verdin prefer trees or shrubs with plenty of thorns and complicated branching like Texas ebony or graythorn (*Zizyphus obtusifolia*).

Diversity is the key to providing plenty of food plants that will encourage a wide range of bird life in the garden. Goldfinches, sparrows, and house finches are seedeaters; using plenty of bee bush (*Aloysia gratissima*) entices them into the garden. Doves, thrashers, wrens, mockingbirds, and cardinals eat a lot of fruit from the wolfberry, desert hackberry, or bitter condalia (*Condalia globosa*), to name just a few. Verdin cannot resist the fruit of creosote (*Larrea tridentata*), and a Say's phoebe used to come to my garden specifically for the fruit of my firebush (*Hamelia patens*).

Gardens Near a Natural Area

If you are fortunate enough to have a natural area adjacent to your garden, whether it is a park, a preserve, or the endless wildness of public lands, it is important to consider both the garden and the wild area in your plant selection. When living with the natural world as your next-door neighbor, the gardener faces both ecologically practical considerations and aesthetic concerns.

The first and most important consideration is to forego planting any invasive species—species known or suspected to be able to escape and grow on their own without the intervention or attention of people. These species include the grasses like buffel grass (*Pennisetum ciliare*) and fountain grass (*Pennisetum setaceum*), or annual weeds like African daisy (*Dimorphotheca* sp.), as well as feathery cassia (*Senna artemisioides*) and Mexican palo verde. Other regions have their own potent pests and it is wise to know what they are.

What qualifies as a pest species is usually a local situation; rare indeed is the species that is a pest no matter where it grows. Check with the local County Extension or counseling program or native plant society for lists of what species are known or suspected to be pests in your area. Woody species that escape and become ecological thugs are the exception rather than the rule in ornamental plants. In addition, problem plants are not universally problematic in all areas: a tame, responsible ornamental in one region can be a monster in another region. Knowing which plants are problems or pests will save you a lot of grief and will spare your neighboring natural area even more.

Striking a balance between the style of your garden and the surrounding landscape is a matter of both design and plant selection. When not only the view but the natural area itself is literally part of the visual space of the garden, it is best to try to blend them together. In many cases the easiest way to

achieve balance between a planted space and a natural space is to incorporate many of the species growing naturally into the garden boundary so there is a blurred line between the two rather than an abrupt edge. Use a mix of species on the edge of your property, letting some of the toughest, most native trees, perennials, or shrubs fade into the natural landscape. Reserve the most exotic and least visually compatible species for parts of the garden nearest the house or areas inside courtyards and enclosed places. In this way your garden and the wildness beyond it blend gracefully, preserving the visual grandeur of the setting and incorporating it into the overall scheme of your garden.

To achieve a good blend between your garden and an adjacent natural area, inventory the views that are particularly exciting. Take special note of areas in the garden that allow for the spectacle of a sunset or approaching storms, so they are an integral part of your garden. Set up seating areas intended only for those times when you need to gaze at the garden that is never tended.

Chilopsis linearis (desert willow)

Mixed planting of firebush (*Hamelia patens*),
Texas olive (*Cordia boissieri*), and yellowbells
(*Tecoma stans*) in the back and cape plumbago
(*Plumbago articulata*) in the front.

2 Care and Cultivation

Woody plants are an investment in a garden, installing permanence and a solid foundation wherever they are grown. These plants are not the fillers of space, although they do that as well, but the architects of space, defining and creating not only the amount of room left after they mature but the character and style of the garden itself.

Almost all woody plants and many palms live a long time, often much longer than a gardener's life span. Like us they grow quickly in youth, often outrageously so, then settle into a calmer middle life, spreading out to become an immutable feature of the life of the garden. These species are rugged, well suited to the rigors of arid conditions—in many cases extreme desert conditions—but as for all living things, good care helps them to have a long, healthy life.

Good care of woody plants begins early and shifts and modifies over time as they age. All plants, even local natives, require attentive care when they are first planted and for the first few years thereafter. The great payoff with well-adapted species is their ease of care and modest cultural requirements as they age. Light care of such splendidly adapted plants extends their life and keeps them vigorous and looking their best even in dire conditions. Success hinges on their getting a good start, and that begins with where you intend to plant them in your garden.

Soil

Soil is the heart and soul of a garden. Soil is where all the success of the garden begins and where most failures originate. The more you understand your soil and the part it plays in the overall success of the plants in your garden, the more your garden will reward you. Plants and soil are interwoven into an elegant living system, one depending on the other, and the more we encourage each to play its role well, the more satisfying and successful the garden becomes.

In simplest terms, the duty of soil is to provide a place for plants to grow. Root systems thread through the soil, holding plants upright and in place, and they support the plant throughout its life. Roots are also the conduit through which the plant absorbs the water, air, minerals, and nutrients available in the soil that are vital for photosynthesis. This absorption is greatly enhanced, in some cases solely performed, by a range of fungi we know as mycorrhizal fungi.

Soil is not one uniform material—an inert

substance into which we place plants. It is a cacophony of living and nonliving elements blending and melding together to create the living organism that we call soil. Soil has two basic materials, one mineral and the other organic, and it is colonized by a wide range of insects, invertebrates, worms, bacteria, and fungi.

The organic component of soil is a stew of fallen leaves, spent flowers, dead branches, seeds and their husks, rotting fruit, and ultimately the entire plant when it dies. This vegetable conglomeration combines with the residue left over from the decay of all the animals—tiny and large—that have lived among the rocks and plants. All of this organic matter is present in various states of decay, a situation that in turn provides a food-filled haven for the hordes of fungi, bacteria, worms, and other invertebrates, as well as for insects and their larvae that depend on decaying matter for their food. These creatures not only eat up the residue; by working it through their minute digestive systems, they transform nutrients into solutions and chemical formats that are easily taken up by plants. These elements all function like a complex metropolitan area with a spectacular internal order where everything is interconnected and interdependent. The soil's health and vigor is dependent on a careful balance and its steady replenishment. Without doubt, soil is one of the most breathtaking of all natural systems and, unlike oceans, forests, or deserts, most of the activity of the system happens outside our view.

The mineral composition of any soil is derived from the rocks of the region. Over thousands of years, wind and water wear down rocks into ever-smaller pieces. Bits of the rock, which may have been previously formed from volcanoes, sedimentation, or the metamorphosing action of pressure and movement, are worn down into increasingly smaller fragments from boulder to cobbles, gravel to sand. Eventually the particles become small enough to unite with the organic parts. This aggregation transforms an inert pebble into a soil particle.

Most of the current Southwest was once part of a huge ocean that spread from modern-day Texas to the eastern half of California. Eventually the ocean receded, leaving a complicated array of abandoned shorelines, sand dunes, coves, estuaries, and isolated lakes. There, relicts became the foundation of the areas with deep sandy soils. A few locales, particularly in southern California and New Mexico, have vast sand deposits overlying the limestone, another remnant of long lost lakes. While these soils offer wonderful drainage, they contribute little else and are so poorly consolidated, they shift and move like the dunes they are. The water and its creatures have disappeared, but immense layers of the shells of tiny, unimaginably numerous sea creatures piled up. Gradually the calcium in the shells coalesced and was transformed into an undercoating of the limestone and other forms of so-called chalky or alkaline rock that lie beneath the region today.

Over time these huge beds of shells became rock, were covered with other rock formations, and then were uplifted, tilted, or bent, and finally began to erode. These vast limestone formations underlie the hills and mountains of region when exposed from the rocky, tumbled hillsides so common in the region. In many parts of the region, these exposed limestone beds are near the surface, and the soil that sits atop them is merely a thin patina.

In some parts of the region the limestone base has been covered, often to great depth, by the debris that floated off the mountains as the wind and water wore down the mountains. In these areas there are tight clay soils, which are probably the most difficult soils to work with because they combine the tendency of clay to hold too much moisture, stay cold, and resist easy cultivation, as well as being highly alkaline.

In other parts of the region, water percolated through these chalky soils, especially in areas that were flat. As the climate dried out and the soil moisture continued to evaporate, calcium carbonate within the soil precipitated, hardened, and over time formed the rock we know as caliche. Caliche may be found in a thick layer that is impenetrable by either pick or roots, or and it may be fractured and fragmented into a rocky, rough-looking, but usable soil.

As the southwestern United States has dried out over time, the organic debris that falls on the ground races through the decomposition process, leaving only minimal residual nitrogen in the soil. The increasing aridity of the region has also reduced the total number of species growing in a given area, thereby reducing the total amount of organic matter. Together, these two forces left most of the region—particularly the deserts—with beautifully drained soils, rich in all nutrients and minerals except nitrogen.

What this means to a Southwest gardener is that in order to grow more than just the species that are locally native, you must familiarize yourself with the soil that you inherit and find species that can grow well in it. The soils in the region grow a vibrant mix of species; it is when we start trying to accommodate newcomers—our garden plants—that the fundamental nature of the soil and our gardening desires come into conflict. Making a match between an idealized garden soil and what you find in your particular garden requires an understanding of the soil, selection of species that thrive within its parameters, and a few techniques to gently modify its limitations. Here are three strategies that may help.

First, grow an abundance of local or regional natives. Most of these species are already suited to the soils of your garden and do not need arduous soil-building to grow them well. Simply being native, however, does not mean that a species will thrive in your rocky, dry soil if it comes from the banks of creeks, or that a species that lives only in gravelly washes will do well in your thick clay soils. In addition, species that grow in extreme soil conditions or that come from odd or rare soil types, like gypsum fields or serpentine hills, may present huge challenges when grown outside those soils. Most species, even those from desert or arid regions, are less demanding, thriving in soils with a pH from 6 to 8.

Second, to expand your choices beyond local or regional natives, choose species from areas of the world that have analogous soil conditions. The most critical criterion when choosing species from other regions is to select ones that accommodate to the inherent alkalinity of our region's soils.

Third, learn to live with the soil you have. If you live in the Southwest, you garden in the Southwest. Naturally, there is room for modest improvement, and in this region that means the introduction of more organic matter either as mulch or compost, the holy grail of gardening.

Another common condition found throughout the region is soil compaction, usually the result of human activities. In countless new housing developments, it is routine practice to scrap all vegetation, including the top layer of soil, from the site, then grade the site and build the house. Building alone causes violent disruption; the soils become greatly compacted with heavy equipment rolling over them time and again. But the loss of the top layers of soil is the loss of most of the life of the soil. Homeowners in new subdivisions often find that they have considerable difficulty getting new plantings to grow well.

There are two ways to bring the soil back to life when it has been deeply disturbed in this way: add copious amounts of organic matter in the form of compost, manures, clippings, or mulch to renew and encourage the swarm of soil microorganisms that are vital to a healthy soil; and grow things as quickly as possible in the soil. If you aren't ready to plant a full-fledged garden, spread a wide array of annuals that fill in quickly and aid in bringing in the invisible organisms that the soil needs to come back to life.

Planting

Placement

All shrubs, trees, palms, and pines will grow considerably larger than they are in the container you bring home from the nursery. So before you consider putting in a shrub,

and especially a tree, look around and look up, and consider its ultimate size. If a tree is able to spread to 30 ft. (9.1 m), that means it spreads at least 15 ft. (4.6 m) from the trunk on each side. Use a measuring tape and measure that point, and don't forget to look up. If there are power lines or other obstructions above the direct path of growth, there will come a day of reckoning. If the power lines are not entirely within your property, the local utility will be along someday to either top or shear your tree in a quick but ugly way. It is considerably wiser, and less costly, to either give up choosing a tree for such a location, or choose one that will not grow large enough to cause problems with power lines.

Timing

The plant profiles in Chapter 3 provide recommended times for planting particular species. A few general guidelines that apply to all woody plants and palms follow.

SPRING PLANTING Species that are frost sensitive and grow most actively when it is warm, like red bird of paradise (*Caesalpinia pulcherrima*), firebush (*Hamelia patens*), or yellowbells (*Tecoma stans*), are best planted in the spring. Plant as early as possible in the spring, but be certain that all danger of frost is past. Many of these species are dormant or deciduous in the winter. In that case they transplant better if you wait until the buds are formed or just beginning to break. This gives the plant ample time to establish a root system before both its chief growing season and the rigors of a desert summer.

In the hottest deserts, spring planting begins as early as February and continues through April. In mid-elevation deserts, it

Leucophyllum laevigatum (Chihuahuan rain sage)

begins about a month later and extends for about another month, depending on temperatures. In the milder areas of the region, push everything up yet another month.

SUMMER PLANTING While most container-grown woody plants and lots of cold-tender species may be planted in the summer, that season is a difficult time for all newly planted plants, particularly in the hottest deserts. For the home garden, I urge restraint and believe it is best to resist planting after mid-May. High heat coupled with extremely low humidity makes summer a demanding time to plant almost anything in the hottest deserts and much of the mid-elevation deserts

as well. You can resume planting of warm-season ornamentals when the summer rainy season appears, the humidity increases, and overall temperatures decrease.

Palms are the great exception to this rule. No matter which palm species you choose, all palms prefer to be planted in warm to hot soils. These plants do not establish well in cool soils, and winter planting is doomed. Palms are not actively growing during most of the cool season, and new plants with insecure root systems may rot out quickly. For this group, summer is definitely the preferred time to plant. In the hottest deserts, summer planting begins as early as April and extends through late August or early September. In the mid-elevation areas, discontinue summer planting in August, and in milder areas by the beginning of August.

FALL PLANTING In the deserts, fall is the most active and successful planting season. For woody plants, fall gives the plant a chance to establish a significant root system over the long, benign, cool growing season. Rainfall is considerably more reliable during this time of the year, further enhancing the success of the planting. The temperatures are low enough to drastically reduce the drying out or dessication that is inherent after planting because of a reduced root system.

All deciduous species are more successful when planted in the fall, and some species can be planted through the winter. The exception is cold-tender species. Resist putting in any cold-sensitive species within two months of the first expected frost date. The growth that erupts from newly established plants is particularly sensitive to cold snaps, and you greatly reduce the chances of good establishment by planting such species in the fall.

For species that are spring blooming, like redbud (*Cercis canadensis* var. *mexicana*), it is critical to plant them in the fall because they begin to grow in the fall and maintain steady growth throughout the winter. By the time they have bloomed in the spring, they are shifting into a slower growth cycle that results in a semidormant state for the summer. Because of this natural cycle, planting such species in the spring in the hottest deserts and the warmer parts of the mid-elevation deserts may result is high losses if you do not pay close attention to their care.

In the milder areas or areas with regular freezes, fall planting must be carefully considered. Species need to be winter hardy and able to withstand intermittent or late frosts in order to survive being planted in the fall in these areas. The window for fall planting in these areas is shorter, with late August and September being recommended, and spring planting is more widely recommended for most species.

In the hottest deserts, fall planting extends from September to November. In the mid-elevation areas, stop planting by early November and possibly earlier, depending on temperatures. And in the milder areas, fall planting extends only to late September or early October.

Selecting the Plant

Successful planting begins with a sturdy, healthy plant that has a well-developed root system for its size. The root systems of woody plants perform two vital functions throughout their lives: they are the anchors that hold up the plant and they conduct water and vital dissolved nutrients from the soil into the plant. When plants are growing in nurseries, usually in containers, they mainly grow young, fine, feeder roots that ideally spread and branch. While these roots are easily damaged, they also quickly regenerate. Although you cannot see through a pot (and most gardeners are not as shameless as I am about nudging the plant out of the pot to look around at the roots), there are clues that help you know a healthy choice from a doomed one.

First, the plant must be firm and secure in the pot. When you give the plant a gentle tug or push, you should get resistance. If the plant falls over, comes out in your hand, or feels loose in the soil, move on to another selection.

Second, the plant should be an appropriate size for its pot. It is a fantasy to think that, when faced with a tree in a five-gallon (20-liter) container that is 6 ft. (1.8 m) tall and one next to it that is 3 ft. (0.9 m) tall, the taller one is the bargain; that is rarely the case. The larger one may simply be wildly overgrown for the size of the pot, indicating that it has probably been in the pot too long and is also in danger of having badly formed or damaged roots.

Third, roots should be freely extended into the soil, branched, and have no circling or girdling around the stem or within the pot. If you see girdled roots, at some point in its life the roots of the plant got too crowded and began to wind around in the container, growing ever larger. Root girdling is a difficult to nearly impossible condition to correct once it has taken hold. When a plant with this condition is put in the ground, its roots may fail to spread. The plants either fail to thrive right away, remain stunted, or grow for only a short while and suddenly keel over. Avoid girdled roots, and if you find them in the plant you picked out, put it back, even if the plant is your heart's desire. Growers have adopted strategies to inhibit or arrest this problem in the nursery, including the use of copper compounds and porous containers, but you will still occasionally find potted plants with girdled roots at nurseries.

Fourth, you should never see roots coming from the bottom of the pot. At the extreme end of this condition, plants become rooted in the soil where they are sitting. This is a certain sign that the plant has been in the pot and in that location much too long. Such a plant has often grown significant roots, and when you lift it up, you rip roots out of the ground or are forced to cut them to move the pot, causing damage to the plant. Resist any plant with roots coming out of the pot and especially if the roots extend into the ground.

Fifth, select plants with as natural an appearance as possible. In most species this means that they show a strong leader and have both intact terminal shoots and juvenile branches throughout. In some species that are multitrunked, the trunks must be firmly joined with an angle of attachment that is less than 45 degrees.

Making the Hole

Begin planting by digging a hole that is as deep as the root-ball. Near the base, the width of the hole needs to be about twice the width of the root-ball. Flare out the hole as it rises to the surface so that at the top the hole is three to five times wider than the root-ball. This sloped, wok-shaped hole provides ample room for young roots to grow and spread, and it collects water at ground level and directs it down the slope to the roots.

For example, if you are planting a shrub from a five-gallon (20-liter) container that is about 12 in. (30.5 cm) deep and about 11 in. (27.9 cm) wide, then the hole should be 12 to 14 in. (30.5 to 35.6 cm) deep, about 22 in. (55.9 cm) wide at the base, and 3 to 4.5 ft. (0.9 to 1.4 m) wide at the top. The precise dimensions hinge on your ability to dig, but you always want the hole to be much wider than it is deep. And never set a plant in a hole that is exactly the width of the container.

Depending on how you dig or what kind of tool you use, the sides of a hole may sometimes end up slick and firm. It is better to rough up the sides to make them irregular and loose. The tiny roots need to spread, and

...ughing up the hole's slope makes it easier ...r them to work through the soil.

It is also a good practice to make sure the ...ottom of the hole is firm. Tamp it lightly ...ith the end of the shovel or the pot so that ...e soil is firm. This helps to prevent sinking ...ubsidence) once the hole is backfilled and ...atering begins.

In areas where caliche is a problem or you ...uspect that it might be, dig the hole to the ...ppropriate size, then fill it up with water. ...eave it for a few hours or even overnight. If all the water is not gone from the hole when left overnight, there is a bed of caliche beneath the hole. This is bad news for trees and shrubs with their large root systems. If water cannot find its way out of the hole, neither can the roots of your plant. And your

tree or shrub will be either stunted or seriously held back if planted in that spot. Find another spot, dig another hole, and try again. But you can use the first hole for something smaller, like an agave, a small cactus, or even a perennial—all of which have smaller and shallower root systems than woody plants.

Watering a hole is also a good practice even if you don't have or suspect caliche. It gives the plant a lush zone in which to start its residence in your garden and it also settles the soil so that subsidence after planting is minimized.

Setting in the Plant

Finally, it is time to put the plant in the hole. Remove the plant from the container carefully, making every attempt not to disturb, mangle, cut, or injure the roots. The plant should come out of its container easily when you give it a sharp rap on the bottom, drop it gently, or lay it on its side and roll it a bit. If the plant won't come out, keep working on it gently. Do not grab the plant by the stem and try to yank it out of the pot. If the plant simply will not give up its pot, cut the pot away from the root-ball.

Position the plant in the hole and check to see that the depth of the hole is right. It is important that the root crown not be buried. Planting too deep is lethal to most woody plants, so take your time and get the plant positioned correctly. When a young tree or shrub germinates, the cells begin to differentiate almost immediately into stems and roots. Stems are able to withstand the wear and tear of growing above the surface but they have little ability to withstand continuous moisture along their surface. For roots, however, the situation is the reverse: roots are

Nerium oleander

well suited to growing in moist conditions but do not do well growing aboveground.

The place where these two types of tissue meet is the crown of the plant, and you can recognize the crown in a number of ways. In most woody plants, especially trees, there is a flared area at the base of the stem where it melds into the root. This flare must be above the surface of the soil. When the flare is either not present or is not clear, then look for the color difference in the two types of tissue. The part of the plant that was belowground in the pot is paler, usually significantly so. The part that was aboveground is darker and often has more significant bark. Situate the plant in the hole so that these areas are growing just as they were in the container, neither higher nor lower. Make whatever adjustments are necessary to achieve this positioning before you begin to backfill.

Backfilling

Once the tree or shrub is well positioned, begin to backfill the hole. Many tree growers recommend that you stop backfilling when the hole is about halfway full of dirt and water the hole. This helps to firm the soil around the roots and fill the air pockets that accumulate in the planting process. It also helps to prevent subsidence of the planting hole.

It is not a good practice to use your foot to mash down the backfill in the hole. This process does remove air pockets, but it also creates others pockets by leaving gaps where your footprints were. Even more significant, this process is usually too firm, causing a concretization of the soil when you want loose, light soil in the hole for the plant's tiny roots.

For all trees or shrubs from desert regions it is unnecessary to add anything to the backfill when you plant. Some gardeners like to add soil amendments, mulch, compost, or even fertilizer to the backfill. But I am not convinced that this is a good practice unless the soil is almost pure rock. And if that is the case and if you want to add something to the backfill, you add it on the surface and mix it up very well. Do not add layers or piles of unmixed product into the hole.

Once the plant is in and all the backfill has been returned that fits in the hole, water the entire planting area thoroughly. Be sure to soak the plant's entire root zone to a depth and width of the planting hole. You may need to build a berm around the hole to hold the water. Create a berm by piling dirt up around the perimeter of the hole. Don't build the berm by digging soil out of the plant's root zone, which could cause damage to the roots.

Mulching

Mulch is an excellent additive at the time of planting, but don't put it in the hole; put it on the surface of the ground. A 2- to 4-in. (5.1- to 10.2-cm) layer of mulch covering the entire root zone helps hold in moisture and reduce soil heat and evaporation for the newly planted tree or shrub. Use any mulching product you wish: chipped or broken leaves or twigs, grass clippings that have been well dried, commercial products, or rocks and gravel. It is important that the mulch does not touch or mound up around the stem, because it will hold moisture against the bark, offering an opportunity for bacterial and fungal infections to take hold.

When applying mulch, do not use anything that is too green, particularly grass clippings, around your plants. If you happen to have an abundance of green clippings at hand, dry them thoroughly before putting them on the soil surface. Grass that is too fresh wrests available nitrogen from the soil while it is decomposing, a process known as nitrogen robbing. Let the grass clippings dry and slightly decompose in a pile before applying them as mulch to prevent this process from occurring. In addition, grass clippings that are well dried will not resprout and regrow when spread around the garden.

Throughout much of the Southwest, particularly in the hottest deserts, inorganic mulch is widely used. Most of it is crushed rock in an array of sizes. Rock mulch is highly effective in reducing soil evaporation. But inorganic mulch, which is essentially neutral, does not provide nutrients to the soil. It also can build up enormous heat on its upper surface. Some plant species find the extra heat perfectly acceptable while others do not and will fail. Before putting rock mulch beneath a species you are growing, read up on the plant's ability to resist reflective heat.

Staking

There are few aspects of tree care that provoke more contentious debate than staking. The practice is often misunderstood and vastly overused. And I believe it is almost always carried on far too long. But there are some situations that call for staking.

In areas with strong winds, like the Coachella Valley or El Paso, or in regions with strong seasonal winds like those that occur in the summer thunderstorm season in southern Arizona, newly planted trees may benefit from staking until their roots are firmly established and can hold them up. Trees planted on a steep slope or in shifting or unstable soils

may also benefit from staking, which will give the roots assistance while they are taking hold. In either case, staking is done at the time of planting and is a temporary measure. Stakes are left in place for weeks, not months, and never as long as a year.

Staking is unnecessary for most trees with or without a single trunk, because of the way that trees build bark and grow. Bark is secondary growth in trees and continues to expand for the entire life of the tree. The thickness of the stem and of the bark are greatly affected by the amount of stress placed on the plant while it grows. More stress leads to thicker stems and bark. Less stress leads to weakly formed bark and thinner, more pliable stems. The yanking and tugging, bending and heaving that the stem endures in the face of wind builds strength in the stem, making it grow wider and sturdier more quickly.

I have known many small trees of less than 1 in. (2.5 cm) diameter that when just planted look like a bent twig. I have a palo blanco (*Acacia willardiana*) that was alarmingly thin when it was initially put in the soil. I resisted staking it, and within less than year it stood straight and strong. Years later it is still straight with solid, firm branches and excellent resistance to the wind. I know it is hard to believe in a tree when it is nearly falling on the ground and looks more like a hook than a mast, but be patient. Let the tree grow, and only stake it when absolutely necessary and for as short a time as possible.

While it is a common practice to stake multitrunked trees, they rarely need it. The greater volume of such a tree offers much more wind resistance, which is the point of staking anyway. Multitrunked trees may also be difficult to properly stake so the lines don't beat up the limbs.

While there are a number of effective ways to stake, there is one immutable rule: the single stake that came with the plant in the pot is useless, and frankly destructive, once the plant is in the ground. Those slender stakes tied directly to the main trunk are tools for growers to keep plants tidy, to masquerade poor growth in some cases, or to make the plants easier to move around. While handy and possibly useful in the growing yard, they are the first thing you should get rid of when you plant a tree or shrub.

The best results in staking come from using two stakes that are parallel to each other when tied to the tree. Begin by selecting stakes that are sturdy enough to drive into the ground a foot or so and will stand upright in the wind. They can be made of almost anything, but be sure that they are not flimsy, pliable, or prone to snapping or breaking.

Drive the first stake into the ground on the outside edge of the planting hole that you just made. Do not drive the stakes into the roots or too near the root-ball; you don't want to risk damaging the roots. This usually means that the stake is about 2 ft. (0.6 m) from the trunk or more, but this varies by the size of the hole. Put the second stake on the other side of the trunk so that the two stakes and the trunk form a straight line and the line is parallel with the prevailing wind.

Now, take your hand and put it low on the trunk, then follow the trunk up until you reach the point where the tree begins to bend. At that point, you will put the lines that attach to the stakes. While there is no hard and fast rule, this point is usually halfway to two-thirds of the way up the trunk. There

may or may not be limbs in the way, but what matters is that the stem below the stake lines is more or less straight and above the stake lines tends to bend. You are looking for the lowest point of attachment that will be helpful to the tree.

There are two ways to attach the lines. In one method, attach a line to one of the stakes, then run it around the trunk, and back to the stake to attach again. Repeat for the other side, placing the two lines adjacent to each other on the stem. The result is two parallel loops, one on top of the other on the stem. In the other method, you attach the staking line to one of the stakes, run it alongside the trunk of the tree, loop it around the other stake, bring it back alongside the opposite side of the stem, and attach it at the first stake. The line looks like a figure 8 with the tree in the center. If you are using the figure-8 method, you make only one turn around the tree.

While you may use almost anything to make the staking line, be sure it is a material that does not cut or slice into the bark. Tree tapes are ideal, and you could use old hosiery, pieces of garden hoses, T-shirt strips, or tube socks. Two materials that should be avoided as staking lines are rope and wire. Rope does not stay firmly in place and rubs the bark away. Wire, even when wrapped with hoses or other materials, slices through the bark.

Attach the line firmly enough to the stake and around the tree so that the tree can move a bit within the line but does not lean over. You want the tree to move and benefit from the wind action, but you don't want it to move so much that it is driven out of the ground by a sudden or fierce wind. Grab the trunk and sway it a bit: it needs to move within the harness but still remain upright.

If the stakes are tall, and they usually are, saw them off to below the lowest branch. Tall stakes are destructive to a tree because wind action causes the young branches to whip and snap where they beat against the stake.

Check your tree often for rigidity and to make sure that the lines are firm but not cutting into the tree or have not broken loose. Be observant about the staking lines: they should not cause a crease or mark on the bark, which would mean they are too tight. Within three to six months, the stakes and lines should be removed so your tree can be independent. No tree needs to be staked for longer than a year. If the tree blows over or is otherwise unstable after a year, it is likely that it has girdled roots and you will need to replace it.

Watering

Watering is an endless conundrum of gardening in arid climates: when to water, how much to water, and how to deliver water most efficiently. There are innumerable ways to successfully water, and the combinations of soil types, plant selection, and weather make the issue all the more challenging. But once you have chosen species that are well suited to your garden's soils and climate conditions—species like the ones detailed in this book—you are far down the road to finding a successful watering solution. Taking it one step at a time helps.

When to Water

When to water is not just a matter of what time of day or season, but also how long to go between intervals of watering. Plants, with few exceptions, draw in all the water they use through their roots. When the soil is suffi-

ciently moist to meet their needs, they take up water in an uninterrupted and steady fashion. As the soil dries out and less water is available, plants may begin to show symptoms of either wilting and decline. Wilting may be temporary, like the late-afternoon collapse that is prevalent during extremely hot weather, or it may be so profound that the plant cannot rehydrate. Wilting is a condition to avoid and requires finding a proper balance between how much water to use and how often to water.

Many woody desert species have an array of adaptations for dealing with ever-declining soil moisture that may not signal imminent death or ill health in the plant. These adaptations are simply their ways of dealing with long periods of time between rains and the related drying of the soil. The most dramatic of these adaptations is that some species drop their leaves.

Leaves are like a faucet, releasing water vapor and gases as the by-products of photosynthesis. Many trees and shrubs native to arid or desert regions simply shed their leaves until there is enough moisture in the ground to support the leaves again. Some, like creosote (*Larrea tridentata*), are able to draw on reserves stored in their stems and roots to see them through until there is enough moisture to regrow their leaves. Others, like palo verdes (*Parkinsonia* spp.), have shifted chloroplasts, the workhorse cells of photosynthesis, to their bark and retain leaves only during very wet times. The bark is therefore green, and for the plant this is an ideal solution: many fewer stomata release precious water but the plant has a continuation of photosynthesis without the vast water loss inherent with leaves.

Others, like shrubby alfalfa (*Medicago arborea*), simply go dormant, losing all their leaves, shutting down, or at least slowing down all metabolic process to the bare minimum until soil moisture is adequate again. In times of severe drought, many desert trees, in particular mesquites (*Prosopis* spp.) and palo verdes, also begin to release the outer branches to protect the life of the tree. In these species, you find dead branches at the tips of limbs commonly at the end of the summer. These symptoms do not necessarily signal great stress or life-threatening decline in the plant. But consistent watering in a garden helps to keep the trees in optimal condition.

Water needs, of course, change with the seasons. As a general rule, plants need much less frequent watering in the winter than in the summer. In summer, plants experience huge evapotranspiration rates and the soil has greatly increased soil evaporation rates as well. Many desert species grow most actively during the spring, so it pays to know a bit about the species you are growing so you can adjust for these situations. Details of growing times are found in the plant profiles in Chapter 3.

It is a truism that young or newly planted individuals need more frequent watering than established or mature plants. But just how much is that, and how often should water be applied? All woody plants respond best to long, deep soaks that wet the entire root zone, and there should be enough time between the soaks for the soil to dry out slightly. The soaking of a root zone in most plants means watering the area encompassed roughly by the drip line or edge of the plant to a depth of about 3 ft. (0.9 m) for mature trees and to 2 to 3 ft. (0.6 to 0.9 m) for shrubs,

Eucalyptus microtheca (coolibah)

depending on their size. Palms need water to the same depth as trees once they are large enough to have a visible trunk; before that, they have water needs more like shrubs.

While most active roots are found within the top 8 in. (20.3 cm) of the soil, deep watering provides an important reserve for the plants. Soil water moves toward the surface as water evaporates or is taken in by the roots of plants. The greater the reserve, the less frequent the need for supplemental watering and the less potential for stress on the plant. Allowing the soil to dry out somewhat between waterings enables the spaces between the soil particles to fill once again with air, which is also vital to the health of the plant. When soil is fully saturated, there are no spaces for air, and if that continues for a prolonged amount of time, the plant basically drowns from lack of air. Only species of the swamps and marshes have adaptations that allow them to survive while their roots remain saturated most of the time.

Here are some general guidelines for woody plants and palms by age and size and by season. Try out the guidelines and see how they work for your plants in your garden. Do not simply take them on faith and stick with one watering schedule no matter what. A good way to know whether these schedules work for you and your plants is to wait

Gossypium thurberi (desert cotton)

about 30 minutes after watering and then plunge a long screwdriver, metal rod, or similar instrument into the soil near the drip line of the plant. If it doesn't go in with minimal resistance to a depth discussed above, then you need to run the water longer. If after what appears to be adequate watering of the soil out near the drip line still appears to be dry, then the soil may be either too sandy and water is running more or less straight down and not outward, or the soil is highly compacted and water is sheeting along only a few inches below the surface. In either case, it is helpful to use a berm to slow down the water or hold it in place longer so it percolates through the root zone.

For a plant that is set out in the fall, begin by watering it every three days for up to two weeks. Then gradually increase the number of days between waterings, so by the end of six weeks you are watering every 10 days. Continue to water the plant every 10 days through the following summer. In areas outside the hottest deserts, begin watering in the same way, but at the end of six weeks extend the watering interval to every two weeks. The same is true in the milder areas for the initial period of establishment. In the first summer after planting, even if planted in the fall, water at least every 10 days in the hottest deserts and every two weeks in the other two areas. The next cool season, the plant may be watered on a schedule of every three weeks if there is no significant rainfall.

In the hottest deserts continue to water at least every other week for the next two summers, but you may need to water more often if temperatures become extreme. In midelevation deserts, this schedule is excellent, although in the southern and eastern parts of the region more reliable summer rainfall may make it unnecessary. In the milder areas, continue summer watering every three to four weeks.

For plants planted in the spring, cut these watering frequencies in half for the initial establishment and the first summer. After that, the suggested schedule applies until the plants are fully established. Establishment means that the tree, shrub, or palm has a mature and fully functional root system. For trees, establishment occurs in about three years, for large shrubs two to three years, for small shrubs two years, and for palms about two years although some may be faster.

Particular watering requirements for established or mature plants are included in the species descriptions in Chapter 3. Regardless of frequency, it is always best to water long and deep rather than doing shallow watering for short intervals.

How to Water

There are a lot of ways to apply water to woody plants and palms, and every approach has good points and limitations. You may also find that some ways are easier or more available to you because of the condition, size, or configuration of your garden.

BASINS A basin is formed by a ridge or dike around the base of the plant. To create a basin, mound 3 to 4 in. (7.6 to 10.2 cm) of soil to form a berm in a circle at the drip line of the plant. For plants that are extremely susceptible to rotting if water stays against their bark, you may also make a similar berm a few inches from the stem to prevent standing water from touching it.

Water is applied in one of two ways. Fill up the basin to the top and then let the water completely soak in. Repeat this once or twice more, depending on the size of the tree. For small or young trees, once is sufficient, but large trees may need three or more repeats.

For the other method, fill the basin almost to the top, then turn down the flow of the water so that the water level is maintained but doesn't overflow the berm. When the soil is fully saturated, the water will overflow, indicating that you have applied enough water.

OVERHEAD SPRAY Using a sprinkler that sprays overhead is an inefficient way to water, but it does have the advantage of covering a lot of space with one spraying unit. There are many sprinkler types, from oscillators that run back and forth and attach to a hose, to heads set on pipe that are part of a garden-wide system. This type of watering generally does not deliver enough targeted water for large trees or shrubs and is more suitable for perennial beds or lawns that are intensely planted and have shallower roots.

DRIP IRRIGATION Drip irrigation is king in the much of the Southwest, especially in the hottest deserts. But this watering system is not necessarily ideal for woody plants. The bewildering array of drip irrigation emitters boils down to three general styles: fixed-rate emitters, variable-rate emitters, and bubblers.

Fixed-rate emitters look like buttons, flags, or little spaceships, but in all cases the amount of water is set by the size of the opening on the emitter. This type of emitter usually delivers a one-half, 1, or 2 gallons (2, 4, or 8 liters) per hour.

Variable-rate emitters look something like the pod of a poppy, with a cap that turns to reveal up to 10 openings in the rim. Although they are rated to deliver from 1 to 10 gallons (4 to 40 liters) per hour, their accuracy is a matter of controversy. I find this style useful and extremely flexible, regardless of precisely how much water is emitted. Although all types of emitters may be turned off if you aren't using them, these are the easiest to turn off and on in my experience. Variable-rate emitters also let you give very small or new plants increasing doses of water per watering interval as they grow, at least up to the limits of the emitter.

Bubblers are larger, often with a head up to 1 in. (2.5 cm) across, and deliver much more water. This type of emitter is built to supply one-half to 2 gallons (2 to 8 liters) per minute, which is 160 gallons (640 liters) per hour at the highest setting. These emitters are extremely effective for trees or other large plants. They are best used with some sort of basin around the plant, unless you are certain that the water will not run off.

How many emitters to use is a voodoo art at best, but there some general guidelines to follow. The Arizona Municipal Water Users Association (AMWUA) in Phoenix has developed a guide for watering in the hottest deserts that offers useful guidelines on how many emitters to use (see the bibliography for the reference). The goal is to start with enough emitters to get the breadth and depth of soaking that you need for the plant. The guidelines suggest that for a tree with a canopy up to 10 ft. (3 m) in diameter, it takes three to five emitters, each of which sends out water at 2 to 4 gallons (8 to 16 liters) per hour, running for six hours, to achieve the 38 gallons (152 liters) it takes to soak the entire root zone of this tree. A shrub up to 6 ft. (1.8 m) across needs two to three emitters issuing water at 2 gallons (8 liters) per hour, running for about eight hours to get the 16 gallons (64 liters) needed to soak the root system. You can see how detailed this gets.

If you can't get the detailed booklet, try this. For trees, use no less than three emitters and up to six each, and no less than two but up to four emitters each for shrubs and palms. Initially, use emitters that deliver at least 2 gallons (8 liters) per hour and run them for at least three to four hours. Then check to see how well they are doing in soaking the root system. If this type of emitter doesn't soak down at least 2 ft. (0.6 m) for the shrubs and 3 ft. (0.9 m) for the trees, then run it longer until it does. This process will give you a guideline for how long to run your emitters for the first year. You will need to check your emitter results often through the seasons and adjust the timing accordingly.

The secret for emitters like this when used with trees and other large plants is that as the plant grows so must the number of emitters. While three emitters are adequate for a newly planted tree for two years, they will not provide enough water beyond that. You should double the number of emitters for the growing tree annually, and you must spread those emitters out to the larger drip line. Sad are the trees that got their requisite number of emitters when planted and did very well for a couple of years, but are still trying to eke out a living on two or three emitters adjacent to the trunk. The closer to the trunk, the farther away the emitters are from the action of the root system—the zone where absorption of moisture and nutrients occurs.

For these reasons, I use drip emitters only to establish trees and large shrubs. After about three years, and certainly by five years, drip emitters, no matter how many you put in, are woefully inadequate for the needs of a tree. I switch to laying down a hose, or building a slight basin, and I let the water drip slowly overnight once every few weeks.

In areas with salty or mineral-laden water, and that includes most of the deserts of the United States, water often becomes increasingly salty over the course of the summer. This common regional problem causes havoc with drip irrigation systems. Emitters plug up with crusted salt and lines becomes scarified and often leak. To deal with this problem, I do two things. Once or twice over the summer, I run the system at two or three times the normal duration. This procedure leaches salts out of the soil, returning them to a state of solution and driving them below the root system.

In the second procedure, I turn on the system and take a close look at each of the emitters. They tend to plug up fast with salt. I remove the emitter cap and let the water shoot out for a few seconds to restore each emitter line to usefulness. If you find an emitter cap that is white or so encrusted it cannot be cleaned out, either replace it or soak it in full-strength white vinegar for a couple of hours, then put it back on it. At least once over the summer, I take off the end cap from the whole system and let it run for a few minutes to clear out the salts. This step is especially useful with soaker hoses and systems that have a lot of small emitters.

SOAKER HOSES A soaker hose is porous, flexible hose that oozes water from the walls of the hose. When used for trees, shrubs, or palms, you set it in a ring around the outer perimeter, or drip line, of the plant. It may be left on top or slightly buried in the soil, whatever you prefer. Soakers emit water slowly, so you need to experiment to determine how long to run the hose in order to get sufficient water to the root system of each individual plant; but expect the length of time to be long, often overnight. Soaker hoses are effective devices for young trees that are becoming established. They are easy to hook up to a battery-operated timer connected to a faucet. They also develop problems with salt buildup over the years, so replace them every five years or so.

TIMERS Automating a watering system with a timer gives you back your life. Not only are automated watering systems extremely convenient but when properly set and maintained, they provide plants with the appropriate amount of water—no more and no less. The most common type of timer is electronic, and it seems that each version, like most electronic equipment of my experience, is just a bit different. It is definitely worth the time and trouble to learn how to use the timer and to program it to suit the needs of your garden. But you can avoid a few pitfalls with timers if you are forewarned.

First, it is important to put plants with similar watering needs on a single station (valve). When you water all plants, trees, shrubs, perennials, and succulents from one valve, some plants starve for water and some become inundated. Unfortunately, this situation is common, especially with new houses. Take the time and care to add enough stations so that only plants with the same watering needs are being serviced by the same station.

Jacaranda mimosifolia at the gate

Second, electronic timers are touchy about power interruptions and lightning. Power outages, even the most minor blip in the power supply, can shut off the timer, sending it into its default mode, which typically is a daily watering for 10 minutes. A strong lightning strike in the vicinity of your yard, even if it doesn't touch your house or yard, may run through the ground, up the wires, and blow out an electronic timer. Most have battery-operated backup systems to hold your program, and a few restart after such an interruption, but be aware of how your timer handles power interruptions and be prepared to reset or reprogram if necessary.

I find that battery-operated timers that attach directly to a faucet or hose bib are especially useful. They can be used for plants that are not near an existing irrigation system, and they are particularly handy when only one or two plants have unusual requirements. They are also excellent for running the irrigation just for trees or shrubs that are establishing themselves. These two situations are difficult to accommodate with an irrigation system that serves a lot of plants. It is good practice with these timers to watch them carefully; batteries have an annoying habit of going out just when you aren't looking.

RAINWATER HARVESTING One of the simplest ways to water trees and other large plants is to direct the water that comes to us as rain into the garden and hold it there. The basic principle of rainwater harvesting is simple: trap all the water that falls on your site during a rain and either store it or direct it in such a way that it provides additional water for plants. There are numerous ways to do this. You can capture water that falls off the roof into gutters that are then directed into bermed or low areas of the garden that are small, temporary holding areas for water. Anything that slows water down and makes it stay in one place for a while allows more water to percolate through the entire soil column. By directing the water from the roof into either cisterns or lower areas of the garden, you capture precious water that is so infrequently available.

It is astounding how much rain falls off a roof. Workers at the University of Arizona report that for every inch of rain that falls, 0.6 gallon (2.4 liters) of water is collected per square foot of roof. So in one rainfall, a modest house with a roof of 1500 square feet sheds about 900 gallons (3600 liters) of water. That is about what a 10-ft. (3.0-m) tree needs in a year.

It only makes sense to try to keep the rain that you get; we get rain so irregularly. If you don't have gutters, you can save the roof runoff by building a ditch directly under the roofline and fill it with rock. This is often known as a French drain. The rocks absorb the force of the falling water and the ditch directs the water underground, where it spreads out and is held in reserve.

Another way to direct water throughout the garden is by contouring the land or by channeling. In the first instance, gentle ups and downs of the land in the garden automatically make pathways for water to follow when it rains. You can link such contoured runs to basins throughout the yard around trees or entire beds.

Many years ago my neighbor perfected this technique but wasn't too concerned about concealing it. Her garden looked like moles had taken over, but it worked splendidly. I recommend a little more camouflage by planting around the contours, not making them more prominent than gentle runs, and unless you intend the contours to be a design feature don't outline them in small, rounded rocks.

An old Spanish version of this method, known as an *acequia*, was popular in Mexico and then in the Southwest until irrigation pumps replaced it. An *acequia* is basically a ditch that moves water from a big source, like a river, to a smaller locale, like a farm, usually by gravity flow. It can be a delightful feature in the garden when it is lined with native rocks, planted lushly with overhanging trees or vines, and snakes through the yard, channeling precious water wherever you need it.

In areas with some slope you may also create small lenses, or open berms, on the downhill side of your trees or other plantings. Then, when rain comes, the water runs into the obstruction, slows down, or perhaps even pools, and slowly percolates into the ground. Similarly, if you have a more defined waterway, you could place a weir, check dam, or a rock-filled mesh cage called a gabion at intervals along the wash to slow the water down and hold it for your plants' use.

If you have impermeable pavement on your property, consider replacing it with bricks laid on sand or with open paving materials. Such materials create a hard surface for walking or driving, but allow water to filter to the ground, eliminating or reducing a lot of the racing runoff that is so wasteful over asphalt or concrete.

The entire realm of rainwater harvesting is as simple or as complicated as you care to undertake. But remember the basic principles: capture all water that falls on your garden, slow down water so that it percolates deeply, and don't let any water run into the street or alley if you can help it.

Fertilization and Soil Maintenance

Many of us are quick to think our plants need fertilizer, as if the soil in which they grow is some kind of dead load of cardboard. Most soils, even in the deserts, are lively and full of the nutrients, minerals, salts, and other compounds that plants need to thrive. Problems may arise when plants are chosen that are from areas much different from where you live, or that have high requirements for nutrients that your soil has in short supply. Fertilization is a quick fix, and needs to be done only in light doses at long intervals. Even better, don't fertilize until after you have the garden soil tested. You may be surprised at what your soil already contains.

Most commercial fertilizers are blends of three nutrients that are highly important for all plants: nitrogen, which is indeed often in short supply in desert soils, and phosphorus and potassium, which are rarely in short supply in our soils. A good soil test may help you to avoid applying too much of these nutrients to your soil over too short a time.

Excessive amounts of potassium have been shown to shut down the work of various organic compounds that permit plants to take up iron, and also to reduce the effectiveness of those miraculous little mycorrhizal fungi found on the roots of most woody plants. Excessive potassium and nitrogen also cause unusual or erratic growth, inhibit blooming (in the case of nitrogen), and lead to symptoms that look like diseases and other problems.

I am not a strong advocate of regular or steady fertilization, except for plants grown in pots. Fertilizers yield dramatic short-term results, but none of them, regardless of type or origin, is as effective in building and maintaining a healthy soil as are compost, layers of mulch renewed annually, and other organic additives.

Most fertilizers are formulated to be fast acting, serving as a supplement to existing soil nutrients. But they do not stay around long. Once in solution and taken up by the plant, they are gone, and it is then necessary to continually replenish them if you want the effect to continue. In addition, alkalinity and aridity work to cause some fertilizer formulations to build up toxic loads of mineral salts if you aren't religious about leaching the ground regularly. Most fertilizers supply nitrogen, often in extravagant doses, but most arid- or desert-adapted plants have an innate ability to thrive in soils that are low in nitrogen because most desert soils come that way.

So I prefer the slower approach. In my view, it is critical to maintain and enhance the health of your soil as a whole. The continual nurturing and renewal of the soil ensures that your plants will thrive over their entire lives. It is a long-term relationship between you, your garden's soil, and the plants in the garden.

My own scheme for maintaining the soil is simple and has yielded excellent results over the life of the garden. At least once a year, ideally twice, to the entire garden I add a generous layer, up to 4 in. (10.2 cm), of a combination of homemade compost and composted forest mulch or similar products,

often with a small amount of composted manure included. These components are in roughly equal parts, except for the manure that is added less generously. I add this feeding mulch in either April or September, but you may apply it any time that is convenient.

This feeding program has been the lifeblood of my garden for years. Desert- and arid-adapted ornamentals thrive with this diet of a gentle increase in the organic content of the soil. There is a delicate line between providing enough nutrients for desert- and arid-adapted ornamentals so that they thrive and not creating a situation that is too rich for them—a situation where they may overgrow and overreach, then become weak and short lived. In any garden, over time the plant litter, leaves, fruit, and flowers of the garden plants themselves also provide their own mulch and enrichment to the soil.

Composted steer or chicken manure is widely available and is used as a fertilizer by many gardeners. Often gardeners are hesitant to use these products because they are salty if they are not composted properly, increasing an already salty soil and water condition. There are ways to handle manure products to minimize the salt problems and get the most effect from the product.

First, know your products and buy ones that work the best in your soils. While this may involve some experimentation, it is worth it.

Second, do not overuse these products. It is not necessary to add them often: once or twice during the growing season is more than enough. Using such products too often can indeed build up unhealthy amounts of salts, release too much nitrogen, and cause plants to grow leaves at the expense of bloom.

Third, water both before and after applying

manure products. This helps leach out any residual salts and settles the product into the upper reaches of the soil so that it won't wash away in the next rain.

Fourth, whether you start with fresh manure or are buying a dried manure product, be sure that it is well composted before you apply it to the ground around your plants. A product called composted manure must be slightly dry, not powdery, in the bag and have no smell. If it is otherwise, throw it on your compost pile for a few weeks or months before using it. If you are fortunate enough to have a ready supply of fresh manure, put it along with other vegetable leavings in a pile and let it break down for a season before applying it to the ground.

Pruning

I love to prune. I find it satisfying to see a wild array of unruly stems, stalks, and flowers end up as a neat bundle of tidy splendor. But pruning is not a task to be taken up lightly, and it should not be performed on a calendar date or because you have nothing better to do in the garden. Pruning is a technique to enhance the appearance of a plant, to correct damage or poor growth, and to train young trees or shrubs. The plant profiles in Chapter 3 offer specific timing and pruning style recommendations. But here, let's consider why to prune as well as how to prune a shrub, tree, or palm.

I prefer plants to grow into their natural form. If they become too large or too unruly or look out of place, it is usually for one of three reasons. First, the plant is the wrong choice for the site. Second, the plant was planted too close to others, making no

allowance for the plant's growth and spread. Third, the plant may be overwatered, causing it to grow bigger than normal. No amount of pruning will resolve these conditions.

If the primary cause is that the wrong plant was put in the wrong place, consider replacing it. If the plants are much too close together, look at them hard and take out a few plants to correct the spacing. If the cause is overwatering and its associated overgrowth, then cut back the shrub to a more desirable height and width while gradually reducing the watering to a more appropriate amount; then watch the plant and see how it grows.

While I am convinced that far more pruning takes place for the mental health of the gardener than for the physical health of the plant, there are situations when pruning is necessary or desired. It is best to remember that pruning is a practice full of promise and opportunity, but when done improperly or too often it may be the death of your plant. Proper pruning is a fine art that improves with practice. While there is nothing mysterious about pruning, I subscribe to six general guidelines for pruning all plants.

ONE Always prune to a junction between the main stem and the one you are removing. Pruning in mid stem is an unattractive and destructive practice, particularly for trees. It forces the plant into an immediate disaster response to the injury, which results in a large number of small stems growing around or beneath the cut.

TWO Prune with an eye to the natural form of the plant, unless you are practicing the specialized art of bonsai or topiary. This approach includes understanding whether your style and time of pruning are going to compromise or even destroy blooming.

THREE Use the right tool for the job. Power tools are not pruning tools; they are tools of destruction. Don't get me wrong; I am crazy about my chainsaw. But this tool has limited uses in pruning. Power tools are an excellent choice for making the first cut in large branches, and are invaluable when you are faced with the huge task of removing storm or cold damage. But the final cut in pruning should be done with hand tools, because the location of the cut is so important. Small, sharp handsaws are excellent tools, as are hand-held bypass pruners. Some arborists have a bias against long-handled bypass pruners, but I find them useful if they are sharp and used properly.

FOUR Prune at the right time. This takes information and practice. All species have an optimal time of year in which to be pruned. Conversely, most species have a time of year when pruning is highly destructive. Learn which is which, and unless there is some hazard or storm damage, take this timing to heart and try to prune only at the right time of year for each species. Poorly timed pruning usually means the plant will not heal properly, creating opportunities for damage by pests, disease, or sunburn. Cutting off segments of a plant at the wrong time of year may also shock it so much that it will die simply from the stress of pruning.

FIVE Follow any hard or heavy pruning session with a deep watering. Pruning is stressful and removes many leaves that provide photosynthetic activity for the plant. So give the plant a nice drink to help it maintain health.

SIX Avoid fertilizer applications for at least a month after a significant pruning. This is especially critical if you have been forced to prune out of season, because many fertilizers are too strong for the young growth that will appear after pruning.

Pruning Shrubs

Although these pruning guidelines apply to all pruning, there are some special situations and techniques for pruning shrubs. To prune a shrub, begin by asking yourself what you wish to achieve. Does the shrub have dead wood that needs to be removed? Was it

Leucophyllum langmaniae (Cimmaron sage)

struck hard by a cold spell and has damaged branches and foliage? Does it look bad after a long hot spell, with some branches that are lean or withered? Have one or two branches shot out away from the main body of the plant and are obstructing a path or driveway?

Removing dead wood, old flowers and their stalks, and fruit can occur just about any time you want, and their removal will have no effect on the shrub. The removal of dead wood, if there is a lot of it, however, may make the shrub look awkward. When you take out a lot of dead wood, you can open up a portion of the shrub to light, encouraging more secondary stems and lateral growth. So it is often best to prune dead wood first, and let the plant grow for a bit before you decide whether other corrective pruning is needed.

When taking out old flowers, fruit, or their stalks, just cut back to the first set of leaves. That is all that is necessary to get them off the plant and won't adversely affect the plant. Rosewoods (*Vauquelinia* spp.), for example, are notorious for holding spent flowering heads for months, and because they dry and turn brown, they are not especially attractive to some.

Cold damage is harder to generalize because it generally depends on how much and in what species. Sometimes it is necessary to give a cold-damaged shrub a hard prune, which is a drastic pruning that removes most of the volume of the plant. Hard pruning is not elegant: the plant is cut back at a uniform level, resulting in a dramatic but brief change to the appearance of the plant. This kind of pruning must be done at the right time or it could kill the plant.

In species like red bird of paradise or most tecomas, which are fast summer growers,

hard prunes may be done as soon as all danger of frost is past whether they have begun to leaf out or not. In species that do not grow so fast, prune out cold damage both when all danger of frost is past and when they have begun to put out significant new growth.

Hard freezes present you with hard choices. I have four large hopbushes (*Dodonaea viscosa*) planted at the corners of a patio. These are upright plants and they were a beautifully matched set until they suffered severe freeze damage one January. Two suffered more than the others, with new growth beginning only 2 ft. (0.6 m) from the ground rather than the 4 ft. (1.2 m) or more in the other two. In addition, the stems of each plant responded differently: some came out with new growth right at the tips while others sprouted only at the base of the branches far inside the plant. Pruning this kind of damage requires patient, careful work. Because these plants were part of a group, I started with the hardest-hit individual, the one that would be shortest when fully pruned, and I pruned the others to that size. While time consuming, if you value the symmetry of a planting, this kind of pruning pays dividends.

The most common reason to prune a shrub other than cold or wind damage is to make it smaller. Whether you are trying to reduce the height or the girth, begin by taking out the stem that has grown the most beyond the desired height or width. Follow the stem into the plant as far as you can, then remove it at its junction with the larger branch. If you can't reach that spot, cut the stem back as far into the plant as possible. Now stand back and take a look. If the entire plant is still too tall or too wide, cut the next-largest stem in the same way. Continue like this until the shrub is sized appropriately. This style of reduction pruning maintains the form and symmetry of the plant. Although best done when the plant is actively growing, this type of pruning isn't as time sensitive as tip pruning and may be done whenever it does not strongly affect blooming or vigor.

Thinning out a shrub to either open up a view or let in more light is a similar process. Plants such as the smooth-leaf chaste tree (*Vitex trifolia*) and San Carlos hibiscus (*Gossypium harknessii*) often grow an abundance of branches on the outer edge, and the inner branches are so shaded that they become naked stems. When thinning, you are clearing out the middle of the plant so it gets more light, and the plant will then fill out.

Tip pruning, also known as shearing, is so poorly practiced and misunderstood that it should probably be banned. It is disheartening to see acres of luscious Texas ranger (*Leucophyllum frutescens*) plants with exquisite natural form and charming clouds of bloom turned into rigid balls, boxes, or bullets without a shred of charm or a hint of blooming. I once was called to a house to help the owners decide what to plant around a newly refurbished pool. Once that was done, they asked me how to get more color in their front yard. I looked around and noticed that there were several Texas rangers and red fairydusters (*Calliandra californica*) that were well arranged but each had been pruned into a ball and few flowers were showing. I told them they already had exactly what they needed; they should just quit pruning. Months later, they were ecstatic with their new yard, and could not believe how much blooming erupted from their unpruned shrubs.

In addition to all the aesthetic reasons

for not subjecting plants to the absurdity of shearing, there are practical reasons. A plant that is sheared all the time grows more quickly to compensate for the devastating loss that you have exacted on it. So your pruning style, ironically, is encouraging even more pruning. In addition, massive pruning creates mountains of yard waste that landfills have to deal with. Many cities have sharply curtailed the amount of yard waste that may be put into their already overstretched landfills, so do your part by stopping the practice of shearing. Finally, in the severe climates of the Southwest, repeated shearing encourages sunburn and stresses plants, making them more susceptible to pests and disease. Sheared plants require increased water to produce more and more new growth.

Timing of pruning is critical. As a rule of thumb, prune evergreen woody plants when they are at the beginning of their growth cycle, whenever that is, but at least six weeks before blooming. Alternatively, you may wait until they flower and prune directly after that.

In the hottest deserts do not prune evergreen shrubs or spring-blooming shrubs in the summer unless you must remove storm damage. Fall-blooming shrubs are also at risk when subjected to summer pruning because you remove the stem tips where the flowers emerge. Plants are easily stressed by the reduction of so much mass. In an already stressful time of year, summer pruning of these shrubs may be debilitating, causing more damage that you corrected, shortening the plants' lives and reducing their vigor.

Summer-growing, tropical species may be pruned in the summer and they will recover quickly. Species that are actively growing in either the spring or the fall can be severely damaged by pruning in the heat of the summer. Pruning opens up new stems to sunburn and the resulting damage. When damage is caused by severe heat (and stems can be lost in a protracted heat wave), timing is also important. Wait to prune out dead or damaged stems until the temperatures have moderated in the fall.

Pruning Trees

Caring for a tree is a long-term commitment that begins with its selection, planting, possible staking, and watering. As the plant matures, judicious and well-timed pruning becomes a significant feature of its care. To understand why proper pruning practices are so important in trees, it helps to know how trees grow. Growth in height in trees, in fact in all woody plants, is by the elongation of the branch from the apical meristem, which is located at the tips of the branches. Most trees have a branch in the middle, referred to as the leader, which is taller than most of the rest of the branches. All other branches arise from the leader as secondary branches, each of which may also have additional branching. That central leader is the focal point of the tree's growth: it controls the vast swarm of hormones and chemical signals that determine how much and what kind of growth occurs lower in the tree. In trees that are naturally, or sometimes even unnaturally, multitrunked, more than one leader shares the responsibility and the tree is then described as being codominant, or having codominant growth. Many desert and arid-region legumes fall into this category, for example foothills palo verde (*Parkinsonia microphylla*). Training such a tree to have a single, and therefore dominant, leader is

often desirable if you want the tree to gain height and spread into a shade tree. But codominance is not necessarily undesirable. Such plants form graceful trees with two, three, or even five main branches.

The role of the leader in the growth of a tree is the reason topping is such a destructive practice. When the leader is removed, most trees respond by flooding the tree with chemical signals that result in numerous new branches below the cut. These branches often grow like the fingers on a hand. In addition, one or more of the secondary branches resumes the duties of the leader, generally resulting in horizontal branches that may be too large to be supported properly.

When trees form branches, two things happen. The vascular tissues, including the cork cambium and associated tissues, melt into each other from the originating branch into the new one. This process allows the free flow of nutrients to the new branch. Bark ultimately forms over the union, and where the initial buds once were, the tree forms a collar that is chemically equipped to seal off the rest of the tree when it is injured and to heal a wound.

Good pruning practice is to cut just in front of this union—that is, toward the secondary branch—leaving the collar intact. The tree will almost instantly compartmentalize the wound, cutting it off from the rest of the tree, and prevent the introduction of bacteria, fungus, insects, and other disease bearers into the vulnerable vascular system of the tree. The tree begins to grow bark from the collar at that location and will eventually surround and cover the wound.

The use of paint when pruning prevents this natural healing process. When applied

Vitex agnus-castus (chaste tree)

to a cut, paint seals in whatever was on the outside before the tree has an opportunity to seal off the area. Paint also holds in moisture, which can cause rapid decay. Likewise, cutting farther from the collar, leaving a stump, does not allow either the appropriate sealing by the tree or the formation of the surrounding bark. The stump just stays there, unattractive and an invitation for decay-forming bacteria, fungus, and other disease-bearing organisms. So, anytime you prune, make the cut just above the collar but don't cut into it, and leave the cut to heal itself.

Sometimes, particularly with storm damage, it is necessary to cut off a large limb. In that case, it is prudent to use the proper tool for the job and to cut the limb in segments. Tree limbs are heavy. If you try to take out a large limb in one big cut, you are asking for trouble. The weight of the limb will cause it to rip down the trunk, taking a wide swath of bark and growing tissue with it and injuring the tree. Avoid this by never cutting in one cut a limb that is more than 1.5 in. (3.8 cm) in diameter. For large, heavy limbs, start at the outer edge of the limb and cut one small segment at a time to reduce its weight. Then continue to cut segments until you have a small enough stump to make the final cut, by hand, and leave a smooth, finished cut.

Trees routinely have numerous small, low-forming branches when they are young. These juvenile branches are important: they provide leaves that allow enough photosynthesis to get the tree growing and keep it in good condition. Without intervention, trees shed these small branches as they grow and leave only a few to form secondary branches. But we often have different ideas about what we want the tree to look like, and we may remove the juvenile branches too quickly. These branches in the early years of your tree provide not only the nutrients they need but are helpful in holding up the tree. A low-branched tree has better wind resistance, bowing to the wind rather than being snapped by it. Such branching also provides important sun protection on

Chilopsis linearis (desert willow)

young, emerging bark that is not yet ready to face the western sun.

In training a young tree and working with juvenile branches, it is best to go slowly. I shudder when I see someone immediately try to train a tree into a single leader or to induce a spreading crown after planting. Never prune a tree when you plant it, other than to remove the ends of limbs that may be damaged by stakes. Even if it is an ill-formed tree at the time of planting, do not prune it. The business of a tree in the first two or three years in the ground is to grow a root system. Because a tree cannot establish well without its canopy to provide the needed energy, leave the tree alone for the first year it is in the ground and proceed slowly after that. You have plenty of time to fix wayward branches or irregular formations.

Once you are ready to start training a young tree into a beautiful spreading shade tree, do two things. First, look at a mature example of the species to learn what form it will eventually assume naturally. Second, keep in mind that you should not take more than a quarter of the mass off a tree in any one year. Your objective should be to form the tree gradually, not to chop it into shape.

It is difficult to paint a clear picture of how to train and prune each individual tree. In all cases, you are trying to remove branches that have already shown that they want to grow to the ground or lie across other branches (crossing branches). Removing dead wood is like removing flowers or seeds; you may do it any time. But the same rules apply: cut to just above the collar, make a clean cut, use the right tools, and do not put any substance on the cut.

Many of the species native to the desert, like mesquite, palo verde, ironwood (*Olneya tesota*), and creosote, present interesting pruning challenges. Special issues, timing, or procedures for each of these species are taken up in the plant profiles in Chapter 3. Many of these types of plants, particularly desert legumes, begin life with a plethora of small juvenile branches, often from the base, making them more like a shrub than a tree. This characteristic is an adaptation to grazing pressure and both gives the plant the ability to regenerate quickly and ensures that at least one stem becomes the leader of the tree.

Pruning Palms

Pruning palms is simpler than pruning woody plants. But timing and technique change, depending on whether you are removing blooming and/or fruiting stalks, leaves, or stems. Flowering stalks on many palms are large and may be messy when the flowers and fruit drop; it may be desirable to remove the flowering stalk. You can remove the stalk just about any time after it forms, but waiting until it is fully extended ensures that the plant won't try to grow another one. Fruiting stalks are much the same: you can prune them anytime you wish. If you don't want to keep the fruit or don't want the fruit to fall on the ground, remove the stalk when the fruit is green.

Pruning leaves of palms is an entirely different situation. And again, there is so much unnecessary and ill-advised pruning of palms you have to wonder how they put up with it. Although bad pruning can be found on almost all species of palms in the region, the hapless California and Mexican fan

palms (*Washingtonia filifera* and *W. robusta*) seem to be the most frequent victims. Pruning practices inflicted on palms are highly destructive as well as unattractive. Just look at a California fan palm or Canary Island date palm (*Phoenix canariensis*) with a full, well-formed head of leaves: they are magnificent. Now compare that to the pathetic plants with only two or three of their nearly 30 leaves remaining—they look like denuded feather dusters.

In monocots like palms, there is only one growing point, and unlike woody plants, there is no secondary branch growth. Everything begins and ends with the solitary meristem that resides at the base of the leaves in what is called the crown. In palms, the leaves are the entire focus for providing energy and nutrition for the plant. The head of leaves is closely matched to the energy needs of the plant. A plant puts out only as many leaves as it needs to thrive, fewer when young and more as it increases in size and age. In an elegant series of energy transfers, the emergence of a new leaf is simply the replacement of an older one, and the leaves transfer carbohydrates and sugars to the other. As an old leaf dies and a new one begins, by this energy transfer the plant is able to maintain the optimal number of leaves for its needs. A full head of leaves is important—vital in fact—to the health of the plant. In addition to shifting energy from fading leaves to newer ones, the older leaves are also important as a prop and wind shelter for the new tender leaves. The entire head serves as a windbreak for the plant, helping it to meet and bend with the wind so the trunk won't break.

For these reasons, pruning of a palm

involves only the removal of dead leaves, completely dead leaves. When you remove living leaves, you not only affect the entire energy and nutrient balance of the palm, but you make it considerably more susceptible to stress-related diseases, insect infestations, and heat and drought stress, and you reduce the vigor and life span of the plant. Annual pruning of palms is totally unnecessary in large plants and almost never necessary in younger ones. Many species, including the California and Mexican fan palms, are self-pruning. These species tend to hold the leaves and their bases until they are around 15 ft. (4.6 m) in height, and then shed them regularly in high winds.

To prune a palm, cut off the leaf as close to the leaf base as you can with a sharp pair of pruners or a saw. The petioles are fibrous and tough, so be sure your tools are sharp. It is also advisable to clean and disinfect your tools when switching from one tree to another to prevent the spread of disease. When you cut, leave a segment of the petiole attached to the plant. This segment forms what is known as a boot. In some species these boots form an intricate, interesting pattern on the stem. Do not pull or strip a leaf off the plant or leaf base. The bases of the petioles form part of the structure of the stem. In some species the bases remain, while in others the bases die off over the years, leaving a smooth trunk. If the base comes away in your hand, remove it; if not, leave it in place.

If you need to get up high, get a ladder or a lift. Climbing a palm is dangerous and difficult, and when done improperly may damage the plant. Gouges and holes from poorly positioned boots or crampons are invitations to infection. Palms do not have wood or bark and the stem is soft and vulnerable to injury, so take great care not to puncture or wound it.

In multitrunked palms like the Mediterranean fan palm (*Chaemerops humilis*) or Senegal date palm (*Phoenix reclinata*), it is often desirable to reduce the number of stems, either to achieve a more elegant look or to keep the plant within a size range. Choosing five or seven trunks often looks good and helps to maintain the lovely symmetry in these types of palms. The stems of these types of palms may be removed anytime during warm weather. Cut as close to the next stem as possible and make a clean, smooth cut. These stems are much harder than they look; a sharp saw is usually the best tool for the job. Again, avoid gouging or cutting into any adjacent stem. Multitrunked palms often regrow stems vigorously for a while after such pruning. Keep removing the new stems to get the effect you want. This becomes a routine task; you are working against the true nature of the plant. But the task isn't difficult or time consuming and the results are exquisite.

Pruning palms to remove both leaves and stems is strictly a warm-weather activity. Never prune a palm when it is cold. They resent it mightily and it is ruinous to them.

Pests, Diseases, and Other Problems

When I first moved to the Southwest from the Louisiana Gulf Coast, I thought there were no insect pests or plant diseases worth noticing. Along the Gulf Coast you have an unrivaled intimacy with insects and disease in the garden. I soon learned that while these garden marauders are dramatically reduced in the arid Southwest, there are still a few with which to contend.

I have to admit that I take a benign, live-and-let-live approach to almost all insects, even those we traditionally label as pests. Most species are a fleeting presence in the garden. They tend to erupt into stygian hordes of destruction only when plants are deeply stressed, are genetically susceptible to their predations, or when a collusion of environmental conditions creates unnatural numbers of the insect. Learning about the preferences and life cycles of these insects helps keep the challenge in perspective and make for clear determinations of when to proceed with some kind of control. In fact, most of the insects you see in the garden are not the ones causing destruction but are more likely your partners in creating the balance and harmony that is the best safeguard against more destructive insects.

I adhere to a few strategies for dealing with insects and their possible damage to my plants: look often and carefully at your plants, be clear that the insect you see is the one that is causing the damage you notice, and deal only with the exact insect that is causing the problem.

These same strategies apply in dealing with disease; it is critical to know what is going on so you can treat it appropriately. When you see a notched leaf, a wilted stem, or a blackened twig, there is nothing so destructive or wasteful as the conditioned response to launch an assault on the entire garden with a wide-ranging poison. It is never a good idea to just douse a plant with pesticide on a regular schedule with the intent of preventing dam-

age. You are only making your plants and the garden in which they live a sterile, hostile place where ironically a lethal infestation is more likely to get a foothold and cause extensive damage. In fact, a garden full of a wide array of insects that eat each other, along with healthy plants that resist and ward off disease, are more certain steps toward preventing the ups and downs of insects and disease.

Watching plants carefully is simple and fun. We grow them to enjoy them, and getting out and doing that up close is not only your reward for the care you lavish on them but also is the quickest way to spot trouble. Early detection means noticing subtle symptoms like yellowing leaves, chewed segments, browning tips, or a general fading that marks the first stages of decline.

Noticing a problem in its early stages, however, does not necessary reveal the cause. Yellowing leaves may result from heat stress or a mineral deficiency or it may only be old leaves that are ready to fall. Yellowing may also indicate overwatering and simply be common at that particular time of year. Chewed leaves might indicate the feeding of a caterpillar but it might also be the surgical cutouts of leaf-cutter bees or the scar left by a bird pecking at a delectable nymph. Then again it might be the nibble marks of a small rodent. Browning tips may signal salt buildup in the soil but they may also result from drying winds or a mineral deficiency. And old leaves that are going to fall off anyway regularly turn brown.

Plants may look puny because they are water stressed, and a good soak may fix them up. They might be showing incipient signs of root rot that is preventing water and nutrients from rising through the roots to the stems, or they might just be too hot or too cold. Plants that are preparing for dormancy often look peaked and begin to lose a leaf or two shortly before they drop all their leaves for a long rest. Newly established plants can have all kinds of alarming symptoms before they settle in and adjust to their new location.

After you spot a problem, the next necessary step is figuring out what is causing it. Knowing what is wrong and what is responsible allows you to choose what to do about the problem or whether you need to deal with it at all. Ask yourself whether the problem will severely cripple the plant or cause all the fruit or flowers to vanish, or whether it is only a slight blip in the life of the plant. Find out whether this problem is a short-term issue or something that can worsen if untended. Many insects and some diseases are extremely sensitive to changes in their environment, and their activity in your garden is linked to a particular part of their life cycle. It pays to know whether you can just wait it out with gentle control or if an assault is necessary.

In addition, we should take a hard look at our cultural practices. Cultural failings on our part are often the actual source of the problem, and when we don't know that or are reluctant to acknowledge it, we take the easier road of blaming whitefly or powdery mildew for the damage. For most diseases in plants, the surest control is to use species that are either resistant or highly resistant to the diseases common in your area. Maintaining healthy, lively soil and avoiding undue stress on the plants goes a long way toward keeping them disease free.

Destructive Insects

Numerous insects are routinely considered pests because they may cause serious damage to an ornamental plant. But to deal with such insects appropriately, it is crucial to understand a bit about the insect's life cycle. Many insects are just passing through the garden or are only a problem at certain times of year. A few of the insects that commonly cause damage to woody plants are discussed next.

APHIDS These tiny sucking insects are found on plants throughout the year but they are most prevalent in the spring and fall. Aphids have tiny mouthparts that are built to extract food from the leaves of the plant. In woody plants, they are most often seen on new growing tips and flower buds. Their eggs are virtually invisible and the immature stage (nymphs) shows up as small, yellow, or whitish circular eruptions on the underside of the leaf. There are four stages of molt in these insects, and the tiny shells they leave lying around have fooled many into believing that they have whitefly. It pays to look closely to be sure that the white speck moves before you attack it as a pest. Adult aphids look much like the juvenile stage but they have legs and move around. Modest numbers rarely harm a healthy plant.

Vigilance is key in dealing with aphids. You may run your hand over the crowded tip or leaf to brush off and kill the daily invasion, or use a strong jet of water to remove them. You may also smother them with liquid insecticidal soap to keep the numbers down. Outside of a greenhouse, it is nearly impossible to get rid of all aphids. Your goal should be to keep the numbers low so that damage is not overwhelming.

Aphids secrete a substance known as honeydew that ants feed on voraciously, so large numbers of aphids encourage ants, and sometimes vice versa. Honeydew also encourages the growth of black sooty mold. The mold itself is harmless to the plant but is unattractive. It may be scraped off, and so may the honeydew, to reduce either of these problems.

The surest way to minimize aphid damage is to maintain healthy plants and avoid excessive use of fertilizer. Overuse of fertilizer or overwatering encourages tender tip growth which is a magnet for aphids.

LEAF-CUTTER BEES Leaf-cutter bees are not really pests, but their telltale circular or semicircular cutouts on leaves make their presence noticeable. Damage occurs in late spring or early summer when the bees take the leaf segments back to their nest and use them to line the egg-laying site. The damage to the plant's leaves is simply cosmetic. The plant fully recovers and secondary problems from the holes in the leaves are not likely. You may seldom see the bees, so any spraying is merely a shot in the dark. And they are better pollinators that we are, so wise gardeners leave them alone.

SPIDER MITES Spider mites are nearly microscopic creatures that, like aphids, suck nutrition from plant leaves. The leaf of a plant that is heavily infected with spider mites is stippled with yellow dots. Spider mites are frequently red. You can tell if you have them by placing a white piece of paper under a leaf and shaking the leaf. The crawling bits of reddish dust are the spider mites.

Spider mites thrive in dusty, dry conditions. One of the best ways to prevent their damage is to keep plants clean, spraying them with water every few days to ensure that spider mites do not reach huge proportions. Dust is a way of life in areas without regular rain, so giving your plants an occasional gentle spray cleaning is your best defense. Leaves that are heavily infected become mottled and discolored, and they fall off. Clean up any infected fallen leaves to keep down the population of these minute creatures.

WHITEFLIES The adult whitefly is small and extremely mobile. You find them when you flick a leaf and cause an eruption of white particles. Many researchers believe that the adults cause little harm and are using plants only as a resting place, but all gardeners agree that the nymphs are sucking devils. Whitefly nymphs are tiny, rounded creatures that may be almost clear, whitish, or yellow. They are commonly found on the underside of a leaf.

Huge infestations of whitefly may decimate a plant in hours. But whiteflies, whether adult or nymph, are particular: their mouth structure only permits them to feed on thin, soft leaves, such as those of lantana, hibiscus, tecoma, and most vegetables. Symptoms of large infestations include discolored and distorted foliage and copious honeydew on the leaves, which encourages a bloom of sooty mold or premature defoliation. The mold by itself isn't much of a problem for the plant, but it is a clear indication of the presence of this insect or of aphids.

In some parts of the Southwest, especially

near agricultural fields, whiteflies arrive in clouds in the late summer. Major eruptions have decimated miles of melons and other crops and, in unfortunate years, they form a haze in the sky and we not only see them but we also can't avoid breathing them.

There is no way to remove all whiteflies from a garden. You can only hope to keep them down to manageable numbers. The adults are constantly on the move, and the ones you may be lucky enough to remove today are just replaced by new ones tomorrow. Spraying them off your plants daily with strong jets of water or applying insecticidal soaps keeps the numbers down. While insecticidal soaps and a few other insecticides do kill adults, there are usually so many that these controls are only workable within closed systems like greenhouses. Lots of predatory insects eat them or their larvae, so encouraging a bountiful fauna of good bugs is perhaps your best defense.

PSILLIDS These tiny sucking insects strongly resemble whiteflies; it is difficult to tell them apart. They tend to occur quickly in the late spring or early summer, often in great numbers, and then disappear. Psillids are a problem on selected species; members of the genus *Caesalpinia* appear to be particularly susceptible. And a significant infestation defoliates a tree quickly. In my yard, these marauders show up each April. Soon I realized the futility of trying to control them on my large palo colorado (*Caesalpinia platyloba*), so I just let the tree lose all its leaves. That, of course, was the end of the psillids, which I later learned do not hang around long anyway. In a species like palo colorado, which comes from the

wet-dry tropics where the trees are routinely deciduous in periods of drought, it takes only a good watering and a couple of weeks for the tree to completely restore its leaves and look better than ever. Now I just wait them out each year, and when the tree begins to defoliate I make sure I give it a deep soak to encourage rapid regeneration of the leaves.

If you can't wait out the psillids or find the infestation too onerous, use the same control measures recommended for whiteflies.

LERPS Another closely related group of insects known as a lerps has arisen in some areas of the west. The ones that cause the most notice are those that have a taste for a few members of the genus *Eucalyptus*. Infestations are easy to spot: the insects leave a hard, sugary shell on the leaf under which it feeds with impunity. Some work suggests that plants grown where it is somewhat colder than eucalyptus prefer, like Tucson, Arizona, may dilute the defenses of a tree, and lerps are the result. Heavy rains tend to get rid of a lot of the insects, but in some special cases treatment may be advised. Treatments range from foliar sprays and soil soaks to injections into the main trunk of the tree. These types of treatment are difficult, often expensive, and are best left to professionals.

GRASSHOPPERS As with whiteflies, some years you find one or two grasshoppers in the garden and in other years you are fighting them off with brooms. With their long legs and great mobility, grasshoppers in large numbers can be a huge problem. They eat plants voraciously while they are around.

If you only find one or two, as I always

do in the late summer, simply remove them individually and dispatch them with a rock. *Nosema locustae* is a protozoan disease of grasshoppers sold under the trade names NoLo Bait, Grasshopper Spore, and Semaspore. Young grasshoppers are the most susceptible to this disease but some species of grasshopper are not affected at all. The effectiveness of this product hinges on proper timing and use of quality strains, and it is only worth using for huge infestations.

CATERPILLARS Caterpillar is a catchall phrase for the larvae of moths and butterflies. All caterpillars are eating machines; they only live to grow up large enough to pupate and ultimately to harness enough energy to transform into their adult stage. The variety of size, shape, coloring, and other markings is vast. The numbers of caterpillars are the critical factor in determining whether control measures are needed. A few are fairly easy to either tolerate or deal with by directly killing them. Larger infestations may need more dramatic measures.

Tent-forming caterpillars that are the larvae of the genista moth relish the growing tips of Texas mountain laurel (*Sophora secundiflora*) and other members of the genus *Sophora*. In some years these larvae are numerous and may defoliate a plant, while in other years they affect only a few tips. The larvae emerge in the early spring to feed on the new growth of Texas mountain laurel and its relatives. You may pick them off or cut off the stem and put it in the trash. The larvae are drawn to tender new growth, and plants that are overwatered and growing too fast are even more attractive to them. So don't overdo the water or fertilizing of Texas mountain laurel in the spring when these little critters are active.

The less vigilant or more squeamish gardener rejoices in the harnessing of the bacterium *Bacillus thurengensis* (Bt), which has gone a long way in helping to control caterpillars. There are numerous Bt formulations. Many target only one species, so be sure you know which is the useful form for your situation before applying it. Apply Bt regularly as soon as you notice the first caterpillar.

I urge caution in dealing with caterpillars. These off-putting creatures last only a short time in the garden and then become the exquisite butterflies that we all enjoy and go to so much trouble to attract. Many also become the humble moths that pollinate vast numbers of species throughout the year. So deal only with the ones that are truly a problem.

PALO VERDE BEETLES These impressive insects are native to the hottest deserts of the Southwest. The adult is 3 to 4 in. (7.6 to 10.2 cm) long, dark black, with two long, forward-facing pinchers. It flies at dusk, and it is so large you might think a hummingbird has become drunk and is having trouble finding its way home. They may not fly well but they certainly get your attention. In the way of many insects, the adult does not live long. It is consumed with finding a mate, hence the mad dashing around, and it deposits eggs in the ground at the base of a tree or shrub. While numerous woody species are acceptable to the palo verde beetle, it carries the name of the palo verde because it is rare to find an old plant without larvae at its base.

The larvae are equally impressive, 5 or 6 in. (12.7 or 15.2 cm) long, as big around as a decent cigar, and white. These larvae live a long time deep underground, by some estimates up to five years, and by that time they are truly revolting. They feed on the roots of the plant, although in vigorous, healthy plants they are rarely the cause of injury or decline. But in old plants or those that are weakened by age, drought, disease, or disaster, they deliver the final blow, killing enough of the root system to cause the tree to die and sometimes fall over. It is when you go to dig out the stump that you find all those big, white, writhing larvae. There is little to do to prevent these larvae.

GIANT PALM BORER This boring insect is the larva of a large beetle that lays its eggs in the crown base of a palm tree. These larvae become large, over 6 in. (15.2 cm) long, and live up to 10 years in the tree. As they grow they feed their way through the plant toward the ground and eventually emerge from a quarter-sized hole in the trunk.

Like most borers, they damage trees that are already under stress from overpruning (particularly removal of too many living leaves over too long a time), water or heat stress, or nutrient deficiencies. Palms have natural defenses against these types of insects. But when they are stressed, defenses can break down or become ineffective, resulting in sudden loss or collapse of leaves or even the entire crown and, when the infestation is severe enough, structural collapse of the trunk.

The best strategy is prevention. Do not overprune palms, especially the living leaves,

and keep palms healthy, watered appropriately, and in good condition.

TERMITES Termites are primarily feeders on dead wood. But one species forms mud tunnels on the outside of the plant, and while they look bad, the tunnels usually aren't a problem. The tunnels are routinely found running up the stem of a large cactus like saguaro (*Carnegiea gigantea*) but may be found nestled up against anything. I once saw a large group that had formed a colony on a bromeliad in the genus *Hechtia*. These insects are not feeding on your plants; they are just using it as a prop. So go get a cup of tea, and don't worry about them.

THRIPS Thrips are tiny, sucking insects that favor the growing tips of a wide range of ornamental species. One of the surest ways to know they are on a plant is the characteristic curl of the leaf around the insect associated with a dimpling of the leaf. While thrips in vast numbers can cause serious problems on small plants, this rarely occurs. The damage is usually just cosmetic on woody plants. Rose growers loathe them because they adore the new flower bud and ruin it right at the time when you want to enjoy a perfect bloom.

Beneficial Insects

In a revolution in pest and disease control methods there is an increasingly large number of advocates for what is known as integrated pest management (IPM) or ecologically based pest control. This is a version of the quaintly termed method known as organic gardening. But the terms are not synonymous: pure organic gardeners never use a synthetic product for any type of control. Both methods hinge on the concept that pest control is best done in a targeted fashion, with prevention and accurate identification as the key to success. One of the chief resources of these methods is the use of so-called beneficial insects—those little warriors of the insect world that are parasites or predators on the insects that we deem pests. Supplying beneficial insects has become a flourishing industry, and when properly encouraged, an army of these warriors may be your best assurance of healthy plants.

But first a couple of caveats. Many of the insects sold as beneficial ones are not native to or comfortable in your area. Many of them last only a few weeks and never set up the colonies you hope for; this is particularly true of ladybugs. Take great care in buying beneficials. You need to make sure they will attack just the intended insects and that they will live well where you do. It is also vital that their life span coincides with your insect problems.

The long-term plan is to encourage these helpful predators to flourish in your garden by the dual methods of creating a diverse and healthy garden from the soil up and by eschewing spraying pesticides that kill broadly and without discrimination.

Destructive Animals

Gardeners find that in most of the region they share their place with a number of destructive animals. This problem is increased if you live adjacent to a park or preserve, or on the outskirts of town. Such animals include rabbits, gophers, round-tailed ground squirrels, chipmunks, and a host of other small rodents. Some areas have invading javelinas and deer.

These unwelcome critters are fully capable of chewing their way through a garden in a matter of days or even hours.

Gardeners plead for a sure and certain fix for the invasion by these animals, believing that lures, repellants, and other fantastic formulations will ward them off. I think that medieval charms or exhortations would work just as well as most of the lures and repellants on the market. The only thing that works permanently for these creatures is a fence.

Fences come in many forms and, depending on your budget and your garden, you may want to use any or all of these suggestions. If you are able to fence the entire perimeter of the garden, that can be a serious deterrent to most animals, although ground squirrels and their relatives are excellent climbers and resist almost any fencing effort. Javelinas are unable to move through a block fence or other sturdy wall, but rabbits are geniuses at finding even a tiny slit beneath a gate. Deer can be fenced out but the fence must be extremely tall, well over their leaping height. Ground-dwelling rodents, like gophers and the other smaller rodents, simply burrow under a fence.

Fences may also be temporary. Rabbits are extremely common throughout much of the region and represent a significant pest in the garden. Rabbits are especially fond of the plants you put in yesterday and will devastate new plantings without protection. A small temporary fence of chicken wire, hardware cloth, or similar material is the only deterrent I know that works. Although the fence is hideous, it need not be permanent. Once the plant is large enough both to survive a minor chewing attack and to have some semiwoody growth at the base, the corral may be removed. Rabbits eat absolutely anything if they are hungry enough, including cactus, agaves, and other plants that are not normally touched, so protection for new or tender plants is necessary.

Ground-dwelling rodents are the most trying animal invaders. Every part of the region has its own species, but in my garden they are ground squirrels and small mice that tunnel throughout areas of the garden, creating well-turned soil. I cannot bring myself to use the baits and poisons on the market, but they may be effective. These products are not selective, and if you choose to use them, be sure they are not accessible to pets or young children.

Even when using such products there are no guarantees. Rodents are prolific. The loss of one clan creates an opportunity for another clan to move in and quickly recolonize your garden. I once fought these creatures with a host of removal techniques in a nursery yard I managed, and only a cat kept them at bay and even then only when she was right there.

Diseases

A plant gets diseased when it is invaded by bacteria, fungus, or a virus. Although the incidence of some of the most devastating plant diseases is low in the Southwest, a few do plague selected ornamentals in the region.

BACTERIAL DISEASES Bacterial diseases are often the direct result of injury to a plant. Some of the most common reasons for bacterial infection are poor pruning practice or timing, too much damage to the roots during planting, sunburn, or frost damage. Good

hygiene and good cultural practices dramatically reduce the probability of many bacterial infections. The black goo oozing out of leaves or stems that is a symptom of overwatering is the work of bacteria that attack weakened plant tissues.

Oleander scorch is a devastating infection of oleander (*Nerium oleander*) by the bacterium *Xylella fastidiosa*. There are several strains of these bacteria and associated diseases, some of which infect crops like grapes. All are devastating, almost inevitably killing the infected plant. This particular strain affects oleander and is spread by the glassy-winged sharpshooter, smoketree sharpshooter, and other sharpshooters. These tiny flying insects feed on the xylem of a vast range of species. Damage from the insects' feeding is negligible, but their vectoring of this disease has made them the target of intensive research and quarantines throughout the region. Like most quarantines of flying or wide-ranging insects, this effort has only been mildly successful. There are pockets of this disease in parts of Phoenix and around the region. Some years ago, it raged through the desert cities of the Coachella Valley of California and other locales, killing thousands of mature oleanders.

There is at present no cure for this disease and no real way to control the sharpshooters that move it around. If you find that you have an oleander that has been infected, remove it as soon as possible and dispose of it quickly, because sharpshooters renew their supply of the bacteria in live, infected plants.

Galls are the result of an infestation by the soil-borne bacterium *Agrobacterium tumefaciens*. It is a ubiquitous bacterium that is present in a wide variety of both fruit trees and ornamental woody plants. Galls begin as soft green formations but become a round, rough fissured growth on the stem. In general, except for fruit producers, the presence of galls is benign and causes no serious problems or injury to the plant. They may look unattractive and you can certainly remove the offending branch, but the infestation may recur. There are no controls and no known prevention strategies.

Oleander gall is caused by a different bacterium, *Pseudomonas syringae* var. *svastanoi*. These bacteria grow up to 1 in. (2.5 cm) across and enter cylinders through wounds, frost injury, or natural openings in the plant. This problem is cosmetic for the plant. If it is localized, you may halt its spread by cutting out the infected area and cleaning with a 1:10 mixture of bleach and water.

FUNGAL DISEASES Fungal diseases are more common in woody plants than bacterial diseases and affect a wide range of other plants as well. These diseases often show up when conditions are optimal, usually based on temperature but often a combination of temperature and soil moisture. As for bacterial disease, wise cultural habits and pruning practices can discourage both the eruption of these diseases and their spread.

Cotton (sometimes called Texas) root rot is a disease that infects a huge array of woody plants. It results from the infestation of the root by the fungus *Phymatotrichopsis omnivora*. The fungus is indigenous to vast areas of the Southwest and northern Mexico that are characterized by alkaline soils with low organic content. The fungus lives deep in the soil, sometimes many feet down, and produces thin strands known as hyphae that can infect the roots. These hyphae are parasitic and eventually will kill the root.

Aboveground, you rarely see symptoms of cotton root rot until it is much too late. Initial symptoms are dead leaves that dry and stay on the plant. This sudden dying of the foliage then spreads quickly over the entire plant. The plant is often dead within days of the first dead leaves. In higher elevations above 3500 ft. (1067 m), the disease may progress more slowly but the result is the same. In areas with cold winters, it may take an entire growing season to kill the plant. The hyphae extend from plant to plant, creating a characteristic pattern of first one plant dying, then a couple years later another, and a couple of years later another, and so on.

There is no cure and almost no prevention for this disease except to use species with low or no susceptibility to it. Whether a particular species has high or low susceptibility to this disease or is virtually immune is covered in each plant profile in Chapter 3. We know that monocots are immune to the disease, which means that all the palms share this immunity. Woody plants that are native to the region are tolerant of growing where the fungus is present and rarely succumb to it.

Crown, collar, and root rots are caused by various forms of the fungus *Phytophthora*. Symptoms are vague and include general decline of the plant, wilting that cannot be reversed by watering, stunting, loss of good color in the leaf, and eventually death of the plant. Most of the activity is underground where the fungus lives. Warm soils, over 85°F (29.4°C), encourage its growth, and overwatering or poor drainage is usually present when it arises.

Fungicide drenches around the base of infected trees may be quite effective in preventing the spread of such infections but have mixed results as a cure. The best strategy is prevention. Provide excellent drainage, don't plant a tree too deep, and do not overwater. It is tempting to water continuously, or more often than necessary, when it is hot. Just because we are hot, be careful not to overdo the watering, because these fungi are ready to pounce.

In Texas another fungal disease, oak wilt (*Ceratocystis fagacearum*), has devastated vast numbers of both Spanish oak (*Quercus buckleyi*) and its close relatives and the plateau live oak (*Q. fusiformis*) and its close relative live oak (*Q. virginiana*). This fungus invades the vascular system of the oak, causing a sudden leaf drop, typically in the summer, and death quickly after that. It is spread by beetles moving from an infected plant to a healthy one, particularly in the Spanish oak group, and by movement through the vast intertwined root system of the plateau live oak and the live oak. While there are no sure cures, prevention currently appears to be the key. Although identified for over 60 years, oak wilt has not moved west of Texas.

If you live in an area where this disease is common, I highly recommend turning to the Oak Wilt Information Partnership and their informative website, www.texasoakwilt.org, for information on susceptible species, control recommendations, and substitute species that are not susceptible.

Two other genera of fungus cause a wide array of rots in plants, *Pythium* and *Rhizoc-*

tinia. But both of these are more commonly associated with disease in young seedlings or small plants that are still herbaceous. Neither disease is particularly effective in debilitating established woody plants.

Keeping a sense of perspective about pests and disease is essential for both your peace of mind and your garden's health. If you recognize that a healthy and diverse garden with living soil is your goal, then a few yellow leaves or nibbled stems is a small price to pay for the range of life that lives in your small area. If one species or one plant continues to be plagued by certain diseases or insects, it is easier to just remove it and try something else. There are plenty of excellent replacements around that would enjoy a home in our gardens.

Water and Heat Stress

When you are assessing disease or insect damage, look for signs of under- or overwatering, too much or too little sun, bad timing when planting, or poor timing for pruning. Many diseases and insect infestations are secondary symptoms of things we gardeners may have done.

Sun stress and associated heat stress is a common occurrence in the desert and shows up as yellowing, occasionally browning, of leaves or stems. This condition usually comes on suddenly, within a day or two of a plant being transplanted or moved into a sunnier location, or when a sheltering limb is pruned away. Sunburn or heat stress also occurs after ill-considered pruning in the summer.

All parts of woody plants may be sunburned or show heat stress. Heat stress is most often seen on the leaves, but it may show

Mixed planting, *Caesalpinia pulcherrima* (red bird of paradise)
C. pulcherrima 'Phoenix Bird', and *Yucca rostrata*

up on the bark as well, particularly in trees with soft or thin bark like tenaza (*Havardia pallens*) or palo colorado. Plants with thin bark are easily sunburned when the bark is exposed to the western sun too quickly. Heat stress symptoms range from a yellowing or fading of the leaf to leaf drop. In some cases, the tip of the shrub or tree may be withered from intense or prolonged heat. In the hottest deserts, some of the most challenging gardening conditions are when the temperatures are severe, over 110°F (43.3°C), for days and sometimes weeks at a time. During those episodes, heat stress and sunburn may show up on plants that are otherwise well adapted for the area.

Over- and underwatering are difficult to diagnose. The symptoms may sometimes be the same as for heat stress: pale, yellowing leaves. Stems and leaves that become soft or blackened may indicate root rot brought on by overwatering or extremely poor drainage or both. Wilting makes underwatering a snap to diagnose.

Water and Soil Salinity

Throughout the Southwest, increases in the use of reclaimed, recycled, gray water is contributing to an increasing problem of saline conditions for many ornamental species. When you add that to the already inherent salty conditions of many regional soils, in some areas the problem is already acute and in others it looms large for the future.

In arid areas, salts normally held in solution in the soil begin to precipitate out as the soil dries out. Over time a much higher than normal concentration of salts forms in the root zone of plants and sometimes even on the soil surface. When more water, especially irrigation with gray water, is applied, those salts again go into solution, but then they are in even higher concentrations. For some species such elevated salinity levels are lethal, and for most species they create some level of stress, depending on the species' tolerance for saline conditions.

The typical symptoms in plants of higher than acceptable salinity, known as salt burn, are crisp brown leaf edges, leaf loss, stunted growth, and, less obviously, root injury. Often these symptoms are subtle, with a general loss of vigor or vitality in the plant being the first sign of trouble. It is something like a general malaise and it takes you by surprise, particularly when the plant has been thriving for some time and then suddenly begins to fade.

The best way to deal with the problem of overly high salinity is prevention. Deep watering of woody plants, soaking the root zone 2 to 3 ft. (0.6 to 0.9 m) with each watering, is important. It has been reported that 24 in. (61 cm) of water in the soil removes up to 90 percent of the soluble salts to below the root zone. Even a modest 12-in. (30.5-cm) soak reduces the salinity by about 80 percent. One of the best practices in areas where salty soils and water are a concern is to extend the watering duration to two or three times what you normally provide once or twice during the summer when the salt buildup is most pronounced. These few extra-deep soakings push the salts lower into the soil column and disperse and dissolve them more widely.

Symptoms

A number of conditions in plants look alarming but don't represent any real problem. Becoming familiar with the most common of these conditions removes the temptation to treat something that was never a problem, saving you time, money, and worry.

WEEPING SAP Many desert legumes, mesquites and palo verde trees in particular, ooze sap at some time during the year. During cooler weather mesquites weep out a thick sap that is jet black and quite gooey. Known as lac, this product was prized by Native American peoples for use as a sealer for baskets and as a dye. It causes no harm to the plant and is entirely benign.

Because the vascular tissue in woody plants is directly below the bark when plants grow quickly, it often causes the bark to yield or split and sap weeps out. In most cases, this type of sap loss is only visible when the plants begin to grow in the spring, but it may also be the result of overwatering plants, which causes them to overgrow. Woody plants grow both up and out at nearly the same rate, and if growth is going too fast for the bark to form and adjust, something has to give. Rarely, if ever, is it a problem for the plant, and it may be either ignored if it is entirely seasonal, or corrected by adjusting the watering scheme.

WOODY LESIONS AND CRUSTY FORMATIONS
As palo verde trees age, rough, oddly crusted areas and dark, split bark forms along the main trunk of the tree. The phenomenon is common in all species and their hybrids. These growths often ring the stem, but they may also just show up anywhere on the bark. When newly formed, these eruptions display erratic patterns of dark growth surrounding the greener bark. This is simply part of a normal aging process in these trees, where the green, thin bark is being replaced by a darker, rough bark. It looks strange but it is not harmful to the plant. This rough tissue may also form on these trees as a result of injury. Rarely a serious problem for the plant, the dark bark is the seal that the plant makes to heal the injury. Unless there are other related problems, there is no cause for concern. I have seen such injuries from innocuous things: impulse watering that too routinely pounded the stem, plant stakes that were not far enough from the bark of the stem or a branch, woodpeckers and other birds poking around for insects, and scraping by nearby trees or by the palo verde's own limbs.

PINE NEEDLE DROP All conifers, including pines, lose needles on a regular basis. In the Southwest, pines in ornamental settings often do not receive enough water and they lose excessive needles. To most arborists, excessive needle loss means losing more than three growing years' worth of needles. This condition often is called pine blight and has been attributed to a number of insects, including mites, and to other diseases. But it is almost always the result of drought conditions or water stress to the plant. Other infestations,

by insects or other pathogens, may be secondary when the real culprit is severe water stress.

This condition is difficult to control in some ornamental settings. Often the trees are large, with root systems that may be far outside the confines of your own garden. In years that are dry with minimal natural rainfall, the stress starts to build up, and when it goes on a long time, needle drop is the result. To mitigate this, be sure to plant pines in areas that have adequate water for their needs, or where there is plenty of root room and you can provide intermittent supplemental water when necessary.

BRANCH DIE-OFF In all species of woody plants, one of the most critical adaptations to drought is the ability to kill off small branches when times are lean. In the garden, we may notice that the tip branches or the lower limbs of some mesquites are dying off and we think it must be a disease or a problem. But it is just the plant's way of controlling its size in response to how much water is available. In general, it is best to take a cautious approach: don't overwater the plant in an effort to ensure that there are no dead limbs. Rather, if there has been a long run of dry weather, especially in the winter, water with one or two long, deep soaks which should be enough to help the plant sustain itself.

Propagation

Propagating plants is so much fun it is a wonder we don't do it more. Basic propagation skills also allow you to grow species or varieties that are not widely available in your area and to give some of your favorites to your friends and relatives. For trees and shrubs, there are two types of propagation: by seed and by cuttings.

Propagation by Seed

Most desert- and arid-adapted species have strong protections in the seed to delay germination until conditions are just right. Therefore some pretreatment of the seeds is often necessary. Seeds may be coated with chemical inhibitors, have impermeable seed coats, or have an interior clock that prevents the seed from completely maturing until after it falls from the plant, a condition known as after-ripening.

Some species need cool soils to germinate while others need hot soils, making the time of year or your ability to control these conditions important to success. It is helpful to find out as much as you can about the particular species you want to grow before you set out to propagate it.

In the hottest deserts if you are unsure about the requirements of a particular species, then plant seed from September to February. Extremely hot weather is hard on seedlings, and many lethal fungal infections occur when tender seedlings are transplanted when it is warm. Unless you know that the species loves these conditions, try to get plants up and growing well before the hottest weather sets in. In mid-elevation deserts and milder areas of the region, plant seed from late winter to early summer.

The seed of many woody plants and virtually all legumes is hard or has strong chemical germination inhibitors. And so scarification is a good practice to increase germination success. Scarification simply opens up the seed coat to permit water to penetrate the embryo and allow for germination. There are two easy ways for the home gardener to scarify seed and another common method that I think is best reserved for professional growers.

The first method is a hot-water soak. Soak the seed for a few hours or overnight in hot water to soften the seed coat. To get water hot enough, run it through a coffee maker or bring it to a boil on the stove, then let it sit for about two minutes before pouring it over the seed. Although overnight is plenty of time, seed may be left in the water for up to three days before being planted.

The second method involves cutting the seed coat. Nick or cut the seed with a file, razor blade, or other sharp object, being careful not to wound or destroy the embryo. The idea is to provide a tiny opening for water to get in so the embryo will swell and begin to germinate.

The third method is to use an acid bath. Soak the seed in a strong acid, usually sulfuric acid, to break down the seed coat. Don't try this method unless you know what you are up to and have plenty of protection at hand for your eyes, mouth, and clothing. The other two methods are more than sufficient to get almost all seed germinated in a home garden.

I plant all seed in a mix of equal parts vermiculite and perlite to prevent problems with fungal disease like damping off. After making up the mixture, wet it thoroughly, and then fill clean containers. If you prefer to add some good-quality, sterile potting soil, by all means do so, but watch closely for signs of fungal infections. After sowing the seed, water again. Newly germinated seedlings are fragile; using a powerful hose spray may drown or damage them. Misters or fine-spray nozzles are much better and cause fewer problems.

Put the containers in a place that has bright but indirect light and cover them to prevent moisture loss. If you have a greenhouse or a cold frame, that is ideal. Otherwise, cover the entire container with a loose shroud of plastic. Plastic food storage (not freezer) bags are excellent because the plastic is slightly permeable. You may also cover the pot or container with a milk jug or a one-liter clear, plastic beverage container from which the bottom has been removed. Secure the plastic around the container with a string or rubber band. As long as there are droplets of water on the inside of the covering there is no need to water the seeds.

Most seedlings do not need any supplemental nutrients until they are growing true leaves. So they may be left in a sterile mix until they germinate and have grown up to five true leaves. Then it is time to move them out of the sterile mix and into a good-quality, well-drained potting soil. Move seedlings by taking hold of the leaves rather than the stem or better yet by inserting a spoon or small trowel into the pot and lifting out the entire plant, soil and all. The seedling's stem is so fragile that if you break it, the plant is lost, but if you break a leaf it will regrow quickly. Roots are also fragile so you want to disturb them as little as possible. When the mix is moist the roots usually hold together well. Once you have transplanted the seedlings, water them thoroughly and return them to the same location where they germinated for at least a week or two. For seedlings, too many changes at once in the growing environment can be lethal.

Seedlings must not be allowed to dry out but they also must not be saturated. To achieve this fine balance, spray nozzles or misters are excellent tools for getting just the right amount of water to the seedlings. After a week or two, gradually allow the seedlings more and more light, and move them gradually to a semishaded location where they are subject to normal air temperature. Soluble fertilizers, whether natural or synthetic, give young seedlings a boost as they begin to grow. Slow-release fertilizers used at half the recommended amount or less are also helpful because you do not have to remember to apply them on a schedule.

Keep shifting the seedlings to successively larger pots until they are large enough to plant in the ground. Many woody species are large enough to plant in the ground a year after germination, but a year or so in a 1-gallon or 5-gallon (4-liter or 20-liter) container results in an even larger root system. During the summer, be sure the plants are in large enough pots so that they do not dry out daily. Keep them well watered and in the shade throughout the summer.

Propagation by Cuttings

Basically three kinds of cuttings can be identified by the age of the stem. Hardwood is the oldest part of the stem and is at least two years old. This part of the stem is nearly impossible to bend without breaking and is usually a darker color than the rest of the stem.

Semihardwood is last year's growth and is hard or nearly hard but is more pliable than the oldest part of the stem. It, too, can break when bent, but with gentle pressure it will curve. It can be darker than the newest stems.

Softwood is the growth of the current year and may be as young as just a few weeks old. It includes the tip, which is the newest extension of the stem. Softwood, as the name implies, is extremely pliable: it can be curled around your finger without breaking. When the cut stem piece is just a few weeks old, it is often referred to as tip growth. When it is just a bit older, a few months old, it is known as softwood. Either way, such a cutting is young and delicate.

The greatest success in almost all desert- or arid-adapted species is from cuttings of semi-hardwood or softwood that is at least a few weeks old. Take cuttings only from a plant that is healthy, vigorous, and robust, and is not stressed by heat, cold, or lack of water. Also, it is often best to take cuttings from a plant that is not in bloom, although you can work around this by simply removing all the flowers from the cutting. It is critical that the plant be actively growing when you take the cutting, although there are some woody species that root from a cutting when dormant.

The growing medium for rooting cuttings is the same as for germinating seedlings. It is also helpful to use a rooting hormone. There are many root hormone formulations, both liquid and powder, and all of them work well. Dip 'N Grow, Horminex, or Hormodin are some of the most commonly available products. All hormone formulations need to be used within the stated shelf life on the container and kept refrigerated when not in use.

Take cuttings that are about 4 in. (10.2 cm) long; longer stems can be cut into pieces. If you are not able to work with all the cuttings right away, or the weather is hot and dry, plunge the cuttings immediately into a container of water while you work. For longer storage, keep them cool in a refrigerator or cooler. Putting cuttings in freezer bags with a moist paper towel keeps them fresh for a few days if you cannot get to them right away. Cuttings rarely survive longer than a week without being put in the growing mix, and some last only a day or two.

Remove all the leaves from the part of the stem that will be beneath the soil. It is better to strip them with your fingers rather than to cut them off, because the wounding action of stripping exposes more of the bud to the rooting hormone which helps induce the nodes to begin the rooting. If there are flowers anywhere on the cuttings, remove them. If there are large leaves on the stem remove them or cut them in half; they will rot in the moist atmosphere necessary for rooting.

Use a growing container—almost any kind will do—that has drain holes and is immaculately clean. More than one cutting may be put in the container but it is best if cuttings are not touching each other. Water the potting mix well before putting in the cuttings and pat it down so it is firm. Dip the end of the cutting and all visible nodes in the rooting hormone. Then push the cutting into the potting mix deeply enough so that it stands up on its own.

Like seedlings, cuttings need to be kept in a place that has bright indirect light and is consistently moist. If you don't have a greenhouse, cold frame, or mist system, then cover the container in the way described for seedlings. After about a week, remove the plastic, check for any signs of disease, water if needed, and gently prod the cutting. Cuttings have grown roots and are set when they do not pull out of the pot with gentle pressure and won't rock around in the mixture when pushed gently. The time a cutting takes to establish roots is variable, depending on the species and on the growing conditions; it can range from two to eight weeks.

Once roots are well set transplant the cutting into an individual container. Keep these young plants in the same gentle atmosphere for at least a week before letting them begin to grow in normal light, heat, and air. Once growth has resumed you can start to fertilize with a soluble fertilizer or a minute amount of time-release fertilizer. Be careful not to overfertilize young cuttings too quickly; they are easily shocked and burned.

Bougainvillea

3 Plant Profiles

Abutilon palmeri
Indian mallow, superstition mallow

FAMILY: Malvaceae.

DISTRIBUTION: In the United States in California from San Diego County east through the Gila River drainage of central Arizona at 1000 to 3000 ft. (305 to 914 m). In Mexico from northeast Baja California into Sonora to the Yaqui River.

MATURE SIZE: Shrub 4 to 7 ft. (1.2 to 2.1 m) tall and 3 to 4 ft. (0.9 to 1.2 m) wide.

BLOOMING PERIOD: Heaviest bloom is from March to May, but blooms repeat through fall following rain or heavy watering.

EXPOSURE: Full sun to light shade. In the hottest deserts, provide protection from the afternoon sun especially in the summer.

HARDINESS: Cold hardy to at least 25°F (−3.9°C), but recovers quickly.

Indian mallow is a multistemmed shrub of desert hillsides and arroyos. In nature, plants are short and often look sparse, but in the garden they are lush and full.

The leaves are more or less heart-shaped and have three distinct, deep lobes. The gray-green to light green leaves are 1 to 4 in. (2.5 to 10 cm) wide. A thick coat of fine hairs gives the upper surface of the leaves a gray cast and makes them velvety soft.

Flowers are on loose, pyramidal, branched stalks far above the foliage. There may be numerous showy stalks, each with dozens of flowers. Occasionally plants have solitary flowers in the axils as well. The 1-in. (2.5-cm) corolla lobes are soft, pastel orange, and are much longer than the calyx.

Depending on temperatures, plants are either spare in the winter or fully deciduous. So it is best to plant this shrub in the early spring. While growth is deliberate in the spring and early summer in the hottest deserts, plants shoot up fast during the thunderstorm season of late summer.

I once tried to prune an Indian mallow that had grown too large. I learned the hard way that this plant does not take well to heavy pruning. I cut too much and the plant subsequently died. It is best to prune lightly at intervals when the plant is actively growing, in early spring or late summer. Flowering stalks may be pruned as soon as they are spent. If the plant suffers cold damage, wait until it shows leaves before pruning out the damage.

This abutilon is not particularly common,

Abutilon palmeri (Indian mallow)

although everyone who has one loves it. I have found that it gently reseeds in the garden where there is abundant water, yielding just enough new plants to give to friends.

This plant lends a softening effect in the garden, creating a delicate backdrop for hard-leaved plants. It also looks outstanding against a wall, in a low-light corner, or beneath a large tree such as palo verdes (*Parkinsonia* spp.) or ironwood (*Olneya tesota*). When used abundantly it makes a good filler for lightly shaded areas or along a path where its soft foliage is welcome.

The similar *Abutilon parishii*, which is scarce in most of its range in Arizona, may be differentiated from this Indian mallow by its more sharply pointed leaves that are dark green above and silvery below, as well as other floral distinctions.

Acacia aneura
Mulga

FAMILY: Fabaceae.

DISTRIBUTION: Australia, where it is abundant and widespread in the states of Western Australia, South Australia, New South Wales, and Queensland. Reported to cover nearly a fifth of the dry interior of the continent.

MATURE SIZE: Multitrunked shrub or tree 15 to 20 ft. (4.5 to 6 m) tall and spreading 10 to 16 ft. (3 to 4.8 m).

BLOOMING PERIOD: March, June to October.

EXPOSURE: Full sun in all areas but tolerates partial shade in the hottest deserts.

HARDINESS: Reports of cold hardiness vary and may reflect the origin of the seed. Many growers report plants undamaged at 15°F (−9.4°C), while others report moderate branch damage at 20°F (−6.7°C).

Mulga is an evergreen large shrub to small tree. The new branches are dark reddish brown but age to gray. In older plants the bark becomes fissured.

The leaves are rigid with fine hairs and are 1.5 to 3 in. (3.8 to 7.6 cm) long. The narrow to broadly linear, leathery phyllodes range from dull dark green to gray-green or silver and are 1 to 3 in. (2.5 to 7.6 cm) wide and up to 10 in. (25 cm) long. This species offers a spectacular range of phyllode shape and color: they may be straight or curved, rounded, keeled, or flat.

The flowering heads are short, stalked spikes that are up to 0.5 in. (1.3 cm) long and are crammed with tiny, bright yellow to golden flowers. They are followed by straight, oblong, flat brown pods that are up to 4 in. (10 cm) long.

Mulga grows in almost any soil as long as the drainage is superb. Because it does well on monthly watering in the deserts, it is a favored choice for areas that are irregularly irrigated or outside the reach of regular irrigation. Plants that show yellowing leaves are usually being overwatered. The plants grow

Acacia aneura (mulga)

at a rate that is slow to moderate. Plants are long-lived, with a life span over 100 years reported in nature.

Mulga has a graceful conical to rounded natural form that does not need regular pruning. Any pruning is best done in October; then only cut enough to reinforce the existing structure of the plant. Mulga sunburns readily when pruned in the summer, so avoid any pruning then.

Mulga is a name used for a number of

Australian species of *Acacia*. It is an Aboriginal word that refers to a shield that was made from the wood of this species.

Tough and durable, mulga is a wonderful choice for areas that are hot, even those with reflective heat from a wall or a pool. It makes a good screen and can be placed anywhere a large screening shrub is desirable. Because litter is minimal, it may be used near pools or other areas where tidiness is required. Its highly symmetrical form makes it useful for filling a corner or an odd space.

There is wide variability in the species in both phyllode size and color. Many forms are deep green while others are nearly silver. Some grow as large, round shrubs while others are more treelike.

Acacia angustissima

Fern acacia, whiteball acacia, prairie acacia

FAMILY: Fabaceae.

DISTRIBUTION: In the United States in western and southern Texas, southern New Mexico, and in central and southeastern Arizona along the drainages of the Verde, Salt, and Gila Rivers at 3200 to 6500 ft. (970 to 1950 m). Fern acacia also occurs in disjunct and isolated populations in Oklahoma, Kansas, Missouri, Arkansas, and Louisiana, and in isolated populations on the Gulf side of southern Florida. In Mexico it occurs in central Sonora, Coahuila, and northern Nuevo León, and south to Guatemala and Costa Rica.

MATURE SIZE: Low-growing shrub. Some individuals are barely woody from 1 to 3 ft. (0.3 to 0.9 m) tall and spreading from 2 to 5 ft. (0.6 to 1.5 m), although in some parts of the range the plant grows larger.

BLOOMING PERIOD: May to September.
EXPOSURE: Full sun in all but the hottest deserts, where light shade or an eastern exposure is recommended.
HARDINESS: Hardy to at least 25°F (−4°C); records for Tucson, Arizona, indicate tip damage at 20°F (−7°C).

Fern acacia is a spineless, short shrub that is at home in the dry deserts as well as the open reaches of the prairies. This species is highly variable, and some accepted varieties reflect these differences across its vast range. Most plants form extensive colonies from rhizomes. In the colder parts of the range, plants are deciduous. But where winters are mild, they remain evergreen, only losing their leaves when newer ones push them out.

Young branches are somewhat hairy but become smooth with age. There are fine spines (stipules) in the leaf nodes, but they are tiny and rarely significant. Most stems remain herbaceous and become woody only at the base in old age.

The leaves are bipinnately compound, 4 to 10 in. (10 to 25 cm) long, and composed of 2 to 14 pairs of pinnae, each with 6 to 30 pairs of leaflets. Leaflets are tiny, much less than 0.25 in. (0.6 cm) long with either an acute or rounded tip. Leaflets are deep green to yellow-green.

The pure white flowers form in either a terminal or axillary raceme that is congested into a globe. The flowering head is up to 2.5 in. (6.4 cm) in diameter. Flowers are frequently tinged with pink or lavender, and the entire head may appear to be that color in some individuals. This species blooms extravagantly, with 100 or more flowering heads on the plant.

The reddish brown pod that forms after flowering is linear, flat, and 1.25 to 2.5 in. (3.1 to 6.4 cm) long. It is smooth and opens soon after maturity.

Fern acacia is entirely unfazed by the type of soil it is placed in; it grows well in sand and loams as well as in rocky caliche. Good drainage is essential, however.

In the hottest desert, fern acacia needs to be watered every month. Natural rainfall is sufficient in areas with regular summer rains. In all areas, the plant needs minimal or no winter watering. Growth is moderate to rapid in all areas.

Fern acacia is valued as a perennial ground cover or for erosion control because of its rhizomatous habit. For some reason, it is not commonly grown despite its good performance in most areas.

There are five recognized varieties of this species, with a great deal of overlap and dispute over some of them. The type, *Acacia angustissima* var. *angustissima*, is rhizomatous, often semiwoody, especially at the base, while var. *hirta* has more pinnae and more leaflets. Var. *texensis* occurs across the southern part of the range into most of eastern Mexico, and is a low-growing, smaller form with the flowers held within the leaves. All of these varieties intergrade where their ranges overlap. There is a huge amount of variation in both nature and in the nursery.

Var. *chisosiana* has leaves that are sparsely hairy and is limited to far western Texas and south into Mexico with only two to four pairs of pinnae. And some authors recognize var. *shrevei* as the form found in southeastern Arizona.

In the garden, this shrub is lovely, light, and small and makes a good backdrop for

Acacia angustissima (fern acacia)

smaller perennials. It is well suited to filling in small or tight places, so it is a good choice for use along a driveway or walkway, or as a small, loose, informal hedge.

Acacia berlandieri (guajillo)

Acacia berlandieri
Guajillo

FAMILY: Fabaceae.

DISTRIBUTION: In the United States in far western Texas to south Texas on dry, limestone slopes near the Rio Grande at 1000 to 3000 ft. (305 to 914 m). In Mexico in southeast Chihuahua through Coahuila, Nuevo León, and Tamaulipas, south into northeastern Durango, extreme north Zacatecas, south and eastern Querétaro, northwest Hidalgo, and also in Veracruz up to 6200 ft. (1860 m).

MATURE SIZE: Multistemmed shrub or small tree from 6 to 15 ft. (1.8 to 4.5 m) with an equal spread.

BLOOMING PERIOD: March, and continues intermittently until November or December.

EXPOSURE: Full sun; partial shade to full sun in the hottest deserts.

HARDINESS: Hardy to at least 20°F (–7°C) with no damage; but there are reports of it withstanding temperatures to 15°F (–10°C). It is killed at 10°F (–12°C).

Guajillo is a deciduous to semievergreen species that has numerous stems arising from the base, particularly when young. Guajillo grows at a moderate rate and will form a small tree with moderate pruning over the life of the plant. Although it has spines, they are tiny and rarely noticeable, and some individuals do not have spines. Branches are gray to white with a modest amount of pubescence. The bark on older stems turns gray and has shallow fissures and broad, flat ridges.

The bipinnately compound leaves are 3 to 6 in. (7.6 to 15 cm) long. There are 5 to 11 pairs of pinnae, and each is 1 to 2.5 in. (2.5 to 6.4 cm) long. There are 15 to 35, sometimes more, pairs of leaflets per pinna. Leaflets are linear to oblong with an acute tip and are tiny, less than 0.25 in. (0.6 cm) long; they have a light fuzz when young but quickly become smooth.

The sweetly fragrant, white to cream flowers are held in congested, rounded terminal heads that are 2.5 in. (6.4 cm) around. The species is widely regarded as a heavy bloomer and is prized for the outstanding honey made from its flowers.

The thin, flat, dark brown pod is 2 to 6 in. (5.1 to 15 cm) long and may be straight or slightly curved. When young the pod is quite pubescent but becomes smoother with age. At maturity the pod is thick and leathery, and seeds bulge through the pods, and the pod opens long after the seeds are mature.

Acacia emoryana, which has a more elongated flowering head, is a well known but not always available hybrid of this species and *Acacia greggii*.

Guajillo grows in almost any well-drained soil and has excellent drought tolerance. It is capable of growing on annual rainfall of as little as 6 in. (15 cm) but is a more desirable garden plant with summer irrigation every two to three weeks in the hottest deserts. A branch elongation study performed in Texas found that this species does most of its growing in the fall and early winter.

This small tree is one of the species recommended by local utilities in the Phoenix area for use under power lines. Any pruning is best done in the late spring or early summer, but the species rarely needs more than the removal of dead wood or a stray branch or two. This species is attractive to rabbits when young, so a protective cage or other device is advisable until the woody base forms.

Guajillo has such exquisite spring flowering that it demands being placed where it can be enjoyed fully when in bloom. Otherwise, it is a good addition to a mixed hedge or as a backdrop to desert plantings because of its delicate, lacy foliage. Its great heat and drought tolerance makes it a good choice for areas that don't have regular irrigation or are on the edge of the garden. The lush, full look of the tree softens any planting, and its extreme durability makes it useful in almost any garden in the region.

Acacia constricta
Whitethorn acacia, white thorn

FAMILY: Fabaceae.

DISTRIBUTION: In the United States abundant in southern Arizona and New Mexico at 1500 to 5000 ft. (450 to 1500 m). In West Texas widespread in dry areas and in scattered locations along the Rio Grande drainage mainly west of the Pecos River, becoming rare farther south. In Mexico abundant in dry areas of Baja California and northern Sonora, as well as in Chihuahua, Coahuila, western Nuevo León, Tamaulipas, to Durango, Zacatecas, San Luis Potosí, as far as southern Puebla.

MATURE SIZE: Shrub to small tree 4 to 10 ft.

(1.2 to 3 m) tall with some individuals up to 20 ft. (6 m); plants spread 10 to 15 ft. (3 to 4.5 m) wide.

BLOOMING PERIOD: May to August, but is most prolific in late spring.

EXPOSURE: Full sun in all areas.

HARDINESS: Hardy to at least 15°F (−9°C), probably lower.

Whitethorn acacia is a multibranched, deciduous shrub that forms a small tree as it matures. In nature, plants often form thickets. New stems are reddish, but the smooth bark ages to dark brown or black with a reddish cast. With age the bark turns gray and becomes slightly roughened with small scales that often flake away.

The branches and new growth are thornless when young, but a pair of straight, smooth, somewhat rounded spines forms at the base of the leaves. These thorns range from barely visible to over 1.5 in. (3.8 cm) long and become white with age, hence the common name.

The bipinnately compound leaves are 1 to 2 in. (2.5 to 5.1 cm) long. They are usually alternate but may also be clustered around the node in fascicles. Leaves are made up of 3 to 7 pairs of pinnae, each of which has 6 to 16 pairs of leaflets. Leaflets are oblong to linear, somewhat thick, smooth, or hairy, and less than 0.25 in. (0.6 cm) long with a rounded tip. Although winter deciduous, plants also shed their leaves in prolonged drought.

The fragrant, dark yellow flowers are held in a dense, globular head that is up to 0.5 in. (1.3 cm) around. Flowers are dark yellow and fragrant. They are followed by red pods that are 2 to 4 in. (5.1 to 10 cm) long, straight, and somewhat flattened. The pods have a distinct constriction between the seeds that accounts for the scientific name. Pods open quickly after maturity.

Whitethorn acacia grows at a slow to moderate rate in almost any well-drained soil. It has moderate tolerance for saline soils. In the hottest deserts, water it once a month in summer to prevent early leaf drop, although it survives on natural rainfall in most of the region. Some growers report that both caterpillars and mistletoe may invade plants, but both are easily controlled by vigilant removal of affected areas.

Current research indicates that unlike other species of *Acacia*, whitethorn forms nitrogen-fixing nodules on the roots. This activity is particularly abundant when tem-

Acacia constricta (whitethorn acacia)

peratures reach 97°F (36°C), making it one of the few species that performs this vital activity in soils of high heat, with salty conditions and a medium high pH.

Whitethorn acacia is popular in many desert cities for its delightful, roselike fragrance as well for its attractiveness to wildlife. Its seeds are a feast for birds and the nectar makes excellent honey. Because of its smaller size, this species is recommended for use under power lines.

Whitethorn acacia is a species for the edges and boundaries of the garden and for those areas where you want a natural look. While it is tough and durable, the flowers are lovely during the spring with a light, delicate aroma.

Acacia craspedocarpa
Leatherleaf acacia

FAMILY: Fabaceae.

DISTRIBUTION: Endemic to the state of Western Australia, where it is common near watercourses and often forms thickets.

MATURE SIZE: Small tree or shrub 9 to 12 ft. (2.7 to 3.6 m) tall and 10 to 15 ft. (3 to 4.5 m) wide.

BLOOMING PERIOD: Blooms intermittently from April to September.

EXPOSURE: Full sun in all areas; tolerates light shade in hottest deserts.

HARDINESS: Cold hardy to 15°F (−9°C).

Leatherleaf acacia is a dense, evergreen, rounded shrub to small tree. Although some individuals tend to spread wider than they are tall, most are a generally upright, symmetrical tree. Young branches are dark red-brown but gray with age.

The thick, gray phyllodes are broadly elliptic, rounded or broadly obovate, and up to 1 in. (2.5 cm) long. They are rounded at the tip and firm and leathery to the touch.

The golden yellow flowers are held in short, dense, axillary cylindrical heads. These flowering heads are less than 1 in. (2.5 cm) long and occur in pairs near the end of the branch.

Following the flowers, pods form, which are markedly veined (which is the meaning of *craspedocarpa*); although they begin with a fresh shade of green, they fade to dark brown. The pods are flat, rounded at the tip, and up to 1.5 to 2.5 in. (3.8 to 6.4 cm) long. They continue to hang in clusters on the tree and open long after they mature.

Leatherleaf acacia grows in almost any well-drained soil but performs best in rocky,

Acacia craspedocarpa (leatherleaf acacia)

alkaline soils. It tolerates any level of heat. Growth rate is slow to moderate.

This evergreen tree is good looking and durable. When left unpruned it forms a dense, upright shrub that makes a good evergreen hedge. Its small stature makes it a good choice for smaller gardens, around patios or pools, or various restricted situations.

Acacia cultriformis
Knife acacia, knife-leaf wattle

FAMILY: Fabaceae.

DISTRIBUTION: Australia from southeast Queensland to southern New South Wales, mainly along the western slopes of the Great Divide.

MATURE SIZE: Erect shrub 6 to 12 ft. (1.8 to 3.7 m) tall and wide.

BLOOMING PERIOD: January to March.

EXPOSURE: Tolerates full or reflected sun in all areas, as well as partial shade in the hottest deserts.

HARDINESS: Hardy to at least 25°F (−4°C).

Knife acacia is a large, open shrub with angular, often fancifully twisted, branches, giving it an unusual, intriguing look. It is well named: *culter* is Latin for knife. In nature, it forms thickets, but this is rare in cultivation.

As in all Australian acacias, what appear as leaves are the flattened petioles called phyllodes. In this species the phyllodes are 0.5 to

Acacia cultriformis (knife acacia)

1 in. (1.3 to 2.5 cm) long, triangular, flat, leathery, and with a sharp tip. One edge of the phyllode hugs the stem, and they are densely crowded along the stem. These unusual phyllodes range from gray-green to light blue-green but are more often a scruffy silvery gray.

Rounded heads of creamy yellow to deep golden yellow flowers are held in short spikes of 10 to 20 flowers. The flowering heads are each 0.5 to 2 in. (1.3 to 5.1 cm) around and cluster at the nodes in either a pair or groups of 6 to 8 flowering heads. These flowering heads are profuse on the plant and often are so congested that from a distance it appears that there is a huge beehive of bloom on the stem. Flowers are followed by linear pods 2 to 3.5 in. (5.1 to 8.9 cm) long that are covered with fine hairs.

Knife acacia grows in any well-drained, even rocky, soil with little or no amendments. Water it monthly in the growing season of the winter and when heat is severe in the summer.

In Australia the selection 'Australflora Cascade' (registered by the Australflora Nursery in 1980 and sold with or without this name) has a more than average pendulous habit and spreads over walls and the ground. This form is rarely seen in the United States.

I like this odd-looking plant, particularly when it is in bloom. I admire its rugged regularity in difficult conditions. It makes a good accent or focal plant, chiefly because of its intense flowering. It is a good choice for a mixed border or a loose, informal hedge. This species is especially useful to residents of the deserts who want color in the winter season but want to leave the plant somewhat on its own for the summer.

Acacia erioloba (camel thorn)

Acacia erioloba
Camel thorn

FAMILY: Fabaceae.

DISTRIBUTION: In Africa through the dry woodland and arid stony or sand areas of Angola, Zambia, Namibia, Botswana, Zimbabwe, and South Africa. It is a protected species in South Africa.

MATURE SIZE: Highly variable in nature, often attaining only 6 ft. (1.8 m) in height, probably due to grazing. As a tree, grows up to 50 ft. (15.2 m) tall with the crown spreading up to 30 ft. (9.1 m) across.

BLOOMING PERIOD: July to September.
EXPOSURE: Full sun in all areas.
HARDINESS: Hardy to 15°F (−9°C).

Upright and multibranched when young, camel thorn is a many-branched shrub. As it matures, it will retain most of these branches without pruning. Select one or several sturdy stems and prune out the rest to encourage a taller, more erect plant. Once selected, the leaders grow tall and straight, and the crown, while somewhat columnar when young, spreads and flattens with age, and the tree develops into a handsome shade tree.

The bark is green to dark brown or black and becomes deeply furrowed as it ages. Young branches are shiny and often a rich reddish brown. Stems have sturdy, straight, axillary white spines that are profuse on young branches but drop as the branches age. Spines are up to 2.5 in. (6.4 cm) long and are often swollen at the base.

The bipinnately compound leaves are 1 in. (2.5 cm) long and have two to five pinnae per leaf. There are 8 to 18 pairs of leaflets that are 0.25 to 0.5 in. (0.6 to 1.3 cm) long on each pinna. Leaflets are smooth and dusky gray green. The leaves are held in pairs at the nodes and are widely spaced along the stem.

The flowers are bright golden yellow in rounded heads that are up to 0.75 in. (1.8 cm) long. They are followed by pods that are 3 to 4 in. (7.6 to 10.2 cm) long. These pods range from straight to slightly curved and are densely covered with gray, velvety hairs. They are so hard that they are virtually impenetrable and do not open on their own.

The wood of camel thorn is hard and resistant to both borers and termites. It fulfills a wide variety of functions in its range, including firewood, food, and building materials. In the past, the strong wood was used for mine timbers. This tree is invaluable for shade and is frequently the only large tree growing in a given area.

The common name comes from a mistranslation of the Afrikaans *kameeldoring*, which means giraffe thorn. When I first encountered this species at the Desert Botanical Garden in Phoenix, the plant's previous botanical name was *Acacia giraffae*.

The species is intermittently available but ought to enjoy much greater use. It is a tall, durable tree that thrives in the rocky, alkaline soils of the region on minimal supplemental irrigation. It makes a good alternative to the ubiquitous South American mesquites where tall shade trees are desirable, and with its dusky, gray leaves it dominates the visual field as much as those trees do.

Acacia farnesiana
Sweet acacia, huisache

SYNONYM: *Acacia minuta* and *A. smallii*.
FAMILY: Fabaceae.
DISTRIBUTION: Sweet acacia is cultivated throughout the warm parts of the world, but its exact natural distribution is uncertain. Many botanists believe it originated in South America. It is now found growing outside of cultivation along the Gulf coastal plain and down the entire length of the Rio Grande Valley in Texas, through southern Arizona, southern California, as well as the Gulf states to Florida, tropical Central and South America, and the West

Indies at 2500 to 5000 ft. (762 to 1524 m). Sweet acacia is considered a pest species in tropical islands, especially Hawaii, and is also considered invasive in other areas.

MATURE SIZE: Multibranched shrub to small tree from 8 to 30 ft. (2.4 to 9.1 m) tall with an equal spread.

BLOOMING PERIOD: Blooms prolifically from January to March, but in milder areas it continues through May.

EXPOSURE: Full sun in all areas; it tolerates partial shade in the hottest deserts.

HARDINESS: Hardy to 20°F (−7°C) without appreciable damage, but records from Tucson, Arizona, indicate minor tip damage at 18°F (−8°C). Plants grown from populations in the northern part of its range are hardy to 10°F (−12°C).

Sweet acacia is a spiny, multistemmed shrub to small tree with complicated branching: branches often grow in a zigzag pattern. The bark is light red-brown with narrow ridges and shows deep furrows with age. Stems are punctuated by pairs of straight, white spines that are 1 to 3 in. (2.5 to 7.6 cm) long.

The bipinnately compound leaves are 1 to 4 in. (2.5 to 10.2 cm) long and are composed of two to six pairs of pinnae, each with 10 to 25 pairs of leaflets, but may become fascicled in old age. The leaflets are linear to oblong, have a sharp tip, and are less than 0.25 in. (0.6 cm) long. Leaflets are bright, dark green, but there are individuals with gray-green leaflets.

Sweet acacia is drought deciduous if conditions are severe and winter deciduous in the most northern parts of its range. If the leaves do not fall during the winter, they are replaced as the new ones emerge in spring.

Golden yellow flowers are held in con-

Acacia farnesiana (sweet acacia)

gested globular heads that are up to 0.5 in. (1.3 cm) across. Each leaf axil has one to three flower heads and flowering is profuse. Plants in full bloom have a golden hue even from a distance. The flowers exude a strong, sweet perfume that is noticeable far from the tree.

Flowers are followed by dark brown, cylindrical, woody pods that are 1 to 3 in. (2.5 to 7.5 cm) long. The pods open long after maturity and are the source of brown dye in many parts of Mexico.

Some authors, particularly in Texas, recognize two growth habits for this plant: those with a single trunk and drooping branches that appears more along the coast, and those found more inland with several trunks and ascending branches.

Over the years there has been immense confusion and indecision regarding the name of this taxon and its various geographic forms. Currently *Acacia farnesiana* is the recognized name and includes all those formerly known as *A. minuta* and *A. smallii*. While there are forms that tend to bloom more in the fall and others that bloom more prolifically in the spring, and there is a wide variety in cold tolerance, it is the current botanical thinking that these differences are no more than the expected variability of a wide-ranging species.

Sweet acacia grows best in deep, somewhat enriched soils with good drainage, and it struggles in rocky, dry soils. Sweet acacia has excellent heat tolerance, although it is short lived and disappointing when grown where there is strong reflective heat such as from walls, buildings, or gravel mulch.

Sweet acacia grows best when watered every 10 to 14 days in the summer in the hottest deserts. In other areas, it grows almost entirely on natural rainfall unless there is a prolonged dry spell.

Plants are brittle and break in high winds. This tendency is exacerbated by two cultural conditions common in the region: watering too shallowly and too frequently, which creates the twin perils of a poorly grown and insufficient root system to anchor the plant, and dense, crowded branching that makes the plant more susceptible to wind throw.

Sweet acacia is not a particularly long-lived tree. Most reports state that it survives 25 to 50 years in cultivation.

It is reported that sweet acacia was first brought to Europe in 1611 from Santo Domingo and was originally cultivated in the garden of Cardinal Odoardo Farnese at his sumptuous Italian villa. It is still grown in southern Europe for the perfume trade. Sweet acacia is one of the species recorded by Thomas Jefferson in his extensive collection at Monticello. It has been grown in Australia since 1845 and older texts cite it as native, but it is probably not.

Acacia greggii
Catclaw, catclaw acacia

FAMILY: Fabaceae.

DISTRIBUTION: In the United States in southern California, extreme southwestern Utah, southern Nevada, western and southern Arizona and New Mexico, and in Texas from far West Texas south and east into the South Texas Plains and the valley of the Rio Grande at 1000 to 5500 ft. (305 to 1676 m). In Mexico it is found in Baja California, Sonora, eastern Chihuahua, all of Coahuila, northeast Nuevo León, and northeastern Durango in areas with dry plains and rocky hillsides.

MATURE SIZE: Grows as both a shrub 5 to 6 ft. (1.5 to 1.8 m) tall and about as wide and as a tree to 15 ft. (4.6 m) with a crown spread of 6 to 20 ft. (1.8 to 6.1 m).

BLOOMING PERIOD: April through July, and to October outside the hottest deserts.

EXPOSURE: Full or reflected sun in all areas.

HARDINESS: Cold hardy to 0°F (−18°C).

Acacia greggii (catclaw)

Catclaw, even when tall, forms an irregular, loose shrub or multitrunked tree. It has numerous spreading branches covered with small, less than 0.25-in. (0.6-cm), stout, curved spines that are flat at their base, giving the plant its common name. These tiny, tightly curved, sharp spines help distinguish this acacia from all other similar acacias that occur within its range. Plants are often abundant and form virtually impenetrable thickets. The bark is rough and dark gray. Catclaw is chiefly winter deciduous, with the leaves often shedding late in the season.

Leaves are bipinnately compound and usually alternate with a noticeable red petiole.

There are one to three pairs of pinnae, each of which has three to seven pairs of leaflets that are minute, much less than 0.25 in. (0.6 cm) long, and obovate or elliptic. Leaflets range from gray-green to deep green. Leaves are persistent through the winter and only drop when pushed out by new growth.

Flowers are held in a dense spike or raceme at the axil. The inflorescence is 2.5 to 5 in. (6.4 to 12.7 cm) long. Flowers are light yellow to cream and have a light, sweet fragrance.

The pod is typically flat, 2 to 4 in. (5.1 to 10.2 cm) long, and may be straight, curved or twisted. It is light brown to reddish and opens along the seams when seed is mature.

Catclaw grows in a wide range of soils but does best in well-drained soils. It thrives in poor, dry soils and is often used for revegetation, restoration, or in areas to encourage wildlife. It grows quickly in response to regular watering, and growth has been recorded at up to 8 in. (20.3 cm) a year under such conditions.

In parts of southern Texas, catclaw freely hybridizes with guajillo (*Acacia berlandieri*). Honey from their hybrids is highly valued and is called Uvalde honey.

Catclaw is distinguished from the equally widespread and often associated whitethorn acacia (*Acacia constricta*) by having a more open spreading habit, curved spines, larger leaflets, and gray bark.

The similar *Acacia wrightii* of Trans-Pecos, the Edwards Plateau, and the southern plains of Texas has larger leaflets and a somewhat larger pod. Otherwise, they are extremely similar and have the same cultural requirements.

Catclaw is a useful species in a dry or naturalistic garden both for its attractiveness to wildlife and its immunity to heat and drought. In the hottest deserts, it should have monthly irrigation in the summer, but in all other areas it grows perfectly on natural rainfall. With its complex branching and tiny thorns, this plant is an excellent choice as a barrier or as part of a mixed shrub planting.

Acacia millefolia
Santa Rita acacia, fernleaf acacia

FAMILY: Fabaceae.

DISTRIBUTION: In the United States in far southern Arizona and extreme southwestern New Mexico at 3500 to 5500 ft. (1067 to 1676 m). In Mexico in Sonora and Chihuahua.

MATURE SIZE: Open, multibranched shrub 3 to 10 ft. (0.9 to 3 m) tall; more typically about 6 ft. (1.8 m) tall and wide.

BLOOMING PERIOD: July and September.

EXPOSURE: Partial shade in all areas; full sun only outside the hottest deserts.

HARDINESS: Reports from Tucson, Arizona, indicate that minor tip damage occurs at 20°F (–7°C).

Santa Rita acacia is a loosely branched shrub with weak, nearly insignificant spines at each leaf node. The bark is smooth and pale gray.

The leaves are bipinnately compound, 2 to 6 (5.1 to 15.2 cm) long, and formed of 5 to 10 pairs of pinnae. Each pinna supports 20 to 30 pairs of linear leaflets that initially are softly hairy but are smooth with age. The leaflets are tiny, 0.5 to 1.25 in. (1.3 to 3.2 cm) long,

Acacia millefolia (Santa Rita acacia)

giving the plant a full-leaved appearance. The leaves are both cold and drought deciduous, although this species has extremely good drought tolerance even in the hottest deserts.

The white to pale cream flowers are held in crowded, cylindrical spikes that are 1 to 2 in. (2.5 to 5.1 cm) long. These small spikes look like fuzzy caterpillars on the plant and are held in pairs near the end of the stem. They are followed by flat pods that are 2.75 to 6 in. (7 to 15.2 cm) long with a slight constriction between the seeds.

Santa Rita acacia can be distinguished from nearly all other acacias in its range by the combination of bipinnately compound leaves with relatively few pinnae, flowers in spikes, and tiny to no spines along the stems.

This small shrub is charming and delightful. Its delicate lacy appearance is completely at odds with its performance in rugged hot and dry conditions. The plant is not commonly found, although specialty and native nurseries in the region occasionally carry it. It is excellent as a small hedge or light backdrop for a naturalistic planting or for smaller succulents. Its small size and ferny appearance work well in tight corners, around a patio or seating area, or in any spot that needs softening.

Acacia notabilis
Notable acacia, stiff golden wattle

FAMILY: Fabaceae.
DISTRIBUTION: Endemic to Australia in New South Wales and Victoria, where it is listed as endangered in nature but is commonly cultivated.
MATURE SIZE: Tree growing 6 to 10 ft. (1.8 to 3 m) tall and spreading 6 to 12 ft. (1.8 to 3.7 m) wide.

BLOOMING PERIOD: March to April.
EXPOSURE: Full sun in all but the hottest deserts, where partial shade is best.
HARDINESS: Hardy to 15°F (−9.4°C).

Notable acacia is a fine, small tree for gardens with limited space. It has a multibranched, spreading form with pendulous reddish-brown branches.

The phyllodes are 2 to 6 in. (5.1 to 15.2 cm) long and are elliptic to narrowly oblanceolate and up to 1 in. (2.5 cm) wide. The phyllodes are leathery and smooth gray-green with a prominent midrib.

The flowers are held in axillary racemes that are 1 to 2.5 in. (2.5 to 6.4 cm) long. There

Acacia notabilis (notable acacia)

are up to 40 flowers in each rounded head and they are bright golden yellow.

The seedpods are narrowly oblong, up to 2.75 in. (7 cm) long, and are dark red-brown. Seeds are reported to be edible when roasted.

Notable acacia grows at a moderate to rapid rate in any well-drained soil. In areas where there is at least 12 in. (305 mm) of rainfall, it thrives on rainfall alone.

This plant is a lovely choice for a small patio or seating area that needs a gentle accent or focal planting. It is tall enough to be a shade tree, and provides light shade for smaller plantings of perennials or succulents beneath it. It has a spreading form that is enhanced by the long, firm phyllodes, and rarely needs more than occasional pruning to remove dead wood. Pruning is best done in the late fall or early winter.

The species was named by Ferdinand Mueller, a famous worker in Australian botany, who thought the epithet a double attribution to its beautiful blooming and the fact that it was first collected by him near Mount Remarkable in South Australia.

Acacia redolens

Prostrate acacia

FAMILY: Fabaceae.

DISTRIBUTION: Endemic to Australia from the far southwestern part of West Australia in slightly saline or alkaline soils or along the margins of salty lakes.

MATURE SIZE: Shrub 2 to 5 ft. (0.6 to 1.5 m) tall and spreading 6 to 12 ft. (1.8 to 3.7 m) wide.

BLOOMING PERIOD: February to April.

EXPOSURE: Full or reflected sun in all areas; tolerates partial or light shade especially in the hottest deserts.

HARDINESS: Hardy to at least 20°F (−6.7°C), with some reports of no damage in temperatures in the high teens.

Prostrate acacia is a low-growing, sprawling, evergreen shrub. The highly attractive reddish bark is largely obscured by the foliage.

Phyllodes are dull gray to olive green and up to 3 in. (7.6 cm) long. They are normally oblanceolate to narrowly oblong and may be straight or incurved.

The tiny, rounded flowering heads of golden yellow flowers are less than 0.25 in. (0.6 cm) in diameter. The subsequent pods are narrowly linear up to 2.5 in. (6.4 cm) long, smooth, and thick.

This species was once so commonly used along highway rights of way in the Phoenix area that it became known as the freeway acacia. This rugged species is able to tolerate almost any well-drained soil, even saline ones, as well as the intense heat along a roadway even in the hottest deserts.

Poor pruning easily ruins this plant. It is best to prune in April, taking only small amounts from the tip if it needs to be filled out, or removing a long limb from the base if has grown too far out. It does not recover well from shearing, and usually will lose the middle of the plant. Plants that are overpruned have also shown more extensive cold damage during a hard freeze.

Prostrate acacia has excellent drought tolerance once established, and while something of a yawn from overuse, this plant is a good choice to stabilize a slope or fill in an area that does not receive regular irrigation.

Acacia redolens (prostrate acacia)

Plants that fail are almost always overwatered and overpruned, resulting in too much growth both up and out, and the dead middle that has become a hallmark of pruning abuse in this species. When left to its natural form, it is a good low shrub. The selection 'Desert Carpet' grows shorter and tends to sprawl closer to the ground; in California, the selection 'Low Boy' is similar.

Acacia rigidula
Black brush, blackbrush acacia

FAMILY: Fabaceae.

DISTRIBUTION: In the United States in Texas from the southern coastal prairies and southern plains into the Rio Grande Valley at 1100 to 1800 ft. (335 to 549 m) and is scarce in western Texas. In Mexico, from Sonora, eastern Coahuila, Nuevo León, western Tamaulipas, San Luis Potosí, to northern Veracruz.

MATURE SIZE: Shrubby, multistemmed tree or large shrub growing 3 to 15 ft. (0.9 to 4.6 m) tall and 9 to 12 ft. (2.7 to 3.7 m) wide.

BLOOMING PERIOD: April to May, before the leaves emerge.

EXPOSURE: Grows well in full sun in all areas.

HARDINESS: Hardy to 15°F (−9.4°C).

Acacia rigidula (black brush)

The bipinnately compound leaves are formed of one to two pairs of pinnae, each of which has two to three pairs of leaflets. Leaves are up to 1 in. (2.5 cm) long, and the elliptic to oblong leaflets are 0.25 to 0.5 in. (0.6 to 1.3 cm) long. They are a dark, lustrous green with conspicuous nerves and a blunt tip, and are often crowded into fascicles.

The fragrant, pale yellow to whitish flowers are held in spikes that are 1 to 2.5 in. (2.5 to 6.4 cm) long. Blooming may occur before the leaves emerge and, because flowers are profuse, makes a brilliant show.

The pod is linear or curved, somewhat constricted between the seeds, red-brown to black, and 2 to 3.5 in. (5.1 to 8.9 cm) long. It is eventually dehiscent.

Black brush forms a spectacular small tree when pruned carefully as it grows. The deep green leaves contrast well with other desert plantings, offering a green blanket of relief in the intense heat of summer. The lightly fragrant flowers are welcome near patios or seating areas where the aroma may be enjoyed. This species has an especially interesting form, with its angular branches and dark, closely set leaves. Placing it where this silhouette is visible adds drama and interest to the garden. Although a splendid specimen tree, when left unpruned black brush forms a thorny, barrier hedge.

Black brush is not widely grown outside its native range, for some reason. It grows best in well-drained soils with moderate enrichment. In the hottest deserts, water it deeply every three to four weeks in the summer, but in areas with at least 20 in. (508 mm) of rainfall a year, it thrives on natural rainfall.

Black brush is a deciduous shrub to small tree that frequently forms dense thickets in nature. It has a slow to moderate growth rate. The bark is light gray to nearly white but ages to dark gray and is smooth and tight. It may become fissured when plants are old. Stems have a pair of white, straight thorns at the axils that are 1 to 1.5 in. (2.5 to 3.8 cm) long and hidden within the dense leaves.

Acacia salicina
Willow acacia

FAMILY: Fabaceae.

DISTRIBUTION: Endemic to Australia mainly in central Queensland and western New South Wales but also in Northern Territory, South Australia, and Victoria.

MATURE SIZE: Large shrub or tree 10 to 40 ft. (3 to 12.3 m) tall with a crown spread of 10 to 20 ft. (3 to 6.1 m).

BLOOMING PERIOD: October to December, but it may bloom at almost any time during the year.

EXPOSURE: Full sun in all areas.

HARDINESS: Hardy to 20°F (−6.7°C); severely damaged at 18°F (−7.8°C).

Willow acacia is an attractive tree, with its high, rounded crown and long, flowing branches. It has a moderate growth rate and tolerates alkaline soils well. The bark is smooth and gray when young, but darkens and furrows with age.

The narrow phyllodes are 2 to 7.5 in. (5.1 to 19.1 cm) long, elliptic to narrow oblanceolate, and are held on slender branches causing them to fall toward the ground. Most forms have gray-green phyllodes but there are forms that are blue-gray.

The creamy white flowers are held in small rounded heads that are up to 0.5 in. (1.3 cm) around. The heads of flowers are collected in an axillary raceme that is 1 to 8 in. (2.5 to 20.3 cm) long and holds two to eight heads.

The pods are straight or slightly curved, flat, sometimes constricted between seeds, and 1.25 to 4.75 in. (3.2 to 12.1 cm) long. They are thick, gray-green, slightly woody, and wrinkled when dry.

Acacia salicina (willow acacia)

Willow acacia grows in virtually any soil, including moderately brackish ones, as long as there is excellent drainage. Plants do best with long, deep soaks at long intervals. Even in the hottest deserts, watering every three to four weeks in the summer is sufficient. Frequent, light watering or overspraying encourages shallow rooting and wind throw problems.

Plants, particularly in nature, form root suckers and colonies, but in cultivation this is usually only reported after severe injury or pruning. This species is thought to have a 10- to 15-year life span in cultivation but plants growing without abundant water may last much longer.

Willow acacia is an excellent shade tree for a garden that needs a moderate-sized shade tree with minimal litter. It tolerates almost any soil, as long as it is well drained. Its tolerance for high heat and especially reflective heat have made it a favorite choice for roadside plantings. Willow acacia has a graceful, weeping form: the hanging phyllodes sway in the lightest breeze, making a delicate display in a harsh climate.

Willow acacia is easily confused with its close relative, blue-leaf wattle (*Acacia saligna*). Although there is great variability in phyllodes among individuals as well as when they age, the phyllodes of blue-leaf wattle are usually thick, leathery, and blue-gray and are about the same size as those of willow acacia. Branches do not tend to hang down as prominently as they do in willow acacia, so blue-leaf wattle has a more upright or rounded appearance. In flower, blue-leaf wattle has distinctive 1-in. (2.5-cm) bright golden globes along the stems. Blue-leaf wattle also blooms from February to April rather than in the winter. The bark of willow acacia is smooth and gray when young, only darkening with age, while in blue-leaf wattle it is smooth and red-brown throughout its life.

Acacia schaffneri
Twisted acacia

FAMILY: Fabaceae.

DISTRIBUTION: In the United States only in the plains of south Texas and the extreme southern portion of the Rio Grande Valley. In Mexico in southern Chihuahua, northeastern Coahuila, Nuevo León, Durango, Zacatecas, San Luis Potosí, Querétaro, Hidalgo, and south to Oaxaca.

MATURE SIZE: Sprawling tree or complex shrub 13 to 25 ft. (4 to 7.6 m) tall, occasionally to 30 ft. (9.1 m), and 15 to 25 ft. (4.6 to 7.6 m) wide.

BLOOMING PERIOD: March and April.

EXPOSURE: Full sun in all areas.

HARDINESS: Hardy without damage to 15°F (−9.4°C).

Twisted acacia is a semideciduous tree that freely branches from the base, often forming complicated branching patterns. It often requires attentive pruning to maintain one or a few trunks as the plant matures. The dark brown bark is rough and fissured. Each node has a pair of sharp but almost invisible reddish thorns.

Acacia schaffneri (twisted acacia)

The leaves are bipinnately compound and often fascicled with two to three pinnae. There are 10 to 25 dark green, linear leaflets per pinna. The leaflets are tiny, much less than 0.25 in. (0.6 cm) long, and rounded but end in a sharp tip.

The bright golden yellow flowers are held in rounded 0.5 in. (1.3 cm) heads. There are from one to five heads collected at the nodes.

The pods are linear, straight or with a slight curve, solitary, or clustered at the leaf nodes. The pods are 2.75 to 6 in. (7 to 15.2 cm) long, thick, velvety, and dark brown, with only a slight constriction between the seeds.

Twisted acacia is tolerant of any well-drained soil including the rocky, alkaline dry soils of the deserts. Established trees need only intermittent supplemental irrigation, even in the hottest deserts, during the summer. But leaves remain longer on the plant if it is watered at least monthly during the summer.

Ill-considered pruning ruins the graceful twists of the branches of this plant When pruning twisted acacia, it is wise to carefully remove only juvenile branches or damaged ones and to check often to be sure that the symmetry and character of the tree are maintained. Pruning is best done in May; avoid pruning in the summer in the hottest deserts.

Twisted acacia is a spectacular specimen or focal plant for smaller gardens. This species used to be seen more than it is today, which is a shame. Its handsome branching and deep green leaves make it a fine choice for any garden. While its slower growth rate makes some people impatient, this lovely tree is well worth the wait.

There has been much taxonomic confusion over the populations of this species found in the Rio Grande Valley of Texas. To some authors, those plants are the West Indian and Florida species, *Acacia tortuosa*. The current botanical thinking considers those plants to be of the same taxon as *A. schaffneri* var. *bravoensis*, which continues its range through northeastern Coahuila and Nuevo León, and all other populations in the range listed here to be of the type, var. *schaffneri*.

Acacia stenophylla
Shoestring acacia

FAMILY: Fabaceae.

DISTRIBUTION: Shoestring acacia is common and abundant in the arid areas of northeast Western Australia, in Northern Territory, Queensland, New South Wales, Victoria, and South Australia.

MATURE SIZE: Erect tree 20 to 30 ft. (6.1 to 9.1 m) tall and spreading to at least 20 ft. (6.1 m).

BLOOMING PERIOD: April to July.

EXPOSURE: Grows well in full or reflected sun in all areas.

HARDINESS: Hardy to 20°F (-7°C) with minimal to no damage.

Shoestring acacia begins as a tall, vertical tree with rough, maroon to gray bark and long, hanging branches that give it a weeping willow look. As the plant matures, the crown fills out and the tree takes on a more rounded form. Some individuals, however, tend toward the more rounded form and others toward the long, weeping form. Plants are able to form root suckers when the roots are disturbed or injured or when growing under difficult conditions or on poor sites.

Phyllodes are 6 to 12 in. (15.2 to 30.5 cm),

Acacia stenophylla (shoestring acacia)

pods are straight, they are deeply constricted between the seeds and look like a green or tan string of pearls on the tree.

Shoestring acacia grows equally well in well-drained alkaline clay soils or dry, rocky soils. This species has great heat tolerance and has been a favorite choice for street plantings in the Phoenix area for many years. While there have been a few recorded cases of cotton root rot, the species is not considered highly susceptible to that fungal infection.

This is a symmetrical and graceful tree that does not need regular pruning. If you need to remove damaged or erratically growing limbs, prune in January in the hottest deserts and a month or two later in the other areas.

This species lives longer than some other Australian members of this genus, with plants living up to 50 years in cultivation. As for most Australian acacia species, over-watering is not helpful and can greatly shorten their life span.

Shoestring acacia is an excellent choice to provide high, light shade, growing tall enough to shelter a building or a roof. The weeping habit is attractive, particularly from a distance, and in large gardens may be used to good effect. Shoestring acacia is a good choice near a patio or pool area where its minimal litter is appreciated.

There is much variability in shoestring acacia, some of which is the result of cultural practices and some of which is inherent in the individual plant. Trees may be tall and rounded or thin and weeping. These two conditions may occur through the life of one plant, or a plant may retain a particular growth habit throughout its life. If you care about the ultimate form, look closely at the

narrow, and silvery gray. They are straight and hang down from the branches.

The creamy white to pale yellow flowers are held in axillary round heads 0.5 in. (1.3 cm) around. There are two to six heads in a cluster, giving the bloom more prominence than the size of the individual heads suggests.

The distinctive pods are 8 in. (20.3 cm) long or more and held in clusters. Although plant in the nursery and select the form you prefer.

The other renowned Australian acacia with a strong cacading habit is weeping acacia (*Acacia pendula*). This imposing tree, which is 20 to 40 ft. (6.1 to 12.2 m) tall with a crown spread of 15 to 25 ft. (4.6 to 7.8 m), is endemic to central and western Australia. In the United States it blooms from April to May and again in August to September. Its bright, golden flowers are held in round, congested heads in groups of three to five at the nodes. Hardy to 20°F (−7°C) with tip and leaf damage at 18°F (−8°C), this immensely heat-tolerant tree is a good choice as a focal or accent tree. It also serves well near patios or pool areas because, as for many of the Australian acacias, litter is minimal.

Acacia willardiana
Palo blanco, white bark acacia

FAMILY: Fabaceae.

DISTRIBUTION: Endemic to Mexico in western Sonora and northwest Sinaloa and islands of the coast from sea level to 3000 ft. (914 m).

MATURE SIZE: Spare, erect tree 10 to 25 ft. (3 to 7.6 m) tall, occasionally to 30 ft. (9.1 m), and spreading 5 to 10 ft. (1.5 to 3 m) wide.

BLOOMING PERIOD: February to April.

EXPOSURE: Full sun in all areas.

HARDINESS: Temperatures near 25°F (−4°C) cause the leaves to fall but there is no stem damage.

Palo blanco is a tall wisp of a tree with few branches that form a distinct vase shape. The thin, white bark peels readily from the tree,

Acacia willardiana (palo blanco)

and older trees are remarkable for the long sheets of papery bark that hang from the unarmed stems.

The bipinnately compound leaves are formed of one to three pinnae that are 1 to 2 in. (2.5 to 5.1 cm) long. Each pinna has 4 to 15 minute leaflets that are less than 0.25 in. (0.6 cm) long. These true leaves are held at the tip of a petiole that is 4 to 12 in. (10.2 to 30.5 cm) long; the petiole functions in the same manner as the phyllodes of the Australian acacias. While the leaves are ephemeral and appear briefly in the spring or after summer rains, these phyllodes are persistent year-round and give the plant its distinctive evergreen, weeping form.

The creamy white flowers are clustered into dense, cylindrical spikes that are 1 to 3 in. (2.5 to 7.6 cm) long. The flowers are followed by flat pods 2 in. (5.1 cm) long.

Palo blanco grows in any well-drained soil, even dry, rocky native soils of the deserts. Once established they grow on natural rainfall even in the hottest deserts, although in these areas plants retain better vigor if given monthly deep waterings. This tree has exquisite natural form and needs to be pruned only to remove dead wood or crossing branches. Pruning is best done in April.

This spectacular tree is a wonderful choice for a small area that needs some drama or lift. It is particularly effective when planted in groves. Palo blanco forms a unique statement with its tall, spare, whitish stems and light phyllodes that float on the lightest breeze. It has astounding heat and drought tolerance while being such a delicate-looking plant.

Aloysia gratissima
Whitebrush, bee brush

SYNONYMS: *Lippia lycioides*, *Aloysia lycioides*, and *Lippia gratissima*.

FAMILY: Verbenaceae.

DISTRIBUTION: In the United States from southeastern Arizona through the southern third of New Mexico and into most of western Texas and extending east through the Edwards Plateau and south down the Rio Grande to its mouth at 1100 to 5000 ft. (335 to 1524 m). In Mexico from Sonora to Nuevo León throughout the Chihuahuan Desert and south to Oaxaca, and into South America in Brazil, Bolivia, Paraguay, Uruguay, and Argentina.

MATURE SIZE: Loosely branched shrub 4 to 10 ft. (1.2 to 3 m) tall and spreading up to 6 ft. (1.8 m) wide.

BLOOMING PERIOD: March to November intermittently, particularly in response to rain.

EXPOSURE: Full sun in all areas.

HARDINESS: Hardy to 15°F (−9°C).

Whitebrush is a densely branched shrub with slender, stiff, aromatic, tan branches. Individual plants and their abundant seedlings may form dense thickets in some parts of the species' natural range, a trait that has made it unwelcome in some areas. Plants are evergreen or may lose some or all of their leaves in response to cold, drought, or at the end of the season as new leaves emerge.

The tiny leaves are less than 1 in. (2.5 cm) long, opposite, narrowly oblong to elliptic, with an entire or a toothed margin. Leaves often form dense clusters at the nodes with even tinier leaves nearest the stem. Leaves are dark green but the minute rough hairs give them a grayish cast and a scruffy texture.

The numerous flowers are arranged in loose 1- to 3-in. (2.5- to 7.6-cm) spikes. There may be one or two flowering stalks per node and they extend far beyond the leaves. The individual flowers are minute, less than 0.25 in. (0.6 cm) long, and are white or tinged with pink. They have a strong vanilla fragrance. Flowers are reported to be poisonous to horses, mules, and burros, but the pollen is immensely attractive to butterflies and bees. The honey from the flowers is delicious and highly regarded in its natural range.

The fruit is a drupe composed of two tiny nutlets that are significantly less than 0.25 in. (0.6 cm) long. Lesser goldfinch and other seed-eating birds devour the fruit as soon as it sets.

Whitebrush grows in any well-drained soil, including poor, rocky, native ones. Although it tolerates growing in the shade, both its form and blooming are much improved when it grows in full sun.

Used as part of a mixed hedge or to form a border area, whitebrush is an excellent choice to attract wildlife. Extremely drought tolerant once established, it does not need routine care, but it thrives on watering two or three times a month in the summer in the hottest deserts. Within its vast natural range, it grows on natural rainfall.

The sweet fragrance of the flowers is delightful and the leaves have a pungent aroma like that of oregano. The combination is magnificent and seductive, so be sure to put it where you take full advantage of the dual fragrances. Prune in the spring just as a new flush of growth begins. Better yet, do not prune until the goldfinches and other birds have stripped off the fruit, because birds are one of the best reasons to have this charming shrub in the garden.

Whitebrush may be aggressive, forming thickets, especially on disturbed ground, but it is only a minor problem in the garden unless it receives too much water. Seedlings arise where there is ample water; they should

Aloysia gratissima (whitebrush)

be pulled as they appear because their deep roots take hold quickly.

The similar oreganillo (*Aloysia wrightii*) is distinguished from whitebrush by its smaller, hairy, almost oval leaves with strongly toothed or wavy margins and its strongly congested flowering spikes. The flowers and leaves have the same delightful fragrances, and this species enjoys the same cultural conditions.

Amyris texana (Texas torchwood)

Amyris texana
Texas torchwood

FAMILY: Rutaceae.

DISTRIBUTION: In the United States in Texas along the southern coast and prairies. In Mexico in Nuevo León and Tamaulipas and extreme northern Veracruz.

MATURE SIZE: Shrub 3 to 5 ft. (0.9 to 1.5 m) tall, occasionally to 9 ft. (2.7 m), and as wide.

BLOOMING PERIOD: April to October.

EXPOSURE: Full sun or filtered shade in all areas; filtered shade in the hottest deserts.

HARDINESS: Hardy to 20°F (−7°C).

Texas torchwood is a dense, round shrub that is usually evergreen but may drop its leaves during a hard freeze. The bark is smooth and light gray.

Leaves are compound with three glossy, deep green leaflets. The leaflets are 0.5 to 1.25 in. (1.3 to 3.2 cm) long and much longer than they are wide. When crushed, they have a light, crisp, citruslike fragrance.

The flowers are lightly fragrant and held in terminal clusters 1 to 3 in. (2.5 to 7.6 cm) long. Individual flowers are white and less than 0.25 in. (0.6 cm) long, but the collected blooms are showy. Flowers are followed by a dark black, juicy fruit that is favored by birds.

The similar *Amyris madrensis* has 5 to 11 rounded aromatic leaflets and larger fruit. The wavy margins of the leaves make this species showier, but it is less cold hardy. Both species occur in similar areas, although *A. madrensis* ranges into Coahila, Mexico.

Texas torchwood is a good specimen in a smaller garden, where its pleasant fragrance and shorter height are welcome. Texas torchwood's size also makes it appropriate for use in large containers or planters. This species enjoys a strong following in Texas, but because of its great heat tolerance and ability to grow in dry soils it should be considered for more parts of the region.

Anisacanthus puberulus
Pinky anisacanthus, red Chihuahuan honeysuckle

FAMILY: Acanthaceae.

DISTRIBUTION: In the United States in far west Texas at 2800 to 6300 ft. (853 to 1920 m). In Mexico this Chihuahuan Desert endemic plant ranges intermittently through Chihuahua, Coahuila, Zacatecas, and San Luis Potosí at 2600 to 4900 ft. (792 to 1494 m). It is not common anywhere in its range.

MATURE SIZE: Sprawling shrub 3 to 8 ft. (0.9 to 2.4 m) tall and 6 to 10 ft. (1.8 to 3 m) wide.

BLOOMING PERIOD: March to April and October to December.

EXPOSURE: Full sun in all areas.

HARDINESS: Root hardy to 15°F (−9°C).

Pinky anisacanthus is a rambling, intricately branched shrub with fine hairs along the young stems. As the bark ages it turns

Anisacanthus puberulus (pinky anisacanthus)

gray and often peels away, but this feature is rarely noticeable because the bark is well hidden beneath the leaves. Plants are winter deciduous, but during mild winters they may not lose their leaves until new ones begin to emerge.

Leaves are broadly lanceolate to ovate and 2 to 3.5 in. (5.1 to 8.9 cm) long. They are light green with a slightly gray cast from the fine hairs.

Flowers are held in a crowded inflorescence that is 0.5 to 2.75 in. (1.3 to 7 cm) long at the nodes of the leaves. The individual flowers are 1.5 to 2.25 in. (3.8 to 5.7 cm) long with the corolla lobes formed into a narrow tube that is deeply split and flared at the ends. They are pale pink and occur both before and after the leaves emerge.

Pinky anisacanthus is a drought tolerant, colorful shrub that has not enjoyed much use, perhaps because of its sprawling, loose habit. Judicious tip pruning in the late spring improves the appearance of the shrub. Severe pruning in the summer, however, risks sunburn, and pruning too late in the fall impedes bloom.

Pinky anisacanthus appears to have no preference about soils as long as drainage is superb. Water every two weeks in the summer in the hottest deserts but be careful not to overwater, which increases its tendency to create long, floppy branches.

Pinky anisacanthus provides excellent winter color in a mixed planting or as an accent plant in a hot, dry location. Even in the hottest deserts it thrives in full sun and so it is particularly useful where watering is intermittent and care is minimal.

The closely related dwarf anisacanthus (*Anisacanthus linearis*) is also uncommon in the trade. This is a more erect shrub with narrow, linear, light green leaves. Flowers are orange-red in this species, and it blooms from June to September. Hybrids of dwarf anisacanthus with flame anisacanthus (*Anisacanthus quadrifidus* var. *wrightii*) have been offered occasionally. Despite its name, dwarf anisacanthus is larger than *A. puberulus* or *A. quadrifidus* var. *wrightii*, and also thrives in areas with dry, rocky soils and minimal supplemental watering. Hummingbirds flock to the tubular flowers as they do for all members of the genus.

Desert honeysuckle (*Anisacanthus thurberi*) is a less well-known desert relative. It is an erect, multibranched shrub growing 3 to 8 ft. (0.9 to 2.4 m) tall and spreading 3 to 4 ft. (0.9 to 1.2 m) wide. Desert honeysuckle flowers from February to June and again from October to December. The blooms are pale orange to deep, copper red, tubular, 1.25 in. (3.2 cm) long, and held in axillary clusters. This columnar shrub has numerous thin stems arranged in an intricate branching pattern. The smooth, linear leaves are deep green, 2.5 in. (6.4 cm) long, and end with an acute tip. While desert honeysuckle is grown in full sun throughout the region, it is best to offer it shade from the afternoon sun in the hottest deserts. Use it in any part of the garden that receives minimal watering; overwatering or poorly drained soils will quickly kill it. Hummingbirds are strongly attracted to its flowers. It is an excellent addition to the background of a native or naturalized planting as well as within wildflower beds.

Arenga engleri
Formosa palm

FAMILY: Arecaceae.

DISTRIBUTION: The islands south of Japan including the Ryukyu Islands to Taiwan. It has also been reported in India.

MATURE SIZE: Multitrunked, clumping palm 10 to 20 ft. (3 to 6.1 m) tall with a spread of 10 to 16 ft. (3 to 4.9 m).

BLOOMING PERIOD: April to May.

EXPOSURE: In the hottest deserts protect from western or afternoon sun. In milder areas or near the coast, filtered sun is best. Formosa palm grows well in significant shade in all areas.

HARDINESS: Mature plants are hardy to 20°F (–7°C) for brief periods of time, with leaf damage at 22°F (−6°C) and stem death below that temperature for extended periods of time. Mature plants have been reported to be hardy to 15°F (−9°C) for short periods of time.

Formosa palm is a handsome, sturdy palm with nearly invisible stems that rise from a crowded base and are shrouded in black fibers. Stems are 5 to 6 ft. (1.5 to 1.8 m) tall.

The pinnate leaves are 8 to 15 ft. (2.4 to 4.6 m) long with 70 to 100 leaflets in pairs. Each leaflet is dark olive-green above and silvery below, 1 ft. (0.3 m) long, and with a ragged edge. Leaflets are folded into a sharp V, a rare and distinctive leaf form that is known as being induplicate.

The flowering stalk emerges within the leaves and is up to 7 ft. (2.1 m) long. Each plant has both female and male flowers on the stalk and is self-fertile. Flowers are bright orange and fragrant. This species has a most unusual flowering cycle. On each stem a flowering stalk emerges first from the oldest leaf node. Then in successive years a new flowering stalk arises from next-oldest leaf, and so on until the final, or youngest, leaf node has sent out a flowering stalk. Once that final flowering is complete, the entire stem dies. This flowering cycle takes decades to complete.

Fruit is globular and bright red and is less than 1 in. (2.5 cm) around. The fruit of this palm is known to cause severe allergic reactions on the skin so it is wise to wear gloves when handling fresh fruit or seeds.

Formosa palm has moderate tolerance for salty soils and drought conditions. It has extraordinary heat tolerance. It grows best in a slightly fertile, well-drained soil. Most ref-

Arenga engleri (Formosa palm)

erences indicate a preference for slightly acid, evenly moist soils. My plant has been growing in a lightly amended, raised bed with weekly summer watering for over a decade with no loss of vigor or beauty. It is important in the hottest desert to expose it to almost no direct sun, especially in the summer.

Formosa palm is moderately susceptible to the ravages of lethal yellowing disease. Fertilizer applied annually, particularly as slow release spikes, encourages both good health and leaf color. High winds may damage the leaflets, causing them to become frayed and unsightly.

Pruning is rarely required except for dead leaves, spent stems, and spent flowering stalks. The latter may be pruned out anytime, but living leaves must not be pruned except in the early summer. The low-growing form and dense set of stems make this a lovely choice to provide screening or a backdrop in a dry, shady location.

Atriplex canescens
Four-wing saltbush

FAMILY: Chenopodiaceae.

DISTRIBUTION: In the United States the species is widespread and often common in all states west of the Mississippi River and extending north into adjacent Canadian provinces. It is found in rocky, dry soils from sea level to 7000 ft. (2134 m). In Mexico it extends south into Baja California and western Sonora, south into Sinaloa, and east to Coahuila, Nuevo León, Zacatecas, San Luis Potosí, and Tamaulipas.

MATURE SIZE: Erect shrub 3 to 8 ft. (0.9 to 2.4 m) tall, averaging 4 to 5 ft. (1.2 to 1.5 m), and with a spread 4 to 6 ft. (1.2 to 1.8 m) wide.

BLOOMING PERIOD: March to September, but in colder areas, July to August.

EXPOSURE: Full sun in all areas, although it grows successfully in light or partial shade in the hottest desert.

HARDINESS: Because of its immense range, hardiness is as low as −30°F (−34°C); it is reliably hardy to 15°F (−9°C) regardless of its origins.

Four-wing saltbush is a sturdy, dense, evergreen shrub. In many individuals the plant begins round but mature plants have a flat-topped or compressed appearance. The plant is woody throughout, and the branches are stout and gray and shed the bark as they mature. This species is especially long lived. Researchers have compared photos of individual plants growing in the Grand Canyon and are able to document some that are over 100 years old.

The leaves are oblanceolate to linear with a sharp or rounded tip. But there is great variation in leaf length over the range of the species, with some shorter and others longer than described. The thick, sessile leaves are usually 1 to 2 in. (2.5 to 5.1 cm) long, are covered with prominent white scales, and have a scruffy, tan to whitish color.

Plants are usually dioecious. Pistillate (female) flowers occur in dense, leafy, 2.75 to 8 in. (7 to 20.3 cm) spikes at the ends of the branches. Staminate (male) flowers are held in dense, 1 to 6 in. (2.5 to 15.2 cm) terminal spikes, but the tiny bracts do not form the distinctive four-winged enclosure. The pollen carries significant allergens that affect many people.

Intriguingly, plants are able to switch the sex of their flowers in response to both water availability and cold. When water resources are scarce or after a particularly heavy blooming year, a plant may switch to male flowers for the following year or until conditions improve. It is believed that internal stresses in the plant are more pronounced in females because of seed formation, and this trick has evolved to lessen that pressure.

After blooming, the bracts extend and flatten into the distinctive four-winged receptacle for the seed. The edges of the pod are usually wavy but may also be sharp toothed.

Atriplex canescens (four-wing saltbush)

Here, too, there is wide variation particularly in the pods' size over the range. These charming pods begin light green but fade to tan and range from 0.5 to 1 in. (1.3 to 2.5 cm) long. They are persistent on the plant often for months and are crammed into the terminal spikes. They can be used in dry arrangements.

Many desert species delay seed maturity as a strategy to maximize seed germination success. In four-wing saltbush, seed takes about 10 months to mature. It is also reported that the bracts themselves have a germination inhibitor and that their removal is important for germination success.

Four-wing saltbush tolerates a wide range of soil and drainage conditions, although it has the lowest salt tolerance of this most salt-tolerant genus. It requires only minimal watering after establishment, regardless of where it is grown. So it is a particularly good choice for edges and boundaries of a garden that are not regularly irrigated, or to fill in a wild or naturalistic garden. It is widely used in erosion control.

Overwatering is the easiest way to kill this shrub outright and certainly to modify its tight, dense form. Overwatered plants become soft with floppy leaves and encourage a host of insect predators, especially a gall midge.

Four-wing saltbush is attractive to numerous species of birds, but especially quail, for its seeds and the dense cover it provides. Native peoples of the Southwest ground the seeds into a leaven, much like baking powder, for baking bread. This species is also browse for both wild and domesticated animals, so it's advisable to cage young plants to protect them from rabbits and other critters until they are 3 to 4 ft. (0.9 to 1.2 m) tall.

All species in the genus *Atriplex* collect and ultimately remove excess salts in the soil through bladders in their leaves. These structures act as salt sinks, keeping the toxic salts from the plant's cells. As the old leaves are shed or eaten, the salt is handily removed from the plant.

Atriplex hymenelytra
Desert holly

FAMILY: Chenopodiaceae.

DISTRIBUTION: In the United States in the lowest and hottest desert areas of southern California to southwestern Utah and extreme southern Nevada and along the Colorado River in far western Arizona below 2500 ft. (762 m). In Mexico it is found only in the driest parts of Baja California; although it has been historically reported from northwest Sonora, recent researchers have been unable to verify this distribution.

MATURE SIZE: Erect, compact shrub growing 1 to 3 ft. (0.3 to 0.9 m) tall and as wide.

BLOOMING PERIOD: January to April.

EXPOSURE: Full sun in all areas.

HARDINESS: Hardy to 28°F (−2°C) with severe damage at 20°F (−7°C); particularly susceptible to cold damage in wet soils.

Desert holly is an evergreen shrub of diminutive proportions that provides a dramatic splash in a desert garden. The young twigs and leaves are silvery white and appear to glow in the strong desert sun. As the season progresses and the leaves dry out, the salt bladders that move salt out of the leaf become prominent on the leaf, giving it even greater reflectance. Plants appear to gleam and are astounding by moonlight. Branches begin tan but age to gray and may become fissured with age.

The leaves are 0.5 to 1.75 in. (1.3 to 4.4 cm) long, more or less triangular, and have sharp, pointed lobes that give them a resemblance to holly. There has been a modest industry in using the leaves for holiday decorations in its native range because of this similarity. Leaves are covered with scales that make them silvery

Atriplex hymenelytra (desert holly)

white. As leaves age they turn purple or reddish and ultimately are shed from the plant. In the cool season, leaves are pale green but as the weather gets hotter and the land gets drier they become white to gray and more brittle. Leaves are steeply angled, almost vertical on the branch, which is an adaptation to the intense heat of their native range.

Desert holly, like all members of this genus, is dioecious. There are dense, leafy terminal panicles of female flowers on some plants and dense, short spikes of male flowers on others. Individual flowers are minute and innocuous.

Desert holly can be difficult to grow, especially when it is overwatered or grown in soils that hold too much water between irrigation. It prefers culture that is closest to its native situation and is therefore truly well suited for the hottest areas of western Arizona and southern California in native or naturalistic gardens.

Desert holly demands perfect drainage; almost pure sand is excellent, with supplemental water only in the winter growing season and during long, dry spells. When grown well it is a glorious little mound of silvery holly out in the most desperate parts of the garden.

Desert saltbush (*Atriplex polycarpa*) is another excellent ornamental member of this genus from the extreme deserts of western Arizona, southern Utah and Nevada, and California and Baja California. This erect, intricately branched shrub is 3 to 6 ft. (0.9 to 1.8 m) tall and spreads up to 6 ft. (1.8 m) wide. It tolerates full sun even in the hottest deserts. Although bloom is not showy, it occurs intermittently throughout the year in response to rainfall, particularly from July to October. This species is hardy to 10°F (−12°C)

and possibly lower. Plants form a dense mound with slender twigs and tiny, graygreen leaves that are less than 0.5 in. (1.3 cm) long and are crowded into clusters (fascicles) at the nodes. Desert saltbush tolerates wet or poorly drained soils, particularly when coupled with cold, better than the other desert saltbush species described here. It has a slow to moderate growth rate, and is well regarded in dry but not desperately hot regions, like southern California. It is extremely drought tolerant and is favored for revegetation or erosion control projects.

Atriplex lentiformis
Quail bush, lens scale

FAMILY: Chenopodiaceae.

DISTRIBUTION: In the United States in southeastern California, southwestern Arizona, far southwestern Utah, and extreme southern Nevada at 300 to 2000 ft. (91 to 610 m). In Mexico it is found in desert flats in Baja California and western Sonora below 3000 ft. (914 m).

MATURE SIZE: Large, spreading or ascending shrub ranging 5 to 10 ft. (1.5 to 3 m) tall and spreading 6 to 15 ft. (1.8 to 4.6 m) wide; almost always much wider than it is tall.

BLOOMING PERIOD: February to April, June to August.

EXPOSURE: Full sun in all areas.

HARDINESS: Hardy to at least 0°F (−8°C) and is more tolerant of cold, wet soils than most other members of the genus.

Quail bush is a densely branched shrub whose smooth branches spread at broad angles and often hang to the ground. The young branches are white or pale gray but darken with age

Atriplex lentiformis (quail bush)

and grow fine scales. Branches may become slightly thorny after the leaves are shed but this feature is not a problem.

The leaves are small, gray-green to blue-gray, 0.5 to 1.25 in. (1.3 to 3.2 cm) long, and heart shaped. They form on a small petiole, a feature unique among the Sonoran members of this genus. The leaves are persistent as long as there is ample moisture, but fall quickly with drought.

The innocuous whitish flowers are held in dense, crowded clusters or panicles and are either pistillate (female) or staminate (male) on the plants. Plants are occasionally monoecious. Seeds are held in long, drooping spikes, and are prominent although not particularly attractive.

Quail bush is tolerant of a wide range of soils but it must have excellent drainage for best results. It is tolerant of alkaline and saline soils and also grows quickly under cultivation. Once established, and particularly in deeper or richer soils, plants rarely need supplemental irrigation.

The shrub is well named: quail are mad for its fruit. It is also highly desirable as a nest location for quail, which prefer to lay their eggs on the ground in the shelter of the dense, low-hanging foliage. Along the waterways of western and southern Arizona, this species is so common it forms an impenetrable barrier and you only hear, not see, the wildlife within its sheltering branches.

Use quail bush wherever you need a screen, windbreak, or border that does not have regular irrigation. Although it is not the handsomest of *Atriplex* species, it is one of the easiest to cultivate and its wildlife value alone makes it highly desirable.

All of the plant is considered edible. Native American peoples favored its young shoots as a spring green and enjoyed its salty character.

Young or newly planted individuals are highly attractive to rabbits, so plants should be caged until they are about 3 ft. (0.9 m) tall and able to withstand their ravages.

There is a form that is sometimes known as *Atriplex griffithsii* or *A. lentiformis* var. *griffithsii* although neither name is now valid. It is a beautiful shrub from southern Arizona and southwestern New Mexico with leaves that are a bit larger, more triangular, and bright silvery white.

Atriplex lentiformis subsp. *breweri* from southern California, southern Nevada, and far southwestern Utah is much favored by some in the trade. It is smaller and slower growing. Its leaves are dense, gray, triangular, and 2 in. (5.1 cm) long.

Atriplex nummularia
Old man saltbush

FAMILY: Chenopodiaceae.

DISTRIBUTION: From inland Australia; naturalized in parts of coastal southern California.

MATURE SIZE: Mounding shrub 6 to 9 ft. (1.8 to 2.7 m) tall and 4 to 6 ft. (1.2 to 1.8 m) wide.

BLOOMING PERIOD: Summer.

EXPOSURE: Full sun in all areas.

HARDINESS: Hardy to 22°F (−6°C).

Old man saltbush is a big, rounded, more or less evergreen shrub. Its fine, intricate

Atriplex nummularia (old man saltbush)

branches fall in a cascade with age and plants are dense all the way to the ground.

The leaves are thick, up to 1.25 in. (3.2 cm) long, and elliptic to round with slightly serrate margins. They are prolific on the stem, covering it completely. Leaves range from blue-gray to pale gray and are rough to the touch.

Plants are dioecious. The innocuous, tiny, green to tannish flowers are held on a branched flowering stalk up to 8 in. (20.3 cm) long. The female flowers are held along this flowering stalk while the male flowers are clustered in dense bunches at the ends of the branches. Female flowers have a bract, which grows to surround the fruit and becomes 0.5 in. (1.3 cm) wide and fan shaped as it matures.

This shrub is another rugged choice for an area that is hot and dry with only intermittent irrigation. Old man saltbush is tolerant of all alkaline, well-drained soils and also thrives in brackish soils. It grows fast and is therefore handy if you need a quick screen or covering hedge. It works well as a hedge either singly or when mixed with other drought-tolerant species. Birds, particularly quail, are fond of its fruit, and the dense plants provide cover for nesting and resting.

Baccharis sarothroides

Desert broom

FAMILY: Asteraceae.

DISTRIBUTION: In the United States wide-spread and common in southern California, far southern Nevada, central and southern Arizona, but rare and local in southwestern New Mexico at 1000 to 5500 ft. (305 to 1676 m). In Mexico ranges into Baja California, far northern Sonora, and Sinaloa from sea level to 5500 ft. (1676 m).

BLOOMING PERIOD: September to February, but intermittent throughout the year.

MATURE SIZE: Erect, multistemmed shrub growing quickly to 3 to 9 ft. (0.9 to 2.7 m) tall with equal spread.

EXPOSURE: Full or reflected sun in all areas.

HARDINESS: Hardy to 15°F (−9°C).

Desert broom is a deep green array of countless leafless stems of all sizes, giving it a broomlike look. The branches are stiff, upright, and sticky, and the plant has an almost perfectly round shape. The gray-brown bark is restricted to the oldest stems, usually at the base.

The ephemeral leaves are small, nearly scales, and are 0.5 to 1.25 in (1.3 to 3.2 cm) long. They are linear, narrow, and rigid. They are covered with a varnishlike, sticky exudation.

Pistillate flowers are held in dense, 2-in. (5.1-cm) heads on elongated branches. An abundance of white, silky pappus surrounds the flowers and is the most noticeable aspect of the plant's flowering. Staminate flowers are in shorter heads and have minimal pappus at the base, so those flowers are not as showy.

The seeds are attached to the silky pappus and float anywhere the wind takes them. This feature makes this species nearly a pest. To germinate, the seeds have a way of finding the interior of the nastiest cactus or cholla in the garden. Because the plant grows a sturdy, long taproot, they are difficult to remove. Pick them out as soon as you notice them.

Desert broom is not fussy about soil and drainage, and grows quickly in almost any condition. It is tolerant of extremely alkaline soils and appears to be free from all pests and diseases. It grows quickly with supplemental moisture, so keep it in bounds by withholding water. It is a highly drought-tolerant species, capable of growing on natural rainfall even in the hottest deserts.

A hybrid form between *Baccharis sarothroides* and the slightly smaller and less heat-tolerant *B. pilularis* was first released as 'Centennial'. This cultivar proved to be female, and it produced profuse amounts of pappus. Later Ron Gass of Mountain States Wholesale Nursery in Glendale, Arizona, crossed 'Centennial' back with *Baccharis sarothroides*. One of those crosses became Thompson, a male plant that bypasses the detrimental feature of the former cultivar as well as hav-

Baccharis sarothroides (desert broom)

ing good heat tolerance and disease resistance. Thompson is now patented as 'Starn'.

Coyote bush (*Baccharis pilularis*) is a more prostrate form than the tall desert broom. It forms dense mats in old age that are 3 to 13 feet (0.9 to 4 m) across. This species is widely regarded in coastal areas and cooler climates for its use in soil stabilization and bank improvement. If you plant individuals close together, they grow over each other and you end up with a higher groundcover. The numerous light green leaves are evergreen, resinous, oval, and are 0.5 to 1.5 in. (1.3 cm to 2.2 cm) long. Coyote brush is found in coastal sage scrub and chaparral on hillsides and in canyons below 2500 ft (762 m) along the California and Oregon coastal ranges. It is not very reliable in the hottest deserts.

Bauhinia 'Blakeana'

Hong Kong orchid tree

FAMILY: Fabaceae.

DISTRIBUTION: Grown throughout the tropical and semitropical parts of the world; the original plant was found near Hong Kong.

MATURE SIZE: Small tree with rounded crown from 15 to 30 ft. (4.6 to 9.1 m) tall and with an equal spread.

BLOOMING PERIOD: December to March.

EXPOSURE: Full sun to partial shade in all areas.

HARDINESS: Leaves are damaged at 28°F (−2°C) with severe damage at 22°F (−6°C)

Hong Kong orchid tree is a semievergreen tree with a distinctive, rounded, umbrella-shaped crown. The bark is smooth and light tan to nearly white.

The large light green to gray-green leaves are from 6 to 8 in. (15.2 to 20.3 cm) long. They barely split into two leaflets, giving them a heart-shaped, occasionally round, appearance.

The flowers are 5 to 6 in. (12.7 to 15.2 cm) across, with the five corolla lobes deeply divided and opened widely. Flower color ranges from deep magenta to rose-red. The lightly fragrant flowers are prolific on the plant, often obscuring the leaves.

Plants are sterile and do not produce pods, which is one reason why they are so valued ornamentally.

Hong Kong orchid tree thrives in well-drained, moderately fertile soils that are not highly saline. Wind may damage both the

Bauhinia 'Blakeana' (Hong Kong orchid tree)

leaves and branches, and in particularly windy regions the plant must be sheltered from the full force of the wind. Water mature plants every week or so during the summer in all regions, but especially in the hottest desert. The plant will become chlorotic in alkaline or poorly drained soils, a condition that is common in the region. All individuals are derived from grafting onto other *Bauhinia* stock or from cuttings.

This taxon has a fascinating ornamental history. A single tree was originally found in the 1880s by French missionaries in an abandoned house in Pokfulam on the western end of Hong Kong Island. These unnamed clerics propagated it and grew it at the Pokfulam Sanatorium, and then it was introduced into the Hong Kong Botanic Garden as well as to the grounds of the Catholic Cathedral of Guangzhou. In 1908, S. T. Dunn, superintendent of Hong Kong's Botanical and Forestry Department, wrote up the first description of this plant and named it *Bauhinia blakeana* for the governor of Hong Kong, Henry Blake. By 1914, this form was being cultivated extensively in the regions around Hong Kong. It is still much revered in that city and is the emblem of the city as well as the image on their flag.

There is no evidence to refute the long-held assumption that all trees are derived from this single, chance encounter. This fact, which some authors note with despair, makes all forms clones and therefore hugely susceptible to some as yet unknown pathogen.

In 2005 Lau, Ramsden, and Saunders published results of their work on establishing whether the plant was truly a hybrid, what the presumed parents were, and whether the plant was able to produce seeds or otherwise propagate itself. They reached the conclusion that this plant is indeed a hybrid form, almost certainly between *Bauhinia purpurea* and *B. variegata*. Whether the hybrid occurred naturally is unknown, but since the two parents occur together in nature, it is entirely possible that it happened by chance. In addition, they found that this taxon is entirely sterile; they were not able to make it produce seed under any conditions. Therefore, this sterile hybrid form cannot reproduce itself and must be considered a horticultural species, and hence the change in the name to *B.* 'Blakeana'.

One of those putative parents, orchid tree (*Bauhinia variegata*), is a popular flowering tree in many parts of the hottest deserts. This tall, upright plant grows 10 to 30 ft. (3 to 9.1 m) tall and spreads up to 20 ft. (6.1 m) wide. Orchid tree suffers leaf drop at 26°F (–3°C) and is severely damaged at 20°F (–6°C). The deep green leaves are 4 to 6 in. (10.2 to 15.2 cm) long. The five irregular corolla lobes of the flowers overlap slightly and are 3 to 5 in. (7.6 to 12.7 cm) wide; flowers range in color from pink to magenta or white. Plants with purple to pinkish flowers are sometimes offered as *B. purpurea*, but that species is not as common as *B. variegata*.

Orchid tree requires deep, enriched soils and regular, deep watering to thrive. In the hottest deserts of Arizona, it suffers from serious salt burn damage throughout the summer. Trees also become chlorotic in alkaline soils or when watering is intermittent or shallow.

While these showy, full-flowered orchid trees are spectacular spring-blooming trees, they are most suitable in areas with mild winters such as southern California, central and western Arizona, and far southern Texas.

Bauhinia divaricata
Mexican orchid tree

SYNONYM: *Bauhinia mexicana*.

FAMILY: Fabaceae.

DISTRIBUTION: In Mexico widely distributed from Sinaloa to Coahuila and south and east through most of the country. Also found from Guatemala to Nicaragua and into the Caribbean Islands. There is a disjunct population in the cape region of Baja California Sur.

MATURE SIZE: Spreading shrub or small tree from 6 to 10 ft. (1.8 to 3 m) tall. Tropical specimens are larger, up to 20 ft. (6.1 m) tall and spreading up to 26 ft. (7.9 m); most plants are within the limits described here.

BLOOMING PERIOD: April to October.

EXPOSURE: In the hottest deserts, protect from western and afternoon sun. In all other areas, full sun to partial shade.

HARDINESS: Hardy to at least 20°F (–7°C), but often sheds its leaves at these temperatures. Freezes to the ground at 15°F (–9°C) but recovers quickly.

Mexican orchid tree is a spreading, often much branched low shrub or small tree. Branches are unarmed and the plants have an open aspect. Leaf and flower size, flower color and stature and form vary widely over the plant's geographic range.

The leaves are compound, formed of two leaflets that are united for about two-thirds of their length having a vague resemblance to a hoof. This low style is typical of the entire genus. Each leaflet is 1.5 to 2.5 in. (3.8 to 6.4 cm) long and about as wide. The leaves are bright green, fuzzy below and smooth above, and are elliptic, ending with a sharp tip.

The flowers are 1 in. (2.5 cm) long and have five deeply split corolla lobes. They are elliptic, end in a sharp tip, have wavy margins, and are held in congested sessile racemes among the leaves. The flowers open pure white and fade to light pink; the pink may be darker in selected individuals. Plants may have either perfect or single-sexed flowers on the same plant. The five corolla lobes are uneven: the lower ones are much enlarged with a pointed tip and the other three are much reduced.

The pod is oblong, flat, and dehiscent. It ranges in size from 0.5 to 1 in. (1.3 to 2 cm) long and has a sharp tip at both ends.

Mexican orchid tree is a rugged, forgiving species that thrives in both moist and dry soils, heavy alkaline sands or acidic sands, and is reportedly more salt tolerant than other species of *Bauhinia*, which is indicated by the coastal distribution of at least the Baja populations. In some areas, the plant reportedly is bothered by chlorosis in soils with low fertility or high pH, but I have not known this to be a problem. It is reported to be resistant, perhaps repugnant, to deer.

Mexican orchid tree does best with weekly deep irrigation in the hottest desert but needs much less frequent watering in the milder areas of the region. The yellowish branches are brittle and often break with high winds. So it is wise to nestle the tree among larger

Bauhinia divaricata (Mexican orchid tree)

plants in areas that routinely experience high winds.

Because Mexican orchid tree blooms almost continuously through the summer, it makes a stunning accent or focal plant in a small garden or near a patio or pool. Butterflies, birds, and even bats are wildly attracted to its numerous flowers.

In my garden, a few seedlings pop up every year—not enough to be a problem but just enough to give them away. Like most legumes, the tree is easy to grow from seed as long as the seed is soaked in hot water or mild acid before being planted.

Bauhinia lunarioides
Anacacho orchid tree

SYNONYM: *Bauhinia congesta*.
FAMILY: Fabaceae.
DISTRIBUTION: In the United States only in limited sites in southern Texas. In Mexico in central and eastern Coahuila and eastern Nuevo León.
MATURE SIZE: Multitrunked upright shrub growing 6 to 12 ft. (1.8 to 3.7 m) tall with a spread of 6 to 10 ft. (1.8 to 3 m).
BLOOMING PERIOD: March to May.
EXPOSURE: Prefers afternoon shade in the hottest deserts but full sun in all other areas.
HARDINESS: Hardy to 18°F (−8°C).

Anacacho orchid tree is a semievergreen to deciduous shrub. It is often seen in horticulture as a rounded shrub, but it grows taller and nearly vertical, reminding me of a desert version of dogwood (*Cornus* spp.).

Like all *Bauhinia* species, the leaves are composed of two leaflets united near the base forming a distinctive hooflike shape. In this species, the dark green to gray-green leaves are less than 1 in. (2.5 cm) long, somewhat asymmetrical, and often have a wavy margin. They are rounded at the tip.

The numerous flowers are 0.5 to 1 in. (1.3 to 2.5 cm) long with five free corolla lobes. They are ovate with a rounded tip and are held in short, crowded racemes among the leaves. In nature most flowers are pink with occasional white-blooming individuals, but nurserymen much prefer the white so it is the most common one sold. Flowers are followed by a reddish brown pod that is 1.5 to 3.25 in. (3.8 to 8.3 cm) long. It opens quickly, often twisting or curling as it drops the ripe seed.

Anacacho orchid tree thrives in rocky, thin, alkaline soils. It is immune to heat, although in the hottest deserts a break from the afternoon sun improves their looks and

Bauhinia lunarioides (Anacacho orchid tree)

health. In areas that receive up to 18 in. (457 mm) of rain per year, it never needs irrigation. The tree is reported to be resistant to browsing by deer. Fertilizer is usually not needed although a rock mulch or leafy mulch may be used to cover the roots.

Pruning is seldom needed and is used only to eliminate crossing branches or dead wood. The best time to prune is directly after blooming. In older plants the tallest stem often dies, leaving numerous smaller stems at the base. Prune out this dead stem at any time and the other stems will grow quickly to reform the shape of the plant.

Anacacho orchid tree is lovely as an understory plant near larger trees. It is small enough to surround patios and clean enough to work well around pools.

Bauhinia macranthera
Chihuahuan orchid tree

FAMILY: Fabaceae.

DISTRIBUTION: In Mexico in Coahuila, Nuevo León, and Tamaulipas, and possibly in San Luis Potosí and Hidalgo.

MATURE SIZE: Widely branched, open tree growing to 20 ft. (6.1 m) tall and spreading up to 15 ft. (4.6 m) wide.

BLOOMING PERIOD: May and June.

EXPOSURE: Full sun in all but the hottest deserts, where relief from the summer afternoon sun of is advisable.

HARDINESS: Hardy to 20°F (–7°C) with only light tip damage.

Chihuahuan orchid tree is an open-branched, small tree with only a few widely spaced branches. The tan bark is smooth and gives the tree an overall lightweight look.

The deep green leaves are 1.5 to 3 in. (3.8 to 7.6 cm) long. They are composed of two united leaflets with a wide, deep cleft between them, and they have a broad, rounded tip.

The flowers, like those of most of the genus, are composed of five, freely split corolla lobes and are lavender to pink. The flowers of Chihuahuan orchid tree are 2 to 3 in. (5.1 to 7.6 cm) across and are held either singly or in loose clusters along the top of the branches. The flowers are laid out along the branch like pink corsages on a tray. The flowers are followed by a flat pod that is 1 to 3 in. (2.5 to 7.6 cm) long and remains on the plant long after it matures.

I first saw this species many years ago in a nursery in Austin, Texas, and at the time they had none to sell. But they were kind enough

Bauhinia macranthera (Chihuahuan orchid tree)

to sell me a few seeds from their plant. I grew one of the trees with ease and I had it for many years near the house until a mighty monsoon wind finally shattered it. It was a wonderful small tree for that spot or any spot that does not need a large shade tree.

This tree is an excellent choice for a small patio or limited space. The late spring bloom is a good addition to a larger perennial planting or other mixed garden. Root suckers spring up from time to time and the plant gently reseeds where there is ample water. Seedlings may be lifted out in the spring and either planted elsewhere or placed in a pot.

Wind is an issue for all bauhinias. This one has weak branches that break easily and often. Plants will quickly grow another branch or two and the plant will be no worse off. But the best course is prevention: avoid planting this species in open areas, particularly in areas of strong or persistent wind. Nestle it among other species and be careful not to overprune the plant.

Berberis haematocarpa

Red barberry

SYNONYM: *Mahonia huematocarpa*.

FAMILY: Berberidaceae.

DISTRIBUTION: In the United States from southeastern California and southern Nevada through central and southern Arizona and central and southern New Mexico, far southeastern Colorado, and western Texas at 3000 to 7200 ft. (914 to 2195 m). In Mexico from northern Sonora to Chihuahua east and south to Coahuila, Nuevo León, San Luis Potosí, and Hidalgo in scattered or local populations at similar elevations.

MATURE SIZE: Much-branched thick shrub or small tree usually 6 to 8 ft. (1.8 to 2.4 m) tall; grows to 12 ft. (3.7 m) tall in some conditions and 5 to 6 ft. (1.5 to 1.8 m) wide.

BLOOMING PERIOD: February to June.

EXPOSURE: Partial shade or eastern exposure in the hottest deserts; full sun in all other areas.

HARDINESS: Hardy to 21°F (−12°C) and possibly lower.

Red barberry is an evergreen shrub with a stiff, rigid form. Stems branch repeatedly and create a thick ball that is difficult to penetrate. Bark is rough and fissured and turns a grayish-purple tone with age. A beautiful yellow dye is derived from the bark and the roots.

The stiff, firm leaves are made up of five to

Berberis haematocarpa (red barberry)

nine leaflets and are 1.25 to 2.5 in. (3.2 to 6.4 cm) long. Each leaflet has small teeth along the margin and a sharp tip, giving them a strong resemblance to holly leaves. The leaves are a bright blue-green and crowded together on short stems.

The profuse, bright yellow, fragrant flowers are held on short, lax racemes that are 1 to 1.5 in. (2.5 to 3.8 cm) long with five to seven flowers on each. Flowers are profuse on the plant and followed by prolific numbers of red to purple berries that are up to 0.5 in. (1.3 cm) around. The tart, juicy berries are relished by birds and other wildlife and also make a tasty jam or jelly.

Red barberry is a tough and hardy species that grows best in well-drained soils but otherwise is not particular about the soil type. Occasional, not more than annual, fertilization may help plants grow faster but in most areas even that is not required. Red barberry grows on natural rainfall where rainfall averages 16 in. (406 mm) per year. In the hottest deserts, water it every two weeks in the summer but much less often in the winter.

Some authors treat this species as a part of *Berberis fremontii*, which grows at 4000 to 7000 ft. (1219 to 2134 m). The ranges of the two species overlap in central Arizona and along the eastern edges of the Mojave Desert. Some of the higher-elevation examples of this species may indeed be *B. fremontii*, for while the differences sound significant—*B. haematocarpa* has narrow, ovate or lanceolate leaflets and bright red to yellowish, juicy fruit while *B. fremontii* has ovate to orbicular leaves and brownish red to yellow dry fruit— many intergrade and intermediate populations have been recorded that show different

combinations of leaflet shape and berry size, color, and inflation.

Berberis trifoliolata
Agarita, algerita

SYNONYM: *Mahonia trifoliolata.*
FAMILY: Berberidaceae.
DISTRIBUTION: In the United States a widely distributed species from southeastern Arizona and southern New Mexico into Trans-Pecos and coastal south Texas from sea level to 3000 ft. (914 m). In Mexico it is common from eastern Chihuahua east and south through Coahuila, Durango, Nuevo León, southwestern Tamaulipas, and northern San Luis Potosí.
MATURE SIZE: Multibranched, somewhat spreading shrub growing 3 to 8 ft. (0.9 to 2.4 m) tall and spreading to 4 ft. (1.2 m) wide.
BLOOMING PERIOD: February to April.
EXPOSURE: In the hottest deserts, partial shade or eastern exposure; full sun in all other areas.
HARDINESS: Hardy to at least 10°F (–12°C).

Agarita is an evergreen shrub that may be either rigid and upright or somewhat spreading. The bark turns gray to grayish purple with age.

The thick, firm leaves are gray-green to deep blue-gray and are composed of three distinct leaflets with the middle much longer than the other two. The leaf blades are 2 to 4 in. (5.1 to 10.2 cm) long and lanceolate to oblong or elliptic and two to three times longer than they are wide. Each leaflet has distinctly lobed margins with fine spines at the tips and a sharp terminal spine. The leaves are usually two to three times longer than they are wide.

The flowers are bright yellow with a distinctive spicy fragrance, and are held in a loose raceme of up to eight flowers that is 0.5 to 3 in. (1.3 to 7.6 cm) long. The flowering stalk is much shorter than the leaves.

Flowers are followed by round, juicy, bright red fruit. The delicious fruit is feasted on by birds and is renowned locally, especially in southern Texas, for the jelly that can be made from it.

Agarita is a tough shrub throughout the region. It thrives in strong heat as well as significant cold and grows in any well-drained

Berberis trifoliolata (agarita)

soil. In the hottest deserts, it is best to water it every week in the summer. But where rainfall is at least 16 in. (406 mm) or more per year, it grows well on natural rainfall.

Old-timers collected the berries by putting a sheet under the bush and thrashing the plant with a stick. There are historic reports of the seeds being roasted as a substitute for coffee but I haven't tried that. I can vouch for the delicious, tart jelly made from its fruit.

As for many other members of the genus, the wood and roots are a source of a beautiful dark golden dye. It is reported to be deer resistant and is tolerant of salty soils and salt spray near the coast.

There are forms whose leaves are strongly marked with fine hairs and are silver to gray. These forms were once thought to be separate varieties, but now they are considered just variants that occur in numerous populations.

Agarita is a great choice for a wildlife or naturalistic garden. Its stiff, hollylike leaves offer stunning contrast to softer-leaved shrubs and perennials in a mixed planting.

Bismarckia nobilis
Bismarck palm

FAMILY: Arecaceae.
DISTRIBUTION: Madagascar.
MATURE SIZE: Solitary palm growing 30 to 60 ft. (9.1 to 18.3 m) tall with a crown spread of 20 ft. (6.1 m) or more.
BLOOMING PERIOD: Summer.
EXPOSURE: Full sun in all areas.
HARDINESS: Hardy to 26°F (–3°C), with minor leaf damage when the freeze is of short duration. Young plants are more susceptible to freeze damage.

Bismarckia nobilis (Bismarck palm)

Bismarck palm is a sturdy-trunked, solitary palm. Young individuals retain the leaf bases, but these are not persistent as the trunk ages. Old specimens are stunning with their heads of wide, blue-gray leaves and smooth trunks.

The palmately compound leaves are divided into about 20 segments that split for only about 3 in. (7.6 cm) from the tip and are 8 to 10 ft. (2.4 to 3 m) long. The full crown has up to 25 leaves. These huge leaves are a bright blue-gray, although there are green forms in nature and occasionally in cultivation. The sturdy petiole is up to 6 ft. (1.8 m) long and rimmed with small, sharp teeth. The petiole of young leaves is covered with fine, white hairs, giving it a soft, fuzzy look.

The flowers are small and held on a stalk that is up to 4 ft. (1.2 m) long. Plants are either male or female. Fruit is brown drupe that is a 1.5 in. (3.8 cm) long.

This palm is well suited to the high heat of the hottest deserts. Adaptable to almost any soil as long as it is well drained, Bismarck palm is drought tolerant once established.

This palm grows best with a combination of hot, dry summers and mild, nearly frost-free winters. California growers report that the green-leaved forms appear to do better in the coastal climates, while the gray- or blue-leaved forms prefer higher heat.

This tree is truly one of the most extraordinary and gorgeous of all palms. The heads are stunning and prominent even when the plant is young. The palm needs to be given plenty of room for its eventual size. As with all palms, only dead fronds from the lowest rank of leaves may be pruned once they are completely dead. This palm is more or less self-pruning, and dead leaves do not remain long on the plant.

Bismarck palm can rot quickly in cold, or even cool, wet soils, because like most palms it has roots which are inactive during the winter, making the plant virtually dormant. It grows best in well-drained soils, even rocky ones.

Provide minimal supplemental water in the winter. In the summer plants in the hottest deserts grow well when watered two or three times a month. Potassium deficiencies have been noted for this species, but that is easily corrected with a balanced palm fertilizer applied once a year.

Years ago a good friend who owns a nursery asked me to do a talk for her. She found pubic speaking an anathema and knew I did not. Instead of a fee, she gave me a Bismarck palm, which at the time was just beginning to be offered in the region. It is without question one of the handsomest palms I have ever grown or even seen. Although it is not yet large, I can't wait to see that smooth trunk rise up, crowned by the stunning silver leaves.

Bougainvillea Hybrids
Bougainvillea

FAMILY: Nyctaginaceae.
DISTRIBUTION: Coastal Brazil; grown throughout the warm parts of the world as an ornamental.
MATURE SIZE: Fountain-shaped shrub or large vine growing up to 30 ft. (9.1 m) tall with an equal spread. Dwarf and shrubby forms grow 10 to 12 ft. (3 to 3.7 m) tall and as wide.
BLOOMING PERIOD: A cool-season bloomer from December to May, but may hold its colorful bracts much longer and bloom intermittently throughout the year.
EXPOSURE: Full or reflected sun, even in the hottest deserts.
HARDINESS: Leaves are destroyed at or near 32°F (0°C), stems are hardy to 25°F (−4°C) sometimes more, and most forms are root hardy to 20°F (−7°C).

Bougainvillea is a vigorous, shrubby vine that loses all or most of its leaves in the coldest part of the winter especially when temperatures are near freezing. *Bougainvillea glabra* is a smaller plant with less thorny canes, and some of the more shrublike forms exhibit these characteristics. *Bougainvillea spectabilis* is the rampant grower most gardeners are so familiar with. But after decades of hybridization and back crossing, it is difficult to assign any given selection to one of the two species. Despite this, many forms present characteristics that are closer to one or the other of the two species, causing even more confusion.

One of the first well-known, documented hybrids is sold as *Bougainvillea ×buttiana*.

Bougainvillea

This hybrid is credited to a Mrs. R. Butt who is reported to have made, or perhaps found, the cross in a garden in Trinidad. In England it became known as 'Mrs. Butt'. Later when it was grown in the United States it was given the name 'Crimson Lake'. Now it has a dozen other names as well.

Bougainvillea peruviana is the most stable species. When plants are grown from seed, there is little variation in the general shape of bracts and leaves. A representative plant of this species has long branches and is sometimes bare of leaves in the juvenile stage. The bracts are usually small, wrinkled, and a pale pink. It is easy to distinguish *B. peruviana* from the other two species, but this species is rarely offered in this country.

The leaves of bougainvillea are slightly fuzzy, thin, and soft, and grow up to 3 to 4 in. (7.6 to 10.2 cm) long. They are held on a short petiole and are usually more or less heart-shaped. Color ranges from a light chartreuse to a rich forest green.

The species have marked leaf differences: *Bougainville glabra* has small, smooth leaves, while the leaves of *B. spectabilis* are hairy below. And the hybrids of the two species show a wide array of intermediate leaf forms.

The flowers are small, white, and tubular and are held in short clusters of three flowers at the leaf nodes. Each flower is surrounded by three large, showy bracts that are often mistakenly regarded as the flowers. These bracts come in a bewildering array of colors from red and magenta to pink, white, orange, salmon, purple, and mauve. Bracts are elliptic with a sharp tip and range from 1 to 2 in. (2.5 to 5.1 cm) long.

In many bougainvillea varieties, the flower color changes based on sun exposure, age, or growing conditions. For example, while a variety in a cool coastal climate flowers a scarlet red, in the interior with strong sun and harsher conditions it flowers an orange red. This trait and the long breeding history of the plant mean that there are forms that are identical but carry numerous varietal names.

Bougainvillea is a species for the heat and does best when grown in full sun, regardless of the locale. Although it tolerates wet conditions well, flowering and therefore bracts are more numerous and of better color when it is grown without excessive moisture. It is a truism that bougainvillea only looks great when you neglect it a bit.

Planting bougainvillea requires some special attention. The roots bind to soil loosely, even in a pot, so when planting, care must be taken not to disturb the roots any more than necessary. If possible, put the plant in the hole and cut away the container in place. Alternately, get the root ball wet and pull it out and place it in the hole without disturbing the roots. Many growers notice that bougainvillea is slow to recover (months, sometimes a year) and begin growing after transplanting usually as a result of root disturbance.

Although bougainvillea is renowned for its drought tolerance, this characteristic is most evident in older, established plants. Young plants need to be watered deeply and often for the first year or two, so they will establish well. After that, in the hottest deserts, water every two weeks in the summer, much less often in the winter. Overwatering not

only encourages plants to get large, but also increases the growth of leaves at the expense of flowers.

Bougainvillea rarely needs fertilizing, but any that is applied must be done moderately and only once a year at the beginning of the growing season. Too much fertilizer and you get leaves and no flowers.

Pruning bougainvillea is a daunting task. Unless there has been extreme cold damage or you are trying to reinvigorate an old plant, it is best to give it one or two light tip prunings in the early summer rather than whack it back to the ground regularly.

Bougainvillea may or may not have been introduced into horticulture in the U.S. in the late 19th century in southern California by the San Diego horticulturist Kate Sessions. She certainly promoted and popularized it, and set off an explosion of interest and ultimately breeding in the plant that continues to this day.

There are too many *Bougainvillea* cultivars to count and many look much alike. Among the most common and popular in the region are 'Barbara Karst', which is red in the sun, magenta in the shade, and the most common bougainvillea variety; 'San Diego Red', which is the same as 'Scarlett O'Hara' and 'American Red', has larger leaves and fewer flowers per cluster, and blooms later than Barbara Karst'; and 'Texas Dawn', which is nearly pink and does well in high heat and some humidity. The numerous orange-toned varieties include 'Rainbow Gold', with burnt orange bracts; 'Orange King' with orange bracts that fade to copper then pink; 'California Gold', with golden bracts; and 'Superstition Gold', also with golden bracts.

'Jamaica White' has white bracts that turn pink in cooler weather. 'Torch Glow' has become popular in recent years, with its dark reddish pink closely spaced flowers on upright stems that point straight up. Dwarfs like 'Temple Fire' with reddish bronze bracts are also available. This is just a selection of the colors and forms that are found in this group.

Bougainvillea was discovered during the around-the-world voyage of Louis Antoine, Conte de Bougainville (1729–1811). The actual collector of these then unnamed plants was French botanist Philibert Commerson, who named them in honor of the French navigator.

Brahea armata
Blue hesper palm, Mexican blue fan palm

FAMILY: Arecaceae.

DISTRIBUTION: In Mexico along the east side of the mountains and some interior drainages and canyons of Baja California at 700 to 1300 ft. (213 to 396 m).

MATURE SIZE: Solitary palm grows 15 to 40 ft. (4.6 to 12.2 m) tall with a crown spread of 8 to 16 ft. (2.4 to 4.9 m).

BLOOMING PERIOD: February and March.

EXPOSURE: Full sun in all areas, but grows in partial shade in the hottest deserts.

HARDINESS: Hardy to 15°F (–9°C), but withstands temperatures to 10°F (–12°C) for short periods with only minor foliage damage.

Blue hesper palm has a sturdy, solitary trunk that is 18 in. (45.7 cm) in diameter and slightly swollen at the base. While the leaf bases do not persist on the plant, a scar remains where each one was attached, creating an interesting pattern on the otherwise smooth, gray trunk.

The slightly costapalmate leaves are held on a petiole that is 3 to 5 ft. (0.9 to 1.5 m) long and lined with sharp teeth. The leaves are 3 ft. (0.9 m) in diameter and broken into 40 to 60 leaflets that are split up to 22 in. (55.9 cm). They are rigid with a waxy coating and range in color from a pale bluish green to a striking blue-gray. There may be as few as 25 or as many as 60 leaves forming the rounded, mature head. Leaves persist on the plant for a long time and, if not removed, form a continuous skirt along the trunk.

The cream-colored flowers are held on remarkable, distinctive flowering stalks that

Brahea armata (blue hesper palm)

are up to 15 ft. (4.6 m) long and project out and down from the plant, often hanging to the ground in young plants. This feature is one of the palm's most striking characteristics. The flowers are perfect and plants are therefore self-fertile.

The oval fruits are shiny, yellowish with brown stripes, and 0.75 in. (1.8 cm) around. Each contains a single seed.

This palm, which is endemic to the Baja Peninsula, is one of the most striking of all Sonoran palms. Blue hesper palm thrives in high heat and grows well in any well-drained soil including dry, rocky soils. It prefers alkaline soils; strongly acid soils will cause it to fail.

Although it may be large in old age, this species grows slowly. This slow growth makes it an excellent choice in a garden, near a pool, or where its gorgeous, blue-gray head of leaves may be featured. It needs good drainage and cannot tolerate a situation where it is consistently wet. Watering is best done by a long, deep soak at infrequent intervals in the summer. It is particularly susceptible to various root rots when overwatered or in situations of poor drainage. In areas with higher rainfall than the deserts, it is important to pay strict attention to providing the plant with excellent drainage or grow it in a particularly dry location.

This species is reported to be sensitive to moving, particularly when older, and every effort must be made to minimize, or avoid, root damage, and minimize root disturbance. Some gardeners recommend planting the entire pot. Two reports from palm experts indicate that significantly damaged blue hesper palm roots may be slow to heal, and this slow healing may initially and adversely affect the plant's health and ultimate size. These problems are pronounced in hot, humid areas, and while there are few reports of such problems in the deserts, fewer large plants of this species have been moved around.

Brahea brandegeei
San Jose hesper palm

FAMILY: Arecaceae.

DISTRIBUTION: In Mexico in localized populations both along the Gulf Coast of Baja California Sur and western Sonora, and in disjunct, distinct populations as far inland as the Rio Yaqui drainage from sea level to 3800 ft. (1150 m).

MATURE SIZE: Solitary palm 35 to 45 ft. (10.7 to 13.7 m) tall with a crown spread of 6 to 7 ft. (1.8 to 2.1 m).

BLOOMING PERIOD: February and March.

EXPOSURE: Full sun in all areas, but tolerates light shade in the hottest deserts.

HARDINESS: Hardy to 20°F (–7°C) but often there is minor leaf damage below 25°F (–4°C).

San Jose hesper palm is a slender-trunked, solitary species. The leaf bases remain on the plant for a long time and form a distinctive, attractive crisscross pattern. Eventually they release; old specimens have a smooth trunk with only the scars remaining.

The leaves are slightly costapalmate and are held on a long petiole that is well armed with sharp teeth. The leaf itself is up to 3 ft. (0.9 m) long but including the petiole it is up to 10 ft. (3 m) long. Leaves are light gray-green, stiff, and waxy and they are grayer or lighter on the underside.

The small cream-colored flowers are held in a branched inflorescence that is 3 to 4 ft.

Brahea brandegeei (San Jose hesper palm)

it does not have high salt tolerance. It does not thrive in areas of high humidity and has rarely been grown outside of the hottest parts of the region.

This palm carries the name of one of the most famous of California botanists, T. S. Brandegee. The species was brought into horticulture by the equally famous California horticulturist Kate Sessions, of San Diego, from seed she and Brandegee collected in 1903 near Cabo San Lucas, Baja California. Those plants were ultimately planted in Balboa Park in San Diego.

San Jose hesper palm is similar to the more widely used Mexican fan palm (*Washingtonia robusta*), especially from a distance. Mexican fan palm is distinguished by its persistent leaf scars, long petioles, and blue-green leaves.

Bursera microphylla
Elephant tree, copal

FAMILY: Burseraceae.

DISTRIBUTION: In the United States in eastern San Diego and Imperial Counties in California and east to western Maricopa and Pima Counties of Arizona at 1000 to 2000 ft. (305 to 610 m). In Mexico in Baja California and Sonora in extremely arid conditions from sea level to 3000 ft. (914 m).

MATURE SIZE: Multitrunked tree growing 12 to 18 ft. (3.7 to 5.5 m) tall and as wide. Individual specimens in the southern part of its range reach a height of 25 ft. (7.6 m) or more.

BLOOMING PERIOD: July.

EXPOSURE: Full sun in all areas.

HARDINESS: Leaves and young stems damaged at 30°F (–1°C), and plants are frozen

(0.9 to 1.2 m) long, which is slightly shorter than the leaves. Flowers are perfect so the plant is self-fertile. The flowers are followed by brownish yellow, 0.5-in. (1.3-cm) round fruit that is shiny; the fruit is edible.

San Jose hesper palm is a slow-growing palm with enormous heat tolerance. It prefers to grow in alkaline to highly alkaline soils with outstanding drainage. Despite growing near the coast in some parts of its range, to the ground at 24°F (−4°C) or lower but often regrow from the base.

Elephant tree has a large, swollen, semi-succulent trunk in old age, and even young trees have an interesting, unusual form. The branches are reddish brown and the thin, greenish to cream bark peels away from the trunk as it ages. Even when large, the tree appears to spread and hulk rather than have a tall, spreading stature, and it is usually wider that it is tall. Old ones are astounding and gorgeous.

The sap is red, and all parts of the plant are strongly fragrant with a sharp, clean smell.

Plants are highly drought deciduous but even modest cold causes them to drop all their leaves. The reddish stems, deep green leaves, and creamy peeling bark are unlike those of any other trees but its close relatives. It makes a stunning statement in gardens that meet its required cultural conditions.

Peeling or exfoliating bark is fairly common in trees of the Baja California region of Mexico. In this extremely dry area, the thin sheets of bark admit light so that the photosynthetic tissue beneath functions properly. The adaptation of photosynthesis somewhere other than in the leaves is a common strategy in desert trees. Many botanists also believe

Bursera microphylla (elephant tree)

that in addition to opening up the bark to light, shedding older bark also discourages the growth of light-inhibiting lichen on the trunk, which is also common in the region.

The leaves are oddly pinnate with 7 to 35 dark green leaflets. Leaves are 1 to 3 in. (2.5 to 7.6 cm) long, and leaflets are small at less than 0.25 to 0.5 in. (0.6 to 1.3 cm) with an acute tip.

The white flowers are in clusters of three on the side branches, and plants are dioecious. However, isolated populations have some trees that produce perfect flowers (flowers with both female and male flower parts), which may indicate an adaptation to maintain its ability to reproduce in the absence of other individuals. Small, red, round drupes form late in the summer.

Elephant tree is an easy plant to grow in hot, dry areas. It prefers extremely sharp drainage and monthly watering in the summer. Natural rainfall in the winter is usually sufficient unless the year is exceptionally dry. Its remarkable and unusual form and its strong, crisp, camphorlike aroma make it an interesting specimen plant. It makes a unique potted plant and grows well under such conditions.

This species was first known to botanists by collections in Mexico, but it wasn't until the 1930s that American botanists confirmed its distribution and presence in this country. Donald Peattie, the spectacular naturalist, forester, and writer, relates the tale of this "discovery:" around 1910 "a mysterious old desert rat" who was prospecting for a gypsum mine told of finding an odd tree that had bleached white bark, boughs like an elephant's trunk, with wood that bled like an animal. One Edward Davis heard this story

and somehow received a crude map on which this man drew the location. The prospector vanished, but Davis found the trees in eastern San Diego County. About 10 years later, another man appeared in San Diego and began to tell of a grove of trees in the eastern part of the county that looked like a herd of elephants. Although he disappeared and left no map, workers from Scripps, the San Diego Museum of Natural History, and the state parks set out in 1937 and found those trees, finally documenting that elephant trees occurred in the county.

Elephant trees are the northernmost members of their family, and are undoubtedly relics from an earlier and wider distribution. They are widely used for both their incense and gum in Mexico. The gum is thought to cure venereal disease, work as an adhesive, and act as a varnish base. The bark is used as a dye.

White bark tree (*Bursera fagaroides*) is also a thick-trunked, semisucculent tree that resembles this species but has white, peeling bark that reveals a distinctive reddish orange to gray underbark. Like all *Bursera*, all parts including the stem are fragrant, and in white bark tree the fragrance has a citruslike quality. This species is extremely rare in Arizona; its range extends into northern Mexico.

Another species found in Baja California, *Bursera hindsiana*, is a large, swollen-trunked tree that over many years becomes a rambling, erratically branched tree or shrub. The leaflets are similar to those of the other two species but twice as large. The bark is a rich cinnamon-brown and peels away to reveal an underbark that is much the same color.

Butia capitata
Jelly palm, pindo palm

FAMILY: Arecaceae.

DISTRIBUTION: In South America in a wide arc from northern Argentina to southern Brazil, Paraguay, and Uruguay.

MATURE SIZE: Solitary palm growing only 10 to 20 ft. (3 to 6.1 m) tall and 6 to 8 ft. (1.8 to 2.4 m) wide.

BLOOMING PERIOD: May to July.

EXPOSURE: Full sun in all but the hottest deserts, where partial shade is best.

HARDINESS: Hardy to 15°F (−9°C) but possibly to 5°F (−15°C).

Jelly palm is a single-trunked palm whose stem grows wider at the base and tapers toward the top, giving the plant a vase shape. The leaf bases persist for many years and form a distinctive, attractive crisscross pattern over the stem.

The leaves are pinnately compound, and the petiole arches significantly so that in young plants the leaves curve back toward the trunk, almost covering it. There are 18 to 32 leaves on each petiole, each of which is 7 to 10 ft. (2.1 to 3 m) long of which the petiole is 2 to 4 ft. (0.6 to 1.2 m). The petiole is marked with coarse spines. Each leaf is broken into 50 to 140 leaflets that range in color from light green to blue-gray.

Butia capitata (jelly palm)

The tiny cream flowers are virtually count-less. They are held on a stalk that is up to 30 in. (76.2 cm) long. Both female and male flowers are formed on each plant.

The bright orange, oblong fruit is 1 in. (2.5 cm) long and is delicious. Jellies and other condiments are made from the fruit wherever jelly palm is grown.

This palm prefers enriched soils with regu-lar watering, weekly or more in the summer in the hottest deserts. In other parts of the region, monthly watering is sufficient in the summer. It grows slowly, and while it has sig-nificant heat tolerance, it is not very drought hardy. It has a tendency to become chlorotic in highly alkaline soils or those with poor drainage.

Butia capitata var. *odorata* is a short, com-pact plant with a bushy look. Var. *strictior* is more upright than typical, with a sparse, few-leaved crown. While these varieties are rarely offered with their names, over the years numerous collections from the wild have made them available, usually just called jelly palm. This mixing of varieties has contrib-uted to the noticeable and extensive variabil-ity of the species. In addition, several other species in this genus are similar and difficult to distinguish one from another, the most popular of which is *B. yatay* which grows taller and has a thicker trunk than jelly palm. All of these varieties and species hybridize readily when grown in close association, and some authors suggest that many of the plants offered as *B. capitata* are in fact hybrids. To make identification even more confus-ing, individual plants grown in dry or highly infertile soils tend to be smaller and with reduced leaves than those grown in deeper soils and more abundant water.

Jelly palm makes an excellent accent plant around pools and seating areas or in smaller gardens. Its graceful, falling leaves are attrac-tive and make a good focal point in lushly planted gardens. This palm is the most cold hardy of all the pinnate-leaved palms, mak-ing it useful in the far edges of the region as well in the deserts.

Jelly palm has also been crossed with Queen palm (*Syagrus romanzoffianum*) to produce the handsome palm called ×*Buti-agrus*. This plant is more widely grown in the southeastern United States.

Caesalpinia cacalaco
Cascalote

FAMILY: Fabaceae.
DISTRIBUTION: Tropical Mexico in Sinaloa, Jalisco, Colima, Michoacán, Querétaro, and Vera Cruz from sea level to 3500 ft. (1060 m).
MATURE SIZE: Round-crowned tree 10 to 20 ft. (3 to 6.1 m) tall and spreading as wide.
BLOOMING PERIOD: November to March.
EXPOSURE: Full or reflected sun in all areas.
HARDINESS: Flowers may be damaged at 30°F (–1°C) but plants tolerate cold to 20°F (–7°C) with minimal damage. Plants have endured temperatures as low as 16°F (–9°C) and recovered as multibranched shrubs.

Young cascalote trees have numerous low branches that are well armed with stout, curved spines reminiscent of rose spines. The dark brown stems thicken over time, shed-ding the thorns, so that well-grown trees become excellent single- or few-branched specimen shade trees. New growth is strongly tinged with red or purple, making the plant attractive even when young.

The leaves are 4 to 8 in. (10.2 to 20.3 cm) long and twice pinnate with three to six pairs of pinnae. The dark green, elliptic to rounded leaflets are arranged in three to five pairs per pinna and are 0.5 to 1 in. (1.3 to 2.5 cm) long.

The flowers are held in an erect, elongated, pyramidal flowering stalk that rises 4 to 12 in. (10.2 to 30.5 cm) above the foliage. Individual flowers are up to 0.5 in. (1.3 cm) wide and are bright, sulfur yellow. Up close you can see that the lower petal has a dark orange spot. The entire effect is of upraised candles illuminating the brilliant winter sky.

Fruit is a reddish pod that is 2 to 4 in. (5.1 to 10.2 cm) wide. It is deeply constricted and often distended by the seeds. The pods are an attractive feature but quickly shatter when the seeds are ripe. As for all members of this genus, the seeds and pods are reported to be toxic or poisonous when eaten.

Cascalote is an excellent choice for a smaller garden where modest shade is required. The blooming is beautiful and dramatic, so the tree should be placed where that feature may be easily viewed. Cascalote tolerates dry, rocky soils but grows much faster and into a better form with moderately enriched but well-drained soils. It is immensely heat tolerant but does best with deep watering twice a month or more in the summer in the hottest areas. Cascalote grows in response to the amount of watering it receives and grows fast if watered amply when young.

To reduce the low-forming stems of young trees, prune regularly in the early spring, leaving one or two main leaders as desired. In some individuals this pruning needs to be

Caesalpinia cacalaco (cascalote)

performed annually, while others discontinue producing so many suckers after a while. Otherwise, only prune after bloom is finished in the early winter. Plants bloom at the end of new wood, and fall pruning severely hampers flower formation.

There is a selection from Mountain States Wholesale Nursery in Arizona that lacks thorns and is called 'Smoothie'.

Caesalpinia gilliesii
Yellow bird of paradise

FAMILY: Fabaceae.

DISTRIBUTION: Native to Argentina and Uruguay. It has naturalized in parts of western Texas, southern New Mexico, and southern Arizona below 6000 ft. (1829 m) as well as in southern Florida and throughout much of Mexico.

MATURE SIZE: Loosely branched, openformed shrub 5 to 10 ft. (1.5 to 3 m) tall and spreading 3 to 6 ft. (0.9 to 1.8 m) wide.

BLOOMING PERIOD: May to September.

EXPOSURE: Full sun in all areas, but also grows well in partial shade in the hottest deserts.

HARDINESS: Although temperatures around 25°F (−4°C) cause leaves to drop, stems are hardy to 10°F (−12°C), and the plant recovers quickly from any cold damage.

Caesalpinia gilliesii (yellow bird of paradise)

Yellow bird of paradise is typically grown as a loose, open shrub although it can be trained as a small tree. It has an irregular, loosely branched form. Young branches are smooth, thornless, and green but age to a light tan or brown. They are strongly glandular and feel sticky when touched. The plant is cold deciduous but in warm winter areas it retains all or most of its leaves until new growth pushes them off.

Leaves are bipinnately compound and are 3 to 5 in. (7.6 to 12.7 cm) long with 7 to 25 pairs of pinnae. The yellowish green leaflets are tiny, less than 0.25 in. (0.6 cm) long, with 7 to 15 pairs of leaflets on each pinna. The number and size of the leaflets gives the plant a ferny, tropical appearance.

The flowers are held in congested 4 to 5 in. (10.2 to 12.7 cm) flowering stalks at the tips of the stems. Petals are about 1 in. (2.5 cm) wide, bright yellow, and showy, with brilliant red stamens 5 to 6 in. (12.7 to 15.2 cm) long that reach far beyond the petals. The entire flower looks like a red-beaked bird ready to take flight.

The pod is 4 to 5 in. (10.2 to 12.7 cm) long, flat and glandular, and reddish brown. Once mature they open explosively, expelling seeds in a wide arc around the plant with a noticeable pop.

Yellow bird of paradise is tolerant of a wide range of soils from rocky, dry alkaline soils of the desert to the slightly acidic soils of parts of southern California. It also shows good salt tolerance. It tolerates extreme heat; in fact in areas outside the hottest deserts, full sun and a hot location are necessary for best growth and blooming.

For best growth and to maintain leaves throughout the summer and to secure repeat blooming, provide water at least monthly in the summer in the hottest deserts. Plants that are deeply water stressed lose their leaves but regrow them quickly once water is available.

Pruning is best done in either early winter before new leaves emerge or in June after the first burst of blooming. Hard pruning should be restricted to these times, but light tip pruning may be done almost any time except in winter. Because of its loose-limbed form, prune carefully to remove only unnecessary branches. Removal of spent flowering stalks helps maintain a tidy look and may encourage continued blooming.

Yellow bird of paradise is a wonderful choice around pools, patios, or seating areas. It blooms almost year-round in the warmest parts of the region and is a colorful addition to mixed perennial or shrub plantings. I am especially fond of this species placed near colorful walls. The cheerful color and exuberant bloom are simply unrivaled.

Caesalpinia mexicana
Mexican bird of paradise

FAMILY: Fabaceae.

DISTRIBUTION: In the United States it is rare and local in far southern Texas in Cameron and Hidalgo Counties. The Texas populations are listed as native, but it is also widely cultivated, so it is not clear whether these are escaped and naturalized populations or truly native ones. In Mexico it is widespread and common in Sinaloa east to Tamaulipas and south to Guerrero.

MATURE SIZE: Large shrub or small, upright tree growing 10 to 15 ft. (3 to 4.6 m) tall and 6 to 10 ft. (1.8 to 3 m) wide.

BLOOMING PERIOD: February to July, often continuing as late as October.

EXPOSURE: Full sun or partial shade in all areas.

HARDINESS: Hardy to at least 25°F (−4°C) and is damaged at 20°F (−7°C) but recovery is quick.

Mexican bird of paradise is a rounded, well-formed shrub or a multistemmed small tree. The smooth gray bark and lack of spines make it an excellent choice for small patios, along walkways, and other areas where it can be easily enjoyed.

The dark green leaves are bipinnately compound and evergreen except in the most

Caesalpinia mexicana (Mexican bird of paradise)

severe cold. There are five to seven pairs of pinnae per leaf, each with four to five pairs of leaflets. Each rounded leaflet is less than 1 in. (2.5 cm) long.

The flowers are held in terminal spikes that are 3 to 6 in. (7.6 to 15.2 cm) long with up to 30 flowers in a cluster. They are bright, clear yellow and are lightly fragrant, which is unusual in this genus.

Fruit is a flat tan-to-yellowish pod that is 2 to 3 in. (5.1 to 7.6 cm) long. It splits open to release the seeds when they are mature. As with all members of this genus, the seeds and pods are reported to be toxic or poisonous when eaten.

Mexican bird of paradise has great heat tolerance but does best when it receives weekly watering in the hottest deserts during the summer. In areas with more reliable summer rainfall, it needs less frequent irrigation. It tolerates almost any kind of soil from clays to dry, rocky native soils.

Mexican bird of paradise is a good choice for a smaller garden where it can be used as either a colorful shrub or a small patio tree. It serves well as a focal point, fills a small, hot corner, or may even be massed to great effect where there is room.

It is fast growing, and in the colder parts of the region it may be grown as a low perennial, 3 to 6 ft. (0.9 to 1.8 m) tall, because it is knocked back by the cold every year.

Caesalpinia platyloba
Palo colorado

FAMILY: Fabaceae.

DISTRIBUTION: In Mexico it is found from southern and central Sonora and Sinaloa east to Chihuahua and south to at least Oaxaca from sea level to 2500 ft. (762 m). Also reported to occur along the Caribbean side of Central America to at least Panama, and into South America in Colombia, Ecuador, and Amazonian Peru and Brazil, as well as in the Caribbean Islands.

MATURE SIZE: Tall, open-branched tree growing 15 to 30 ft. (4.6 to 9.1 m) tall and as wide.

BLOOMING PERIOD: April to June, and again in late summer in response to rain.

EXPOSURE: Full sun in all areas; also tolerates partial shade in the hottest deserts.

HARDINESS: Hardy to 25°F (−4°C) but sheds leaves below this temperature. Plants may freeze to the ground below 20°F (−7°C) but recovery is quick even when severely damaged.

Palo colorado is a thornless, moderately fast-growing, small tree in most of the region. In some parts of its range, trees are reported to reach heights of over 100 ft. (30 m) tall. Young twigs are reddish brown but age to a smooth gray. The bark is pocked with small, white lenticels, and it often flakes and peels erratically as the stem matures. In some cases, the feature looks like bark damage, but it is a natural characteristic of this species.

The leaves are up to 8 in. (20.3 cm) long and composed of two to four pairs of pinnae. Each pinna has four to seven pairs of leaflets that are round to oblong and 0.75 to 2.5 in. (1.8 to 6.4 cm) long. Leaflets are shiny, bright green above and gray below. Young leaves are softly hairy but lose this feature as they mature. In the fall, leaves turn bright red before they die and drop off. This tree also becomes leafless when drought stressed, but leaves quickly regrow when the plant is rehydrated.

The flowers are held in short racemes that are 2 to 6 in. (5.1 to 15.2 cm) long. They are small, 0.5 in. (1.3 cm) across, bright yellow, and on close inspection may have an orange spot at the base of the petal. The pod is more or less oval, flat, and 2.5 to 4 in. (6.4 to 10.2 cm) long. It is initially bright red but ages to a reddish brown or tan and remains closed on the plant long after the seeds mature. As for members of this genus, the seeds and pods are reported to be toxic or poisonous when eaten.

Although palo colorado is somewhat frost tender in some parts of the region, it makes a splendid small tree for an enclosed patio or against a south-facing wall. My own tree has sheltered a south-facing bedroom window for over 15 years in a small raised bed, which leads me to wonder about its suitability as a street tree or its use in other constricted locations.

In the hottest deserts, water at least once or twice a month, and much less often during the winter. Psyllids are a common invader of this species in the late spring and can defoliate a plant within days of their arrival. Strong jets of water or other treatments may hold down the number of these sucking insects, but they are reminiscent of white flies with their habit of appearing in overwhelming numbers in some years and creating more modest infestations in other years. But they feed only for a short time, and the tree is perfectly suited to recover from a seasonal leaf drop. It leafs out within a week or so of their moving on.

The wood of this species is highly valued throughout its range for all kinds of build-

Caesalpinia platylobu (palo colorado)

ing uses, including fence posts. It is reported to last in the ground up to 100 years. Woodworkers know it by the two other common names: curly paela for wood with a noticeable burl, and chakte viga for all other wood. They give it high marks for its beauty and ease of use, as well as its great durability. The interior wood is yellow but turns a deep, toasty red, and some individuals' wood has an iridescent quality. With exposure to sunlight, the wood darkens to a rich red-orange.

Caesalpinia pulcherrima
Red bird of paradise, dwarf poinciana, pride of Barbados

FAMILY: Fabaceae.

DISTRIBUTION: Although its origins are uncertain and poorly understood, red bird of paradise is thought to be native to tropical Mexico and the West Indies. It is now established and naturalized from central Sonora throughout all of tropical Mexico, Central America, and along the Gulf of Mexico in Florida to most of the Caribbean Islands.

MATURE SIZE: Sprawling, irregular shrub or trained to a small tree 6 to 12 ft. (1.8 to 3.7 m) tall, spreading 4 to 10 ft. (1.2 to 3 m) wide. In truly tropical areas, it may grow up to 20 ft. (6.1 m) tall.

BLOOMING PERIOD: March to November.

EXPOSURE: Full or reflected sun even in the hottest deserts.

HARDINESS: Foliage is damaged and falls at 30°F (–1°C) and is severely damaged below 25°F –4°C). But recovery is quick even when plants freeze to the ground.

Red bird of paradise is a cold- and drought-deciduous shrub with a number of irregularly placed stems. The stems, branches, and petioles are red when they are young and are covered with soft-looking but prickly spines. When plants have not been frozen back repeatedly, the stems become much enlarged and the bark hardens to a dull gray.

The leaves are bipinnately compound and are 8 to 12 in. (20.3 to 30.5 cm) long. There are 3 to 9 pairs of pinnae and each holds 5 to 12 pairs of small, thin leaflets. The leaflets are much less than 1 in. (2.5 cm) long and two or three times longer than wide, giving the leaf a fernlike appearance. Leaflets are bright green above and duller beneath and turn a vivid yellow when they begin to fall in the winter.

The flowers are held in a tall, open raceme

Caesalpinia pulcherrima (red bird of paradise)

high above the foliage. Each flower is roughly bowl shaped and 2 to 3 in. (5.1 to 7.6 cm) across. The corolla lobes are thin, papery, and often crinkled or wavy, giving them extra pizzazz, which they hardly need because they are yellow, orange, and red. The top lobe is small and bright yellow and the rest are yellow marked with reddish orange. In some plants, flowers begin yellow and change to the redder tones. There are occasional pure yellow-flowered forms—one of which is known as 'Phoenix Bird', another is 'Flava'—and this trait has shown up from time to time throughout the range of this species. The stamens extend far from the petals and are bright red, adding to the gaudy display. There are also forms that have flowers that are almost entirely red, one whose flowers are an odd but lovely pinkish tone, and one rarely encountered form with cream and yellow bicolor flowers.

The fruit is a flat, oblong pod up to 5 in. (12.7 cm) long. When dry, it is brown and twists open to expel the seeds with a loud pop. If you are not prepared for the sound and are standing nearby, it is loud enough to startle you. As for all members of this genus, the seeds and pods are reported to be toxic or poisonous when eaten.

Red bird of paradise is one of the workhorse ornamentals for the cities of the hottest deserts. There is no exposure too hot for it, although it may be devastated by a brief cold snap. The brilliant blooming and soft, ferny foliage contrast beautifully with each other. The species is a reliable and common choice for roadside plantings, pool areas, or around patios, where its luscious blooming may be enjoyed. Butterflies are mad for the flowers and legions of butterflies crowd it in late summer.

Red bird of paradise blooms best when watered at least twice a month in the summer, although it accepts more water and will survive on less. If the plant needs to be reduced in size, prune it in the late winter or early spring just as the new leaves emerge. Light pruning may be done throughout the summer, and spent flowering stalks may be removed at any time.

Caesalpinia pumila
Copper caesalpinia

FAMILY: Fabaceae.

DISTRIBUTION: In Mexico endemic to central Sonora along the margins of the southeastern Sonoran Desert from Carbo to Guaymas.

MATURE SIZE: Open, spreading shrub growing 6 to 10 ft. (1.8 to 3 m) tall and spreading up to 8 ft. (2.4 m) wide.

BLOOMING PERIOD: July to October in response to rain.

EXPOSURE: Full sun in all areas, but tolerates partial shade in the hottest deserts.

HARDINESS: Hardy to 25°F (−4°C).

Copper caesalpinia is a deciduous, loosely branched, unarmed shrub clearly at home in the hottest and driest parts of the region. The bark begins a dark red-brown but ages to gray and is marked with small, circular, white lenticels.

The leaves are bipinnately compound with two to three pairs of pinnae, each of which has two to four pairs of leaflets. The main rachis of the leaf is 2.5 to 3 in. (6.4 to 7.6 cm) long and each pinna is the same length. The dusky-green leaflets are nearly round and are 0.25 to 0.5 in. (0.6 to 1.3 cm) across. In the

Caesalpinia pumila (copper caesalpinia)

It makes a fine addition to a border or boundary mixed hedge, and is a good screening plant within a larger garden. It has not become commonly known, which is a shame because of its durability, toughness, and the beauty of its foliage and form.

Calliandra californica
Baja fairy duster, red fairy duster

FAMILY: Fabaceae.

DISTRIBUTION: Widely distributed and locally common in Baja California but especially in the cape region from sea level to 4000 ft. (1219 m).

MATURE SIZE: Openly branched shrub 4 to 6 ft. (1.2 to 1.8 m) tall and up to 5 ft. (1.5 m) wide, occasionally more.

BLOOMING PERIOD: Blooms virtually year-round, but blooms heaviest in the spring from February to April and again from August to September.

EXPOSURE: Full or reflected sun in all areas.

HARDINESS: Minor tip damage and leaf drop at 25°F (−4°C), but is killed or severely damaged when temperatures fall below 20°F (−7°C).

fall, the leaflets turn a dusky, coppery red and remain that way for a long time before they fall.

The clear yellow flowers are held in short racemes with few flowers. The flowers are up to 0.5 in (1.3 cm) wide. Pods are nearly round or elliptic and range from 0.5 to 1 in. (1.3 to 2.5 cm) across. The pods are dusky pink and remain on the plant for a long time over the fall and winter, offering another round of color and interest for the plant. As for all members of this genus, the seeds and pods are reported to be toxic or poisonous when eaten.

This species can endure considerable drought, needing only monthly watering in the summer, even in the hottest desert. But excellent, even rocky, drainage is best.

Baja fairy duster is an intricately branched shrub with upright stems that cross and wind around each other. The stems are light gray, becoming brownish gray and woody with age. Stems, leaves, and even the short inflorescence are coated with fine, smooth hairs. In warm climates plants are usually evergreen but the species is both cold and drought deciduous.

The bipinnately compound leaves are 1.5 to 2.5 in (3.8 to 6.4 cm) long and are composed of 1 to 4 pairs of pinnae, each of which has from 5 to 15 pairs of leaflets. The leaflets are shiny green above and a dull gray-green below. In many forms, the leaves are a dark, dusky, gray-green. The tiny, oblong, rounded leaflets are up to 0.25 in. (0.6 cm) long and 1.5 to 3 times longer than they are wide. These fine, closely spaced leaves are distinctive, both in color and form, and may only be confused with the leaves of its close relative *Calliandra peninsularis*.

The flowers are composed of a tightly compressed head of numerous, tiny, virtually petalless flowers. The vivid red filaments are up to 1 in. (2.5 cm) long and give a distinctive puffball look to the bloom.

The flat pod is 1.5 to 2.5 in. (3.8 to 6.4 cm) long. It opens abruptly, expelling the seeds when they are ripe; then it curls backward and remains on the plant for a long time.

It is hard to beat Baja fairy duster for both heat and drought tolerance. The most exquisite individuals are those grown in unrelieved full sun. They bloom longest and brightest and have the best natural form. While it is common to see the plant severely pruned, even sheared, that is a crime: it shortens the life of the plant, ruins its lovely, natural form, and dramatically reduces the blooming, which is its most appealing feature.

Baja fairy duster is tolerant of almost any kind of soil, from clays to rocky desert soils. But good drainage is essential. Growth is rapid to moderate, depending primarily on how much water the plant receives.

If pruning is needed at all, prune lightly in the spring after the first flush of flowering. It is unwise to prune in the summer, because it sends the plant into a torpor similar to being drought deciduous and it will not fully recover until late in the year.

Calliandra californica (Baja fairy duster)

Water once a month in the summer in the hottest regions, and much less often anywhere else. In areas with regular summer rainfall, the plant grows on natural rainfall.

A hybrid between this species and the shorter, more northern-growing fairy duster *Calliandra eriophylla* is known as 'Sierra Starr', with a tighter, denser form. While the flowering is similar, the color is closer to a watermelon tone than the brilliant scarlet of the species. Countless individuals in the trade are hybrids showing a range of less than red coloring or are actually *C. peninsularis* unwittingly labeled as *C. californica*. All are lovely, but I think that no selection rivals the form, durability, and extreme red beauty of the species itself.

Baja fairy duster has only been commonly grown for about 20 years. I remember when owning it or selling it was unusual. It is a great pleasure to have hung around long enough to see such a great plant become commonly known and used.

Hummingbirds adore the plant so it is a good idea to place it where both you and they can enjoy it. My plants are outside the windows of the kitchen and dining room so I can see them often and daily spy on the antics of their tiny visitors.

Casuarina cunninghamiana (beefwood)

Casuarina cunninghamiana
Beefwood, river she oak

FAMILY: Casuarinaceae.

DISTRIBUTION: Australia from southern New South Wales to northern Queensland, particularly along rivers. It has naturalized in warm parts of California and Florida as well as Hawaii.

MATURE SIZE: Erect, columnar tree 40 to 80 ft. (12.2 to 24 m) tall, rarely over 60 ft. (18 m) in the region, with a crown spread of 30 to 35 ft. (9.1 to 10.7 m).

BLOOMING PERIOD: Cones form in the summer.

EXPOSURE: Full sun in all areas.

HARDINESS: Hardy to at least 20°F (–7°C) and possibly lower.

Beefwood is a tall, columnar tree that makes a stunning silhouette against the skyline. The bark is dark red and is the source of the common name. The tree's tough wood once enjoyed a minor interest in the timber trade.

The true leaves are minute scales, hardly visible to the naked eye, held in clusters of 8 to 20 at the nodes. The long, dusky-green, jointed stems are also arranged in clusters and look much like the needles of pines; they are easily misinterpreted as foliage.

The plants are dioecious and flowers are also minute. The female flowers are red. The male flowers are crowded in rings equipped with grayish scales; each has one brown stamen. The seeds are held in rounded, woody cones that are 0.25 in. (0.6 cm) long, occasionally longer.

Beefwood grows best in deep soils and it tolerates soils that are wet or dry, alkaline or saline. This species is drought resistant; established plants need to be watered only once a month even in the hottest deserts. It is tolerant of extreme heat and grows best in full sun.

This tall, commanding species is useful in large gardens to shade roofs or tall structures. It is also a good choice at the edge of the garden to cast long shadows over the entire area.

The similar Australian pine (*Casuarina equisetifolia*) looks much the same but the jointed stems hang down in great clusters. This species grows 40 to 65 ft. (12.2 to 25 m) tall and is more tolerant of dry soils than beefwood. It, too, does well with monthly watering in the deserts but is cold hardy only to approximately 25°F (−4°C).

The genus name *Casuarina* comes from the resemblance that Linnaeus saw between the plant's foliage and the plumage of the cassowary, a flightless bird from New Guinea and Australia.

Ceanothus greggii
Desert ceanothus, desert buckthorn

FAMILY: Rhamnaceae.

DISTRIBUTION: In the United States in California from eastern Santa Barbara and Kern Counties to southern Utah, southern Nevada, central and southern Arizona, southern New Mexico, and Trans-Pecos Texas at 3500 to 8000 ft. (1067 to 2438 m). In Mexico from Sonora and Chihuahua south to Oaxaca at similar elevations in chaparral or juniper-pinyon forest.

MATURE SIZE: Rigid, complexly branched shrub 3 to 6 ft. (0.9 to 1.8 m) tall and as wide.

BLOOMING PERIOD: March to April.

EXPOSURE: Full sun in all areas, but in the hottest deserts it is best to provide afternoon shade or relief from the western sun.

HARDINESS: Hardy to at least 15°F (−9°C) and possibly lower.

Desert ceanothus is an evergreen shrub of the chaparral and dry hillsides of the west. Its complex branching pattern and rigid leaves give the plant a rounded, symmetrical form. The bark is gray, and while the branches are stiff they do not have true spines.

The leathery leaves are small and show a wide range of size, color, and margin types over the range of the species. The most typical forms have elliptic or obovate leaves that are small, only 0.5 in. (1.3 cm) long. The margins are entire and the upper surface is a dark gray-green while the lower surface is paler with prominent veins. The leaves are more or less cupped and are opposite on the stem, which helps distinguish this plant from many

Ceanothus greggii (desert ceanothus)

other species of *Ceanothus* with which it occurs.

Varieties have been described by relying on the leaf differences, such as leaves that are yellow-green above, those that have sharply toothed margins, or those with rounded leaves. While these differences and others are noted by botanists, they have not been much noted or selected by horticulturists.

The tiny flowers, which are less than 0.25 in. (0.6 cm) long, are held in dense umbellike clusters, making them showy and spectacular in some individuals. They are white, although some individuals may show a bluish or pinkish cast to the flowers. The flowers are followed by fruit that is a tiny, rounded capsule.

Desert ceanothus, despite its name, is tricky to grow in the hottest deserts of the region. I have known some individuals to do well in special circumstances, but ultimately the prolonged, intense heat of the hottest deserts does them in.

Desert ceanothus grows well in alkaline soils that are well drained and moderately enriched. In the hottest deserts, plant where it can avoid reflective heat or exposure to unrelieved afternoon sun. It does, however, need only moderate supplemental irrigation in all areas. Even in the hottest deserts, watering twice a month in the summer, sometimes less, is sufficient.

Desert ceanothus is a fine choice for a mixed hedge or boundary planting. The gorgeous but fairly brief blooming lights up a planting in the spring. The plant's dense form and virtually evergreen habit provide a good visual barrier along a border. It is also a good choice as a background for more colorful or exuberant plantings.

Celtis ehrenbergiana
Desert hackberry

SYNONYM: *Celtis pallida.*
FAMILY: Ulmaceae.
DISTRIBUTION: In the United States from southern Arizona, extreme southern New Mexico, and in Texas from the Trans-Pecos to the Edwards Plateau and down the Rio Grande Valley to the Gulf of Mexico at 1500 to 4500 ft. (457 to 1372 m). In Mexico from the Sonoran Desert of Baja California and Sonora east to Chihuahua and south to Oaxaca at 3000 to 8000 ft. (914 to 2438 m). The range extends south to Argentina among various subspecies.
MATURE SIZE: Irregularly branched, rounded shrub or tree from 8 to 15 ft. (2.4 to 4.6 m) tall, occasionally to 20 ft. (6.1 m), spreading up to 8 ft. (2.4 m) wide.
BLOOMING PERIOD: March to April and with summer rains July to October.
EXPOSURE: Full sun in all areas, although it grows well in partial shade in the hottest deserts.
HARDINESS: Loses leaves at 20°F (−7°C), but stems are fully hardy to 10°F (−12°C); recovery is rapid from frost damage.

Desert hackberry is an irregularly branched species that is large enough to be a tree but is densely branched enough to be a shrub. It is most often evergreen although it may be cold deciduous if temperatures plunge low enough. The stems are smooth and gray to begin but mature to brown and are heavily armed with paired, small, straight, sharp spines. Branches form in a complicated zig-zag pattern.

The leaves are simple and entire, but in

some individuals the leaf margin may be wavy or even have small teeth. The leaves are thick, 1 to 2 in. (2.5 to 5.1 cm) long, and rough like sandpaper. They are broadly elliptic or ovate, with either a rounded or an acute tip, and are bright green above and pale green below.

The flowers are tiny and held in a cyme. Their greenish-white color and minute size make them almost invisible. Flowers are either pistillate, staminate, or perfect, often on the same inflorescence.

The fruit is a red, reddish-orange, or yellow, juicy, tart, and tasty. It is relished by people, all manner of animals, reptiles, and most birds. Because the fruit is only 0.25 in. (0.6 cm) in diameter, most gardeners leave them for the birds.

Desert hackberry is an effortless shrub to grow anywhere within its range. Although it grows on natural rainfall, it is a better-looking plant and longer lived if given deep irrigation once every month or two, particularly in the summer. It tolerates a wide range of soils but requires sharp drainage.

Desert hackberry has a shallow root system, making it an excellent choice for erosion control where its large size can be accommodated. It is reputed to make good honey as well. This shrub is a splendid choice for mixed hedges at the edges or borders of the garden. It has such great wildlife value that it easily forms the basis for a wildlife or naturalistic garden.

There is much confusion over the botanical name of this species. It was originally placed in *Celtis* as *C. ehrenbergiana* in 1851. But Torrey, probably unwittingly, published the name *C. pallida* for this species in his 1859 boundary survey work of the United States and Mexico border. The name stuck, but

Celtis ehrenbergiana (desert hackberry)

considering the laws of nomenclature many authors have returned to the original name, *C. ehrenbergiana*, as used here. This problem was common in the days of poor communication, long distances, and species with huge ranges that have wide geographic variability.

Desert hackberry is renowned for its wildlife value and for its close association with a couple of butterfly species. It is a host for the Empress Leilia (*Asterocampa leilia*) butterfly and for the snout butterfly (*Libytheana carinenta*), whose larvae feed on the leaves. The bright green caterpillars of the former are shaped like leaves and have a pair of horns on the head that look remarkably like the plant's own thorns.

Many of the leaves on fresh spring growth

are blistered, curled, and oozing sticky honey-dew as a result of feeding by nymphs of a psyllid. Although the condition looks severe, it is temporary and causes no true damage to the plant.

Celtis reticulata
Netleaf hackberry

FAMILY: Ulmaceae.

DISTRIBUTION: In the United States widely distributed from Washington to Wyoming and Idaho south to California, Utah, and Nevada, as well as Colorado, Kansas, and Oklahoma and south to Arizona, New Mexico, and Texas. Commonly found in canyons, along streams or wet areas, at 2500 to 6000 ft. (762 to 1829 m). In Mexico from Baja California east to Sonora, Chihuahua, and Coahuila at similar elevations.

MATURE SIZE: Upright, often irregularly branched tree 20 to 30 ft. (6.1 to 9.1 m) tall and spreading as wide.

BLOOMING PERIOD: March to August.

EXPOSURE: Full sun in all areas.

HARDINESS: Hardy to 0°F (−18°C), but it is also reported to be hardy to −20°F (−29°C).

Celtis reticulata (netleaf hackberry)

Netleaf hackberry is a deciduous tree of the canyons and waterways of the region. The thick, reddish-brown to ash-gray bark is rough, and it often has short protruding edges that look like warts or bruises but is thornless. Some populations, particularly the more southern ones, have smooth, uninterrupted bark.

Plants when young are sprawling with complicated and irregular branching. In maturity they form a fine shade tree with a classic rounded crown. The twisted branching habit coupled with the odd, gnarly bark makes for a striking specimen.

Leaves of netleaf hackberry are thick with conspicuous veins that are arrayed like a net. The leaves are rough and feel like coarse sandpaper. They are held on a short petiole and are 1 to 3 in. (2.5 to 7.6 cm) long. The leaf margins are entire but serrate in the middle, and the leaf tip may be either rounded or acute. Leaves are asymmetrical at the base, with one side shorter than the other. The top of the leaf ranges from yellow-green to gray-green, and the underside is paler.

The flowers are tiny, inconspicuous, greenish-white, and are held in clusters of one to four flowers in the axils of the leaves. The fruit is a rounded drupe almost 0.5 in. (1.3 cm) around. Fruit color ranges from black to reddish-black or orange-red and is copiously consumed by birds and other wildlife.

Despite its origins in the wetter and cooler parts of the region, netleaf hackberry does well as an ornamental tree in cultivation even in the hottest deserts. It grows best in deep soils rather than shallow, rocky ones. It grows well on as little as 12 in. (305 mm) of rain a year, but will be healthier if given deep irrigation twice a month in the hottest deserts. The tree's wood has been used for a wide array of products, from fences to boxes and crates and furniture mimicking the look of elm. There is an old tale that the wood will make stairs that don't creak, but you couldn't prove it by me since I have neither stairs nor hackberry wood in the house.

Netleaf hackberry is parasitized by mistletoe, and both powdery mildew and gallflies may attack the foliage. Neither causes much more than cosmetic damage, however, in healthy trees. The gallfly leaves a leaf that looks bubbled up, which is unattractive but not harmful.

This species is highly adaptable, tolerating high heat, cold, and some drought. Unfortunately, attention has not been paid to making selections that combine good form and tolerance of particular conditions. This species is strongly tolerant of cotton root rot and most other diseases.

There is confusion over what to call this species. Most authors agree to *Celtis reticulata*, although there are adherents to the name *Celtis laevigata* var. *reticulata* and my botanical sources are among them. *Celtis laevigata* is a species of the southeastern United States, and the two species converge in some parts of the range. Frankly, there is so much confusion over the taxonomy of this entire genus that some enterprising botanist could make a nice living sorting it all out for us.

The name hackberry probably came to us from early English or Scottish colonists who used the term *hag* to refer to many different types of berries. Looking a bit like something they knew, they gave the plant the name hag, or hackberry, and it stuck.

Cercis canadensis var. *mexicana*
Mexican redbud

SYNONYM: *Cercis mexicana*
FAMILY: Fabaceae.
DISTRIBUTION: In the United States in far western Texas and southern New Mexico in arroyos, canyons, and among limestone hills at 2300 to 5000 ft. (701 to 1524 m). In Mexico in the mountains of Coahuila and Nuevo León and along the southeastern Sierra Madre Oriental at 2600 to 6000 ft. (792 to 1829 m).
MATURE SIZE: Multistemmed shrub or small tree 10 to 15 ft. (3 to 4.6 m) tall, occasionally to 20 ft. (6.1 m), and as wide.
BLOOMING PERIOD: March and April.
EXPOSURE: In the hottest deserts, in partial shade or eastern exposures. In other areas, full sun or partial shade.
HARDINESS: Hardy to −5°F (−21°C).

Mexican redbud is a deciduous shrub or small tree with densely pubescent to woolly petioles and small branches even when mature. In its natural range, Mexican redbud

Cercis canadensis var. *mexicana*
(Mexican redbud)

has a flat-topped or round form with graceful, spreading branches.

While the new leaves are often fuzzy, mature leaves are thick, leathery, and glossy dark green. The leaves are variable in shape, ranging from gently heart-shaped to nearly round, and with somewhat to distinctly wavy margins. Leaves range in size from 2 to 3 in. (5.1 to 7.6 cm) long and 1.75 to 2.5 in. (4.4 to 6.4 cm) wide.

The flowers erupt before the leaves and are held in sessile clusters that are 4 in. (10.2 cm) long. Individual flowers are small, less than 0.5 in. (1.3 cm) across, and range in color from a light rose to a rich, dark, pink-purple shade. The pod is oblong, flat, and up to 4 in. (10.2 cm) long. It can persist on the plant for a long time in some individuals.

Mexican redbud is tolerant of a wide range of soils, from rocky desert soils to deeper, more traditional garden soil. But it will fail quickly in poorly drained soils.

In the hottest deserts regular irrigation in the summer keeps the plants healthy. In milder areas, they are considerably more drought tolerant. The wood is brittle and fragile, so it is important to provide the protection of other shrubs or trees, especially in areas prone to high winds. Unfortunately, deer like to browse this plant, so it also needs to be protected from them.

Prune Mexican redbud while it is dormant to reduce the height, eliminate diseased or damaged stems, or enhance the form. This species forms numerous suckers at the base as it grows, and some gardeners choose to leave them to achieve a full, multibranched form, while others select out a few stems and eliminate the rest. Pruning is a matter of pure preference.

Cercis canadensis has three varieties recognized by botanists. *C. canadensis* var. *canadensis* is a more eastern species and occurs naturally outside the range of this book. With thinner leaves that usually exhibit a sharp tip on heart-shaped leaves, it also requires more water and deeper soils than the other two varieties. Var. *mexicana*, as noted here, is the smallest of the three varieties, tending more toward being a shrub; it is more drought tolerant than the other two.

Var. *texensis*, known as Texas redbud, occurs in the Edwards Plateau region of Texas, south into adjacent Mexico, and north into Oklahoma where it mingles with var. *canadensis*. It is more treelike than Mexican redbud. While it also tolerates lean, alkaline soils, it is not as drought tolerant as Mexican redbud. It is distinguished from Mexican redbud by the larger leaves and lack of woolly pubescence on the branches and petioles, especially when mature.

Madrone Nursery in Texas has named two selections of Mexican redbud. 'Sanderson' is reported to be taller and more drought tolerant than other redbuds, especially Texas redbud. In 1989, the nursery introduced a weeping form of Texas redbud called 'Traveller', which was subsequently patented by Dan Hosage, the owner. This unique form has received several national horticulture awards, and in 2000 the Native Plant Society of Texas presented Dan Hosage with the Lynn Lowrey Memorial award for this tree.

The western redbud, *Cercis occidentalis*, is a small tree that is found in a wide swath of central and southern California to eastern Utah, Nevada, and northern Arizona. It has somewhat thickened leaves that are a blue-green color. The flowers are much the same as those of other redbuds, occurring before the leaves in shades of magenta and pink from February to April. The leaves of this species turn yellow, sometimes red, in the fall as they drop, a feature not shared by the more xeric members of the genus. It blooms best in areas that receive some winter chill, and does not thrive in either alkaline or saline soils of the hottest deserts.

Chamaedorea seifrizii
Bamboo palm

FAMILY: Arecaceae.

DISTRIBUTION: In Mexico in the states of Tabasco, Campeche, Quintana Roo, and Yucatán south into Belize, Guatemala, and Honduras up to 1700 ft. (518 m), often found in areas that are seasonally inundated by water.

MATURE SIZE: Clustering palm growing 7 to 12 ft. (2.1 to 3.7 m) tall and 1 to 2.5 ft. (0.3 to 0.9 m) wide.

BLOOMING PERIOD: May to August.

Chamaedorea seifrizii (bamboo palm)

EXPOSURE: In the hottest deserts, bamboo palm grows best in either dense or filtered shade. While it tolerates a remarkable amount of sun, western or reflected sun is not desirable. In all other areas, full sun to dense shade is advisable and partial shade is best.

HARDINESS: Hardy to 30°F (−1°C), severe leaf and stem damage at 23°F (−5°C), but recovers quickly. Temperatures below 20°F (−7°C) are lethal.

Bamboo palm is well named. The tall, erect stems are jointed at intervals, and when the spent fronds are pruned, the stem looks precisely like bamboo. The stems have as few as 5 to as many as 15 leaves per stem. Because the palm clusters freely, it has a dense, compact appearance.

The leaves are pinnately compound, with 5 to 18 leaflets per leaf, and are up to 24 in. (61 cm) long. Leaflets are dark green and linear. Each leaflet is up to 14 in. (35.6 cm) long but rarely more than 1 in. (2.5 cm) wide and more or less flat. The leaflets are dark green and show ribbed margins. The terminal leaflet is similar to the rest but it is sometimes wider.

The flowers are held on a stalk that is 6 to 12 in. (15.2 to 30.5 cm) long. The orange flowering stalks arise from the leaf bases, and although each flower is minute their dull yellow color makes them show up.

The fruit is a pea-sized berry that begins green, then turns orange or red, and finally is black. Although birds are fond of the fruit, people need to be wary. These fruits are renowned for causing strong skin irritations when handled, particularly if the berry is broken.

This species was reportedly cultivated by the Maya. In modern times it is one of the most widely cultivated of all bamboo palms. It grows in almost any moderately rich, well-drained soil. It has astounding heat tolerance, much more cold tolerance than most other bamboo-style palms, and is remarkably drought tolerant.

Plants need steady and regular watering through the summer. In my garden this species has thrived on the same irrigation system that waters my desert perennials every four to six days in the summer, depending on the temperature. Application of good compost, well-composted manure, or palm fertilizer at the beginning of the summer keeps the plant growing strongly. Heavy mulching also helps, particularly in areas with drying winds or in dry soils.

Pruning out the old fronds keeps the plant tidy. But resist trimming out the leaf bases until they dry. Once dry, they can be removed to reveal the lovely, ringed, bamboolike stem.

Bamboo palm is widely grown in houses throughout the world. It is one of the best bamboo palms for outside cultivation in the warmest parts of the region. Although this species, like all of this genus, is an understory plant in the rainforests of Central America, it adapts well to cultivation in even the hottest deserts of the region. Its reasonable drought and great heat tolerance make it suitable for any shady part of a dry garden. It is also gorgeous in large containers in or outside of the house.

Chamaedorea microspadix is similar but has larger, papery-textured leaves. It is even more cold hardy, although a bit harder to find. Many growers in Florida have named a selection with wider leaves or thicker stems, but it is not often available in our area. Dwarf forms have been noted and sold from time to time as well.

Chamaerops humilis
Mediterranean fan palm

FAMILY: Arecaceae.
DISTRIBUTION: The western Mediterranean from Algeria, Spain, and France to Italy.
MATURE SIZE: Multistemmed plant 10 to 20 ft. (3 to 6.1 m) tall and spreading up to 20 ft. (6.1 m) wide.

BLOOMING PERIOD: Summer.

EXPOSURE: Full sun or partial shade in the hottest deserts; full sun all other areas.

HARDINESS: Hardy to 15°F (–9°C), but has survived brief spells down to 6°F (–14°C).

Mediterranean fan palm is a multistemmed plant that may be pruned to maintain as many of the trunks as you wish. Plants that are left unpruned become attractive, round, tight balls but they become large in old age.

The leaves are palmately compound and up to 3 ft. (0.9 m) long. There are from 12 to 30 leaves on each stem and up to 32 segments on each leaf. Segments are split for 2 to 8 in. (0.6 to 2.4 cm) and are rigid. Leaves range from olive-green to gray-green and almost blue.

The petioles are armed with short, curved or straight thorns.

The flowers are held on 6 in. (15.2 cm) stalks, and plants are dioecious with male and female flowers on separate plants. Flowers are followed by numerous round, brown or yellow fruits that are 0.5 to 1.5 in. (1.3 to 3.8 cm) across.

Mediterranean fan palm grows well in almost any well-drained soil, although an enriched soil yields the best results. Once the plant is established, provide monthly deep watering in the hottest deserts but much less frequent watering where there is reliable summer rainfall. The palm is much slower-growing than most of the other common fan-leaved palms.

Chamaerops humilis (Mediterranean fan palm)

This is the only palm native to continental Europe and has been in cultivation for a long time. It makes a gorgeous specimen or focal point where there is plenty of room. Many gardeners select a specific number of stems to create an open, symmetrical plant. Prune out unwanted stems in late spring or early summer. Plants regenerate the stems often from latent buds, so maintenance pruning will be needed over the years to keep a tidy, multi-stemmed form.

Chilopsis linearis
Desert willow

FAMILY: Bignoniaceae.

DISTRIBUTION: In the United States in the desert regions of southern California east to extreme southern Nevada and Utah, central and southern Arizona, and central and southern New Mexico below 5000 ft. (1524 m). It also occurs throughout western Texas, down the Rio Grande Valley into the plains of south Texas. In Mexico it is widespread in Baja California, Sonora, Chihuahua, Coahuila, Nuevo León, Zacatecas, and San Luis Potosí below 6000 ft. (1829 m).

MATURE SIZE: Upright or sprawling tree from 10 to 20 ft. (3 to 6.1 m) tall, rarely over 25 ft. (7.6 m). Spread depends on growth habit and is from 8 to 30 ft. (2.4 to 9.1 m).

BLOOMING PERIOD: May to October.

EXPOSURE: Full or reflected sun even in the hottest deserts.

HARDINESS: Hardy to at least 10°F (−12°C) with minimal or no damage. Naturalized in areas of northern Texas and grown as far north as Kansas and Chicago in sheltered locations where it freezes to the ground but recovers rapidly to be a small, blooming shrub.

Desert willow is one of the few truly deciduous trees native to the Sonoran Desert. Grown as either a large multitrunked shrub or a small, multitrunked tree, it has dark gray bark that is smooth when young but becomes fissured with age. Small branches and leaves of some individuals are sticky, which is a mark of one of its named varieties.

The narrow, linear leaves may be either opposite or alternate and are thin, pale green, and 4 to 12 in. (10.2 to 30.5 cm) long, usually with prominent veins. The leaves have a sharp tip and are nearly winged at the base. There is wide variability in the leaves both in their size and in the intensity of the green color.

The flowers are irregular, composed of five unequal corolla lobes. The central lobe of the three lower corolla lobes is the longest and these lower lobes have distinctive nectar guides in shades of purple, lavender, or white. The two upper lobes may be the same shade of pink, purple, or lavender, or not, which makes for some intriguing color forms in this species.

The flowers are congested in terminal inflorescences that may be either a short raceme or panicle. Each flower is 1 to 2.5 in. (2.5 to 6.4 cm) long, and ranges in color from pure white to light lavender to dark purple, or pink. There are also bicolored forms. Flower color is darker and flower size is increased in the southern end of its range. The flowers are sweetly scented and some forms perfume the entire area around them.

The fruit is a thin capsule that is 7 to 12 in. (17.8 to 30.5 cm) long. This capsule, which superficially resembles a legume's pod, opens quickly to release the thin, papery seeds but persists on the tree even after the leaves have fallen for the winter.

Desert willow is tolerant of almost any well-drained soil and grows well in saline soils. Growth is rapid, particularly just after the plant breaks dormancy or when it receives supplemental watering. Once established, the species is highly drought tolerant, growing on modest summer irrigation or nearly natural rainfall throughout the region. Bees love the flowers as do hummingbirds, finches, and other nectar-feeding birds and insects. This species is highly resistant to cotton root rot.

The pliable, but strong, young branches have been favored over the years for making bows, as well as for fencing and fuel. In some parts of Mexico the branches are also used in basketry.

There are three recognized forms over its wide range, accounting for the variability of flower color and size and leaf color and size that is seen in the trade. In nature, there is a significant intergrade among the subspecies where their ranges intersect.

Chilopsis linearis subsp. *linearis* has nearly straight or erect leaves with prominent veins. Leaves are not usually sticky but young stems may be hairy. It occurs chiefly in the eastern end of the range from eastern New Mexico to western and southern Texas, and into eastern Mexico where it is widespread and abundant.

Subsp. *arcuata* has arching, curved leaves that are up to 5.5 in. (14 cm) long and not sticky. This is the westernmost form, ranging from Baja California to western Arizona, New Mexico, and grows in the most xeric part of the range.

Var. *tomenticaulis* has young stems that are densely woolly and occurs in Mexico in Nuevo León and Tamaulipas.

Out of all this natural variation, a number

Chilopsis linearis (desert willow)

of named selections have arisen. They include 'Alpine', with short wide leaves and large pink flowers; AZT Bi-color, with abundant flowers over a long season and narrow, weeping, deep green leaves; AZT Desert Amethyst, with dark purple flowers and upright leaves; 'Barranco', with curved leaves and ample pink to lavender flowers; 'Bubba', with dark purple flowers and a muscular trunk and branches; 'Burgundy Lace', with two-toned white and pink to magenta flowers (this one is possibly self-sterile); 'Dark Storm', with almost

solid, deep magenta flowers; 'Lois Adams',
with minimal pod set and light pink flowers,
'Lucretia Hamilton', with purple flowers with
a white throat and fewer pods; 'Marfa Lace',
with semidouble pink and rose flowers and
short, wide leaves; 'Hope', which is white and
exceptionally hardy; 'Tejas', which has pink
to reddish purple flowers and wider leaves;
Warren Jones, with light lavender flowers in
large clusters and a more upright form; Art's
Seedless, with bright pink flowers with purple
accents and virtually no pods; and Timeless
Beauty (also known as 'Monhew'), which is
also essentially podless with dark pink to
purple lower corolla lobes and lighter pink
upper ones.

×*Chitalpa tashkentensis*

×*Chitalpa tashkentensis*
Chitalpa

FAMILY: Bignoniaceae.
DISTRIBUTION: A hybrid between *Catalpa
    bignonioides* and *Chilopsis linearis*.
MATURE SIZE: Multitrunked tree 20 to 30 ft.
    (6.1 to 9.1 m) tall and as wide.
BLOOMING PERIOD: April to September.
EXPOSURE: Full sun or partial shade.
HARDINESS: Hardy to 10°F (–12°C).

Chitalpa is a tree with numerous stems that
grow upright from the base, forming a dense,
rounded shrub. It is commonly trained into a
single- or few-stemmed small tree. It is deciduous in cold climates, but in the warm winter
areas of the region it is only briefly deciduous.

The leaves are 4 to 5 in. (10.2 to 12.7 cm)
long and 2 in. (5.1 cm) wide and taper to a
sharp tip. Leaves are deep green and thick
enough to cover the stems.

The flowers are held in clusters of 15 to 40

near the end of the stem. Individual flowers
are 1 in. (2.5 cm) long with a deep tube that
ends in ruffled, open, corolla lobes. Flower
color ranges from pale pink or lavender to
white, often with prominent nectar guides
and a yellow throat. This hybrid forms no
seed or pods.

Chitalpa grows best in well-drained, moderately fertile soils. Although it has tremen-
dous heat tolerance, in the deserts chitalpa
grows best when watered every week or two
in the summer. In milder areas, provide deep
watering monthly during the summer.

Chitalpa is a lovely choice for a summer
flowering tree in a small garden or patio. It
blends well with perennial plantings and
when left unpruned forms a dense but colorful shrub. There are two named forms of this
hybrid, 'Pink Dawn' and 'Morning Cloud'.
'Pink Dawn' is by far the more widely grown
and is light pink to lavender with a yellow
throat and pale nectar guides. 'Morning
Cloud' is a white-blooming form.

Chitalpa is a purposeful hybrid between catalpa (*Catalpa bignonioides*) and the Southwestern native desert willow (*Chilopsis linearis*) made by F. N. Rusanov of the Uzbek Academy of Sciences Botanical Garden, in Tashkent, Uzbekistan, around 1964. On an expedition to that area, staff from New York's Cary Arboretum brought back cuttings to the United States, and this hybrid was subsequently introduced in 1977 by Robert Hebb of the New York Botanical Garden. In 1991 Rancho Santa Ana Botanic Garden, in Claremont, California, assigned it the name ×*Chitalpa tashkentensis*, the first part of the binomial being a combination of the two parent plants' genera and the species name recognizing the city where the hybrid was developed. The two forms listed above were subsequently named by Rancho Santa Ana Botanic Garden as well.

Cleome isomeris
Bladderpod

SYNONYM: *Isomeris arborea*.

FAMILY: Capparaceae.

DISTRIBUTION: In the United States from the Mojave Desert regions of California at 200 to 3000 ft. (61 to 914 m). In Mexico in northern Baja California and Sonora at similar elevations.

MATURE SIZE: Loosely branched shrub 3 to 6 ft. (0.9 to 1.8 m) tall and as wide.

BLOOMING PERIOD: February to May.

EXPOSURE: Full sun in all areas, but tolerates shade in the hottest deserts.

HARDINESS: Hardy to 15°F (–9°C).

Bladderpod is an openly branched, somewhat rounded shrub. It is evergreen and emits a strong, astringent scent.

Cleome isomeris (bladderpod)

The leaves are palmately compound, with three leaflets that are oblanceolate and 1 in. (2.5 cm) long or less. They are light green, smooth, and end in a sharp point.

The flowers are in terminal racemes that are up to 12 in. (30.5 cm) long. The flowers are yellow with bright yellow stamens reaching far beyond the lobes.

The fruit is the most noticeable part of the plant. It is a pod that is 1 to 2 in. (2.5 to 5.1 cm) long, inflated, pendulous, rounded toward the end, and begins a pale caterpillar-green but quickly dries to a light tan. The seed is held inside and the pod rattles in the wind. Pods are persistent in loose clusters for months.

Bladderpod is a highly drought- and heat-adapted species from some of the region's driest areas. It needs excellent drainage but is otherwise not particular about soils. Bladderpod is reputed to be easy to grow from seed sown in place, and I can attest that growing it from seed in a more traditional way is also easy.

Once established, the plant will maintain vigor best when provided monthly watering in the summer in the hottest deserts. Make sure that watering or rainfall occurs at least monthly in the winter.

This uncommon species is effortless to grow, even in some of the hottest and driest parts of the region. It makes a charming focal or accent plant because of its bright bloom and interesting fruit. It blends well in a mixed planting, particularly in areas of the garden that do not receive regular irrigation.

Condalia globosa
Bitter condalia

FAMILY: Rhamnaceae.

DISTRIBUTION: In the United States in southeastern California, western and southwestern Arizona, and far southwestern New Mexico below 2500 ft. (762 m). In Mexico in western Sonora, Baja California, and northwestern Sinaloa at similar elevations.

MATURE SIZE: Much-branched shrub or small tree 10 to 20 ft. (3 to 6.1 m) tall and up to 15 ft. (4.6 m) wide.

Condalia globosa (bitter condalia)

BLOOMING PERIOD: March and April and intermittently through the summer.
EXPOSURE: Full sun or partial shade in the hottest deserts, full sun in all other areas.
HARDINESS: Hardy to around 20°F (–7°C).

Bitter condalia is an intricately branched shrub or tree with thorn-tipped branches. The smooth gray bark is well hidden by the dense foliage.

Leaves are up to 1.5 in. (3.8 cm) long and held in bundles along the stem. The leaves have entire margins and are more or less spatulate in shape. On primary branches the leaves are widely spaced and are quickly drought deciduous, but on secondary branches they tend to be smaller and more tightly packed, and the plant looks insubstantial, even floating, from a distance.

The flowers are minute, white, and immensely fragrant. The spicy aroma perfumes an entire garden when the plant is in bloom and this is often how you find this background shrub wherever it is grown. Flowers are held in short clusters at the nodes with up to eight flowers in the tiny inflorescence. The fruit is a dark black berry that is much less than 0.25 in. (0.6 cm) wide and is bitter to people but relished by birds and other wildlife.

Bitter condalia is an effortless choice for the hottest deserts when you need a large, dense shrub that requires minimal care and water. It is tolerant of almost any alkaline soil as long as it is well drained, and it is highly drought tolerant once established.

I have been a fan of this large, delightfully fragrant shrub for a long time. It is an excellent choice for a border hedge or boundary planting. Birds are strongly attracted to it, so it makes a good addition to a wildlife garden or one with a strong naturalistic character. Use it as a backdrop for more intense plantings.

Condalia hookeri
Bluewood condalia

FAMILY: Rhamnaceae.
DISTRIBUTION: In the western part of the Edwards Plateau region of Texas to far western Texas and into the plains of south Texas.

Condalia hookeri (bluewood condalia)

MATURE SIZE: Large shrub or small tree to 30 ft. (9.1 m) tall and up to 35 ft. (10.7 m) wide.

BLOOMING PERIOD: March to May and intermittent throughout the summer.

EXPOSURE: Full sun in all areas, but also tolerates partial shade in the hottest deserts.

HARDINESS: Hardy to at least 20°F (–7°C) and perhaps lower.

Bluewood condalia is a spiny, evergreen, intricately branched shrub that may also become a tree. The smooth, thin, reddish bark furrows and turns dark gray with age.

The leaves are bright, yellowish green and less than 1.5 in. (3.8 cm) long. The smooth-edged leaves are abundant on the plant, often held in short clusters at the nodes.

Flowers are small, green, and insignificant. The berry is bright red, abundant, and turns shiny black at maturity. The fruit is sweet and favored by most animals and birds that are in the area.

Bluewood condalia is an excellent choice for an area with dry soils or where only intermittent irrigation is available. It is attractive to wildlife, especially birds, and makes a good choice for a wildlife or naturalistic garden. It can be used as a background or boundary planting because of its dense form and its tolerance of dry conditions.

Cordia boissieri
Texas olive, wild olive

FAMILY: Boraginaceae.

DISTRIBUTION: In the United States it is found only in the far southern end of the Rio Grande Valley of Texas and is considered rare. In Mexico it is more abundant and is found in southeastern Coahuila, Nuevo León, San Luis Potosí, and Tamaulipas.

MATURE SIZE: Large shrub 10 to 25 ft. (3 to 7.6 m) tall and spreading as wide.

BLOOMING PERIOD: March to October.

EXPOSURE: Full sun in all but the hottest deserts, where relief from afternoon sun is best.

HARDINESS: Loses leaves at around 28°F (–2°C) but recovers quickly. Stems are hardy to 20°F (–7°C).

Cordia boissieri (Texas olive)

Texas olive is a large, loosely branched shrub that can be trained to a small tree as it ages. Its thin, gray bark occurs in broad ridges somewhat like plates, and often has a red tinge to it.

The olive-green leaves are 4 to 5 in (10.2 to 12.7 cm) long and 3 to 4 in (7.6 to 10.2 cm) wide. They are rough to the touch, and the undersides are often coated with fine, brownish hairs. The leaves are more or less oval and have a slightly wavy margin.

The flowers are 2.5 in. (6.4 cm) wide and 1.5 in. (3.8 cm) long, and pure white often with a yellow throat. They are held in short, congested clusters and are extremely showy.

Fruit is a large, whitish drupe, hence the common name. Although the fruit is edible to birds and other wildlife, it is reported that cattle and deer get a bit drunk on it if they eat too much of it. It is said to cause dizziness in people if too much is eaten, but in Mexico jellies are often made from it.

Texas olive is quite drought tolerant when mature but does best with deep irrigation two or three times a month in the hottest deserts during the summer. It is tolerant of a wide range of soils, but it does best in moderately enriched soils with excellent drainage. In the hottest deserts, it often has salt burn problems in the late summer because of the saline soils and water. Occasional deep flooding in the summer mitigates this problem.

Texas olive tolerates any level of heat and is a great choice in the hot, dry parts of the region for a background or screening shrub. It blends well with other desert shrubs to form an interesting hedge, and the extraordinary, profuse flowers occur throughout the summer, lighting up the hedge. In the hottest deserts, it grows and blooms in light shade.

Water established plants once or twice a month in the hottest deserts and much less often where temperatures are less severe. Newly planted individuals need watering every week or two during their first summer to become well established.

A gal I went to high school with was from the southern plains of Texas, far south of Corpus Christi. I vividly remember visiting her there and walking out into the backyard to gaze at the immense, white-blooming shrub her mother grew. I had never seen it before and was told it was a Texas olive. This one was over 30 ft. (9.1 m) tall, towering over the garage, and it served as a windbreak for her mother's entire garden in those dry, windswept plains.

Cordia parvifolia
Little-leaf cordia

FAMILY: Boraginaceae.

DISTRIBUTION: In Mexico along washes and slopes in central Baja California, Sonora, Sinaloa, Chihuahua, Coahuila, Durango, and Zacatecas.

MATURE SIZE: Much-branched shrub 4 to 8 ft (1.2 to 2.4 m) tall and spreading up to 10 ft. (3 m) wide.

BLOOMING PERIOD: March to November.

EXPOSURE: Full sun in all areas.

HARDINESS: Hardiness depends on the populations from which the plant is grown; the hardiest are unharmed down to 15°F (−9°C), while the tenderest are hardy only to 28°F (−2°C), with leaf drop at approximately 25°F (−4°C).

Little-leaf cordia is a multibranched shrub with a more or less central trunk. The bark is smooth and gray with pale gray patches (lenticels) as it matures.

The leaves are small, less than 1 in. (2.5 cm) long, and dusky gray-green. They are ovate to round, with serrate or toothed margins, and show conspicuous veins that make the entire leaf look dimpled.

The pure white flowers are up to 1.5 in (3.8 cm) long and bell-shaped. The corolla lobes are so thin they look like paper. Flowers are held in clusters of four to six. The bloom is profuse and long lasting, recurring throughout the summer in response to either deep irrigation or rain. The fruit is a tiny drupe deeply enclosed within the drying calyx and is often inconspicuous.

Little-leaf cordia is a tough species for dry locations and is tolerant of almost any alkaline, well-drained soil. This species also exhibits excellent heat tolerance and is routinely planted along roadways in the Phoenix area, cooling such hot spots with showers of pure white flowers all summer long. When plants are grown with too little water, leaves are drought deciduous but regrow quickly once watering is resumed. Watering twice a month is sufficient even in the hottest deserts.

Little-leaf cordia makes an interesting and colorful hedge when massed at the border or boundary of the garden. Used generously, as in a long hedge, the sensational bloom becomes a stunning feature. It is also a good

Cordia parvifolia (little-leaf cordia)

choice around patios, in areas that receive reflective heat like a west-facing wall, or where irrigation is intermittent. I am a sucker for white flowers in the summer, and little-leaf cordia is one of the most reliable and satisfying shrubs to provide that cooling color.

Coursetia glandulosa
Coursetia, baby bonnets

SYNONYM: *C. microphylla*.

FAMILY: Fabaceae.

DISTRIBUTION: In the United States in western, central, and southern Arizona at 2000 to 4000 ft. (610 to 1219 m). In Mexico from Baja California Sur, Sonora, and Sinaloa to Chihuahua south to Oaxaca up to 3770 ft. (1128 m).

MATURE SIZE: Loosely branched shrub or small tree 8 to 20 ft. (2.4 to 6.1 m) tall and spreading to 12 ft. (3.7 m) wide.

BLOOMING PERIOD: March and April.

EXPOSURE: Full sun in all areas.

HARDINESS: Hardy to 23°F (–5°C); killed to the ground at 19°F (–7°C) in Tucson, but recovered quickly.

Coursetia is a loose-limbed shrub with relatively thin, flexible branches. It is entirely thornless which helps separate it from a number of other legumes in its natural range. The young branches may be somewhat hairy but

Coursetia glandulosa (coursetia)

become smooth with age, and the bark is uniformly gray.

The leaves are pinnately compound and 1 to 2 in. (2.5 to 5.1 cm) long with 8 to 18 oval leaflets. The leaflets are bright green to gray-green and prolific on the stems.

The flowers are small, less than 0.5 in. (1.3 cm) long, with the complicated structure similar to sweet peas: the upper corolla lobes are reduced and folded into a hood and the lower lobes are expanded. The upper lobes are white and lower ones are yellow. These bicolored flowers contrast dramatically with the burgundy-colored calyx. Two to ten flowers are crammed into an axillary raceme that is just over 1 in. (2.5 cm) long.

The fruit is a sticky, brown pod 2 in. (5.1 cm) long that is markedly constricted between the seeds. When the seed is mature, the pods twist in opposite directions to forcibly eject the seeds.

Coursetia grows best in well-drained soils and has a great tolerance for alkaline conditions. Stems are often covered with an orange insect deposit. This harmless substance was once gathered by local Indian people and was used to treat colds and fevers.

Coursetia is a fine choice near a pool or seating area where its clean branches and delightful flowers may be enjoyed up close. It is also a good choice for a small garden or patio that needs both structure and seasonal color.

Cupressus arizonica
Arizona cypress

FAMILY: Cupressaceae.

DISTRIBUTION: In the United States from southern California through central Arizona, New Mexico, and far western Texas at 3000 to 7000 ft. (914 to 2134 m). In Mexico in extreme northeast Sonora into Chihuahua, Coahuila, and Durango to 7200 ft. (2195 m).

MATURE SIZE: Tall, erect, single-trunked tree 20 to 50 ft. (6.1 to 15.2 m) tall.

BLOOMING PERIOD: Pollen is formed and shed in March.

EXPOSURE: Full sun in all areas.

HARDINESS: Hardy to 0°F (−17.8°C) and probably lower.

Arizona cypress is one of the few tall conifers that grows well in the hottest deserts. It is also highly reliable in the mid-elevation deserts and many other climatic regions.

The plants are tall and erect and exceptionally regular in form. The bark tends to peel when young, revealing the reddish wood below, but in older plants bark is dark brown with deep furrows.

The leaves are minute and scalelike and are held tightly along the stem. Foliage ranges in color from light green to bright silvery blue, a range that has been the source of many named forms in the trade.

Cones are round or somewhat oblong and up to 1.5 in. (3.8 cm) long. They range from gray to brown and are smooth.

Despite its natural range in the highlands and mountains of the Southwest, Arizona cypress shows remarkable heat and drought tolerance. Although it does best in areas with at least 12 to 15 in. (305 to 381 mm) of rainfall, it may be grown successfully in drier areas if it gets ample, although intermittent, deep watering. This species is fast growing and forms a beautiful, pyramidal form early in its life.

Arizona cypress makes a stunning focal or accent plant in a garden large enough to accommodate it. It provides a note of drama in a mixed shrub or tree planting and looks wonderful from a distance.

There are numerous named forms of this plant. Some authors consider the smoother-barked forms that occur in parts of the range as another species, *Cupressus glabra*. But this view has no standing in the botanical community and all forms are considered part of *C. arizonica*. Selections of this species include the Australian 'Hodginsi', which grows to 15 ft. (4.6 m); and 'Pyramidalis', which is also short and compact. Other selections are the silvery blue gray–leaved 'Blue Pyramid', which is dense and grows to 25 ft. (7.6 m) tall; 'Carolina Sapphire', which is a bit taller; and 'Silver Smoke', with vivid blue-gray foliage.

Cupressus arizonica (Arizona cypress)

Dalbergia sissoo
Sissoo tree, Indian teakwood

FAMILY: Fabaceae.

DISTRIBUTION: Indian, Pakistan, and Afghanistan, but cultivated widely throughout the warm regions of the world.

MATURE SIZE: Large, erect, open-crowned tree growing 30 to 50 ft. (9.1 to 15.2 m) tall, occasionally as tall as 80 ft. (24 m), with a spread of up to 30 ft. (9.1 m).

BLOOMING PERIOD: March to May.

EXPOSURE: Full sun in all areas.

HARDINESS: Leaves are damaged at 25°F (−3.9°C), stems die back at 20°F (−6.7°C). Young trees are much more susceptible and are severely damaged at 28°F (−2.2°C).

Sissoo tree is a large, spreading, evergreen to semideciduous tree that provides deep shade beneath its branches. The bark is a reddish brown and becomes shaggy and gray with age. Older trees are noteworthy for the twists and turns of the main trunk and large branches.

The pinnately compound leaves have only three to seven leaflets per pinna. Leaflets are up to 3 in. (7.6 cm) long and are elliptic to oval. Lightly pubescent when young, they become smooth and glossy when mature. Leaves are bright green and a lighter green on the underside.

The small, white, pealike flowers are rarely over 1 in. (2.5 cm) long and are held in tight clusters in the leaf axils. They are followed by short, brown pods that hold up to four seeds per pod.

There is much disagreement about the watering needs of this species. For some it requires great amounts of water and is not appropriate for the deserts of the South-west. Others consider it to have moderate to low watering needs, and support its use because of its great heat tolerance and ability to grow well in the crowded conditions of sidewalks and street sides. I fall into the latter category: I find it a fine tree for large yards, streetscapes, or other public areas.

This species is considered brittle; limbs falling off in high winds are reported regularly. Here, again, there is a range of opinion. Most likely the problem is the result of poor pruning practices. If the lateral branches are left to grow to no more than two-thirds the width of the main trunk, they give the tree

more stability and appear to offer greater wind resistance. Any branch that has formed embedded bark is likely to shatter, so it is wise to prune appropriately so that the tree heals with a strong connection with the main branch. Pruning is best done in January in the hottest deserts.

After teak, sissoo tree is the most important cultivated timber tree in India. The wood makes beautiful cabinetry and furniture and is used for musical instruments, skis, carvings, boats, and floorings. It is also used extensively as a roadside tree or a shade tree for tea plantations. Sissoo tree is cultivated worldwide for lumber and veneers.

This large tree is best used in a place that can accommodate its size. It makes a fine, tall shade tree capable of providing high shade for a house or a roof. It has a denser look than most other legumes and therefore the shade is much heavier. The tree has been in use for some time in the Phoenix area as a street tree, and it appears to do well even with the confined root space and high reflective heat inherent in such situations.

Dalbergia sissoo (Sissoo tree)

Dalea bicolor
Silver dalea, Baja dalea

FAMILY: Fabaceae.

DISTRIBUTION: In the United States in southeastern New Mexico and far western Texas at 1500 to 5000 ft. (457 to 1524 m). In Mexico in Baja California, Chihuahua, Coahuila, and Nuevo León, south to Jalisco and Michoacán, and southeast to Puebla, Oaxaca, and Vera Cruz.

MATURE SIZE: Erect, open-branched shrub 3 to 6 ft. (0.9 to 1.8 m) tall and about as wide.

BLOOMING PERIOD: July to September.

EXPOSURE: Full sun in all areas, but does well in partial shade in the hottest deserts.

HARDINESS: Hardiness depends on the variety: var. *orcuttiana* suffers tip damage at 28°F (−2.2°C), while other varieties are undamaged to 10°F (−12.2°C).

Silver dalea is a loosely branched shrub with a regular, rounded form that is semideciduous in mild winter areas and fully deciduous elsewhere.

The pinnately compound leaves are up to 1 in. (2.5 cm) long with 7 to 13 oval leaflets. Leaflets are covered with fine hairs that give them a silver sheen, hence the common name. *Dalea bicolor* var. *bicolor* has the greenest leaves, while var. *argyrea* has the most silver-colored leaves.

The pealike flowers occur in late summer, occasionally in the spring, in loose spikes that are up to 2 in. (5.1 cm) long. They appear to be dark blue to pinkish purple, but on close examination they are actually bicolored with the banner (upper corolla lobes) white or yellow and the keel (lower corolla lobes) pink-purple to violet, occasionally blue or white. Fruit is a tiny pod that is inconspicuous.

There are five naturally occurring varieties of this species and three of them have come in and out of horticulture in the region over time. The type, var. *bicolor*, is the largest and has deep green leaves. From it came the form Monterey Blue of Mountain States Wholesale Nursery, with its taller growth and deep blue flowers. This variety ranges through the Chihuahuan Desert of Mexico and into southern Mexico and is the most cold hardy.

Var. *argyrea*, usually known as silver dalea, was once commonly offered in the region. It ranges through New Mexico and Texas, and

is much smaller than the type at 4 ft. (1.2 m) tall but is just as cold hardy. Its leaves have the most silvery cast.

Var. *orcuttiana* is from Baja California and is extremely heat- and drought-tolerant. It is the least cold hardy but regrows quickly after experiencing damage.

All varieties of silver dalea have great tolerance for extreme heat and dry, rocky soils. They thrive on limestone outcrops or the poorer soils of the region. Most varieties are at least semideciduous. All benefit from a hard prune in late winter to increase branching, which makes the shrub denser and increases blooming.

Water silver dalea two or three times a month in the summer in the hottest deserts and much less frequently in the milder areas of the region. Its modest watering requirements and great heat tolerance make this species a good choice for an area of the

Dalea bicolor (silver dalea)

garden that may receive only hand watering or intermittent irrigation.

Silver dalea is a good choice for erosion control on dry, rocky slopes and as a ground cover in dry, poor soil or areas that receive reflective heat. Rabbits don't seem to care for any dalea, as I can attest from my rabbit-ravaged front yard where many different daleas have lived over the years.

I have long had a desire to plant all the woody dalea together in a mixed hedge because collectively they bloom throughout the year. I haven't done it yet, but mixing silver dalea with any of the others is a great way to start. Silver dalea is also a good choice mingled with other desert perennials or even succulents. Group plants to form a boundary within the garden or to fill a dry corner.

Dalea pulchra

Bush dalea, indigo bush

FAMILY: Fabaceae.
DISTRIBUTION: In the United States in southern Arizona at 3000 to 5000 ft. (914 to 1524 m). In Mexico from Sonora south and east to Nuevo León and San Luis Potosí.
MATURE SIZE: Multibranched, upright shrub 4 to 6 ft. (1.2 to 1.8 m) tall and 3 to 5 ft. (0.9 to 1.5 m) wide.
BLOOMING PERIOD: October to February.
EXPOSURE: Full sun or partial shade in all areas.
HARDINESS: Hardy to 10°F (−12.2°C), but reported to have survived to 5°F (−15°C) with no damage.

Bush dalea is an evergreen shrub with an open, sparsely branched habit. Plants tend to grow into a rounded form.

The leaves are small, pinnately compound, with three to nine leaflets. The entire leaf is only 0.5 in. (1.3 cm) long. Leaves are gray-green with a deep coating of silvery hairs.

The tiny pealike flowers are held in 0.5-in (1.3-cm) spikes. The individual flowers are barely visible to the naked eye. They appear to be light lavender or pink-purple, but on close examination they are actually purple and white bicolored. The flowers are followed by an equally minute fruit that is a tiny pod.

Bush dalea is a delightful addition to any desert garden. There are so many good shrubby daleas that if you had them all, and planted them near at hand, you could enjoy witnessing that one or another would be in bloom year-round. This plant is perfect for the winter garden, with its coating of delicate pink-purple flowers throughout the cool season.

Dalea pulchra (bush dalea)

Extremely heat- and drought-tolerant, bush dalea needs no particular care to thrive. It requires monthly watering in the summer in the hottest deserts, a full sun location, and excellent drainage. Plants grown with too much water or in too much shade become open and floppy and often succumb to some form of root rot early on. Outside the driest parts of the region, it is wise to provide superb drainage or to place the plant on a mound or in rocky soil. Prune early in the spring to avoid diminishing the fall bloom.

Bush dalea is an outstanding choice for a colorful, woody plant that grows well on the outer boundary of the garden. Mixed with other shrubs, it provides excellent winter color to the blended hedge. Use it freely where heat is intense to soften a hot wall or create a lovely backdrop for more colorful blooming perennials. Bush dalea is rugged enough to be blended into cactus or succulent gardens as well.

The closely related but less commonly grown indigo bush (*Dalea versicolor*) is also from far southern Arizona and into Chihuahua and south to Guatemala. This shrub is open branched, 3 to 4 ft. (0.9 to 1.2 m) tall, occasionally 6 ft. (1.8 m), and as wide. It thrives in full sun in all areas and is hardy to 10°F (−12.2°C). The flowers are like those of most members of the genus, tiny purple to pink flowers crowded in 1-in. (2.5-cm) spikes with prominent plumes at the base of the flowers. Flowering in this species is from October to March. The leaves are pinnately compound and dark green without the silky look or silvery sheen of other similar daleas. Indigo bush is a rugged choice with delicate beauty for areas with dry, rocky, alkaline soils and high heat. Most plants have a fountain or cascading habit that makes them useful in dry corners or as background plants for more colorful plantings.

Dichrostachys cinerea
Chinese lantern tree

FAMILY: Fabaceae.

DISTRIBUTION: From southern and tropical Africa at 3000 to 4800 ft. (914 to 1459 m). Also native to India, Burma, and Australia. Widely introduced and often escaped in the tropical islands of the Caribbean and Hawaii.

MATURE SIZE: Multibranched shrub or small tree 10 to 25 ft. (3 to 7.6 m) tall and spreading about as wide.

BLOOMING PERIOD: March to October.

EXPOSURE: Full sun in all areas.

HARDINESS: Young plants freeze to the

Dichrostachys cinerea (Chinese lantern tree)

ground at 25°F (−3.9°C) but recover with amazing speed. Older plants are heavily damaged at those temperatures but recover just as quickly.

Chinese lantern tree is an erect shrub or many-branched small tree growing much like sweet acacia. It is generally evergreen, although sharp cold snaps barely below freezing may cause it to drop its leaves. Bark is light tan but ages to dark brown with noticeable furrows. The branches are slightly covered with thorns 1 to 4 in. (2.5 to 10.2 cm) long.

The leaves are bipinnately compound, with 5 to 19 pairs of pinnae and anywhere from 9 to 41 pairs of leaflets per pinna. The dark green leaflets are narrow and lanceolate with conspicuous glands on the petiole and the rachis. These ferny leaves are profuse on the plant, giving it a soft, delicate, lacy appearance.

The tiny flowers are jammed into spikes 1 to 3 in. (2.5 to 7.6 cm) long at the axils. They are unusual and striking, with the top half holding bright pink, sterile, male flowers and the lower half holding light yellow, fertile, perfect flowers. These catkins hang down on the branches like delicate lanterns.

The fruit is a cluster of twisted and curled dark brown pods that when stretched out is about 4 in. (10.2 cm) long.

This species is among the fastest growing I have ever encountered, particularly for a woody one. A 3-ft. (0.9-m) plant grew to over 8 ft. (2.4 m) in one growing season. Decimated by a hard freeze, the same plant recovered and was nearly the same height at the end of the next growing season.

The wood is very hard and durable and is widely used as firewood. The tree has many medicinal uses as well. The species is variable: there may as many as 20 subspecies and 11 varieties, but we are familiar with only one.

Chinese lantern tree has great heat tolerance and does well in any well-drained, alkaline soil. While it tolerates some drought, weekly summer watering results in a better-looking plant that blooms more consistently, at least in the hottest deserts. It is a great choice as a focal or accent plant in a large bed or mixed perennial planting. When its aggressive root suckering is a problem, it makes a lovely choice in a large pot or planter.

Chinese lantern is known to aggressively form root suckers where there is abundant water, so it is considered invasive in tropical areas. Seeds also can present problems in these areas because they are long lived in the soil and in the tropics they germinate year-round.

Diospyros texana
Texas persimmon

FAMILY: Ebenaceae.

DISTRIBUTION: In the United States in west, central, and far southern Texas as far east as Harris County. In Mexico in northern Chihuahua, Coahuila, Nuevo León, and Tamaulipas at 1100 to 5700 ft. (335 to 1737 m).

MATURE SIZE: Spreading tree 10 to 15 ft. (3 to 4.6 m) tall, occasionally to 35 ft. (10.7 m), and spreading 15 to 20 ft. (4.6 to 6.1 m) wide.

BLOOMING PERIOD: February to June; may repeat bloom in the fall.

EXPOSURE: Full sun or partial shade in the hottest deserts.

HARDINESS: Hardy to at least 15°F (−9.4°C).

Texas persimmon is a small, deciduous tree that grows in an irregular pattern. The turns and twists of the branches make for a striking specimen plant. The bark is thin and smooth; initially pale gray with reddish tones, it ultimately peels away to reveal the white tissue below. In mild or nearly frost-free areas, trees are evergreen; otherwise it is deciduous. In nature, Texas persimmon grows in a grove with numerous basal stems.

The leaves are alternate and leathery, with entire margins and blades that are oblong to nearly oval but abruptly narrow toward the base. The leaves are 1 to 2 in. (2.5 to 5.1 cm) long, dark green, glossy above and somewhat hairy on the underside.

The female flowers are white, bell-shaped, and 0.25 in. (0.6 cm) wide. Although inconspicuous, they are nicely fragrant. The green male flowers are held in clusters of one to five flowers in leaf axils. They are up to 0.5 in. (1.3 cm) long.

Flowers are followed by a round fruit that is 1 in. (2.5 cm) around. The fruit ripens to a glossy black and the sweet pulp is edible. Wildlife is crazy for the fruit so get there early. Plants tend to bloom when young but the beautiful peeling bark needs up to 10 years to form.

Texas persimmon is a highly adaptable species. It grows in almost any kind of soil but prefers soils with good drainage. It has good tolerance for shallow, rocky, limestone soils and has excellent heat tolerance even in the deserts. Unlike many woody species from its area, it appears to have significant salt tolerance.

In the hottest deserts it is best to provide twice-monthly, deep irrigation for best

Diospyros texana (Texas persimmon)

results. Within its range, it grows beautifully on natural rainfall alone.

This species is a fine choice for smaller gardens that need a dark, evergreen tree. The beautiful exfoliating bark makes the tree useful as a focal or accent plant. Grown as a hedge, it forms a dense, deep green barrier planting and makes a good choice for contrast in a mixed hedge. Wildlife, including birds, is strongly attracted to the fruit, making the species ideal for a wildlife or naturalistic garden planting.

Dodonaea viscosa
Hopbush

FAMILY: Sapindaceae.

DISTRIBUTION: A wide-ranging species from all states of Australia and New Zealand, many Pacific Islands including Hawaii, and tropical parts of Asia, Africa, and South America. In the United States in Florida and southern Arizona at 2000 to 4000 ft. (610 to 1219 m). In Mexico in Baja California, southeast Sonora, northern Sinaloa, southern Coahuila, Nuevo León, San Luis Potosí, and Tamaulipas.

MATURE SIZE: Upright or rounded shrub 8 to 16 ft. (2.4 to 4.9 m) tall and 3 to 5 ft. (0.9 to 1.5 m) wide.

Dodonaea viscosa (hopbush)

BLOOMING PERIOD: May to October.

EXPOSURE: Full sun in all areas.

HARDINESS: Severe damage below 23°F (−5.0°C), especially in forms with longer or purple leaves; many other forms are hardy to 15°F (−9.4°C).

Hopbush is an evergreen, densely branched shrub. Most forms are upright, almost vertical, but there are spreading forms as well. The bark is dark gray and fibrous or stringy.

The leaves are linear to oblanceolate, 2 to 6 in. (5.1 to 15.2 cm) long, and much narrower than they are long. The leaves are simple with entire margins and are shiny green, although there are purple-leaved forms in horticulture. Young leaves are covered with resin, making them sticky, but older leaves are smooth.

Plants are dioecious and flowers of both sexes are innocuous and tiny. The fruit, however, is the showiest feature of the plant. It is held in a three-winged pod that varies from 0.5 to 1 in. (1.3 to 2.5 cm) long and from creamy white tinged with red to deep, burnished red. The fruits persist on the female plants in some selections.

Hopbush is one of the most widely grown evergreen shrubs in the warmer parts of the region. It tolerates any well-drained soil, including highly alkaline ones, and it grows well in rocky or other dry soils. Although hopbush shows excellent drought tolerance in most areas, it retains its leaves longer and is more robust when watered two or three times a month during the summer in the hottest deserts.

Leaf size varies widely in this species, probably the result of its immense natural range. Most of the varieties commercially available have long, linear leaves and are some of the least cold hardy of the species. The purple-leaved variety, usually sold as 'Purpurea', is the most cold sensitive of all the forms sold. In Arizona, the native populations have short, congested, almost fascicled leaves, and these forms are among the hardiest of the species.

In California, this species is considered fire resistant by many cities where seasonal fire danger is high. The common name was given to the entire genus because the winged pods strongly resemble the pods of hop, which is used to brew beer.

A close relative, red hopbush (*Dodonaea microzyga*), is a short shrub 4 ft. (1.2 m) tall. It has tiny, finely cut leaves that are composed of four to six tiny leaflets. The leaves are deep green and so thick on the plant that it looks like a juniper. The flowers are white and innocuous but the 0.5-in. (1.3-cm) pods are bright red to scarlet. This uncommon member of the genus is extremely drought- and heat-tolerant and grows well in rocky, dry soils.

Duranta erecta

Skyflower, golden dew drops

SYNONYM: *Duranta repens*.
FAMILY: Verbenaceae.
DISTRIBUTION: In the United States only in southern Florida and naturalized in southern Texas. Widely distributed in the Caribbean, Central America, and south to Brazil. It is reported to have naturalized in parts of southern Africa.
MATURE SIZE: Intricately branched shrub 8 to 15 ft. (2.4 to 4.6 m) tall and spreading 10 to 15 ft. (3 to 4.6 m) wide.
BLOOMING PERIOD: March to October.
EXPOSURE: Full sun in all areas, but does better in partial shade in the hottest deserts.

HARDINESS: Leaf drop at 23°F (−5.0°C), but root hardy to at least 20°F (−6.7°C).

Skyflower is a dense shrub with dozens of intersecting branches. The bark is pale tan to brown, and in most forms there are few to many axillary thorns. Many selections are virtually thornless, however.

The leaves are pinnately compound, with leaflet size highly variable from 1.5 to 4 in. (3.8 to 10.2 cm) long. Leaves are thin, light green to yellowish green, with a wavy or crenellated margin and an acute tip. The leaves are often held in fascicles at the nodes and profuse along the stems.

The flowers are held on long, terminal, flowering stalks that fall toward the ground.

Duranta erecta (skyflower)

These stalks are up to 6 in. (15.2 cm) long and open sequentially, so that the bloom progresses over time. Individual flowers are tubular, about 0.5 in (1.3 cm) long, and the corolla lobes are flattened out, giving the flower a round, wheellike shape. Flower color varies widely from pale sky-blue to nearly indigo as well as pure white.

The round fruit is less than 0.25 in. (0.6 cm) wide and is bright golden yellow when ripe. It hangs on the stalk for months, creating another attractive feature of the plant. The amount of fruiting is variable, with minimal fruit in some selections and profuse amounts in others.

Skyflower grows best in rocky, alkaline soils that are well drained. Plants are known to be moderately salt tolerant. Where soils are richer, it is important to provide outstanding drainage. In the hottest deserts, weekly watering keeps plants from wilting and maintains good bloom. But in areas with regular summer rainfall, the plant grows on natural rainfall except during prolonged dry spells.

A number of color forms are on the market, some with overlapping names. The Japanese selection 'Geisha Girl' is popular in Australia; flowers are a vivid, deep purple to indigo with a white throat and ruffled corolla lobes. This selection is the same as 'Sapphire Swirl' and probably is also the same as 'Sweet Memory', which is sold in the region. By whatever name, this selection is a vigorous bloomer and the white-edged, deep blue to purple flowers are stunning throughout the summer. It makes little fruit, however. The white-flowering selections are most often sold as 'Alba', although they may also be found as 'White Sapphire'.

In Florida there is a selection known as 'Dark Skies' with intense blue flowers, another known as 'Grandiflora' with flowers to 0.75 in. (1.8 cm) wide, and 'Variegata' with yellow variegated foliage. Another selection known as 'Gold Edge' has bright yellow leaf variegation.

Skyflower is a splendid choice as an accent or colorful focal plant in a small garden, near a patio, or around a pool. It has extremely high heat tolerance, which makes it a good choice in situations of high or reflective heat.

This plant is a great sentimental favorite of mine. We brought our first one with us from New Orleans over 20 years ago. It lived for many years after that and got the attention of many desert gardeners, with its combination of delicate beauty and tolerance of dry, rocky soils and intense heat.

Ebenopsis ebano
Texas ebony

SYNONYM: *Pithecellobium flexicaule.*
FAMILY: Fabaceae.
DISTRIBUTION: In the United States only in the coastal counties and along the Rio Grande in far southern Texas. In Mexico along waterways in Nuevo León, San Luis Potosí, Tamaulipas, and Veracruz.
MATURE SIZE: Upright, densely branched, large shrub or tree 25 to 30 ft. (7.6 to 9.1 m) tall and 6 to 15 ft. (1.8 to 4.6 m) wide.
BLOOMING PERIOD: June to August.
EXPOSURE: Full sun in all areas.
HARDINESS: Hardy to at least 20°F (−6.7°C); severe leaf and some tip damage at 18°F (−7.8°C).

Texas ebony is a thickly branched shrub or tree whose branches turn and twist in a zigzag pattern. There is a pair of small, reddish, slightly curved thorns in the axils of the leaves. The bark begins light gray but ages dark gray to brown and is furrowed with age.

The leaves are bipinnately compound with two to three pairs of pinnae, one of which is often considerably smaller than the other two. Leaves are 1.5 to 2 in. (3.8 to 5.1 cm) long, and there are three to six pairs of oblong, dark, glossy green leaflets that are 0.25 to 0.5 in. (0.6 to 1.3 cm) long.

The numerous cream to white flowers are held in congested spikes or rounded clusters. These elongated puffball heads are 1 to 2 in. (2.5 to 5.1 cm) wide and are lightly, sweetly fragrant.

The distinctive pods are 4 to 6 in. (10.2 to 15.2 cm) long, woody, and covered with fine, grayish hairs. Eventually the pods open to release the seed, but they remain on the plant for months. They are the source of an unusual older common name for this species, ape's ears.

Texas ebony is widely adaptable to many well-drained soils but grows fastest in deep, well-drained, fertile soils. It is immune to heat, but needs watering once or twice a month in the hottest deserts.

Texas ebony is a lovely small, evergreen tree, and it can also serve as an impenetrable hedge when left unpruned. Texas ebony also serves as a hotel for cactus wrens in my garden, which is just fine with me.

Texas ebony grows erratically and with exuberance when young. Like a lot of legumes, it grows numerous small, juvenile stems from the base, which is an adaptation to browsing. These juvenile stems may be removed gradually to form a solitary-trunked, more upright tree. The stems may also be left more or less as they grow, and then the plant will form a dense, thorny hedge.

Ebenopsis ebuno (Texas ebony)

Texas ebony has strong, durable wood with a long history of use for timber, building, jewelry, cabinetry, and small carvings within its natural range.

Ehretia anacua

Sandpaper tree, anacua

FAMILY: Boraginaceae.

DISTRIBUTION: In the United States in central and southern Texas particularly in the Rio Grande Valley but as far north as Hays and Travis Counties. In Mexico throughout northeastern Mexico in Coahuila, Nuevo León, San Luis Potosí, Querétaro, Hidalgo, and Veracruz.

MATURE SIZE: Upright, slightly spreading multitrunked shrub or small tree 15 to 20 ft. (4.6 to 6.1 m) tall and as wide. In areas with permanent water and along creeks, it grows up to 40 ft. (12.2 m) tall or more.

BLOOMING PERIOD: March to April.

EXPOSURE: Full sun, although it tolerates light or filtered shade in the hottest desert.

HARDINESS: Hardy to 20°F (−6.7°C).

Sandpaper tree is a multibranched shrub, occasionally growing to a large tree, with gray to reddish-brown bark that becomes deeply furrowed with age. It has a more or less rounded form. Plants lose their leaves as the newer ones emerge. A hard frost may cause the leaves to drop.

The leaves are alternate, dark olive-green, and 2 to 4 in. (5.1 to 10.2 cm) long. They are oval to oblong, leathery, with toothed margins, and end in a sharp tip. The upper surface has a rough sandpaper texture, hence the common name.

The white flowers are fragrant and are profuse on the plant, making it showy when in bloom. Flowers are held in short panicles 2 to 3 in. (5.1 to 7.6 cm) long; individual flowers are less than 0.25 in. (0.6 cm) long.

The fruit is a bright yellow-orange to reddish drupe 0.25 in. (0.6 cm) wide. Birds love

Ehretia anacua (sandpaper tree)

it. German settlers within its range named it birdberry because it was so attractive to birds. Both flowers and fruit are so prolific that they virtually hide the tree when present.

Sandpaper tree prefers well-drained, alkaline soils, making it suitable for most of the region. While it is extremely heat tolerant, it is only moderately drought tolerant and requires watering two or three times a month in summer in the hottest deserts. In milder areas, or within its natural range, established plants grow well on natural rainfall. Plants grow root suckers and may form dense colonies over time. Mature plants have a fanciful form, becoming gnarled, twisted, and rounded, often with large stems that appear to be intertwined.

The name anacua comes from the Mexican name *anachuite* for this and related species, and is a combination of two Nahuatl words that mean paper and tree.

Anacua is a fine small tree for a small garden or tight situation like a patio or near a seating area. The colorful flowers and subsequent fruit make it a good choice to attract wildlife. It may also be considered for a mixed hedge or boundary planting.

Ephedra spp.
Mormon tea, joint fir

FAMILY: Ephedraceae.

DISTRIBUTION: In the United States from Oregon south to southern California, through Nevada, Utah, Colorado, and south to Arizona, New Mexico, and Texas at 700 to 6600 ft. (213 to 2012 m). In Mexico from Baja California and Sonora to Chihuahua, south to Durango, San Luis Potosí, and Hidalgo, with one species occurring as far south as Oaxaca at similar elevations.

MATURE SIZE: Upright, many-branched shrub 3 to 5 ft. (0.9 to 1.5 m) tall and about as wide.

BLOOMING PERIOD: March to June.

EXPOSURE: Full sun in all areas.

HARDINESS: Hardiness varies by species and ranges from 25°F (−3.9°C) to 0°F (−17.8°C).

Mormon tea, of any species, is an erratically branched, more or less upright shrub that appears to have no leaves. Plants are woody with gray to reddish brown corky bases in old age. The green stems are prolific and often thin with noticeable joints or unions along the stem.

Ephedra (Mormon tea)

The scalelike leaves occur at the joints and are ephemeral and minute, much less than 0.25 in. (0.6 cm) long. There is a sheath at the base of the leaf, and leaves are either opposite or whorled on the stem.

These plants are gymnosperms, related more closely to pines than to other flowering plants, and have no true flowers. Male plants have distinct, often showy, yellow or golden pollen cones. These occur either singly or in groups of up to 10 at the nodes. Seed cones are also in groups of 1 to 10 at the nodes and are covered in thin, papery or fleshy, overlapping bracts. Seed cones occur at or near the joints in pairs or clusters. Seed cones are prominent and up to 0.5 in. (1.3 cm) long.

These distinctive plants are relicts from a much earlier time and are found throughout their range in arid, dry soils. They are challenging, often difficult species to distinguish but most are easily recognized as belonging to the genus by their lack of true leaves, which appear as bractlike appendages at the nodes, the presence of cones, and jointed stems.

Ephedra nevadensis, *E. viridis*, and *E. trifurca* are offered from time to time by specialty or native plant enthusiasts and growers, and it is possible to find the widely distributed *E. torreyana* occasionally. Of the three, *E. viridis* is perhaps the most ornamental, with bright green, densely branched, upright stems and brilliant golden pollen sacs.

These plants are fascinating, and make a lovely specimen or focal plant in a dry, hot location. All thrive in rocky, well-drained soils, and some species are extremely salt tolerant. Native American peoples who lived within their range used many *Ephedra* species for a wide array of medicinal purposes.

Asian species of the genus are the most commonly used to make the various commercial products that are known as Mormon tea.

Eremophila decipiens
Slender emu bush

FAMILY: Myoporaceae.
DISTRIBUTION: Native to the Australian states of South Australia and Western Australia.
MATURE SIZE: Low-growing, intricately branched shrub growing 3 to 6 ft. (0.9 to 1.8 m) tall and as wide.
BLOOMING PERIOD: February to April.
EXPOSURE: Full sun in all areas, but tolerates high, filtered shade in the hottest deserts.
HARDINESS: Hardy to 18°F (−7.8°C).

Slender emu bush is a small shrub with sticky young branches that turn glossy with age. Branches are thin and rise up then arch over, giving the plant a fuller look than the number of stems might suggest.

The bright green, evergreen leaves are linear and thin. They are 1 to 1.5 in. (2.5 to 3.8 cm) long, alternate, have a short S-shaped pedicel, so they appear to cloak the branch.

The tubular flowers are 1 in. (2.5 cm) long, with the top corolla lobes fused into a cap that overhangs the highly recurved lower lobes. Flowers are held on curved peduncles and face downward, which is a feature of the entire genus. Although the flowers are somewhat spotted in the throat, they are rarely as completely so as in spotted emu bush (*Eremophila maculata*). Flowers are a dark, rosy-red, often nearly scarlet-red, and profuse on the plant.

This low shrub is a perfect complement to a dry, full-sun garden meant to attract hummingbirds. The nectar-rich flowers are highly attractive to these and other nectar feeders and the long blooming time makes it a showy plant.

While slender emu bush prefers alkaline soils, it thrives in a wide range of soils as long as drainage is excellent. Perversely, they may have difficulty in deep sands, where top soil or mulch should be added to tighten up the soil.

Watering once a month in the hottest deserts, much less often elsewhere, is best. Avoid overhead watering. Most emu bushes have a lovely natural form, but if pruning is required, prune lightly right after flowering.

Eremophila decipiens (slender emu bush)

Pruning in the summer is destructive, since the plants are virtually dormant during that time and will not recover well.

Eremophila glabra
Emu bush

FAMILY: Myoporaceae.

DISTRIBUTION: Widely distributed in all arid parts of Australia in Western Australia, New Territories, South Australia, Queensland, New South Wales, and Victoria.

MATURE SIZE: Highly variable species that may be prostrate or erect from 1 to 5 ft. (0.3 to 1.5 m) tall and as wide.

BLOOMING PERIOD: February to April.

EXPOSURE: Full sun in all areas.

HARDINESS: Hardy to at least 22°F (−5.6°C).

Most often known in North America by its white-leaved forms, emu bush is a highly variable species with forms that range from entirely prostrate to those that are erect and tightly branched.

The leaves may be smooth and green or hairy and grayish to nearly white. Leaves are alternate and up to 2.5 in. (6.4 cm) long with a sharp tip.

The 1 in. (2.5-cm) flowers are tubular with prominent hoodlike upper lobes over strongly recurved lower ones. Flower color exhibits an equally large range from bright yellow to intense red and shades in between, and most forms bloom profusely.

While most of the variability in this species is restricted to Australia, a few of its more dramatic forms have made it across the ocean. 'Murchison River' has white to gray leaves and bright red flowers and it is sometimes also known as 'Fire and Ice'. A prostrate yellow form known in Australia as 'Kalgoorlie' is occasionally found but rarely with that name. This prostrate form rises only 1 ft. (0.3 m) tall but spreads up to 5 ft. (1.5 m) with bright yellow flowers.

Emu bush grows best in dry areas, although some gardeners in warm, humid gardens have had success with the plant if drainage is outstanding and there is significant air movement to keep down fungal problems. Emu bush, especially 'Murchison River', has been grown for years in the Phoenix area. It has a reputation for being short-lived, which is probably a function of too much water and poor drainage rather than a naturally short life. It also appears to prefer afternoon shade in the hottest desert cities such as Phoenix, although full sun is best in all other areas.

Provide deep watering every month or two in the summer and monthly in the winter in the hottest deserts. In milder areas, it may

need watering only during protracted hot, dry spells. Emu bush hardly ever needs pruning, but when necessary, prune lightly right after blooming in the spring.

Emu bush is a dramatic choice in a hot garden where its glowing foliage and bright flowers can make a brilliant show. It takes heat well enough to be sited around pools or other areas with intense reflective heat. Because it prefers such dry soils it also blends well with succulents and other desert natives.

Eremophila laanii
Pink emu bush

FAMILY: Myoporaceae.
DISTRIBUTION: Western Australia.
MATURE SIZE: Upright, much-branched shrub 6 to 8 ft. (1.8 to 2.4 m) tall and as wide.
BLOOMING PERIOD: January to April.
EXPOSURE: Full sun in all areas, although it tolerates light, filtered shade in the hottest deserts.
HARDINESS: Hardy to at least 25°F (−3.9°C), possibly lower.

Pink emu bush is a large, wildly branched shrub. The pale grayish to tan stems turn and fall in extraordinary patterns and give the shrub its distinctive, complex appearance.

The bright green, evergreen leaves are 2 in. (0.6 cm) long with a sharp tip; they alternate densely up and down the stems. Leaves bend back toward the base of the stem, and because they often lie close to one another this feature gives a scaly look to the stem.

The flowers of this species in nature range from white to dark pink. But the form seen almost exclusively in the United States has

Eremophila glabra (emu bush)
Photo by Nancy Rheinlander

lovely, pastel-pink flowers and is known as 'Pink Beauty'. Flowers are prominent and profuse, up to 2 in. (0.6 cm) long, and last a long time on the plant. They are spotted in the throat, but there can be a lot of variability in this feature.

This large shrub is one of the most reliable for extremely arid gardens. I have known numerous spectacular plants in the Phoenix area that are rarely or almost incidentally watered. Plants do best with winter watering monthly or so and much less frequent watering in the summer. They need some room and excellent drainage.

Pink emu bush blends well into mixed hedges or boundary plantings, particularly

Eremophila laanii (pink emu bush)

where irrigation is not regularly available. The cool-season bloom is prolific, so plants should be placed in the garden so you may enjoy this feature. It is an excellent choice for around pools, seating areas, or in hot, dry areas because of its cooling flower color and soft foliage.

Eremophila maculata
Spotted emu bush

FAMILY: Myoporaceae.
DISTRIBUTION: In arid areas throughout Australia, missing only in coastal or humid, tropical areas.
MATURE SIZE: Upright or spreading shrub 3 to 10 ft. (0.9 to 3 m) tall and as wide, with high variability.
BLOOMING PERIOD: January to May.
EXPOSURE: Full sun in all areas.
HARDINESS: Hardy to 16°F (−8.9°C).

Spotted emu bush is the most commonly seen member of the genus, both in nature and in cultivated landscapes of the arid, hot parts of the Southwest. Plants are indestructible and form a fully branched, more or less rounded shrub. Smaller, almost prostrate or at least flattened forms aren't as common as the shrub.

The leaves are dull green and congested in alternating rows up the stems, so the plant appears to be densely leafed.

The flowers arise in the axils of the leaves and are held on slender, curved pedicels similar to those of slender emu bush (*Eremophila decipiens*). The flowers are 1 in. (2.5 cm) long and range in color from yellow to orange-red and dark red, and the throat is prominently spotted with dark red or magenta.

Spotted emu bush is a sturdy and reliable shrub for arid, hot regions. It prefers excellent drainage but is otherwise unaffected by cultural vagaries. Plants accept regular watering with excellent drainage, but my plants grow superbly with only an occasional good soak or the rare rain.

Prune spotted emu bush lightly in the spring after flowering. This species has erratic, complicated branching but its overall form is regular. It is best to prune it carefully and lightly so you don't compromise the symmetry of the plant.

In January 2007 there was a strong cold

Eremophila maculata (spotted emu bush)

spell when temperatures plunged to 23°F (−5.0°C) in my garden. The spotted emu bushes were in full bloom and not only was there no damage to leaves and stems, which was expected, but the flowers were entirely unmarred.

Many yellow flowering forms are available. Most have clear, yellow flowers and are a lovely addition to the emu bush mix. Out of subsp. *brevifolia*, with its smaller, dusky-green leaves, the selection trademarked Valentine has been offered. This selection has rosy-red flowers that are profuse and it tends to bloom earlier than others on plants that are up to 6 ft. (1.8 m) tall with a spreading, almost flattop form.

Spotted emu bush is an outstanding shrub used either singly or in mixed plantings, particularly in dry soils or where watering is not regularly available. It makes a striking accent or focal plant. Because of its tolerance of intense heat, it is a good choice for around pools or against hot walls. For gardeners who want the strongest color in the garden in the winter, this is an outstanding plant.

While most emu bushes in the region are winter flowering, one hybrid form blooms in the summer. The blue-flowered hybrid of *Eremophila polyclada* and *E. divaricata*, often sold as *E.* Summertime Blue, is a loosely branched shrub with light blue flowers that appear intermittently throughout the summer. The leaves are tiny, almost needlelike. Culture is similar to that of all members of the genus: any soil with excellent drainage, but it does particularly well in dry, rocky, alkaline soils. This emu bush, however, blooms better in partial shade, particularly in the hottest deserts, than the other emu bushes currently offered.

Eremophila racemosa
Easter egg bush

FAMILY: Myoporaceae.

DISTRIBUTION: From a limited area in south-western Western Australia.

MATURE SIZE: Upright, tightly branched shrub 4 to 6 ft. (1.2 to 1.8 m) tall and 3 to 4 ft. (0.9 to 1.2 m) wide.

BLOOMING PERIOD: January to April.

EXPOSURE: Full sun in all areas.

HARDINESS: Hardy to at least 25°F (−3.9°C).

Easter egg bush, a species in need of a better common name, is an upright, densely branched shrub.

Leaves are 1 to 2 in. (2.5 to 5.1 cm) long with a sharp tip. Like all emu bushes, the leaves are packed in alternate rows up the stem and often seem to cling to the stem longitudinally.

The tubular flowers have upper lobes that form a hanging hood over the strongly recurved lower lobes. These unusually formed flowers begin yellow, fade to a tangerine shade, and finally become pink, lavender, or mauve. Flowers of all colors and shades appear simultaneously on the plant, making a charming and colorful show.

Another species that enjoys aridity, Easter egg bush requires excellent drainage, full sun, and a dry climate to perform its best. It tolerates generous summer watering if the other conditions are met, but it is not required for good performance.

I first saw this beauty in California while visiting there with a Phoenix-area grower, and we brought a few plants back. My first ones were all over the garden, and eventually the ones under a tree quit blooming well because of too much shade. I tried to move them in the fall but that was a failure. However, the one I planted in full sun on a rock slope has never faded and is unfazed by its fiercely hot location and modest watering. Gorgeous and reliable, it belongs in any arid garden particularly where inconsistent watering and full sun dominate. It makes a good small hedge or boundary planting and is outstanding in the reflective heat near a pool or a hot wall.

I am always asked to recommend good species to people who don't spend all or most of the summer here. Emu bushes are their pals. These reliable and sturdy shrubs thrive with intermittent deep soaks in the summer and look their best in the winter-spring season of the Southwest deserts.

Eremophila racemosa (Easter egg bush)

Erythrina flabelliformis
Coral bean

FAMILY: Fabaceae.

DISTRIBUTION: In the United States in southern Arizona and extreme southwestern
New Mexico at 3000 to 5000 ft. (914 to 1524
m). In Mexico widespread from Baja California Sur and Sonora south and east to
Sinaloa, Chihuahua, Durango, Zacatecas,
central Jalisco, and northwest Michoacán.

MATURE SIZE: Grows as either a multistemmed, short shrub 4 to 5 ft. (1.2 to 1.5
m) tall in the northern part of its range,
or as an upright tree to 25 ft. (7.6 m) where
freezes are uncommon.

BLOOMING PERIOD: March to May.

EXPOSURE: Full sun in all areas, although
it tolerates filtered shade in the hottest
deserts.

HARDINESS: Damage and leaf drop at 28°F
(−2.2°C) but recovery is quick. Plants may
be killed at 20°F (−6.7°C).

Coral bean in most of its U.S. range is a
multistemmed plant with long stems that
arise from the swollen base. Where frosts
are uncommon or nonexistent, it becomes an
erect tree with a high, open crown. The bark
is smooth and is sometimes copper red with
stout, conical but blunt spines along the surface. These spines are up to 1 in. (2.5 cm) long
and tend to disappear on older wood.

Leaves emerge late in the spring or early
summer. The compound leaf is composed of
three triangular leaflets that are 1 to 3 in. (2.5
to 7.6 cm) long. They are thin, pale green, and
heart shaped with a prominent tip. Plants are
quickly deciduous with drought or cold, so
they are often leafless for significant portions
of the year. Leaves turn a bright clear gold
before they drop.

The flowers are held in terminal inflorescences that are 6 to 8 in. (15.2 to 20.3 cm) tall
which form before the leaves emerge. The
flowers are brilliant scarlet with the banner
lobes much longer than the others and hover-
ing over them so that the flowers look tubular.

The 10-in. (25.4-cm) woody pods follow
and are full of bright red, rock-hard seeds.
The seeds are poisonous if eaten but enjoy
great popularity for jewelry, especially in
Mexico.

In nature coral bean is found growing on

Erythrina flabelliformis (coral bean)

rocky hillsides with the roots firmly tucked under boulders and rocks. In the garden, it is best to provide sharp drainage, and if the soil is rocky, all the better. The brilliant flowers are highly attractive to hummingbirds. Although extremely drought tolerant, coral bean does well with weekly watering in the hottest deserts, and the practice will delay its long deciduous season.

While almost any woody species may be grown in a pot, if you have a large enough one this species is a terrific choice. The large, swollen, storage roots grow well in the inherently dry conditions of a pot.

The flowers are first covered with a bright red cap, which is opened when the dense ball of yellow stamens pushes out. Like all eucalyptus, the flowers have no corolla lobes. The puffball look is made by the large number of stamens congested into a rounded head. Flowers are up to 4 in. (1.2 cm) long and are held in clusters of six to eight flowers. Fruit is a capsule that is more or less cone shaped.

Red-cap gum's open crown and graceful form make it easy to use near walkways or seating areas. The pale bark is a remarkable feature, and the tree even has been recommended for gardens that feature

Eucalyptus erythrocorys
Red-cap gum

FAMILY: Myrtaceae.
DISTRIBUTION: Limited distribution in
    Western Australia.
MATURE SIZE: Tree with an irregular crown
    from 10 to 20 ft. (3 to 6.1 m) tall.
BLOOMING PERIOD: October to March.
EXPOSURE: Full sun in all areas.
HARDINESS: Hardy to at least 25°F (−3.9°C).

Red-cap gum is a single-trunked tree that even when young tends to branch high up the trunk, creating a rounded but somewhat irregular crown. The young branches are reddish but age to light tan or nearly white. The bark of all ages is smooth and often sheds.

Leaves are lanceolate and 4 to 7 in. (1.2 to 2.1 cm) long with a sharp tip. They are bright green to gray-green, thick and glossy, with a noticeable yellowish midrib. The leaves are spaced up to 2 in. (5.1 cm) apart on the branches and are held on long petioles, which gives the tree a full, pendulous look.

Eucalyptus erythrocorys (red-cap gum)

species that shine in the moonlight. This bold-looking plant adds drama and interest to a small space.

Although red-cap gum is tolerant of almost any soil, providing it with good drainage is best. In the hottest deserts, it thrives on watering once or twice a month in the summer and less often in the winter. Plants are often placed in lawns, which they tolerate although they don't need that much water.

Eucalyptus formanii (Forman's eucalyptus)
Photo by Mountain States Wholesale Nursery

Eucalyptus formanii
Forman's eucalyptus

FAMILY: Myrtaceae.
DISTRIBUTION: In limited areas of Western Australia.
MATURE SIZE: Shrub or small tree 15 to 30 ft. (4.6 to 9.1 m) tall and as wide.
BLOOMING PERIOD: April to June.
EXPOSURE: Full sun in all areas.
HARDINESS: Hardy to 10°F (−12.2°C).

Forman's eucalyptus is an evergreen, rounded shrub. The rough, fissured bark varies from tan to silver-gray. The branches turn and twist, but manage to keep a more regular form than many other shrubby eucalyptus.

The thin, light green to yellowish-green leaves are almost needlelike. They grow up to 2.5 in. (6.4 cm) long and have a sharp menthol fragrance.

The small, white flowers are prolific on the plant, and while not showy individually, they make a delightful bloom because of their numbers. Plants usually bloom for a long time.

Forman's eucalyptus grows best in well-drained soils, but it may be subject to root rots when there is too much moisture. This species comes from xeric areas and is well suited to being grown on a lean watering schedule. It is one of the few eucalyptuses that, once established, tolerates growing on natural rainfall in the Phoenix area, although monthly watering keeps it looking more full and lush.

Forman's eucalyptus is a good species to blend into a large hedge or mixed shrub planting. It serves as a barrier, either visual or physical, within the garden, helping to define space in a larger garden.

Eucalyptus kruseana
Kruse's mallee

FAMILY: Myrtaceae.

DISTRIBUTION: Localized distribution in Western Australia; considered rare within its range.

MATURE SIZE: Erratically branched shrub 3 to 6 ft. (0.9 to 1.8 m) tall and spreading as wide.

BLOOMING PERIOD: November to April and intermittent through the summer.

EXPOSURE: Full sun in all areas.

HARDINESS: Not well established, but reported hardy to at least 25°F (−3.9°C).

Kruse's mallee is an odd-looking shrub but that is part of its charm. The branches reach out and bend at odd angles, making it appear much thicker and larger than it really is. The branches are covered with fine, whitish hairs. The older bark is smooth and brown and sheds to reveal greenish-brown bark below.

The round leaves are up to 1 in. (2.5 cm) across. They are widely spaced on the branches and look like dark silver coins.

The creamy yellow flowers are 1 to 1.5 in. (2.5 to 3.8 cm) long. They are held in clusters of four to six flowers that arise between the leaves. Each cluster nearly surrounds the stem. Flowers are followed by seed capsules that resemble acorns with a cap and a pointed end. These capsules make interesting dried objects.

Kruse's mallee grows in any well-drained soil including alkaline ones. Water plants every two to three weeks in the summer in the hottest deserts, for the best form and growth. In milder areas, plants require less frequent watering. Prune in the winter while

Eucalyptus kruseana (Kruse's mallee)

the plant is dormant to shape or encourage a fuller form.

Over time Kruse's mallee forms a mound, and can be an especially attractive feature in a formal planting. The extraordinary form is delightful near a pool or patio area, and the extreme heat tolerance makes it useful in areas with reflective heat. This shrub is also a good choice for hot, dry corners or other small locations.

Eucalyptus microtheca
Coolibah

FAMILY: Myrtaceae.

DISTRIBUTION: Widely distributed in northern Australia from Western Australia to Queensland.

MATURE SIZE: Upright, widely branched

tree 35 to 40 ft. (10.7 to 12.2 m) tall with a spreading crown to 25 ft. (7.6 m) wide.

BLOOMING PERIOD: March to June.

EXPOSURE: Full sun in all areas.

HARDINESS: Hardy to 5°F (–15.0°C), although there may be leaf burn.

Coolibah is commonly seen in gardens in the Phoenix, Tucson, and Las Vegas areas.

Eucalyptus microtheca (coolibah)

It is a slender, multitrunked tree that begins upright, but quickly bends or twists, often in interesting ways. The bark begins smooth and mottled with gray, but as it ages it becomes thick, fibrous, and dark gray with prominent cracks and wrinkles.

The leaves are long, up to 8 in. (20.3 cm), slender, and lanceolate with a sharp tip. Although they range in color from deep green to silver-gray, the gray- or silver-leaved selections are preferred and are mostly what is offered in the trade.

The flowers are small and whitish, held in terminal clusters of three to seven flowers. They are followed by small, innocuous capsules.

This species has a wide range of growing conditions for the region. It grows in almost any well-drained soil. Unlike many of the larger species, this one shows no tendency to get chlorotic in alkaline soils of the deserts.

Coolibah is extremely drought tolerant, although it is often grown within a lawn which it tolerates remarkably well. It is well adapted to long periods between watering, and intermittent deep watering promotes good growth and vigor. It is also tolerant of highly saline soils, which is a great boon in some areas.

Coolibah is good choice for a loosely branched, open-crowned shade tree in a smaller location or placed in groves where its long, hanging silvery leaves can be best appreciated. The vivid color of the foliage and the graceful form complement areas around pools and those that need light shade.

Eucalyptus papuana
Ghost gum

FAMILY: Myrtaceae.

DISTRIBUTION: In both wet monsoon and arid areas of northern and central Australia from Western Australia to Queensland. Also found in Papua, New Guinea.

MATURE SIZE: Slender, upright tree from 20 to 40 ft. (6.1 to 12.2 m) tall with a spread to 25 ft. (7.6 m) wide.

BLOOMING PERIOD: April to June.

EXPOSURE: Full sun in all areas.

HARDINESS: Hardy to 22°F (−5.6°C).

Ghost gum is well named because the bark is a bright, powdery white and so smooth it appears to have been painted on the tree. Trees have an upright, vase shape with few erect, secondary branches which creates an open habit that dramatically accentuates the bark. Some individuals grow more like a large, multibranched shrub rather than a tree.

The leathery leaves are 3 to 5 in. (7.6 to 12.7 cm) long, gray-green with yellow midribs, and they taper to a sharp tip. They have a purplish cast in cold weather. The leaves tend to hang in loose clusters from the smaller branches, giving the entire tree a flowing, draping look.

Flowers are small and white in axillary clusters. They are hardly noticeable on the tree even when it is in full bloom.

The upright growth, smaller stature, and gorgeous color of the bark make this an enduring favorite in the region. Use it where its bright white bark makes a statement, as a garden focal point or at the end of a walkway. This species causes less litter than some of the other eucalyptuses and may be used closer to driveways, patios, and seating areas.

There is much disagreement and discussion among Australian botanists about the exact composition of this wide-ranging species, or perhaps group of species. A few refer to it as *Corymbia papuana,* but in the United States, in particular, it is always found under the name *Eucalyptus papuana.*

Eucalyptus papuana (ghost gum)

Another pale-leaved choice is the lemon-flowered gum (*Eucalyptus woodwardii*). This erect, open-branched tree grows 20 to 40 ft. (6.1 to 12.2 m) tall and 15 to 20 ft. (4.6 to 6.1 m) wide. It is hardy only to about 22°F (–5.6°C), but while seriously damaged at lower temperatures recovers quickly. The light gray-green leaves are up to 5 in. (12.7 cm) long, firm, almost leathery, and hang down to give the plant a weeping form. Bloom is from November to May. Clusters of 2-in. (5.1-cm) pale, lemon-yellow flowers are quickly followed by light, grayish capsules. Lemon-flowered gum requires excellent drainage and full sun to achieve its best form and vigor. It does best in dry alkaline soils, but it is also reported to be tolerant of saline soils. This tree is a lovely accent or focal plant, particularly in a small corner or where its vertical nature will create interest.

Eucalyptus polyanthemos

Silver dollar gum

FAMILY: Myrtaceae.
DISTRIBUTION: Central Australia in New South Wales and Victoria.
MATURE SIZE: Upright tree 20 to 60 ft. (6.1 to 18 m) tall with a crown spread up to 40 ft. (12.2 m) wide.
BLOOMING PERIOD: April to July.
EXPOSURE: Full sun in all areas.
HARDINESS: Hardy to 14°F (–10.0°C).

Silver dollar gum is a few-branched tree with a more or less rounded crown even when young. The bark is rough, mottled with white or cream. When the tree becomes older, the bark will be fibrous, scaly, and reddish brown, easily peeling away from the trunk.

The juvenile leaves are rounded and silvery, hence the common name, and are present on the tree for many years. Mature leaves are more elongated and come to a sharp tip. Young leaves are 0.5 to 1.5 in. (1.5 to 3.8 cm) across with a light gray-green color, while mature ones are 2 to 3.5 in. (5.1 to 8.9 cm) long and deep gray-green. The juvenile form of the leaf is used frequently as a backdrop in floral arrangements.

The creamy white flowers are 1 in. (2.5 cm) long and held in terminal clusters of up to

Eucalyptus polyanthemos (silver dollar gum)

seven flowers. The cluster is up to 6 in. (15.2 cm) long. The flowers' small size makes them innocuous on the plant. They are followed by clusters of cylindrical, cupped capsules.

Silver dollar gum is a graceful, moderate-sized tree that has more than enough heat and drought tolerance to make it well suited to the region. It grows in virtually any soil, although when grown in lawns or with ample water it frequently develops chlorosis. To prevent this condition, be sure the soil is well-drained and the plant is watered every three to four weeks in the summer in the hottest deserts. In milder areas, water even less frequently.

Silver dollar gum is a good shade tree for smaller gardens. The distinctive leaves and intriguing bark allow it to be used as a focal or accent plant as well. It is also a good choice around pools for its interesting look, and also because it has limited leaf drop and is large enough to provide good shade.

Eucalyptus torquata
Coral gum

FAMILY: Myrtaceae.
DISTRIBUTION: Southwestern part of Western Australia.
MATURE SIZE: Upright tree 15 to 25 ft. (4.6 to 7.6 m) tall with a crown spread as wide.
BLOOMING PERIOD: April to June, but blooms intermittently almost year-round.
EXPOSURE: Full sun in all areas.
HARDINESS: Hardy to 22°F (−5.6°C).

Coral gum is an upright tree with a single, straight trunk with a few branches that form a rounded crown. As the plant ages, the branches twist and turn and the crown starts to flatten out. The bark is deep brown, rough, and flaky.

The leaves are light green, firm, and 2 to 6 in. (5.1 to 15.2 cm) long. They are linear, tapering to a sharp tip, but there are forms with blunt or truncated leaves. Leaves begin green but age to blue-green.

The bright red bud caps are waxy with a fluted top and a long tip. These cylindrical bud caps resemble a Japanese lantern and are nearly as ornamental as the showy flowers. The flowers are 0.5 to 1 in. (1.3 to 2.5 cm)

Eucalyptus torquata (coral gum)

across and are held in axillary clusters of three to seven flowers. Flowers are pink to rose-red with yellow tips, occasionally white.

Red-cap gum is tolerant of a wide range of well-drained soils from sands to clays, as well moderately saline soils. It is also tolerant of high heat and wind. As for many eucalyptus that grow well in arid areas, a deep soak at long intervals is the best way to water this species. In the hottest desert, water twice a month in the summer, much less often in less severe areas.

The cinnamon-colored branches and the showy flowers make good contributions to cut flower arrangements. This tree is a fine choice when used generously to form a grove. Its moderate size also makes it a good choice for shade in a smaller garden, near a seating area, or where space is limited and its showy bloom may be enjoyed.

Euphorbia xanti (jumeton)

Euphorbia xanti
Jumeton

FAMILY: Euphorbiaceae.
DISTRIBUTION: In Mexico only in central and southern Baja California.
MATURE SIZE: Shrub 1.5 to 6 ft. (0.5 to 1.8 m) tall and as wide.
BLOOMING PERIOD: December to April.
EXPOSURE: Full sun in all areas.
HARDINESS: Hardy to 25°F (−3.9°C) with minor tip damage.

Jumeton is an upright, intricately branched semisucculent shrub with smooth, gray to gray-green, pencil-thin stems. The base of the plant becomes woody and gray to brown with age. As with all members of the family, the milky sap is irritating to toxic, so care must

be taken not to get it in your eyes, nose, or mouth.

The leaves are 0.5 to 1.5 in. (1.3 to 3.8 cm) long and are held in whorls of three to six leaves. Leaves are also held as opposite pairs. They are smooth, deep green, and linear to ovate. During the growing season of the winter and spring, the leaves are profuse, but with increasing temperatures or dry conditions they become sparse on the stems. In extremely dry conditions, plants become entirely deciduous and new stems die off.

The flowers are 0.5 in. (1.3 cm) wide and are held in terminal clusters. Flowers are white with a purple to rosy-pink throat, deep pink, or pink that fades to white. Although the individual flowers are small, bloom is prolific and makes a showy display. Flowers are followed by a tiny, rounded capsule that is ashy-gray.

Jumeton grows in any well-drained, alkaline soil including rocky, dry, desert native soils. It also grows well in sand or somewhat saline soils. It looks best in the garden when watered monthly in the hottest deserts, although it will take more frequent watering if the drainage is excellent. The stem tips dry and die off naturally when in drought conditions; this is a signal that watering frequency may need to be increased.

This species is immensely heat tolerant, so it is a good choice against hot walls or around pools or other areas with intense reflective heat. The profuse flowering over a long time in the spring and the light green to gray delicate stems make it a handsome plant throughout the year. For a garden that needs a rugged plant able to endure near natural conditions in the summer but is at its colorful best in the winter, this one is a great choice.

The closely related cliff spurge (*Euphorbia misera*) is a low-growing, much-branched, deciduous shrub with gray stems and whorls of deep green leaves spread far apart on the branch. The small, less than 0.25-in. (0.6-cm) flowers are white and profuse during the winter and early spring blooming season This, too, is a rugged species although it does best in sandy soils and is reported to grow best in areas with warm summers that are not intensely hot.

Eysenhardtia orthocarpa
Kidneywood

FAMILY: Fabaceae.
DISTRIBUTION: In the United States in southern Arizona and extreme southwestern New Mexico at 3000 to 6000 ft. (914 to 1829 m).
MATURE SIZE: Open-branched tree 10 to 20

Eysenhardtia orthocarpa (kidneywood)

ft. (3 to 6.1 m) tall and 6 to 12 ft. (1.8 to 3.7 m) wide.
BLOOMING PERIOD: April to September.
EXPOSURE: Full sun, but in the hottest deserts high or filtered shade is best.
HARDINESS: Hardy to 17°F (−8.3°C), although it may lose its leaves at 25°F (−3.9°C).

Kidneywood is a delicate, small tree with few branches that are spaced widely apart. The bark is dark gray to tan and is often shaggy as it ages. Plants may be both cold and drought deciduous.

The gray-green leaves are 2 to 6 in. (5.1 to 15.2 cm) long and are odd pinnately compound. They are composed of 11 to 55 leaflets per leaf that are up to 1 in. (2.5 cm) long. The leaves are highly fragrant, reminding some of tangerine, others of mango, but are pungent and pleasantly sharp in aroma.

The flowers are held in a dense terminal or axillary raceme that is up to 7 in. (17.8 cm) long. Individual flowers are minute, less than 0.25 in. (0.6 cm) long, white, and extremely fragrant with a sharp, sweet vanilla aroma. The flowers are followed by tan pods, each with one seed. The pods are flat and hang on the tree for months; they look like small pagodas suspended from the branch.

Kidneywood is extremely drought tolerant once established, even in the hottest deserts. But plants are fuller and more attractive with intermittent deep soakings during the summer where it is hot. Good drainage is essential, but otherwise these lovely trees are tolerant of a wide range of soils.

Kidneywood is useful in a border or boundary planting, particularly a mixed planting of other woody plants. In smaller gardens, it forms a background shrub or anchors a perennial bed. Its lovely fragrance permeates an entire garden but is most welcome near a seating area or where you walk often. It may be pruned to a single trunk and used as a focal or accent tree on a patio or other smaller garden area.

The similar Mexican kidneywood (*Eysenhardtia polystachya*) was once thought to be the name for the populations found in far southeastern Arizona and southern New Mexico. It is now considered that this species is entirely Mexican from Durango to Oaxaca. All plants in the United States formerly assigned to this taxon are now considered *E. orthocarpa*. Mexican kidneywood is larger, up to 25 ft. (7.6 m) tall, but other differences are fine and difficult to discern.

Eysenhardtia texana

Texas kidneywood

FAMILY: Fabaceae.

DISTRIBUTION: In the United States in western Texas to the Edwards Plateau and through the southern Plains at 2500 to 6000 ft. (762 to 1829 m). In Mexico from Coahuila, Nuevo León, and Tamaulipas to Puebla and Veracruz.

MATURE SIZE: Small shrub 4 to 9 ft. (1.2 to 2.7 m) tall, occasionally to 15 ft. (4.6 m).

BLOOMING PERIOD: May to October.

EXPOSURE: Full sun in all but the hottest deserts, where it also grows well in high, filtered shade.

HARDINESS: Hardy to 15°F (−9.4°C).

Texas kidneywood is much shrubbier than kidneywood (*Eysenhardtia orthocarpa*): it

Eysenhardtia texana (Texas kidneywood)

grows as a dense, multistemmed plant, rarely becoming a small tree. It is winter deciduous, although in mild winter areas it may be late in losing its leaves. It may also be drought deciduous but recovers quickly once rain or irrigation occurs.

The alternate leaves are pinnate and up to 2 in. (5.1 cm) long. Each leaf has 15 to 31 oblong leaflets with a rounded tip. Leaflets are dull dark green to gray-green with the lower side somewhat paler.

The flowers are held in a terminal raceme that is up to 4.5 in. (11.4 cm) long. The flowers are tiny, less than 0.25 in. (0.6 cm) long, white, and extremely fragrant. Flowers are followed by linear to oblong pods that begin green and turn brown when mature.

Texas kidneywood is a lovely shrub for dry gardens. It grows in well-drained, alkaline soils, but tolerates a wide range of soils as long as they have good drainage. Both the leaves, which smell like citrus, and the flowers, which smell like spicy vanilla, are worth having where you brush against them as you walk around the garden. Even the wind causes the delightful aromas to circulate in the garden.

Texas kidneywood is an excellent small shrub in both large and small gardens. It blends well with other shrubs for a naturalistic planting. It is small enough to be included in large perennial beds or in long borders of mixed shrubs.

Fallugia paradoxa
Apache plume

FAMILY: Rosaceae.
DISTRIBUTION: In the United States from southern California to northern Colorado and Utah, into southern Nevada, Arizona, and New Mexico as well as the Trans-Pecos and western Edwards Plateau of Texas at 3000 to 8000 ft. (914 to 2438 m). In Mexico throughout Chihuahua, Coahuila, Durango, and Zacatecas at 2300 to 7000 ft. (701 to 2134 m).
MATURE SIZE: Loosely branched, somewhat irregular shrub 3 to 8 ft. (0.9 to 2.4 m) tall and about as wide.
BLOOMING PERIOD: May to October.
EXPOSURE: Full sun in all areas.
HARDINESS: Hardy to 0°F (−17.8°C).

Apache plume is an irregular, often erratically branched shrub with numerous fine branches arising from a sturdy, woody base. The old stems have peeling bark while young stems have a woolly coating of fine hairs. Plants are most often deciduous, except in extremely warm winter areas. They are rhizomatous and may form small colonies.

The leaves are tiny, up to 0.25 in. (0.6 cm) long, and are pinnately compound with three to seven leaflets. They are dark green above and either rusty-brown or pale whitish-gray below.

The white flowers have five corolla lobes that are free and open wide. They look like old-fashioned roses, which isn't surprising since they are in the same family. Flowers are up to 1 in. (2.5 cm) across.

Flowers are followed by the distinctive fruit that gives the plant its charm and its name. Each seed is attached to a fine, hairy plume that is 1 to 2 in. (2.5 to 5.1 cm) long. The plumes are held in long-persistent clusters on the plant. These cascading seed structures

Fallugia paradoxa (Apache plume)

begin pale tan or whitish and fade to pink and are often prolific enough to shroud the plant in a pink foam.

Apache plume benefits from a hard prune every three or four years to keep it in good shape and to provide a new flush of growth, which increases flowering. Between prunings, remove dead wood, but annual pruning is not advised because it reduces vigor and may impede bloom.

Apache plume grows in most well-drained soils, even rocky ones. Despite its natural range at higher elevations, this species does extremely well even in the hottest deserts, where it is best to water plants monthly through the summer and place them in

filtered shade. In all other areas, once established, plants grow and bloom well in full sun on natural rainfall.

If you have occasion to travel through the spectacular lava fields of northern New Mexico known as the El Malpais, this shrub is abundant there. It is the single most common species on those flows. Flowering profusely in the cracks and crevices provided by the cooled lava, it is a delicate counterpoint to the bleak, rocky field.

Apache plume provides a soft contrast when used as a focal or accent plant. Use it generously as a hedge or in a blended planting of other woody plants at the edge of the garden. It also makes a good background plant within a larger garden to separate or isolate selected parts of the garden.

Ficus petiolaris
Rock fig

FAMILY: Moraceae.

DISTRIBUTION: In Mexico in Baja California and associated islands, west and central Sonora, and in southwestern Chihuahua south to Oaxaca from sea level to 6000 ft. (1829 m).

MATURE SIZE: Shrubby tree 10 to 20 ft. (3 to 6.1 m) tall, up to 45 ft. (13.7 m) in the tropics, and spreading as wide.

BLOOMING PERIOD: Spring and again in the fall, but often does not flower or fruit in cultivation.

EXPOSURE: Full sun or partial shade in all areas.

HARDINESS: Deciduous at or near freezing and stem damage at 25°F (−3.9°C).

Rock fig is a semisucculent tree that may present a number of different forms depending on the growing conditions. In dry, rocky sites with minimal water, it is a multi-branched shrub rarely up to 6 ft. (1.8 m) tall. In better soils or with more consistent watering, it grows into a single or multibranched tree. The bark is white to yellowish, thin, and smooth, and peels off on older wood. The roots grow at or near the surface and in rocky sites cover and cling to exposed rocks, seeking water below them.

The leaves are 4.5 to 12 in. (11.4 to 30.5 cm) long, heart shaped to oval, and are held on a long petiole that is up to two-thirds as long as the leaf blade. Leaves are deep green and either smooth and glossy or covered with fine

Ficus petiolaris (rock fig)

hairs. The veins of the leaf are prominent and are red, pink, or yellow.

The inedible figs are 0.75 to 1 in. (1.8 to 2.5 cm) long and held singly or in pairs. As with all figs, the flowers are embedded within the fruit and are pollinated by tunneling insects seeking the luscious fruit.

The two recognized subspecies are sometimes split into two separate species in older texts. Subsp. *petiolaris* has glossy, green leaves with prominent pink or red veins. Subsp. *palmeri* is the more xeric form and occurs naturally in some of the driest parts of Baja California and Sonora. It has pubescent twigs, leaves, and figs and the veins are yellow. Leaves tend to be slightly smaller in this subspecies as well.

Rock fig is often grown in containers with the extraordinary clinging roots positioned to grow over rocks. But it is also well suited to warm-winter areas as a focal or accent plant in the ground or in large planters. It forms a dense screen or backdrop for other more colorful plantings and is heat tolerant enough to be useful around pools and to cover hot walls.

Numerous other figs are grown in the region but they require careful consideration. The upright, evergreen Indian laurel fig (*Ficus microcarpa*) is a tree 20 to 35 ft. (6.1 to 10.7 m) tall with an upright, dense crown. The waxy, deep green leaves are 2 to 4 in. (5.1 to 10.2 cm) long and come to a sharp tip. Although Indian laurel fig has immense heat tolerance, it needs supplemental water every week or two in the summer in the hottest deserts, and less frequent water elsewhere. It is able to withstand temperatures down to 20°F (−2.2°C) but suffers severe stem damage, and young trees are killed at 25°F (−3.9°C). Var. *nitida* is widely used in the warm-winter parts of the region. This variety has a more upright, regular form than the type, with strongly ascending branches. This species comes from India and Malaysia.

The Chinese banyan (*Ficus benghalensis*) is a huge tree growing up to 50 ft. (15.2 m) tall and spreading at least that wide. It has roots that form near the surface, and as they enlarge they move sidewalks, walls, or any other object in their path. It is best to use this tree as far as possible from buildings, walls, or walkways. The foliage is dense with dark green, evergreen leaves that are 3 to 5 in. (0.9 to 1.5 cm) long on long, drooping branches. I know of one of these plants that had grown into the ground from its pot and towered over the adjacent house, living on only the water associated with the other potted plants. A new owner of the house cut the tree down to the roots, but soon it was back. It took delib-

erate and persistent action to remove that tree. Chinese banyan is a rugged, tough tree that grows under almost any conditions of soil and watering. While it is stunning, it needs plenty of room.

Fraxinus greggii
Gregg's ash

FAMILY: Oleaceae.

DISTRIBUTION: In the United States in limited and local distribution in southern Arizona and New Mexico, but common in West Texas at 4000 to 7000 ft. (1219 to 2134 m). In Mexico from eastern Chihuahua into Coahuila and western Nuevo León and to Zacatecas, Tamaulipas, and San Luis Potosí at 2300 to 6600 ft. (701 to 2012 m).

MATURE SIZE: Multibranched small tree or shrub 10 to 20 ft. (3 to 6.1 m) tall and spreading 10 to 15 ft. (3 to 4.6 m) wide.

BLOOMING PERIOD: March to May.

EXPOSURE: Full sun in all areas, although it does well in high, filtered shade in the hottest deserts.

HARDINESS: Hardy to at least 10°F (−12.2°C).

Gregg's ash is a much-branched shrub, often small tree, that is evergreen. The bark is dark gray, occasionally black, and is smooth with only small scales on older stems.

The leaves are 1 in. (2.5 cm) long and are pinnately compound, with three to seven leaflets per leaf and the terminal leaflet is larger than the other two. The thick, leathery leaflets are pale green to gray-green and are lighter on the underside with distinctive black dots. The leaflets are oblanceolate to elliptical and finely serrate along the margin with prominent wings on the petioles.

Plants are monoecious, with the male and female flowers held on the same plant, often in the same flowering stalk. The flowers are small and are held in panicles that are only 0.75 in. (1.8 cm) long and are pale whitish to yellow. Fruit is a flattened seed surrounded by a pair of elongated wings, which is known as a samara. These distinctive pods are held in long clusters that persist for months on the tree.

Despite conditions of its natural range, Gregg's ash does well in rocky desert soils even in the heat of the hottest deserts. During the summer, however, it does need to be watered regularly, up to weekly, for best results. Water every three to four weeks in milder areas. It is highly tolerant of most soil types, including highly alkaline ones, but must have excellent drainage.

Gregg's ash is a good choice for shade in a small patio or garden. It also forms a dense backdrop or privacy planting. When left as a shrub it is useful as a screen or boundary planting. For a more formal garden, the shrub may be lightly shaped to accentuate its conical form.

Fraxinus greggii (Gregg's ash)

Gossypium harknessii
San Carlos hibiscus

FAMILY: Malvaceae.
DISTRIBUTION: Endemic to Baja California Sur and several nearby islands.
MATURE SIZE: Rounded shrub 2 to 6 ft. (0.6 to 1.8 m) tall and spreading up to 6 ft. (1.8 m) wide.
BLOOMING PERIOD: April to October.
EXPOSURE: Full sun in all areas, but tolerates light shade in the hottest deserts.
HARDINESS: Hardy to 28°F (−2.2°C); at 24°F (−4.4°C) defoliates but recovers quickly.

San Carlos hibiscus is an intricately branched shrub with branches that tend to rise then fall over, giving it a sprawling, cascading appearance. The stems are reddish, particularly when young, but are usually smothered by the foliage so you don't notice them.

The leaves are shiny, deep green, and leathery, more or less heart shaped, often with shallowly undulated margins. They are 1 to 1.5 in. (2.5 to 3.8 cm) wide and are evergreen.

The flowers are 2 in. (5.1 cm) across and are

Gossypium harknessii (San Carlos hibiscus)

bright yellow. The delicate, tissue-thin corolla lobes are marked by a dark purple to brownish throat. The flowers are stunning and are prolific throughout the summer.

In nature, San Carlos hibiscus grows near the coast and therefore has high tolerance for saline soils. It grows well in any well-drained soil, rocky and dry or more amended, highly alkaline, or nearly neutral. Water with intermittent long soaks in the summer in the hottest deserts. I have known plants, however, that grew to great size and with exquisite bloom on just the natural rainfall in the Phoenix area.

San Carlos hibiscus is one of the most colorful large shrubs that bloom throughout the summer in the hottest deserts. Its dense, green foliage make it a good choice for a screen, hedge, or barrier planting. Its extreme heat tolerance makes it useful around pools,

against hot walls or buildings, or anywhere heat is intense. It makes a beautiful addition to a mixed hedge planting and forms a backdrop for succulent plantings. It one of the best choices for a massed planting where regular watering is difficult or uncertain.

Gossypium thurberi
Desert cotton

FAMILY: Malvaceae.

DISTRIBUTION: In southern and central Arizona at 2500 to 4500 ft. (762 to 1372 m). In Mexico from Sonora to Chihuahua and south to Jalisco.

MATURE SIZE: Upright shrub 6 to 12 ft. (1.8 to 3.7 m) tall and about half as wide.

BLOOMING PERIOD: May to September.

EXPOSURE: Full sun in all but the hottest deserts, where it prefers afternoon shade or high, filtered shade.

HARDINESS: Hardy to at least 23°F (−5.0°C) and perhaps lower.

Desert cotton is an upright shrub that is almost a small tree, with smooth, light gray bark. The branches occur at odd intervals and often try to reach toward the ground or twist in interesting ways. Overall the plant is upright, full branched, and leafy. Plants are winter deciduous.

The leaves are palmately compound with three to five leaflets that are linear with a sharp tip. Leaflets range from 2 to 4 in. (5.1 to 10.2 cm) long and are bright green, thin, and with smooth margins.

The flowers are up to 1 in. (2.5 cm) wide and the thin corolla lobes are white, pinkish, or lavender, with pink dots at the base. They begin cupped and open fully during the day,

Gossypium thurberi (desert cotton)

but barely open on cloudy days. The flowers are prolific: blooming lasts for months in the late summer.

The fruit is a prominent capsule that is up to 1 in. (2.5 cm) wide. It splits to reveal the black seeds, but it produces only a few wispy strands of cotton.

Desert cotton is a handsome shrub for small spaces. It may be pruned lightly in the spring when the leaves first emerge to encourage tip growth or to shape the plant. It may also be pruned in the late summer, if necessary, to remove suckers or low branches. The long stems that bloomed often die out during the winter and need to be pruned back in the spring once the plant begins to leaf out.

Desert cotton is moderately drought tolerant but does best with weekly watering in the hottest deserts through the summer. It tolerates a wide range of soils, as long as they are well drained.

This species hosts the pink bollworm, which is a significant pest of commercially grown cotton. Planting it near cotton fields is discouraged. But it is also oddly resistant to the silverleaf whitefly, one of the countless versions of whitefly in the region.

Desert cotton is a charming shrub that provides delicate, late-summer color. It is a good choice in a small garden, around a patio or seating area, or to fill a corner of the garden.

Guaiacum angustifolia

Soapbush, guayacan

FAMILY: Zygophyllaceae.

DISTRIBUTION: In the United States in west and south Texas along the entire Rio Grande and into the Edwards Plateau to Travis County at 1600 to 4000 ft. (488 to 1219 m). In Mexico in Chihuahua, Coahuila, Nuevo León, and Tamaulipas at similar elevations.

MATURE SIZE: Lanky shrub to small tree up to 10 to 30 ft. (3 to 9.1 m) tall and 8 to 10 ft. (2.4 to 3 m) wide.

BLOOMING PERIOD: March to September.

EXPOSURE: Full sun in all but the hottest deserts, where filtered shade is best.

HARDINESS: Hardy to 15°F (−9.4°C).

Soapbush is an irregularly branched, large, evergreen shrub. Older plants often have distinctive gnarled, twisted stems. The bark is gray to black, smooth, and thin.

Guaiacum angustifolia (soapbush)

The leaves are dark green, leathery, and pinnately compound. Each leaf is composed of four to eight pairs of leaflets, each of which is less than 0.5 in. (1.3 cm) long. Leaflets are linear to oblong with a lustrous sheen and strong tip. The leaves are congested along the stems and so small the stems look fuzzy from a distance.

The fragrant flowers are terminal, solitary or in small clusters, and are a deep violet or purple, occasionally white. Individual flowers are small, 0.75 in. (1.8 cm) long, but their brilliant color makes the bloom more extraordinary than the flower size suggests.

The fruit is a heart-shaped capsule up to 0.5 in. (1.3 cm) long. It ultimately splits open to reveal large seeds that are red, yellow, or orange.

This species is extremely tough. It is tolerant of almost any well-drained soil including rocky, alkaline ones. Although the species has excellent drought tolerance and in most areas grows well on natural rainfall, monthly watering will help the plant retain its best form and vigor in the hottest deserts where summer rainfall is unreliable.

The wood is extremely hard and has enjoyed a wide array of uses over the years. The root bark contains saponin: it makes a kind of amole or soap, which historically was used to wash wool and set the color after it was dyed. This species also has a wide array of medicinal uses.

Soapbush is an excellent tall, dark green shrub either massed or mixed with other desert shrubs. It is heat- and drought-tolerant enough to be used on the edges and borders of the garden where watering is intermittent. It is more cold hardy than its close relative *Guaiacum coulteri*, also called guayacan, which extends its use throughout the region. This shrub is also a good choice for a narrow spot where its vertical form is appropriate or to back up a more colorful planting around a pool or patio.

Guaiacum coulteri
Guayacan

FAMILY: Zygophyllaceae.

DISTRIBUTION: In Mexico from central and southern Sonora to Puebla and Oaxaca up to 2000 ft. (610 m).

MATURE SIZE: Upright shrub or small tree from 6 to 25 ft. (1.8 to 7.6 m) tall and 5 to 10 ft. (1.5 to 3 m) wide.

BLOOMING PERIOD: May and June.

EXPOSURE: Full sun in all areas.

HARDINESS: Hardy to 28°F (−2.2°C); tip and leaf damage at 24°F (−4.4°C).

Guaiacum coulteri (guayacan)

This guayacan is an intriguingly branched shrub with rigid branches that fly out at odd, erratic angles despite the fact that the shrub's overall form is tidy and regular. The bark is smooth and gray. While evergreen, the leaves may fall during periods of sudden cold or drought. In either situation, it recovers quickly.

The opposite leaves are 1.5 to 2 in. (3.8 to 5.1 cm) long. They are pinnately compound with three to five pairs of linear to oval leaflets. The leaflets are a deep, glossy green. Although the leaves are spaced widely on the branch, they are prolific enough to give the plant a full appearance.

The flowers are an astoundingly deep, electric blue, nearly indigo—so dark that they don't seem real. While the flowers are only up to 1.25 in. (3.8 cm) wide, they are prolific and coat the plant, making a brilliant show while in bloom.

The fruit is a capsule, which opens to reveal the brilliant scarlet seed coat. The seed inside is yellow to orange.

Guayacan has a following in the hottest deserts of Arizona and with good reason. Although somewhat cold tender, it is a beautiful shrub for extremely hot, dry locations.

It grows in any well-drained soil, including dry, rocky, alkaline ones. While it is naturally drought tolerant enough to grow on natural rainfall in the hottest deserts, it is much more attractive when given monthly deep soaks in the summer although it rarely needs supplemental irrigation in the winter.

This guayacan makes a stunning focal or accent plant in hot, dry locations. It is suitable for small gardens as well as anywhere with intense or reflective heat, like around a pool or against a hot wall. This species blends well with other heat-loving, drought-tolerant shrubs to form a border or boundary hedge at the edge of the garden where watering may be intermittent.

Haematoxylum brasiletto
Brazilwood

SYNONYM: *Haematoxylon brasiletto.*
FAMILY: Fabaceae.
DISTRIBUTION: In Mexico from central and southern Sonora, as well as Baja California Sur and Chihuahua from sea level to 2900 ft. (884 m), and south to Colombia and Venezuela.
MATURE SIZE: Upright, multistemmed tree 15 to 30 ft. (4.6 to 9.1 m) tall and 6 to 10 ft. (1.8 to 3 m) wide.
BLOOMING PERIOD: July to September.
EXPOSURE: Full sun in all areas, but does well in filtered shade in the hottest deserts.

Haematoxylum brasiletto (brazilwood)

HARDINESS: Limbs die back at 25°F (−3.9°C), and may die back to the ground at 20°F (−6.7°C), but recovers quickly.

Brazilwood is a much branched, nearly impenetrable shrub when young but is easily trained to become a small tree. The bark is smooth and gray with indentations and fissures, and as the tree ages the bark achieves a distinctive braided look. There are small, less than 0.25 in. (0.6 cm) long, thorns along the branches. Plants are winter deciduous unless grown in entirely frost-free areas.

The leaves are pinnately compound with 2 to 34 pairs of leaflets. Leaflets are heart shaped and up to 1 in. (2.5 cm) long and often much smaller. They are dark green and spread out over the branches, giving the plant an open, light form.

Flowers are held on flowering stalks that are 2.5 to 3 in. (6.4 to 7.6 cm) long. Individual flowers are 0.5 in. (1.3 cm) wide and are attached to the flowering stalk by thread-thin stalks 0.5 in. (1.3 cm) long. The flowering stalks occur in the leaf axils singly or in pairs near the end of the branches. Flowers are bright yellow, and the lower, much reduced fifth corolla lobe is sprinkled with reddish nectar guides.

The seed is held in a flat, papery pod that is reddish when young and straw colored when fully mature. These pods stay on the tree for months and are like a second bloom.

Brazilwood tolerates almost any well-drained soil but is particularly at home in rocky, alkaline soils. Although immensely heat resistant, it does best with watering twice a month in the summer in the hottest deserts to maintain good form. With less water the leaves drop but they regrow quickly with deep watering or rain.

This species is a good choice for smaller areas. In Phoenix, its heaviest bloom is late in the season with the onset of the summer monsoons, although it shows a few flowers at any time in the warm season. It is among the last tree to leaf out after the winter, particularly if the weather was cold enough to sustain some tip damage.

Hamelia patens
Firebush

FAMILY: Rubiaceae.

DISTRIBUTION: In the United States only in southern Florida. Found throughout the

West Indies, and in Central and South America south to Paraguay and Bolivia.

MATURE SIZE: Multitrunked shrub or small tree 8 to 35 ft. (2.4 to 10.7 m) tall and up to 10 ft. (3 m) wide.

BLOOMING PERIOD: June to October.

EXPOSURE: Full sun in all but the hottest deserts, where it needs afternoon shade or high, filtered shade.

HARDINESS: Minor damage at 28°F (−2.2°C); severe damage at temperatures below 24°F (−4.4°C), but recovers quickly.

Firebush is a fast-growing, multitrunked shrub that rarely gets to be a tree within the region. Over a number of frost-free winters in the Phoenix area, however, some plants got up to 10 ft. (3 m) tall. In mid-elevation parts of the region, it is often grown as a quick-recovering, summer-flowering shrub that dies back routinely in the winter. The smooth bark is tan to darker brown.

The leaves are oval to elliptical, 3 to 6 in. (7.6 to 15.2 cm) long, and clustered in whorls along the branches. In the summer they are bright green to gray-green and lightly covered with hairs. In the cooler temperatures of autumn, they turn a burnished coppery red.

The flowers are held in terminal clusters. The buds are bright red and up to 2.5 in. (6.4 cm) long. They remain tightly closed for over a month and open only when temperatures are hot, over 100°F (37.8°C). Once open, the flowers are tight tubes and are enormously attractive to hummingbirds. The fruit is a black to dark purple drupe that provides a late-season feast for fruit-eating birds as well.

Firebush grows in the hottest part of the summer but prefers partial shade or at least not a western exposure in the hottest deserts;

Hamelia patens (firebush)

elsewhere grow it in full sun. It grows well in a wide range of soils that are well drained but does particularly well in alkaline soils. Water weekly in the summer in the hottest regions to keep the plant fit and in good bloom. But it tolerates much less frequent watering as well. Plants do well in large containers or other restricted planting areas.

This shrub is a great choice for a small patio because of its intense, long-lived, summer color. It is not a particular messy shrub, making it useful near pools. Prune firebush in the early spring just as it begins to break dormancy, to reinvigorate the plant, remove any winter damage, or tighten its form.

Havardia mexicana
Mexican ebony

SYNONYM: *Pithecellobium mexicanum*.
FAMILY: Fabaceae.
DISTRIBUTION: In Mexico in Sonora, Baja California Sur, and south into Sinaloa at 1000 to 3500 ft. (305 to 1067 m).
MATURE SIZE: Upright, spreading tree 25 to 40 ft. (7.6 to 12.2 m) tall and spreading 30 ft. (9.1 m) wide.
BLOOMING PERIOD: March and April.
EXPOSURE: Full sun in all areas.
HARDINESS: Hardy to 18°F (−7.8°C).

Mexican ebony is a deciduous, upright tree with smooth, gray bark. There are tiny, straight spines at the nodes.

The gray-green leaves are 0.5 to 1 in. (1.3 to 2.5 cm) long and bipinnately compound. Leaves are composed of 2 to 4 pairs of pinnae, each of which has 3 to 10 pairs of tiny leaflets less than 0.25 in. (0.6 cm) long.

The flowers are tiny and held in rounded clusters 0.5 in. (1.3 cm) across, giving the flowers a characteristic puffball form. Flowers are whitish to yellow white and fragrant. Pods are oblong and 1 to 3 in. (2.5 to 7.6 cm) long.

Mexican ebony does best in deep soils, although with regular watering plants do well in dry, rocky soils. It is, however, quite drought tolerant and will prosper with a deep soak once a month in the summer in the hottest deserts.

Mexican ebony is a good choice for high, light shade in the garden. It is tall enough to provide significant shade but is not as overpowering in smaller gardens as are many mesquites. It grows quickly and has a spreading crown that shelters a wall, patio, or seating area from the blazing desert sun. The lightly fragrant flowers are an added bonus.

Havardia mexicana (Mexican ebony)

Havardia pallens
Tenaza

SYNONYM: *Pithecellobium pallens*.
FAMILY: Fabaceae.

DISTRIBUTION: In the United States only in far south Texas along the coast and into the southern plains of the Rio Grande Valley. In Mexico in Tamaulipas, Nuevo León, southeastern San Luis Potosí, northern Veracruz, and one locality in Coahuila.

MATURE SIZE: Open-branched, small tree or shrub 10 to 30 ft. (3 to 9.1 m) tall and 8 to 12 ft. (2.4 to 3.7 m) wide.

BLOOMING PERIOD: May to September.

EXPOSURE: Full sun in most areas; high, filtered shade or protection from western sun in the hottest deserts.

HARDINESS: Reported by many authors to be hardy to 15°F (−9.4°C), but individuals in Tucson suffered serious stem damage at 18°F (−7.8°C) and no damage at 23°F (−5.0°C).

Havardia pallens (tenaza)

Tenaza is a small, multistemmed, thorny shrub when young. The slender stems are straight and more or less upright. The bark is thin, gray to brown, and it furrows and peels with age. Stems have a few pairs of short, straight, sharp spines.

The bipinnately compound leaves are up to 1.5 in. (3.8 cm) long and composed of 5 pairs of pinnae. Each leaf has 10 to 14 pairs of dark green to dusky-green leaflets that are less than 0.25 in. (0.6 cm) long.

The flowers are round, creamy white puffballs that are profuse on the plant. They are fragrant, often intensely so, and smell like sweet vanilla. The flowers recur in response to rains or deep irrigation through the summer. The pods are reddish brown, 2 to 5 in. (5.1 to 12.7 cm) long, and open quickly when the seeds are mature.

Tenaza bark is thin and sunburns easily in the hottest deserts, particularly when exposed to western sun. Leaving the juvenile stems on the plant until the bark thickens, or letting the stems hang down to shade the bark, mitigates this problem. If a more solitary plant is desired, these limbs may be pruned in later years after the bark has toughened up.

Tenaza is a good choice for smaller gardens or near a seating area or patio. The fragrance varies in intensity by individuals but is a delicate delight in any garden. To increase the impact use it in groves to fill a corner or leave it more or less unpruned to form a barrier planting. It is also useful in a mixed hedge or boundary planting.

Hyptis emoryi
Desert lavender

FAMILY: Lamiaceae.

DISTRIBUTION: In the United States from the Mojave Desert regions of southern California, southern Nevada, southern Arizona, and as far east as the Rio Grande drainage of New Mexico from sea level to 4000 ft. (1219 m). In Mexico in Sonora and Baja California at 700 to 2600 ft. (213 to 792 m).

MATURE SIZE: Loosely branched shrub 4 to 8 ft. (1.2 to 2.4 m) tall and 2 to 4 ft. (0.6 to 1.2 m) wide.

BLOOMING PERIOD: January to May; intermittently in summer in response to rainfall.

EXPOSURE: Full sun in all areas.

HARDINESS: Foliage damaged below 24°F (−4.4°C).

Desert lavender is a wispy, loose, straight-stemmed shrub of the foothills and rocky mountains of the Sonoran and Mojave Deserts. In youth it is a compact shrub, but as the stems elongate it becomes an erect, open shrub.

The leaves are small, usually less than 1 in. (2.5 cm) long, ovate, serrate, and so densely covered with fine hairs that they appear gray to white. The fine hairs also make the leaves feel soft and fuzzy. Leaves are fragrant and smell like lavender, hence the name.

The minute, barely visible flowers are held in tight clusters that are arranged in pairs around the leaf nodes. Flowers range from pale pink to light lavender. The small size, pastel colors, and lack of contrast with the leaves conspire to prevent this species from being showy except at close range.

Desert lavender grows best in well-drained, even rocky soil. Although it has great drought tolerance, garden plants respond well and look best if given monthly summer watering.

Prune desert lavender in late winter or early spring after all danger of frost is past. It has excellent natural form and rarely needs more than removal of damaged stems.

This plant is strongly attractive to bees, especially native bees. It is a great companion plant for native perennials or succulents because it enjoys much the same growing conditions. Small and discrete, it may also be used where it is touched often to release the delightful, lavender scent, such as along a walkway or a narrow entryway.

Hyptis emoryi (desert lavender)
Photo by Judy Mielke

Jacaranda mimosifolia
Jacaranda

FAMILY: Bignoniaceae.

DISTRIBUTION: In Brazil, Argentina, and Peru chiefly in the Amazon Basin areas of those countries.

MATURE SIZE: Erect tree 25 to 50 ft. (7.6 to 15.2 m) tall and up to 30 ft. (9.1 m) wide.

BLOOMING PERIOD: April to June.

EXPOSURE: Full sun in all areas.

HARDINESS: Hardy to 25°F (−3.9°C); young trees are more sensitive.

Jacaranda is a tall, vase-shaped tree with a thick, feathery crown. Plants are semi-deciduous, but fully deciduous when temperatures are at or below freezing. The bark is light brown to gray and almost black at maturity.

The leaves are 12 to 18 in. (30.5 to 45.7 cm) long, bipinnately compound, and opposite. Leaves have 8 to 20 pairs of pinnae, each of which has 14 to 24 pairs of leaflets. The leaflets are 0.25 in. (0.6 cm) long, oblong to elliptic, and bright green.

The flowers are held in upright, pyramidal stalks 8 to 12 in. (20.3 to 30.5 cm) tall at the tip of the branches. Individual flowers are tubular, 1.5 to 2.5 in. (3.8 to 6.4 cm) long, and are numerous on the stalk. Flowers range from light lavender to deep blue and occasionally purple-blue or white. The entire flowering head is extravagantly showy.

The distinctive fruit is a flat, rich brown, winged capsule that is 2 in. (5.1 cm) wide and more or less round. These disk-shaped fruits are persistent on the tree for a long time after they mature.

Jacaranda mimosifolia (jacaranda)

Jacaranda is tolerant of a wide range of soils and grows well even in rocky, dry soils with adequate water. Trees in drier soils are rarely as tall as those grown in deeper soils. It needs to be watered every week or two in the hottest deserts, and less frequently where summer temperatures are milder or summer rainfall is reliable.

Jacaranda is a stunning tree in the warm winter parts of the region. It has become popular as an ornamental street tree throughout the warm parts of the world, a shade tree in parks or other large properties, and as a colorful flowering tree that provides light shade in yards large enough to accommodate it.

Lantana camara
Common lantana

FAMILY: Verbenaceae.

DISTRIBUTION: Origins are in the tropical Americas, but this species complex has been in horticulture around the world for over 300 years and is now naturalized or grown ornamentally in all warm regions. It has naturalized extensively in the United States in Florida, the Gulf Coast states, and parts of Texas, as well as on tropical islands all over the world. It is a significant pest species in Australia and southern Africa.

MATURE SIZE: Tightly branched, rounded shrub 4 to 6 ft. (1.2 to 1.8 m) tall and as wide.

BLOOMING PERIOD: March to November.

EXPOSURE: Full sun in all areas; filtered shade in hottest deserts.

HARDINESS: Hardy to 28°F (−2.2°C), but even when severely damaged by colder temperatures recovery is quick.

Common lantana is an intricately branched shrub with pale tan to brownish stems. Stems are unarmed or with weak but irritating prickles. Leaves drop quickly in cold weather, but otherwise it is evergreen.

The deep green leaves are ovate to oblong, 2 to 4 in. (5.1 to 10.2 cm) long, and have a pungent aroma. The leaves are covered, particularly on the underside, with small prickles that lie more or less flat against the blade. The base of the leaf is usually abruptly rounded, and the margins show at least some waviness or serration.

The flowers are held in tight axillary clusters of 10 to 30 flowers, with the entire head 1 to 2 in. (2.5 to 5.1 cm) wide. Individual flowers have a long tube and the corolla lobes are open and flat at the tip. Color ranges widely from cream, yellow, to pale or dark pink, magenta, and lavender. There is so much hybridization and selection that almost any color combination within each flowering head is available.

The fruit is a cluster of berries that are dark purple to black. These fruits are much loved by birds but are toxic to people and other mammals.

It is hard to know how to regard this lovely, summer-growing shrub. In most of the tropical world it is considered a thug, listed by some world organizations as one of the 100 worst invasive plants. In our Southwest deserts, it is benign, rarely moving far from reliable sources of water, and even then seldom establishes the astonishing thickets that have blanketed portions of pasture and rangeland in tropical Africa and Australia.

In the deserts, this rugged shrub grows in full sun and is immune to heat, even highly

Lantana camara (common lantana)

reflective heat. Weekly watering in the summer in the hottest deserts keeps plants in good shape and in continuous bloom, but common lantana will grow on much less frequent watering.

Many of the most common selections and cultivars available are hybrids between *Lantana camara* and trailing lantana (*L. montevidensis*). You will find plants that are large shrubs, dwarf shrubs, those that grow upright, those that grow almost flat to the ground, and all sold either as *L. camara* or simply as lantana.

Immense numbers of forms and colors are available, often much the same but under different names. Many of these forms are sterile, which is good where this species has been a problem. Seed-grown plants tend to bloom with a combination of cream, yellow, and pink flowers, a form known in the trade as 'Ham and Eggs'. This coloration represents the more or less original flower colors of the species.

Lantana is unrivaled for excellent color in the heat, even in the hottest deserts. Leaves may become infested with whitefly in areas where those insects are a problem. But even if the plants defoliate following an attacking swarm, they recover quickly and completely once the insects have moved on.

Lantana provides reliable color around pools and patios where reflective heat is intense and is an excellent container plant. This plant is one of the most reliable summer-flowering shrubs for most of the region and even where winters have regular freezing temperatures. The immense range of colors and size in the trade makes lantana easy to blend with a perennial bed or mixed shrub planting of any size or style. All lantana species and forms are beloved by butterflies. They provide a nearly endless run of nectar, and their long and late flowering season means that many butterfly species are able to take advantage of the bounty.

Lantana horrida (calico bush)

Lantana horrida
Calico bush

FAMILY: Verbenaceae.
DISTRIBUTION: In the United States in southern Arizona, and in southern and southeastern Texas but only isolated locales in the Trans-Pecos. In Mexico widely distributed from Sonora and Chihuahua to Tamaulipas, Vera Cruz, and Puebla.
MATURE SIZE: Dense shrub 2 to 6 ft. (0.6 to 1.8 m) tall and as wide.
BLOOMING PERIOD: March to November.
EXPOSURE: Full sun in all areas.
HARDINESS: Hardy to at least 20°F (−6.7°C), but plants have been known to recover from as low as 5°F (−15.0°C).

Calico bush is extremely similar to common lantana, but is distinguished by its slightly smaller leaves and stature and the fact that the flowers are always either completely or dominantly orange. Plants are intricately branched, with hairy or itchy leaves. There are often a few, widely spaced, recurved prickles along the stem that are tan to light brown when mature, but some forms may have entirely smooth stems. Pure forms of this species are usually winter deciduous.

The leaves have a strong scent like those of common lantana and are deep green or yellowish green with toothed margins. They are 1 to 3 in. (2.5 to 7.6 cm) long and have fine, flat hairs on them that make them rough to the touch.

The flowers are held in heads that are 1 to 2 in. (2.5 to 5.1 cm) across and individual flowers are yellow or light orange and fade to dark orange. There may be any combination of colors within a flowering head. Each flower is tiny but has a long tube that ends in flattened corolla lobes. The collection of these lobes makes the head of flowers look like a mosaic.

The fruit is a cluster of black to purple fruit that is much loved by birds. All parts of lantana are somewhat toxic and if eaten in large quantities are dangerous. Most cattle and other livestock won't touch the plant.

Many authors consider this species to be synonymous with *Lantana urticoides* and use that name. Considering how fine the differences are between these species and among most forms of common lantana, as well as how much hybridization and crossing has been done, it is a wonder that anyone can distinguish any of these larger, rough-leaved plants as individual species. In some cases flower color is used, but that approach seems a bit tenuous. And I am always suspicious when otherwise highly reliable botanical keys use native versus cultivated as a distinguishing feature.

Nevertheless, what is generally grown and sold as this species is a hardy, tough, drought-tolerant plant. It is an excellent choice to complement wildflower displays, succulent gardens, or other areas where long-season color and intense heat tolerance are needed. Use it to fill in around pools and patios, or where you can enjoy the clouds of butterflies that adorn the blooms. I have seen these plants put into somewhat raised beds so that the butterflies are at eye height, and the effect was enchanting.

Larrea tridentata

Creosote, creosote bush

FAMILY: Zygophyllaceae.
DISTRIBUTION: In the United States from the desert regions of southern California through Arizona, southern New Mexico, into west Texas, and south down the Rio Grande Valley and east into the Edwards Plateau below 5000 ft. (1524 m). In Mexico common throughout the dry parts of Baja California to Sonora, Chihuahua, and through the Chihuahuan Desert to Tamaulipas and Querétaro.
MATURE SIZE: Open-branched shrub 5 to 10 ft. (1.5 to 3 m) tall and as wide.
BLOOMING PERIOD: Heaviest bloom from February to May, but blooms intermittently in response to rainfall.
EXPOSURE: Full sun in all areas.
HARDINESS: Hardy to 0°F (−17.8°C).

Creosote is an open-branched shrub with few gray to black stems that are ringed with black at regular intervals. The branches are soft and pliable when young, but become rigid when old; long-dead wood is brittle and will break in your hand. Branches grow out or upright, but as they age extend almost horizontally or turn at sharp angles, often declining to the ground. While there is no clear main trunk, the base in old plants becomes large, gray, and fissured. There are rhizotamous populations in the sand dune areas of southern California that are extraordinarily long-lived. Plants are evergreen although they may easily lose over 75 percent of their leaves during drought.

The alternate leaves are composed of two leaflets held on tiny pedicels. The leaves are 0.5 in. (1.3 cm) long and elliptic with a sharp tip. There is a lot of variation in the shape of the leaflet depending on age, condition, and distribution of the plant as well as how many pairs of leaves are found along the rachis.

Larrea tridentata (creosote)

The leaves are dark green and sticky, often with visible golden oil glands. The oil in these glands is the source of the distinctive, sharp smell of creosote so common in the desert after a rain.

The flowers are 1 in. (2.5 cm) wide and bright yellow, with five free corolla lobes, and are prolific on the plant. While the spring bloom is the most intense, flowers are found on plants year-round.

The fruit is composed of five nutlets compressed into a globe that is generously covered with fine, white hairs. The hairs are so prominent that when backlit or wet, they glow with a silver sheen.

Creosote is without question the most common woody species in both the Sonoran and Mojave Deserts, and extremely common in most of the Chihuahuan Desert as well. In many areas of western Arizona and southern California, it grows in nearly pure stands interrupted only by a few blue palo verde (*Parkinsonia florida*) and ironwood (*Olneya tesota*) in drainages and accented by colorful annual wildflower displays following a wet winter.

Its drought- and heat-tolerance are renowned. Research has determined that plants can go up to three years between waterings without losing enough mass to die. It is rarely necessary to push them that hard in the garden, but they are fully capable of growing on natural rainfall anywhere in the region. Plants that are watered regularly lose a lot of the characteristic branching and look more like any other soft, green rounded woody shrub.

Pruning creosote is difficult to do well without losing the character of the plant. On countless occasions impatient gardeners have cut them to the ground and let them come back with two- or three-dozen soft, green branches. But this approach misses the point. Those erratic, sailing branches are part of creosote's charm and are what make it so graceful in the desert garden. Prune out only dead wood, or those branches that are definitely in the way, every three or four years. A heavy watering after pruning as advisable as for almost all woody species so that it begins to fill out quickly.

There are more legends and stories about creosote than almost any other desert species I can name, except perhaps saguaro (*Carnegiea gigantea*). Like all species with vast ranges and huge numbers, it has an equally impressive list of medicinal and other uses, particularly in Native American tradition.

As a garden plant in a desert setting, it is unrivaled, and fortunate gardeners have several creosote plants in their garden. I think they are best used generously, in small drifts or banks so that their lean form is accentuated. Despite folklore to the contrary, other plants grow fine under creosote in a garden setting. Creosote provides light shade for small cacti, aloes, and other succulents and its lean watering requirements make it a good companion for such species. This species secures a garden's place within the greater desert surrounding it. Birds, particularly verdin, adore creosote's flowers and fruit, and scavenge insects and gall with glee from its branches.

The botanical standing of this species is controversial. Five species are recognized in the genus. The other four occur from Peru to Argentina. Some botanists believe one of these, *Larrea divaricata*, is synonymous with the North American species that they consider to be a variety of it. Others accept the species as described here.

Leucaena retusa
Goldenball leadtree

FAMILY: Fabaceae.

DISTRIBUTION: In the United States in far southern New Mexico and western Texas to the western edges of the Edwards Plateau at 1200 to 5500 ft. (366 to 1676 m). In Mexico in Coahuila at similar elevations

MATURE SIZE: Lanky tree 10 to 20 ft. (3 to 6.1 m) tall and up to 25 ft. (7.6 m) wide.

BLOOMING PERIOD: April to October.

EXPOSURE: Full sun in most areas, but it prefers relief from afternoon sun or reflective heat in hottest deserts.

HARDINESS: Hardy to 5°F (−15°C).

Goldenball leadtree is an open-branched, small tree with reddish-brown bark that begins smooth but cracks, fissures, and often peels as it ages. The plants are deciduous and begin multitrunked, but are easy to train to one trunk if that is preferred.

The leaves are bipinnately compound and 3 to 8 in. (7.6 to 20.3 cm) long with three to five pairs of pinnae and three to eight leaflets per pinna. The leaflets are dark green and rounded.

The flowers are clustered in the axils of the leaves with the puffball style so familiar in this family. The flowers are 1 in. (2.5 cm)

Leucaena retusa (goldenball leadtree)

Leucophyllum candidum
Violet silverleaf

FAMILY: Scrophulariaceae.
DISTRIBUTION: In Texas in southern Brewster County at 2200 to 4000 ft. (671 to 1219 m). In Mexico in central and southern Chihuahua through Coahuila, Durango, and Zacatecas at 2000 to 5000 ft. (610 to 1524 m).
MATURE SIZE: Dense shrub 3 to 6 ft. (0.9 to 1.8 m) tall and as wide.
BLOOMING PERIOD: July to October, particularly following rains.
EXPOSURE: Full sun in all areas.
HARDINESS: Hardy to 10°F (−12.2°C).

wide and bright golden yellow orbs that are fragrant. Flowers are profuse on the plant so that blooming is showy. Flowers are followed by a flat pod 4 to 10 in. (10.2 to 25.4 cm) long.

Goldenball leadtree is an excellent choice for a small tree or loose shrub where space is tight. The branches are widely spaced but the blooming is so spectacular that you hardly care. Wood is brittle, much like bauhinias, and in areas with high winds the plant must be protected from the fiercest winds.

Goldenball leadtree grows in almost any well-drained soil, even in rocky soils, with modest watering, particularly in the hottest deserts. Its lack of thorns and its showy flowers make it a fine choice near walkways or seating areas, although the flowers and leaflets make it less than desirable hanging over a pool.

Violet silverleaf is a dense, compact, heavily branched, evergreen shrub. Young stems are coated with fine, closely aligned hairs that are retained, at least to some extent, as they age.

The leaves are alternate and coated with fine hairs, making them gray-green to nearly white. They are held in fascicles and are so profuse that the plant has a tight, symmetrical form.

The flowers are in purple hues, some deep purple, and are coated with silvery-gray hairs. Flowers are up to 1 in. (2.5 cm) wide.

Violet silverleaf is known in horticulture through two selections, both attributed to the late Texas horticulturist Benny Simpson. 'Silver Cloud' has an open, shrubby look and intense, deep purple flowers; 'Thunder Cloud' is similar but rarely over 3 ft. (0.9 m) tall and is more compact with more frequent bloom in profuse, congested clusters. Both selections have nearly white foliage, an illusion created by the congested, fine hairs on the leaves. The contrast between the bright white foliage and intense purple flowers is stunning.

Leucophyllum candidum (violet silverleaf) Photo by Mountain States Wholesale Nursery

This species is intolerant of poorly drained soils or of overwatering. In fact, for a time, it fell out of favor in my area because it rotted out so easily. This species must have well-drained, alkaline soils to grow best. Even in the hottest deserts, only monthly watering in the summer is necessary. To water more frequently, drainage must be extremely sharp. But when violet silverleaf is grown lean with minimal water, it rewards you with its spectacular appearance.

Prune lightly in the spring to increase the amount of new wood for blooming. Hard pruning, if necessary, must be done in the fall or early winter to prevent loss of blooming. Never prune hard in the summer; it reduces blooming, stresses the plants severely, and leads to sunburn and possible loss of the plant.

Violet silverleaf, like most of its relatives, is a fine choice for a hedge or mixed woody boundary planting. Its great heat and drought tolerance make it valuable for areas where regular watering is not available. Use it to cool a hot wall, provide a backdrop for other colorful plantings, or fill in areas with intense, reflective heat around a pool.

Leucophyllum frutescens

Texas ranger, Texas sage, cenizo

FAMILY: Scrophulariaceae
DISTRIBUTION: In the United States in Texas in far west Texas south to the western edge of the Edwards Plateau and in the grasslands of south Texas at 1000 to 4000 ft. (305 to 1219 m). In Mexico from Coahuila to

Nuevo León and southern Tamaulipas at
1300 to 4000 ft. (396 to 1219 m).

MATURE SIZE: Dense shrub 5 to 10 ft. (1.5 to
3 m) tall and as wide.

BLOOMING PERIOD: July to September, especially in response to rainfall.

EXPOSURE: Full sun in all areas.

HARDINESS: Hardy to 5°F (−15.0°C).

Texas ranger is undoubtedly one of the most
commonly used and widely revered woody
shrubs in southwestern gardens. This evergreen shrub is large and thick with fine hairs
on the young stems. Older stems are dark
gray with fissured and peeling bark.

The alternate leaves are oblong to obovate
and up to 1 in. (2.5 cm) long. Most leaves are
covered with fine hairs, giving them a light

Leucophyllum frutescens (Texas ranger)

gray-green color, and they are lighter on the
upper surface than the underside. This pale
color is the source of the common name
cenizo, which means ash in Spanish. The
amount of hairs is highly variable, so leaf
color ranges from nearly white to pure green.

The flowers are 0.5 to 1 in. (1.3 to 2.5 cm)
wide, held in short clusters, and the lower
lobes are fused into an inflated tube while the
upper lobes flare out like a wheel. They are
coated with fine hairs and look soft and fuzzy.
The color ranges from pink to rosy pink,
to nearly magenta, and occasionally white.
They are lightly fragrant especially when the
humidity is high.

Texas ranger is incredibly forgiving of the
exacting conditions of the Southwest. It grows
in any well-drained soil, including dry, rocky
ones, as well as those with more fertility. In
richer soils, such as those that have been
under agriculture, it develops cotton root rot,
but this tendency is highly variable among the
many selections and cultivars.

The plant's watering needs are minimal,
particularly in the summer. Monthly watering is more than ample even in the hottest
deserts, although with excellent drainage,
plants will tolerate more. They easily rot
where drainage is poor or when they are
overwatered.

Texas ranger and many of its close relatives
have enjoyed the attention of some outstanding horticulturists over the years, and so a
number of selections and hybrids are offered
in the trade. 'Green Cloud' was found in
Texas, and its selection and popularity are
attributed to Texas horticulturist Benny Simpson. This selection has completely green leaves
and deep-magenta flowers and usually grows
to 10 ft. (3 m), the tallest height for the species.

'White Cloud', also attributed to Benny Simpson, has much whiter foliage than average and pure white flowers. Plants tend to be in the middle of the size range for the species and are as tall as they are wide so they can look rounded or even flat topped.

'Compacta' is widely grown, particularly in Texas, and is much like the species in leaf and flower color, but it is shorter, only growing up to 5 ft. (1.5 m) tall.

'Convent', released by Norman Maxwell, a Texas nurseryman, is a short, silver-leaved selection with purple flowers. It is a lovely plant that is not seen much in the trade for some reason.

In Texas a selection known as 'Bert-Star' and trademarked as Silverado Sage has been widely promoted as similar but superior to 'Compacta' because it seems to be easier to grow in containers—a problem in much of the genus. It is fuller and denser than the type, 4 ft. (1.2 m) tall and as wide, and has dense foliage to the base.

'Rain Cloud' is a hybrid between this species and Big Bend silverleaf (*Leucophyllum minus*). This cultivar grows up to 6 ft. (1.8 m) tall and 3 to 4 ft. (0.9 to 1.2 m) wide with deep blue flowers. It is also extremely floriferous: the flowers are both profuse and congested on the plant.

Big Bend silverleaf is a small species rarely over 3 ft. (0.9 m) tall. It is covered with fine hairs on the stems, leaves, and flowers. The alternate leaves are gray-green with a silvery coating and are ovate to round. The small flowers are lavender to purple with a narrow, funnel shape.

Another lovely hybrid is 'Heavenly Cloud' which is a cross between 'Green Cloud' and Chihuahuan rain sage (*Leucophyllum laevigatum*). 'Heavenly Cloud' grows to 6 ft. (1.8 m) tall and has the green foliage of one parent with the light blue flowers of the other.

Texas ranger has been subjected to a wide range of pruning abuse. Although it may be formally pruned, that style is inappropriate. The species and all its selections have exquisite natural form, and severe pruning reduces blooming, which is the best reason for using this species. If you must prune, do so in the early fall after blooming, so you do not affect the bloom and the plant has plenty of time to recover. Flowers form on new growth, so continual shearing cuts off the parts that form flowers for the future. However, light tip pruning in the late spring has the reverse effect, forming more new stems and therefore increasing bloom.

Leucophyllum laevigatum
Chihuahuan rain sage

FAMILY: Scrophulariaceae.

DISTRIBUTION: In Mexico in Chihuahua, Coahuila, Durango, Zacatecas, and San Luis Potosí at 4000 to 7800 ft. (1219 to 2377 m).

MATURE SIZE: Wide-spreading shrub 3 to 5 ft. (0.9 to 1.5 m) tall and up to 6 ft. (1.8 m) wide.

BLOOMING PERIOD: May to September.

EXPOSURE: Full sun in all areas.

HARDINESS: Hardy to 12°F (−11.1°C).

Chihuahuan rain sage is a spreading shrub whose upright branches give it a flat-topped look. It has smaller leaves than most other members of the genus and an open-branching habit.

The alternate, sometimes fascicled, leaves are small, obovate, up to 0.75 in. (1.8 cm)

Leucophyllum laevigatum (Chihuahuan rain sage)

long, and rounded at the tips but tapering toward the base. The green to slightly gray-green leaves have folded or wavy margins, giving them a cupped look.

The flowers are small and profuse along the branches, recurring at times of high humidity or rainfall in the summer. They range in color from lavender to purple or violet and occasionally sky blue or white. Most plants in the trade are blue-flowering forms.

Chihuahuan rain sage is a good choice for areas with hot, dry conditions but it tolerates filtered shade better than most members of the genus.

It grows best in well-drained soil. Take care not to overwater this species, particularly in the summer, or to allow water to pond or stand around the plant. Supplemental watering, about once a month even in the hottest deserts, helps keep plants vigorous and in full leaf, and prolongs the blooming season. In other parts of the region, natural rainfall may be sufficient.

'Heavenly Cloud' is a hybrid between this species and *Leucophyllum frutescens* 'Green Cloud'. This hybrid has green leaves and blue to light lavender flowers; it grows up to 6 ft. (1.8 m) tall.

Leucophyllum langmaniae
Cimmaron sage

FAMILY: Scrophulariaceae.
DISTRIBUTION: In Mexico from Nuevo León to Vera Cruz.
MATURE SIZE: Upright shrub 4 to 5 ft. (1.2 to 1.5 m) tall and as wide.
BLOOMING PERIOD: May to November.
EXPOSURE: Full sun in all areas.
HARDINESS: Hardy to at least 10°F (–12.2°C).

Leucophyllum langmaniae (Cimmaron sage)

Cimmaron sage is a tidy shrub with such densely packed foliage it seems impenetrable. It looks like a tighter, lusher version of Chihuahuan rain sage (*Leucophyllum laevigatum*).

The leaves are bright green and held alternately or in tight clusters along the stems. The leaves are small, less than 0.5 in. (1.3 cm) long and often much smaller.

The flowers are 0.5 to 0.75 in. (1.3 to 1.8 cm) long and are lavender to violet. They are prolific on the plant, recurring over the summer in response to rain or deep irrigation.

Like all members of this genus, Cimmaron sage is sensitive to poorly drained soils. This species tolerates more water through the summer than almost all others, up to weekly in the hottest deserts, and tolerates humid conditions when drainage is excellent.

A beautiful member of this group is the selection known as 'Lynn's Everblooming', also called 'San Jose Cenizo', and now widely known as 'Lynn's Legacy' in honor of the late Texas horticulturist Lynn Lowery, who made the original selection. It has profuse large flowers that are up to 1 in. (2.5 cm) long, lavender to blue, with a flat front and crimped lobe edges.

Leucophyllum pruinosum
Fragrant rain sage

FAMILY: Scrophulariaceae.

DISTRIBUTION: In Mexico from southern Nuevo León to southwestern Tamaulipas and eastern San Luis Potosí at 3500 to 5500 ft. (1067 to 1676 m).

MATURE SIZE: Tightly branched shrub 4 to 6 ft. (1.2 to 1.8 m) tall and as wide.

BLOOMING PERIOD: May to October.

EXPOSURE: Full sun in all areas.
HARDINESS: Hardy to 10°F (−12.2°C).

Fragrant rain sage is a tightly branched, upright or lax shrub with young stems marked by fine hairs. The alternate leaves are ovate and up to 1 in. (2.5 cm) long and often smaller. They are more or less rounded and taper broadly to the base of the leaf. They are densely tomentose on both surfaces, making them gray-green to silvery-gray.

The flowers are held in loose clusters and are up to 0.5 in. (1.3 cm) long. They range in color from dark purple to violet and are intensely, sweetly fragrant. The scent is often compared to that of bubble gum, but I find it more delicate than that.

Fragrant rain sage grows well in well-drained, alkaline, and even rocky soils. Water carefully, particularly in the summer. Even in the hottest desert, watering every three to four weeks in the summer is sufficient. Plants must not remain in wet soils for too long.

Like most of its relatives, this shrub is an excellent choice for a hedge or mixed boundary planting. Its heat tolerance makes it particularly well suited to placement around pools or against hot walls. It makes an excellent backdrop for more colorful plantings. The exquisite fragrance makes a good addition to a small patio or seating area where it may be enjoyed up close.

Leucophyllum zygophyllum
Blue rain sage

FAMILY: Scrophulariaceae.
DISTRIBUTION: In Mexico in Coahuila, Nuevo León, Tamaulipas, and San Luis Potosí at 4000 to 6900 ft. (1219 to 2103 m).
MATURE SIZE: Tight, nearly rounded shrub 3 to 6 ft. (0.9 to 1.8 m) tall and about 3 ft. (0.9 m) wide.
BLOOMING PERIOD: June to October.
EXPOSURE: Full sun in all areas.
HARDINESS: Hardy to at least 5°F (−15.0°C).

Blue rain sage, like all members of the genus, has excellent natural form. It is almost round and the branches are so closely packed that it looks like a silver ball. This effect is enhanced by the young stems, which are tightly clustered, upright, and covered with fine, silvery hairs.

The leaves are light dusky-green, often with a tan cast particularly on the edges. They are round and cupped and, unlike other cultivated members of the genus, are opposite on the stem.

The flowers are held in tight clusters and

Leucophyllum pruinosum (fragrant rain sage)

are prolific when in bloom. They range in color from violet to purple, and are usually dark in color, making a stunning contrast with the light-colored leaves.

Blue rain sage grows best in well-drained, even rocky, alkaline soils. Water deeply every three to four weeks in the hottest desert, and do not let water stand or pond around the plant. It is important not to overwater this species. Avoid watering with overhead sprinklers because that encourages root rot problems and removes the leaf hairs that make the foliage so striking.

Use blue rain sage where its small size and intense coloring are shown to best advantage. It is an excellent choice in areas of reflective heat like around pools, or as a short but colorful hedge. I have seen it used to great effect along a walkway or alongside a short wall as a boundary planting, and it is rugged enough to be grown where watering is intermittent or not regularly available.

Lippia graveolens
Mexican oregano

FAMILY: Verbenaceae.

DISTRIBUTION: In the United States, rare in southern New Mexico but widely distributed in Trans-Pecos and central and southern Texas at 1200 to 3200 ft. (366 to 975 m). In Mexico from Sonora to Chihuahua, through Coahuila to Nuevo León, Zacatecas, San Luis Potosí, and Tamaulipas south into Central America at 2000 to 6600 ft. (610 to 2012 m).

Leucophyllum zygophyllum (blue rain sage)

MATURE SIZE: Erect, multibranched shrub
4 to 9 ft. (1.2 to 2.7 m) tall and up to 5 ft.
(1.5 m) wide.

BLOOMING PERIOD: May to September.

EXPOSURE: Full in all areas; filtered shade
in the hottest deserts.

HARDINESS: Hardy to 28°F (−2.2°C), but
may be killed at temperatures below 25°F
(−3.9°C).

Mexican oregano is an open-branched shrub or
small tree in frost-free areas. The slender, resinous stems are tan to brown with some hairs.

The leaves are held in pairs on a long petiole, often with smaller leaves clustered at
their base. They are deep green to gray-green,
elliptical with a rounded tip, with either
bluntly serrate or wavy margins. Leaves

range from 0.5 to 2.5 in. (1.3 to 6.4 cm) long
and are extremely fragrant with the sharp,
acerbic aroma of good oregano.

The flowers are held in pairs of tight clusters that arise from the leaf axil. They appear
white, but on close inspection there is a distinctive pink or yellow cast to the flowers. The
individual flowers are minute, but the short
spike is up to 0.5 in. (1.3 cm) long.

This species is the most commonly grown
culinary oregano from Mexico and Central
America. Many Indian peoples of Mexico
continue to collect it wild for culinary and
medicinal use. There is a thriving commercial trade for the culinary use of this species
in central and southern Mexico.

In the garden, it is outstanding both as
an ornamental and as a culinary herb. It is

Lippia graveolens (Mexican oregano)

immune to heat, although even moderately cold temperatures cause the leaves to either fall or turn black. It thrives in any well-drained soil, even alkaline ones, but it needs regular irrigation in the hottest deserts to look its best and grow steadily.

Tip pruning throughout the warm season tightens up the shrub, giving it a better form for ornamental use. This pruning is easy to achieve since the leaves are such an outstanding kitchen herb.

Livistona chinensis
Chinese fan palm

FAMILY: Arecaceae.

DISTRIBUTION: Japan, Taiwan, and nearby islands.

MATURE SIZE: Solitary plant to 25 to 30 ft. (7.6 to 9.1 m) tall; the head spreads up to 20 ft. (6.1 m) or more.

BLOOMING PERIOD: Summer.

EXPOSURE: Full sun in all areas, although highly tolerant of high, filtered shade, especially in the hottest deserts.

HARDINESS: Hardy to 20°F (−6.7°C).

Chinese fan palm is a solitary palm with a brown trunk that ages to a deep gray. The trunk has closely spaced rings that are leaf scars, and in old age the trunk becomes corky.

The slightly costapalmate leaves are up to 6 ft. (1.8 m) long and are divided into 60 to 100 deeply split segments. This split is up to 2 ft. (0.6 m) long and most of the segment hangs

Livistona chinensis (Chinese fan palm)

down, giving the plant its distinctive weeping look. The leaves are bright yellow to olive-green to light green, and there are noticeable stout teeth along the petiole.

The flowers are held in an inflorescence 6 ft. (1.8 m) long that is nestled within the leaves. The inflorescence is densely branched. The cream-colored flowers are followed by blue-gray fruit.

Chinese fan palm is a moderately drought-tolerant palm that is well suited to areas that receive intermittent but deep watering. It is tolerant of almost any kind of soil and has moderate salt tolerance as well. In the hottest deserts, it does not appear to become chlorotic as long as it is kept regularly watered.

Slow growing but graceful when young, this palm is an excellent choice for smaller gardens where the towering height of a California fan palm (*Washingtonia filifera*) or Mexican fan palm (*W. robusta*) would be too tall. Plant in groups to maximize the effect of the graceful, hanging leaf segments to provide a cooling, lush, tropical backdrop for a pool or patio.

Other members of this genus are not as common and are even rare. A rare desert species, *Livistona carinensis,* from Somalia and Yemen, is marked with exquisite black teeth on the petiole. *Livistona decipiens* (syn. *L. decora*) has an even more exaggerated hanging-ribbon look to the leaves and is offered by specialty growers, as are two similar Australian species, *L. mariae* and *L. australis*. The Australian species are hardy to about 24°F (−4.4°C). All of these less common species are excellent as a focal or accent plant in the garden or for creating small groves near seating areas or pools.

Lycium spp.
Wolfberry

FAMILY: Solanaceae.

DISTRIBUTION: In the United States from California, Nevada, and Utah to Texas, with one species continuing along the Gulf Coast states. In Mexico from Baja California and Sonora to Chihuahua, Coahuila, Zacatecas, and San Luis Potosí.

MATURE SIZE: Erratically branched shrub from 3 to 8 ft. (0.9 to 2.4 m) tall and 3 to 5 ft. (0.9 to 1.5 m) wide.

BLOOMING PERIOD: February to October.

EXPOSURE: Full sun in all areas.

HARDINESS: Depends on the species, but all are hardy to at least 25°F (−3.9°C), some much more.

Wolfberry is a difficult and confusing genus of shrubs that requires attention to tiny and often obscure details to distinguish one species from another. Most are open-branched shrubs with a few thin branches that are light tan to dark brown or dark gray. All are strongly drought deciduous and in nature are leafless for significant portions of the year.

The leaves are small, less than 1 in. (2.5 cm) long, although there may be larger ones occasionally. Most leaves are linear, but a few splay out at the ends, and in the most xeric species leaves may be nearly succulent. Various shapes and sizes of leaves may occur on the same plant or in response to varying growing conditions.

The flowers are small, much less than 0.25 in. (0.6 cm) wide, and are white, lavender, blue, or purple in all species. Fruit is a berry that turns red to orange-red and is edible. It tastes like a tomato and is relished by birds and people alike.

Only a few species are offered from time to time, usually from specialty nurseries or those that grow only native plants. Some that are most likely to be found follow.

Lycium andersonii is a spiny shrub that is native to the Mojave Desert area of California, Utah, and Nevada to New Mexico and Arizona below 1500 ft. (457 m). In Mexico it occurs through Baja California, Sonora, and northern Sinaloa. Flowers are lavender, occasionally white with bluish tinges, and are up to 0.5 in. (1.3 cm) long. Leaves are usually linear and rounded at the tip, smooth, and succulent. This species flowers from February to April, occasionally reblooming with summer rains in August and September. This wolfberry is wide ranging and abundant in its range. This species grows to 6 ft. (1.8 m) tall and is hardy to at least 10°F (−12.2°C) and perhaps much lower.

Lycium berlandieri is a rounded, erratically branched shrub that is native to Texas from the coast to the Rio Grande in south Texas and up to the Trans-Pecos as well as in southern New Mexico and southern Arizona, with one variety found in Mexico in southern Sonora and Baja California. It has smooth, rounded leaves, blue 0.5-in. (1.3-cm) flowers, and bright red fruit.

Lycium brevipes is a much branched, spiny shrub found in Mexico in Baja California and Sinaloa with scattered populations in southern California and its desert islands. Plants range from 3 to 12 ft. (0.9 to 3.7 m) tall. Flowers are white to lilac. The elliptic to spatulate leaves are fleshy and covered with fine hairs. Flowering is from February to April and is followed by bright red fruit.

Lycium exsertum is an open, more or less

Lycium (wolfberry)

unarmed shrub found in south and western Arizona below 4000 ft. (1219 m) as well as in Mexico in Baja California, Sonora, and northern Sinaloa. It is an attractive species with prolific lavender to dark blue flowers that hang down. This species blooms in January and February. Flowers are followed by abundant red fruit. The light green leaves are covered with fine hairs. Plants grow up to 8 ft. (2.4 m) tall and are hardy to 10°F (−12.2°C).

Lycium fremontii is a compact, much-branched shrub that ranges from southern California through western and southern Arizona as well as in Mexico in Baja California and Sonora below 2500 ft. (762 m). The purple or white flowers are more upright than in the previous species, and the red fruit is so prolific that even from a distance the shrub looks like it is red stemmed. The leaves are light green and succulent.

Wolfberry makes a wonderful addition to the garden where attracting wildlife is desired. Birds are wild for the plant's fruit, and hummingbirds swarm to the flowers. In nature, this plant is often one of the earliest flowering food plants for hummingbirds and they crowd around it while it is in bloom.

Wolfberry is an effortless shrub to grow in the hottest deserts. It is fully at home in rocky, dry, alkaline soils. Even in the hottest deserts it does well on natural rainfall. But monthly soaks in the summer prevent complete leaf loss, and in some species induces a second flowering in the late summer. Good drainage is essential, and watering consistently shortens the life of the plants, making them soft and sloppy.

Use any of these *Lycium* species in a native or naturalistic planting or where watering is intermittent or irregular. The shrub makes an excellent dense, screening hedge, either alone or mixed with other woody species.

Lysiloma candidum
Palo blanco

FAMILY: Fabaceae.
DISTRIBUTION: In Mexico endemic to central and southern Baja California.

MATURE SIZE: Upright, few-branched tree 10 to 35 ft. (9.2 to 10.7 m) tall with crown spread of 15 to 20 ft. (4.6 to 6.1 m).
BLOOMING PERIOD: March to May.
EXPOSURE: Full sun in all areas.
HARDINESS: Hardy to 25°F (−3.9°C), with minor tip damage at 23°F (−5.0°C), but young plants may be severely damaged or killed at those temperatures.

Palo blanco is a graceful, slender tree with few stems that branch once or twice, giving

Lysiloma candidum (palo blanco)

it a high, open, vase-shaped form. The bark is pale, almost white, and flakes off as the plant ages.

The gray-green leaves are 2 to 5.5 in. (5.1 to 14 cm) long and pinnately compound. They are composed of 2 to 3 pairs of pinnae, and the leaflets are oblong to ovate with 5 to 17 per pinna.

The flowers are held in rounded heads with the puffball appearance of many legumes. They are creamy white and followed by reddish-brown pods 5 in. (12.7 cm) long.

For areas with minimal cold, this tree is a stunning choice. The pale bark and upright open shape make it easier to use in smaller gardens that its overall size suggests. It needs excellent drainage, but otherwise it is at home in almost any kind of soil.

Water palo blanco deeply but infrequently through the summer in the hottest deserts. If rainfall is scarce through the winter, water deeply at intervals to maintain good form and health. These are rugged trees; mature plants are able to grow on an extremely lean watering regimen.

Long ago I had a customer who fell in love with this species on a trip to Baja. She begged me for a plant for years. I was happy to grow it for her but at the time, the only tree in the collection of the Desert Botanical Garden had been boxed, held, and replanted to make way for some building improvements. It sulked for two seasons but then bloomed spectacularly and offered up lots of seed. Once there was seed in hand, it was an easy plant to grow. It was a great pleasure to visit her from time to time and see the little seedling mature into a beautiful remembrance of her time in Baja.

Lysiloma watsonii
Fern of the desert, feather bush

FAMILY: Fabaceae.

DISTRIBUTION: In the United States in southern Arizona in limited areas around Tucson at 2800 to 4000 ft. (853 to 1210 m). In Mexico in northern Sonora and northern Sinaloa.

MATURE SIZE: Multibranched, spreading tree 10 to 20 ft. (3 to 6.1 m) tall and spreading as wide.

BLOOMING PERIOD: April and May.

EXPOSURE: Full sun in all areas; filtered shade in the hottest deserts.

HARDINESS: Leaf drop at 25°F (−3.9°C) but severe damage at 20°F (−6.7°C) or lower.

Fern of the desert is a multibranched tree that is difficult to train well into a single-trunked specimen; growing it with two or three main stems is usually preferable. The plants tend to grow in a wide, spreading fashion, making them a good choice for light shade. The bark is dark, almost black when old, and fissured. Plants are late deciduous in the winter, in mild areas only dropping all their leaves as the new ones push them out.

The leaves are twice-pinnately compound and 4 to 6 in. (10.2 to 15.2 cm) long. They are composed of 5 to 10 pairs of pinnae, each of which has numerous pairs of tiny leaflets per pinna. New leaves are bright chartreuse but quickly change to darker green for the rest of the summer.

The flowers are large, rounded heads in the puffball style so common in the family, and are numerous on the tree. They are creamy white and lightly fragrant, and are followed by flat, dark brown pods that are up to 6 in. (15.2 cm) long.

Fern of the desert is a graceful, lacy tree that grows well in almost any well-drained soil and under almost any watering regimen. Plants do best when watered once or twice a month in the summer in the hottest deserts, but live on natural rainfall anywhere with at least 10 in. (254 mm) of rain per year.

This tree is beautiful and rugged but comes with a price. The blooming is profuse and the white puffballs fall from the tree soon after blooming. A month or two later, the pods follow, coating the ground once again. While I love this tree and have one near our main patio, be prepared to deal with the large amount of flowers and pods that fall. It is unwise, therefore, to plant it near a pool. This tree is so lovely and so immune to heat and desert conditions; use it as protection from the western sun on the edge of the patio or garden where the free fall of flowers and fruit won't be an issue.

Fern of the desert looks like the old-fashioned mimosa (*Albizia julibrissin*) in the garden, with its fernlike foliage and low, spreading form. But this species needs much less water and is more at home in alkaline soils and high heat.

This species has undergone a wealth of name changes, with most botanists now settling on *Lysiloma watsonii*. You may still find it offered as *L. thornberi*, *L. watsonii* subsp. *thornberi*, *L. microphylla* var. *thornberi*, or *L. watsonii* var. *thornberi*.

Lysiloma watsonii (fern of the desert)

Malpighia glabra
Barbados cherry

FAMILY: Malpighinaceae.

DISTRIBUTION: In the United States in far southern Texas along the coast and in the lower Rio Grande Valley. Also found in the West Indies and northern South America to at least Surinam.

MATURE SIZE: Dense shrub 3 to 10 ft. (0.9 to 3 m) tall and as wide.

BLOOMING PERIOD: March to October.

EXPOSURE: Full sun to partial shade in all areas.

HARDINESS: Minor leaf damage at 25°F (–3.9°C); reported to be root hardy to 20°F (–6.7°C).

Barbados cherry is a variable shrub that is either upright and densely branched or low and spreading. Plants are semievergreen to deciduous, depending on temperature. In warm winters or tropical areas it grows to a small tree.

The leaves are 3 to 4 in. (7.6 to 10.2 cm) long, smooth, and dark green. They are lanceolate to ovate and have a sharp tip.

The flowers are held in short clusters of three to eight flowers, and these clusters are either terminal or in the leaf axils. The pink to purple flowers are 0.5 in. (1.3 cm) wide and have a distinctive pinwheel shape because the corolla lobes are narrow at the base but inflated and ruffled at the end. Bloom is prolific and recurs through the season in response to rainfall. The small, bright red fruit is edible and is sometimes made into preserves or jelly in its natural range. It is also highly attractive to birds.

Barbados cherry tolerates a wide range of soils from deep clays to rocky, dry soils. It has moderate salt tolerance as well. In the hottest deserts, water Barbados cherry every week or two in the summer, much less often in milder areas. It tolerates less frequent watering, but often sheds its leaves under those conditions.

A tidy, dense shrub, Barbados cherry makes an excellent choice for a small hedge or border and is highly valued for this use throughout its natural range. If pruning is necessary, do it in March or April, well before the high heat of summer.

Most of the plants grown in the region are short, rarely over 4 ft. (1.2 m) tall, and densely branched, with close-set, congested leaves. Although it was originally thought to be a dwarf, it is probably just on the low end of the growth range for the species rather than a true dwarf. The large, more open, treelike forms are not as common in the Southwest, but there is no reason to believe they would not thrive in the region.

Another Barbados cherry, *Malpighia punicifolia*, is the species of commerce and trade and is usually known by its Spanish common name *arceola*. This shrub or small tree has a similar range, although it does not naturally occur in Texas. It is a larger plant, often a small tree, with larger fruit, leaves,

Malpighia glabra (Barbados cherry)

and flowers than *M. glabra* and is considerably less cold hardy.

Maytenus phyllanthoides
Mangle dulce

FAMILY: Celastraceae.

DISTRIBUTION: In the United States found only along the Gulf Coast of far southern Texas and Florida. In Mexico along the Gulf of California in Baja California and Sinaloa and in disjunct populations in Nuevo León, San Luis Potosí, Tamaulipas, Puebla, and Veracruz as well as in the islands of the Caribbean.

MATURE SIZE: Dense, freely branched shrub 8 to 12 ft. (2.4 to 3.7 m) tall and as wide.

Maytenus phyllanthoides (mangle dulce)

BLOOMING PERIOD: April to November.

EXPOSURE: Full sun in most areas, filtered shade in the hottest deserts.

HARDINESS: Hardy to 15°F (–9.4°C).

Mangle dulce is a rounded shrub with unarmed, brittle branches that run at odd and irregular angles through the shrub. In nature plants form colonies or thickets from root suckers. This evergreen shrub has light gray bark.

The thick, nearly succulent leaves are 1 to 2.5 in. (2.5 to 6.4 cm) long, smooth, leathery, and light green. They are alternate, and round at the tip, but taper toward the base.

The pale, yellow-green flowers are small and unremarkable and are either solitary or in small axillary clusters. The fruit is bright red and showy and much loved by wildlife.

Mangle dulce resembles a green jojoba (*Simmondsia chinensis*) on first glance, but closer examination reveals that this species has alternate rather than opposite leaves. The leaves in this species are distinctly round at the tip while jojoba leaves form a sharp point, and when present the bright red fruit is unmistakable.

Mangle dulce has great heat tolerance but does best in deep, loose soils rather than the hard, rocky soils of some parts of the region. Once established, it is extremely drought tolerant although monthly watering is advised in the hottest deserts. It is extremely tolerant of salty soils, which is consistent with its maritime distribution.

Mangle dulce makes a great choice where a large, evergreen shrub is desired and when watering is intermittent or heat is intense. It is greener than jojoba if you want that look and provides a smooth backdrop for more colorful plantings. Mangle dulce forms an excellent large hedge either alone or mixed with other desert shrubs. It is also a good choice to screen all or part of a garden or to define a small space.

There is a lot of taxonomic controversy about this species. The name *Maytenus phyllanthoides* is currently accepted for the species in all parts of its odd and disjointed distribution. Some authors, however, believe that the populations in Texas and perhaps those in Florida are a separate species although the differences between them are slight.

Mimosa dysocarpa
Velvet pod mimosa

FAMILY: Fabaceae.

DISTRIBUTION: In the United States in the mountains of far southern Arizona, southern New Mexico, and western Texas at 2500 to 6500 ft. (762 to 1981 m). In Mexico from Sonora and Chihuahua into northwest Coahuila and eastern Durango at similar elevations.

MATURE SIZE: Intricately branched shrub 3 to 6 ft. (0.9 to 1.8 m) tall and 2 to 4 ft. (0.6 to 1.2 m) wide.

BLOOMING PERIOD: May to September.

EXPOSURE: Full sun, although it tolerates light shade in the hottest deserts.

HARDINESS: Hardy to 10°F (−12.2°C).

Velvet pod mimosa is a deciduous, branched shrub with tan to pale reddish-brown bark. The sturdy stems are erratically and intricately branched and are covered with fine hairs and numerous, flattened, curved thorns.

The leaves are up to 2 to 4 in. (5.1 to 10.2 cm) long and are bipinnately compound. They are composed of 5 to 12 pairs of pinnae, each of which has 6 to 16 pairs of leaflets. Leaves are dusky-green and have fine hairs on both the upper and undersides.

The flowers are crowded into spikes 1 to 2 in. (2.5 to 5.1 cm) long and are pink to purple-pink. They are followed by 2.5 in. (6.4 cm) pods that are deeply constricted between the seeds and when mature are covered with fine reddish-brown hairs that are the source of the common name.

This loosely branched, open shrub is a delight through the summer with its lovely spikes of delicate flowers. In most of the region it tolerates extreme heat, although

Mimosa dysocarpa (velvet pod mimosa)

in the hottest deserts does not do well with reflective heat.

Velvet pod mimosa grows well in rocky, alkaline soils as well as in any other well-drained soil. Watering varies across the region. In the hottest zones, water deeply once or twice a month. In the rest of the region, water only during long dry spells or when temperatures are unusually high.

Mimosa dysocarpa var. *wrightii* has smoother leaves, pods that are narrower, and is somewhat less thorny, but there is a great deal of intergrade between the two.

A few other members of the genus show up in the trade from time to time but are not common. *Mimosa pigra* is a thickly armed shrub 2 to 6 ft. (0.6 to 1.8 m) tall with showy, white curved thorns. Despite it wicked thorns, this species has lovely spikes of pink flowers up to 2 in. (5.1 cm) long from March to November.

Mimosa aculeaticarpa var. *biuncifera* (syn. *M. biuncifera*) is a rounded shrub 3 to 10 ft. (0.9 to 3 m) tall that goes by the appropriate common name, wait-a-minute bush. The leaves of this species are dusky gray-green. The white or cream flowers are held in small, rounded heads that are up to 1 in. (2.5 cm) wide. This shrub has a complicated zigzag branching pattern, making it nearly impenetrable when well grown.

Fragrant mimosa (*Mimosa borealis*) has light pink, delicately fragrant, round heads of flowers that are 0.5 in. (1.3 cm) wide. This species is the most cold hardy of these mimosas, hardy to 5°F (−15.0°C). The thin stems have spines they are not as close together on the stem as in the others mentioned here. This is a short, although woody, shrub growing 2 to 3 ft. (0.6 to 0.9 m) tall and up to 4 ft. (1.5 m) wide.

Myrtus communis
Common myrtle

FAMILY: Myrtaceae.

DISTRIBUTION: Possibly has its origins in Iran and Afghanistan, but has been in cultivation for centuries throughout the Mediterranean region, so its exact native distribution is in doubt.

MATURE SIZE: Spreading tree or large shrub 12 to 15 ft. (3.7 to 4.6 m) tall and spreading as wide.

BLOOMING PERIOD: July and August.

EXPOSURE: Full sun in all areas, although prefers filtered shade in the hottest deserts.

HARDINESS: Hardy to 20°F (−6.7°C).

Common myrtle is a slow, deliberate shrub to small tree that at maturity has twisted and angular branching. The bark is smooth and gray when young, but ages to a light brown and eventually becomes papery and shreds, revealing the light tan bark beneath.

The evergreen leaves are 2 in. (5.1 cm) long, deep green, glossy, and densely clustered, usually overlapping, up the stem. They are sharply pointed at both ends and have a sharp astringent scent that is refreshing.

The flowers are less than 1 in. (2.5 cm) wide with creamy white lobes and long, clustered, white stamens. They are sweetly fragrant and arise in the axils of the leaves. The flowers are followed by tiny, blue berries that are edible but not all that tasty.

Common myrtle is an ancient ornamental grown around the Mediterranean for centuries, and there are numerous varieties. One with white-edged leaves is often called 'Variegata'; 'Compacta' is smaller than the type at 2 to 3 ft. (0.6 to 0.9 m) tall; and 'Microphylla', also small, grows to 3 ft. (0.9 m) tall with tiny, dense, overlapping leaves. Far and away the most interesting looking and commonly grown form is known as 'Boetica', which has angular, twisted stems and grows up to a large size.

Common myrtle grows well in any well-drained soil; rocky soils are excellent. It develops chlorosis quickly in poorly drained soils or if watering is shallow and frequent. It is much better to give it long, deep soaks at long intervals, monthly in the hottest deserts in the summer. It is highly resistant to cotton root rot where that is a problem.

Myrtus communis (common myrtle)

Common myrtle, and especially the 'Boetica' form, is a stunning accent or focal plant. Use it where the complicated branching can be featured. It is heat tolerant enough to be useful around pools and other locations with high, reflective heat. Left unpruned it becomes a dense barrier plant, hedge, or boundary planting; use either alone or mixed with other shrubs.

Nerium oleander
Oleander

FAMILY: Apocynaceae.

DISTRIBUTION: Native to Iran and Afghanistan and into India, but cultivated for so long in the Mediterranean region that its exact native distribution is hazy.

MATURE SIZE: Many-branched, dense shrub 4 to 16 ft. (1.2 to 4.9 m) tall, depending on variety and conditions, and 2 to 10 ft. (0.6 to 3 m) wide.

BLOOMING PERIOD: May to October.

EXPOSURE: Full sun in all areas.

HARDINESS: Variable, with tip damage at 20°F (−6.7°C) in some varieties and severe damage or death in others at this temperature.

Oleander is a densely branched, evergreen shrub whose stems arise from near the base and are straight, slender, upright, and sturdy. Old stems become woody and hard at the base. The bark is light green when young and ages to dark gray or brown.

The leaves are deep green, linear, and 3 to 6 in. (7.6 to 15.2 cm) long. They are marked by a yellowish midvein and the margin is smooth. Leaves are alternate or opposite on the stem and densely packed for the entire length of the stem.

The flowers are in terminal clusters that are 1.5 to 3 in. (3.8 to 7.6 cm) across. Oleander flowers are distinctive with five, usually free or at least partially free, corolla lobes with a set of fine appendages at their base that form a crown inside the flower. The shape, size, and overall appearance of this crown vary widely and are often used to distinguish varieties. Flowers may be single or double, with widely separated corolla lobes or overlapping lobes. Flowers may entirely without scent or have a lovely, spicy, sweet fragrance.

The fruit is a long pod that turns tan as it matures. Many varieties are sterile, while others make copious amounts of seed.

Oleander has been cultivated for ages. There are oleander images in the frescoes in the ruins of Pompeii and other sites through-out the Mediterranean, indicating at least 2000 years of cultivation. It is assuredly one of the two or three most heat- and drought-tolerant shrubs in the region, rivaling creo-sote (*Larrea tridentata*) for its incredible endurance to minimal water and maximum heat.

Oleander has often been used in locations with a combination of much more water than required and much less room than it fits, and has therefore achieved a reputation as a mon-strous thug, the hallmark of high-water-use gardens, and a pariah to any right-thinking desert gardeners. All that is a shame, because this beautiful summer-flowering shrub grows and blooms beautifully on natural rainfall in the hottest deserts, and there aren't too many shrubs that make that claim.

Nerium oleander (oleander)

Often used as a hedge, oleander also makes an excellent solitary plant to fill a corner of the garden or provide a focal point. The size and colors of the named varieties are almost endless.

The most commonly grown oleanders in the region are the big, generous-flowering, white 'Sister Agnes'; large reds that have a wide array of names including 'Big Red', 'Tahitian Red', 'Algiers', and 'Casablanca'; as well as numerous pink, yellow, gold, and bicolor forms, and dozens of variations and shades of these colors.

Dwarf forms became available a number of years ago, and most of them are much more cold tender than the taller varieties, particularly 'Dwarf Pink' and 'Dwarf Salmon'. But 'Marrakesh', a stunning red dwarf, is fully hardy and an excellent choice for the region.

Oleanders, particularly the dwarfs that are only up to 6 ft. (1.8 m) tall, make excellent container plants. They tolerate the great soil heat and crowded root conditions of containers extremely well.

The disease known as oleander leaf scorch has been ravaging plants, particularly older plants, first in California and now in isolated parts of the Phoenix metropolitan area. Vectored by a small, sharpshooter insect, the bacteria known as *Xylella fastidiosa* kills the plants it infects. They look as if they have been burned, with all the leaves turning brown, seemingly overnight, but hanging on the plant. At present there is no known cure or even good prevention.

Pruning oleanders is a major undertaking. Because all parts of the plant are poisonous, including the smoke from burning them, use eye protection, gloves, and long-sleeved shirts when pruning. Tip pruning in the summer is a good way to keep a plant tidy, without waiting until pruning is a huge undertaking. But oleanders have a wonderful natural form and rarely need all the pruning they get.

Old plants may have a barren interior due to leaf die out from lack of light. To prevent this, give plants a light tip prune every year or two. Correcting bad growth after years of neglect is a daunting, difficult task that usually requires shearing the plant back significantly and allowing new stems to grow up from the base.

Oleanders are an excellent barrier plant. In many neighborhoods they are appreciated for their ability to substantially reduce noise and dust from busy streets.

Olea europaea
Olive

FAMILY: Oleaceae.
DISTRIBUTION: From the Mediterranean, but in cultivation for so long that its exact origins are uncertain, although North Africa and the eastern Mediterranean are most likely.
MATURE SIZE: A contorted multibranched tree 20 to 30 ft. (6.1 to 9.1 m) tall and as wide.
BLOOMING PERIOD: April and May.
EXPOSURE: Full sun in all areas.
HARDINESS: Hardy to 15°F (–9°C).

Olive is a shrubby tree that slowly grows into a gray-barked, twisted tree of striking character. The base of the tree tends to spread out with age and often sprouts countless small stems. Old trees are magnificent, with contorted limbs and pocked or fissured bark.

Trees are so distinctively shaped that individuals can be easily recognized. Olive is a long-lived plant. Individuals have been documented to be up to 1000 years old, and trees commonly live many hundreds of years.

The stiff, opposite leaves are gray-green above and lighter green or silvery below. They are more or less elliptical with a strong tip and are up to 2 to 3 in. (5.1 to 7.6 cm) long.

The flowers are small, creamy white or yellowish, and occur in the axils of the leaves. Their pollen carries a potent allergen for many people, and therefore some cities in the west have banned their use. The renowned fruit is 1.5 in. (3.8 cm) long; it begins green but turns blue-black in the fall when it is ripe.

This tree is one of many Mediterranean species that have been in cultivation for so long that their true origins are uncertain. Olive is known to have been cultivated over 5000 years ago in Crete and Syria, and some speculate that olive may have first been cultivated in North Africa in present-day Morocco, Algiers, and Tunisia. Olive's uses and cultivation spread over the Mediterranean region through the centuries. By the time written records became available, olive had been long in use both medicinally and for food and oil and was a commodity in some countries. While the modern olive tree's botanical ancestor is not clear, many botanists propose oleaster (*Olea sylvestris*), which still grows wild in North Africa, Portugal, Southern France, Italy, and areas around the Black and Caspian Seas. The entire cultural and cultivation history of olive is fascinating.

Olives were grown in various parts of the Southwest, in southern California, and in the Salt River Valley near Phoenix since the late nineteenth and early twentieth centuries. Relicts of those groves still exist in old neighborhoods in Phoenix.

Olive grows in any well-drained soil although it does best in deep soils rather than rocky ones, and it prefers cool nights where freezing temperatures are infrequent. These conditions are necessary for fruit production, although olive does grow in a much wider array of climatic conditions. In congenial areas, fruit production can be prodigious.

Olea europaea (olive)

'Swan Hill' and 'Wilson's Fruitless' set almost no pollen and therefore no fruit. This characteristic has the twin advantage of reducing the allergenic agents and the voluminous, often messy fruit.

The suckering at the base of olive trees causes problems for many gardeners. There is a longstanding custom of removing these suckers by pulling them off rather than cutting them off. This practice is thought to kill the latent buds so new stems do not grow. Otherwise, prune your olive tree carefully to preserve its natural form and intriguing character.

Water olive thoroughly every three to four weeks in the summer and less often in the winter in the hottest deserts. Olive does not tolerate saline soils well and is susceptible to cotton root rot.

Parkinsonia aculeata

Mexican palo verde, retama, Jerusalem thorn

FAMILY: Fabaceae.

DISTRIBUTION: Native distribution of this species is debated. It grows naturally in south and western Texas, in some areas of southern Arizona, and far into Mexico and South America. Whether this reflects its true native distribution or its ease in naturalizing is not well understood. It is found in these areas below 4000 ft. (1219 m). It is likely that the species is native to Central America and southern Mexico, but it has been cultivated widely for so long it is hard to be sure.

MATURE SIZE: Tall, erect, often erratically branched tree 15 to 40 ft. (4.6 to 12.2 m) tall and spreading as wide.

BLOOMING PERIOD: April to September.

EXPOSURE: Full sun in all areas.

HARDINESS: Hardy to 15°F (−9.4°C).

Mexican palo verde is a deciduous, tall, oddly branched tree. The branches tend to cross often and go in divergent, twisting directions. It is also prone to growing dozens of short, secondary shoots along the main branches. The bark is green to begin but quickly turns brown and scaly.

The bipinnately compound leaves are 8 to 16 in. (20.3 to 40.6 cm) long with 1 or 2 pairs of pinna. There are 25 to 30 pairs of leaflets per pinna. It is common for the leaflets to fall but the long rachis is persistent, so the tree looks like it is still in leaf. The rachis is

Parkinsonia aculeata (Mexican palo verde)

winged and ends in a thorny tip that is 0.5 to 1 in. (1.3 to 2.5 cm) long. Leaflets are linear and less than 0.25 in. (0.6 cm) long.

The bright yellow flowers are held in axillary clusters 5 to 6 in. (12.7 to 15.2 cm) across. One of the corolla lobes is larger than the rest and is usually red or orange.

The narrow pods are 2 to 5 in. (5.1 to 12.7 cm) long and are light brown to reddish. They are deeply constricted between the seeds.

Mexican palo verde grows in almost any soil, but prefers deep, moderately fertile, well-drained ones. It grows extraordinarily fast with ample water, but is capable of growing on natural rainfall even in the hottest deserts.

This weedy species should be approached with caution by all gardeners. There was one in my garden when I moved in and it was lost in a storm over 15 years ago. Be warned: to this day, I still pull its seedlings out of beds in the vicinity. But the long rachis is like pine straw and can be used as a mulch.

Mexican palo verde has reached its best use in the region through a number of excellent hybrids. The most well-known hybrid is 'Desert Museum', which is a three-way hybrid among this species, *Parkinsonia microphylla*, and *P. florida*. This lovely plant has ascending, spreading branches and rich yellow bloom that is brighter than most of the other palo verde. It tends to bloom for a longer time than the others and is as hardy as Mexican palo verde.

Mexican palo verde's aggressive reseeding makes it a poor choice in gardens that are adjacent to or near parks, natural areas, or preserves. All members of the genus hybridize freely when in close contact, so they can become pests on their own and also have the potential to overcome the natural reseeding of native species. All gardeners who live near natural areas need to be aware of this because these species are closely related, and one tree can have a powerful impact on the seedlings of the wash or hillside right outside your home. In those circumstances, it is best to refrain from planting any palo verde other than the native one right outside your door.

When used well within the urban core, this is a quick-growing shade tree. Its long season of bloom with bright yellow flowers against the light green bark and leaves is stunning in the right spot.

Parkinsonia florida
Blue palo verde

SYNONYM: *Cercidium floridum*.
FAMILY: Fabaceae.
DISTRIBUTION: In the United States in far southern California and throughout southern Arizona below 3500 ft. (1067 m). In Mexico in the Sonoran Desert parts of Baja California, Sonora, and northern Sinaloa at the same elevations.
MATURE SIZE: Upright, spreading tree 15 to 25 ft. (4.6 to 7.6 m) tall with as much spread.
BLOOMING PERIOD: March to April.
EXPOSURE: Full sun in all areas.
HARDINESS: Hardy to 15°F (−9.4°C).

Blue palo verde is a tall, spreading tree with a few sturdy branches. The bark, especially when young, is green but quickly turns brown and woody as it ages, with deep fissures, pits, and rings.

The leaves are 1.5 in. (3.8 cm) long and are bipinnately compound with one or two pinnae, each of which has three to four pairs of leaflets. The leaflets are obovate and just over 0.25 in. (0.6 cm) long with a blue-green color.

Flowers are bright, clear yellow and are 0.75 in. (2 cm) wide. They are prolific on the plant, smothering the leaves; the plant looks like it turned bright yellow overnight.

The pods are flat, linear, and 3 to 4 in. (7.6 to 10.2 cm) long. They have two to eight seeds per pod, and the pod is only slightly constricted between the seeds. There are usually innumerable pods.

Found in nature in washes and drainages, blue palo verde tolerates consistent water in the garden. It is not a long-lived tree, particularly in the garden, with documented life spans of up to 40 years.

In the hottest deserts, where it is used extensively as an ornamental, it is immune to heat and drought, although it loses nearly all its leaves when soils are dry. Blue palo verde grows well on natural rainfall, but suffers less stem loss when given long, deep soaks once or twice over the summer. Although it accepts growing in a lawn, it becomes immense under those circumstances and will have a shorter life.

All members of this genus hybridize freely when grown together, and numerous individuals in the trade are hybrid forms, whether intended or not. Most of them are exquisite, and in the garden it hardly matters.

Blue palo verde is a splendid, spreading, shade tree in any desert garden. It offers the high, light shade that is favored by all desert species, including succulents. In a native or naturalistic garden, it brings a strong flavor of the natural desert, and its extraordinary spring bloom makes a stunning statement.

The closely related Texas palo verde (*Parkinsonia texana*) is a smaller tree, rarely over

Parkinsonia florida (blue palo verde)

25 ft. (7.6 m) tall. It looks similar to this species, with blue-green leaflets and green bark, but plants bloom from March to November, particularly in response to rainfall.

Parkinsonia microphylla
Little-leaf palo verde, foothills palo verde

SYNONYM: *Cercidium microphyllum*.
FAMILY: Fabaceae.
DISTRIBUTION: In the United States in southern and western Arizona and southeastern California below 4000 ft. (1219 m). In Mexico in Baja California, Sonora, and Sinaloa at similar elevations.
MATURE SIZE: Multibranched shrub or tree 10 to 20 ft. (3 to 6.1 m) tall and spreading as wide.

BLOOMING PERIOD: April and May.
EXPOSURE: Full sun in all areas.
HARDINESS: Hardy to 15°F (−9.4°C).

Little-leaf palo verde has complicated, criss-crossing branches and rarely shows a clear, central leader. Most branches end in a short thorn up to 2 in. (5.1 cm) long. Short spur branches also end in a thorn. Branches form low on the plant, making it more a huge shrub than a spreading tree. Old trees are sometimes tall enough to serve as shade trees but the shrubbier form is much more common. The bark is thin and pale green, but as it ages it turns deep brown and furrows, ridges, and pits emerge. It is deciduous most of the year.

The leaves are bipinnately compound with two to four pinnae. Each pinna holds four to seven pairs of the elliptic, widely spaced leaflets, each of which is so small you almost need a hand lens to see them. They look more like dots on the rachis than leaves.

The butter yellow flowers are held in short, axillary clusters and on close examination each has a red mark on the lower corolla lobes. The flowers are profuse on the plant but each is less than 0.5 in. (1.3 cm) wide.

The pods are 1.5 to 3 in. (3.8 to 7.6 cm) long and are deeply constricted between the one to four seeds. The pod has a long tail at the tip of the pod. They begin bright pea-green but age to light tan.

Little-leaf palo verde is common on the dry hills of southern Arizona. You hardly notice how many there are until the hills erupt during their creamy yellow bloom. During the spring there is a progression of bloom in the different palo verde species, with the blue palo verde (*Parkinsonia florida*) beginning the parade, followed by this species, and finally ending with the extraordinary palo brea (*Parkinsonia praecox*) bloom.

Little-leaf palo verde is extremely heat- and drought-tolerant. Even in nature, this palo verde is found on dry hillsides rather than along the washes of the desert. Once established, plants grow best and most vigorously with long, deep soaks every month or two in the summer and once or twice through the winter. This species does not grow as quickly as the others, but it is steady and deliberate. In nature plants are extraordinarily long-lived, but there is little known about their life span in the garden.

Use little-leaf palo verde as a large shrub along a border or anywhere where irrigation is not available. The pods are edible and delicious when lightly steamed. Birds and other

Parkinsonia microphylla (little-leaf palo verde)

wildlife are dependent on its flowers and fruit for food. Little-leaf palo verde creates a beautiful light green backdrop for plantings of desert annuals or perennials. It has great presence in the garden even when it is not coated with its lovely flowers.

Pruning is both difficult and rarely necessary. It is hard to train this plant into a spreading tree without ruining the form, and therefore it is much better to let it be what it is. You may remove any of the small, spur branches, however, to reveal more of the bark in the spring. As for all palo verde trees, never prune this plant in the winter or during a cold spell; they do not recover well from pruning then.

Parkinsonia praecox
Palo brea

SYNONYM: *Cercidium praecox.*
FAMILY: Fabaceae.
DISTRIBUTION: In Mexico in Baja California and Sonora, south to Venezuela and Peru from sea level to 2500 ft. (762 m).
MATURE SIZE: Low-branched tree 15 to 30 ft. (4.6 to 9.1 m) tall and spreading up to 35 ft. (10.7 m) wide.
BLOOMING PERIOD: April.
EXPOSURE: Full sun in all areas.
HARDINESS: Loses leaves at 24°F (−4.4°C); at 20°F (−6.7°C) suffers significant tip damage and young trees may be killed.

Palo brea is a heavy-trunked, widely spreading tree with light green bark that is so smooth it looks painted on. Plants are deciduous, holding leaves only when soil moisture is high.

The leaves are 1 in. (2.5 cm) long and bipin-

nately compound with one or two pairs of pinnae, each of which has four to nine pairs of leaflets. The leaflets are dark dusky-green, up to 0.5 in. (1.3 cm) long, and are therefore both larger and fewer than those of the other commonly grown palo verdes. The leaflets are 0.5 in. (1.3 cm) long.

The flowers are profuse on the plant in short axillary clusters. They are bright yellow,

Parkinsonia praecox (palo brea)

0.75 in. (1.8 cm) wide, with red dots at the base on close examination. They are the latest of the three common palo verdes to bloom in the spring. The flowers are so bright and intensely yellow that the plant appears to ignite. Flowers are followed by oblong, flat pods that are 1.5 to 2.5 in. (3.8 to 6.4 cm) long.

This tree is exquisite with a wide-spreading crown that makes it useful in larger gardens where light shade is needed. The remarkable, smooth green bark turns darker brown and woody with small fissures as the stem ages. This darkening and formation of woody lesions and fissures is a common trait in all palo verdes, but is less prominent in this species.

Palo brea grows in any well-drained soil. It thrives on as little as 5 in. (127 mm) of rain a year, but plants are more vigorous if grown with monthly summer watering in the hottest deserts. Some authors describe the plant as short-lived, 25 years or so, but that may be an artifact of cultivation, where plants are grown too fast with too much water.

Palo brea is the least cold-tolerant of the palo verdes of commerce, and for many years was considered too tender to grow in many parts of the region. Young trees are quite sensitive, but as they age they become hardier and recover better.

Pruning must be done carefully to retain the spread and character of the few main branches. Young plants often have long, juvenile stems that turn toward the ground, and those need to be removed regularly. It is also good practice to keep the interior free of crossing branches. Prune in the late spring or late summer, but take care not to expose the thin bark to western sun. If exposure to the western sun as a result of pruning is unavoid-able, either protect the tree with shade or prune it much earlier in the year.

There are two recognized subspecies. *Parkinsonia praecox* subsp. *praecox* comes from Sonora and Baja California and is the common one in horticulture in the region. Subsp. *glaucum* is the South American form; while it is more cold hardy, it also tends to be winter deciduous. This subspecies is not routinely available in the trade in our region.

Phoenix canariensis
Canary Island date palm

FAMILY: Arecaceae.

DISTRIBUTION: The Canary Islands.

MATURE SIZE: Solitary, thick-trunked plant 40 to 60 ft. (12.2 to 18 m) tall with a crown spread of up to 30 ft. (9.1 m).

BLOOMING PERIOD: Summer.

EXPOSURE: Full sun in all areas.

HARDINESS: Leaves are damaged at 20°F (−6.7°C), but mature plants recover quickly.

Canary Island date palm is a tall, solitary palm with a dark brown, thick trunk that is marked by prominent leaf scars. These scars are like stubs and form incomplete circles around the trunk. Near the base, plants often form a collection of old roots and growing buds that is called a boss.

The pinnately compound leaves are enormous, 10 to 20 ft. (3 to 6.1 m) long, and 50 to 100 leaves per plant are more or less stiffly held from the stem. The leaflets are 1.5 ft. (0.5 m) long and there are hundreds of them per leaf. They are dark green, deeply guttered, and stiff; the lower ones are reduced to hefty spines.

Plants are dioecious with yellowish flowers on orange-flowering stalks 3 to 4 ft. (0.9 to 1.2 m) long. Fruit is brownish orange, and while it is edible it doesn't taste good.

Canary Island date palm grows quickly, particularly with ample water, to reach its mature size. It has a wide tolerance for soils but does best in moderately enriched, well-drained soils. It is highly intolerant of poorly drained soils.

This palm does best with regular, deep irrigation and needs to be watered two or three times a month in the summer in the hottest deserts. While it tolerates some drying out of the soil, it is best not to let that get extreme.

A gorgeous and commanding palm, it is so large that it is best used only where the enormous head can be accommodated. It is always sad to see young ones put near the house or next to the front door, because it won't be long before that great trunk begins to rise and takes out whatever is in its way. Use Canary Island date palm where its commanding size is an advantage, in large gardens that need some light shade, to frame a distant view, or in public plantings.

Phoenix canariensis (Canary Island date palm)

Phoenix dactylifera
Date palm

FAMILY: Arecaceae.

DISTRIBUTION: Cultivated throughout the world, but its origins are believed to be in North Africa.

MATURE SIZE: Solitary or clustering palm 40 to 80 ft. (12.2 to 24.4 m) tall and spreading 15 to 25 ft. (4.6 to 7.6 m) wide.

BLOOMING PERIOD: Summer.

EXPOSURE: Full sun in all areas.

HARDINESS: Hardy to 20°F (−6.7°C).

Date palms are tall, towering plants with slender trunks marked with the relicts of old leaves for most of their height. They are often erect, solitary plants but many individuals also produce a copious number of offsets at the base. These offsets commonly occur when plants are under cultivation or production.

The leaves are pinnately compound with the lower pinnae reduced to spines along the petiole, which is typical of the genus. There are 20 to 100 leaves on each head 15 to 20 ft. (4.6 to 6.1 m) long with up to 240 leaflets on

Phoenix dactylifera (date palm)

As an ornamental plant, date palm is unrivaled for its regal beauty and endurance of hot, dry conditions. Fruit sets only in hot climates; date palms have been imported all over the hot parts of the world for commercial production. The Spanish brought them to their missions in Baja California as they moved up the peninsula. Many of these old groves or their progeny still survive, some with modest commercial production. There was a small date industry in the Phoenix area about 100 years ago. A grove of date palms established from seedlings in 1891 at the Saguaro Ranch in Glendale, Arizona, just west of Phoenix are recorded to have begun production in 1897. Many of those plants are still standing in the park now on the site of the ranch.

Date palms are an excellent choice for high, light shade, particularly when planted in groups or groves. If the falling fruit is a problem, the flowering stalk may be removed anytime after it emerges before the fruit sets.

each leaf. Leaflets are dusky gray-green, firm, guttered, and up to 2 ft. (0.3 to 0.6 m) long and 1 in. (2.5 cm) wide.

Plants are dioecious, with female flowers held on a flowering stalk 4 ft. (1.2 m) long. Following flowering, copious amounts of oval fruit appear that are 1 to 2 in. (2.5 to 5.1 cm) long, yellow or orange, and hanging in tight clusters. Fruit ripens from August to October.

Date palms are the oldest known desert species in cultivation. They have been feeding desert peoples in Africa and the Middle East for at least 5000 years. As a consequence the exact origins of the palm have become obscured. There are hundreds of varieties chiefly based on fruit characteristics.

Phoenix reclinata
Senegal date palm

FAMILY: Arecaceae.

DISTRIBUTION: Eastern Africa and Madagascar.

MATURE SIZE: Multitrunked palm 10 to 30 ft. (3 to 9.1 m) tall and up to 25 ft. (7.6 m) wide.

BLOOMING PERIOD: August to October.

EXPOSURE: Full sun in all areas, although it does well in light, filtered shade in the hottest deserts.

HARDINESS: Hardy to 25°F (−3.9°C).

Senegal date palm is a multitrunked palm that may be pruned to maintain only a few trunks or even one trunk. Stems tend to lean and curve gracefully and are covered in fine, brown fibers.

The leaves are pinnately compound and 4 to 13 ft. (1.2 to 4 m) long, with the lowest pinnae reduced to spines. Leaves curve and fall toward the ground in a graceful reverse arch. There are 25 to 40 leaves per stem and the petiole is up to 4 ft. (1.2 m) long. Each leaf has 200 to 260 leaflets that are firm, shiny, and deep green, with a decided gutter down the middle.

Plants are dioecious, with male and female flowers on separate plants. The orange flowering stalks are up to 3 ft. (0.9 m) long and congested with countless, yellowish-white flowers. On female plants flowers are followed by oval, brownish red fruit 0.75 in. (1.8 cm) long.

This graceful palm looks best when it is pruned to leave five or seven stems. This approach keeps the form open and the sinuous curve of the stems prominent. The long, lush leaves make the palm an elegant focal point.

Senegal date palm grows in any well-drained soil and requires summer watering every two to three weeks in the hottest deserts. If you are trying to maintain only a few stems, emerging small stems need to be removed every year or two. Senegal date palm hybridizes freely with other members of the genus, and many of the plants offered are actually hybrids. They look much like the type but usually have thicker trunks and sturdier leaves. Hybrids also tend to be hardy to 22°F (−5.6°C).

Senegal date palm is a wonderful focal or accent plant in gardens large enough to accommodate it. It gives a lush, tropical look to a patio or seating area without requiring much water. Its high heat tolerance makes it

Phoenix reclinata (Senegal date palm)

useful around pools or other areas of reflective heat.

Phoenix roebelenii
Pygmy date palm

FAMILY: Arecaceae.

DISTRIBUTION: From Laos, Vietnam, and south China.

MATURE SIZE: Solitary palm 8 to 10 ft. (2.4 to 3 m) tall and 4 to 5 ft. (1.2 to 1.5 m) wide.

BLOOMING PERIOD: April to June.

EXPOSURE: Full sun in all but the hottest deserts, where it grows in full sun only if soil and water conditions are ideal; otherwise grow in light or filtered shade.

HARDINESS: Hardy to 28°F (−2.2°C); severely damaged or killed at 23°F (−5.0°C) or lower.

Pygmy date palm is most commonly a solitary plant, although clustering individuals are known to occur. Plants show persistent leaf bases that are filled with copious amounts of coarse, black fibers. Trunks are thin, deep brown to almost black. Trunks in young plants are straight and upright, but in older ones often turn and curve.

The leaves are pinnately compound and 2 to 5 ft. (0.6 to 1.5 m) long with up to 100 dark green leaflets. There are 20 to 30 leaves per plant.

The flowering stalk is short, only 1.5 ft. (0.5 m) long, and is enclosed by a large, almost woody, brown bract. Both the bract and the spent flowering stalk are long persistent. Plants are dioecious.

Despite its delicate appearance, pygmy date palm is well suited to gardens in the arid regions of the country. It does best in enriched, well-drained soils but also grows well in rocky soils if there is ample water. In the hottest deserts, it needs to be watered weekly to keep plants fit, but in milder areas it tolerates less-frequent watering. As for most palms, water only once a month or less in the coldest part of the winter.

Pygmy date palm establishes quickly when it is small but it does not move well once it has achieved full size. Transplanting larger plants is rarely successful and takes both excellent timing (cool but not cold weather) and keeping it heavily watered for the first few weeks while it gets reestablished.

Because of this palm's modest size, it is a wonderful choice for small, tight areas like a small courtyard or in a large container and also in groups around a pool or patio. It makes a stunning presentation when planted generously as a grove.

Phoenix roebelenii (pygmy date palm)

Pinus canariensis

Canary Island pine

FAMILY: Pinaceae.
DISTRIBUTION: Canary Islands.
MATURE SIZE: Straight tree 40 to 80 ft. (12.2 to 24 m) tall and spreading 20 to 30 ft. (6.1 to 9.1 m) wide.
EXPOSURE: Full sun in all areas.
HARDINESS: Needles are damaged at 20°F (−6.7°C), and are slowly replaced.

Canary Island pine is a tall, erect tree that has two distinct looks depending on its age.

When young the short branches are widely spaced and the plant has a tiered or layered look. As it matures, it fills out to become a more rounded plant but still with an attractive symmetrical form. The bark is very thick, scaly, fissured, and patterned red-brown and buff.

The needles are 9 to 12 in. (22.9 to 30.5 cm) long and, especially in young plants, hang down slightly at the ends of the branches. Young needles are blue-green but they mature to a dark, rich green. They occur in bundles of three. The oval cones are shiny, a deep rich brown, and 4 to 9 in. (10.2 to 22.9 cm) long.

Canary Island pine grows best in any well-drained soil, including highly alkaline ones. Although this tree is well suited to dry spells, for best form and needle color, provide at least monthly watering in the summer in the hottest deserts. Younger plants grow quickly when watered every two to three weeks in the summer. Elsewhere, once established, the tree needs even less frequent watering.

It has long been a practice to prune out young branches to exaggerate the layered look of this plant. But this is a poor practice because it weakens the tree. It is much better to simply enjoy the excellent, symmetrical form of the plant.

This tree is a tall pole of a plant that is best suited for large gardens or where its strong vertical look is appropriate. It is excellent in groups or mixed with other trees or pines. If you have a place where you can see the silhouette against the skyline, that is the perfect way to enjoy this charming pine.

Pinus canariensis (Canary Island pine)

Pinus eldarica

Afghan pine, mondel pine

FAMILY: Pinaceae.
DISTRIBUTION: Southern Russia, Afghanistan, and Pakistan.
MATURE SIZE: Tall, lean tree 30 to 50 ft. (9.1 to 15.2 m) tall and 15 to 25 ft. (4.6 to 7.6 m) wide.
EXPOSURE: Full sun in all areas.
HARDINESS: Hardy to 5°F (-15°C).

Afghan pine is an upright tree with numerous branches that are more or less the same length up the height of the tree. It has a regular, pyramidal shape.

The needles are medium green and 4 to 6 (10.2 to 15.2 cm) long. They occur in bundles of two. The brown cones are 5 to 6 in. 15.2 cm) long.

ast-growing pine tolerates the heat and alkaline soils of the desert regions

extremely well. It is more tolerant of poor drainage than many other pines. Young plants are more cold sensitive than adults, and once established or mature they have excellent cold tolerance.

Afghan pine is quite drought tolerant but grows somewhat faster and with better form when it gets regular, deep watering, especially in the summer.

Many authors consider this species to be conspecific with *Pinus brutia*, and plants are routinely offered under both names. Afghan pine is one of the species that is widely sold as a tight, pyramidal container plant for living Christmas trees, usually with the name *P. brutia*.

Afghan pine can be distinguished from Aleppo pine (*Pinus halepensis*) by its longer needles and more extensive, regularly spaced branches. Young plants of the two species look very similar. It is distinguished from Canary Islands pine (*P. canariensis*) by its much shorter needles and more closely spaced, longer branches.

This pine is the most regularly formed of the group included here and is beautiful when mature and well grown. It is large, though, so it is best used in gardens that accommodate its mature size. It makes a good shade tree for large areas or to cover walls and roofs. It is also effective for blocking unsightly views or planted in a grove for a soothing, shaded space.

Chir pine (*Pinus roxburghii*) is a less common Asian species of pine that does well in the region. It grows rapidly to 60 ft. (18 m) tall with a full, bushy appearance. The needles are light green, 12 in. (30.5 cm) long, with a slight droop. They occur in bundles of three, and in young plants the needles give the tree

Pinus eldarica (Afghan pine)

a full, lush appearance. The cones are dark brown, usually solitary, and 4 to 7 in. (10.2 to 17.8 cm) long.

Pinus halepensis
Aleppo pine

FAMILY: Pinaceae.

DISTRIBUTION: Found along the Mediterranean Sea from southern Europe to western Asia.

MATURE SIZE: Few-branched pine 30 to 50 ft. (9.1 to 15.2 m) tall and spreading up to 40 ft. (12.2 m) wide.

EXPOSURE: Full sun in all areas.

HARDINESS: Hardy to 15°F (−9.4°C).

Aleppo pine is a fast-growing species that supports a half dozen or fewer large, low-forming branches. The young plants are more or less pyramidal, but later they grow into billowing, round-crowned specimens. The bark is dark reddish brown and deeply fissured.

The needles are held in clusters of two, rarely three, and are light green to yellowish-green. They are 2 to 3 in. (5.1 to 7.6 cm) long. The brown cones are oval to oblong and up to 3 in. (7.6 cm) long.

Aleppo pine is a highly reliable species for dry, rocky, alkaline soils of the hottest deserts. In most parts of the region, it grows well on natural rainfall. But in the hottest deserts

Pinus halepensis (Aleppo pine)

it needs to be watered two to three times a month during the summer. It is also important to provide supplemental water every month or two during the winter in dry years.

In many parts of the Phoenix and Tucson metropolitan areas, this pine has been grown in areas that receive regular, deep, flood irrigation. Under those conditions the plants become towering thunderclouds, immense giants that swamp small urban lots. When grown with much less water, they are tall but rarely so overwhelming.

Although Aleppo pine tolerates a huge range of soils, those with extensive lenses of caliche need to be avoided. Pines have a long, deep, central root, and an interruption or prevention of the growth of this root might debilitate a tree.

Needle drop is common in the spring and may be extreme after a long, dry spell. It is sometimes described as a blight, but it is probably more appropriately considered an environmental condition. After long, dry periods when the soil has virtually dried out, plants drop vast amounts of needles to compensate. Mites are often noted on plants at this time of year and in association with these conditions, but we don't know whether they are the cause of the needle drop or are merely associated with the symptoms. Because this plant grows fast and is large, it may be difficult to manage the watering of a mature specimen, but it will recover well when it gets rain or deep irrigation.

Aleppo pine is best used in large gardens, or in parks and other public places. Its great drought resistance, immunity to heat, and acceptance of almost any soil type make it a great choice where its size can be accommodated.

Aleppo pine has been in cultivation for centuries. The resin of this species was found as an embalming agent throughout Egypt's pharonic tombs. The Greeks had a habit of cutting one tree down annually and decorating it with flowers and ribbons in honor of the dead god Attis. Europeans adopted this practice to honor Christ, and some believe that this may have been the origin of the use of decorated trees at Christmas. This pine and Afghan pine (*Pinus eldarica*) are routinely sold in the Southwest as living Christmas trees.

A related species, stone pine (*Pinus pinea*), is also a tall pine of the Mediterranean region. Young plants of this species are symmetrical pyramids and are difficult to distinguish from Afghan pine and other related species. But with age the plant becomes tall with a straight, dark brown trunk, and the branches are all at the top of the plant, forming a distinctive, deep green, umbrella-shaped crown. The needles are 3 to 7 in. (7.6 to 17.8 cm) long and occur in bundles of two. The cones are 6 in. (15.2 cm) ovals and are full of the edible seed that is the *pignoli* (pine nuts) of southern Europe.

Pistacia lentiscus
Mastic, mastic tree

FAMILY: Anacardiaceae.

DISTRIBUTION: In the Mediterranean parts of France, Spain, Portugal, Greece, Turkey, and North Africa from sea level to 2500 ft. (762 m).

MATURE SIZE: Low-branched tree 15 to 25 ft. (4.6 to 7.6 m) tall and spreading 20 to 30 ft. (6.1 to 9.1 m) wide.

BLOOMING PERIOD: March and April.

EXPOSURE: Full sun in all areas.
HARDINESS: Hardy to 20°F (−6.7°C).

Mastic is a splendid, spreading evergreen tree. The bark is a fine reddish brown when young but ages to dark gray.

The leaves are pinnately compound with three to five pairs of glossy green, elliptic leaflets. Leaflets are up 1 in. (2.5 cm) long and are held on winged petioles.

Both female and male flowers are small, whitish, held in the axils of the leaves on short panicles, and are innocuous. The fruit is a small, round, and begins bright red but matures to black. This species only occasionally fruits in the deserts.

Mastic grows in any well-drained soil and is more drought resistant than most members of the genus. Water established plants once or twice a month in the summer in the hottest deserts and less frequently in milder areas.

The resin from this tree is also called mastic. It is one of the oldest-known, high-grade resins used by people. It is used in perfumes, chewing gums, pharmaceuticals, high-grade varnishes for protecting pictures, and in adhesives for dental caps. The resin looks like golden rock candy and has a distinctive taste and chewiness. Trees are known to live a long time, up to 100 years.

Mastic is a good choice for an evergreen shrub, either singly or mixed with other equally drought- and heat-tolerant shrubs. It is dense enough to serve as a significant barrier or screen. It forms a good background for more colorful plantings or to delineate specific areas of the garden.

Pistacia mexicana
Texas pistache, Mexican pistache

FAMILY: Anacardiaceae.
DISTRIBUTION: In the United States in west Texas, along the Rio Grande as far south as the Amistad Dam near Del Rio and into the western Edwards Plateau. In Mexico widely distributed in Chihuahua, Coahuila, and Durango, and south into Central America.
MATURE SIZE: Spreading, somewhat irregular shrub or tree 15 to 30 ft. (4.6 to 9.1 m) tall and spreading as wide.

Pistacia lentiscus (mastic)

BLOOMING PERIOD: April to June.

EXPOSURE: Full sun in all but the hottest deserts, where it needs relief from afternoon sun or filtered shade.

HARDINESS: Hardy to 20°F (−6.7°C).

Texas pistache is a deciduous or nearly evergreen shrub or small tree with numerous spreading branches and a somewhat irregular form, particularly when young. Young branches are finely covered with grayish hairs but they become smooth and brown as they age.

The new leaves are red but quickly turn green, leaving only a reddish cast at the tip. The pinnately compound leaves are made up of 9 to 19 deep, glossy green leaflets, each of which is 1 to 4 in. (2.5 to 10.2 cm) long.

Plants are dioecious. The female flowers open as the leaves begin to grow in spring. They are less than 0.5 in. (1.3 cm) long, white, and not particularly showy. They are held in loose paniculate heads with pinkish bracts. Male flowers are held in tightly congested panicles with red bracts and are much the same size.

The fruit is bright red at first but turns dark blue to black as it ages. It is not considered edible, but birds and other wildlife feast on it.

Texas pistache grows best in dry, alkaline soils, although it tolerates richer soils as long as they are well drained. In the hottest deserts, deep, lightly amended soils improve its performance.

In the hottest deserts, water two or three times a month in the summer for best results. In milder areas or in its native range, it grows well on natural rainfall.

Texas pistache is a good choice for a boundary planting and for a hedge either singly or mixed with other shrubs. The deep green leaves provide good contrast with more colorful plantings. Its fruit makes it another excellent choice for a garden to attract wildlife. This species is regularly sold or offered as *Pistacia texana*, but that taxon is now considered a subspecies of *P. mexicana*.

Pistacia mexicana (Texas pistache)

Prosopis alba
Argentine mesquite

FAMILY: Fabaceae.

DISTRIBUTION: Argentina, Uruguay, southern Bolivia, and Paraguay.

MATURE SIZE: Tall, vertical tree 20 to 40 ft. (6.1 to 12.2 m) tall and spreading as wide.

BLOOMING PERIOD: April and May.

EXPOSURE: Full sun in all areas.

HARDINESS: Hardy to 15°F (−9.4°C).

Argentine mesquite is an upright tree with a wide, spreading crown. The bark is dark brown or black and deeply furrowed.

The leaves are bipinnately compound and

2.5 to 6 in. (6.4 to 15.2 cm) long. There is one pair of pinnae, each of which has 25 to 50 linear leaflets. Leaflets are spaced less than 0.25 in. (0.6 cm) apart and are less than 0.5 in. (1.3 cm) long, giving them a lacy appearance.

The numerous flowers are held in compact spikes 2 to 3 in. (5.1 to 7.6 cm) long. They are creamy white to greenish.

The pod is up to 8 in. (20.3 cm) long, strongly curved, sometimes even forming a ring. Pod production is variable: in some years pods coat the ground beneath the tree, in others they are barely noticeable.

Pure members of this species are barely distinguishable from *Prosopis nigra*, unless you have the fruit and even then to some authors they are conspecific. Argentine mesquite is distinguished from pure Chilean mesquite (*Prosopis chilensis)* by the size, number, and density of the leaflets as well as the distinctive pods. But nearly all plants in the trade are hybrids between these two highly variable species and even their hybrid progeny have crossed back on each other. There is also significant intergrade naturally between these taxa. Still, any of the South American species, whether they are pure or hybrids, are gorgeous tall, upright, and commanding shade trees, including Argentine mesquite. The more of this species in the mix, the taller the plant. *Prosopis alba* 'Colorado' is a thornless selection that is somewhat more cold hardy than the type.

Argentine mesquite is tolerant of a wide range of soils as long as they are well-drained. Deep caliche may inhibit growth, causing the plants to be stunted. In deep soils and especially when combined with ample water, the tree can become extremely large.

Argentine mesquite is best watered with deep soaks at long intervals at least monthly in the hottest deserts.

Prune in late summer to shape or remove unruly branches. Pruning earlier in the year induces aggressive regrowth from latent buds and you will get even more growth than if you never pruned at all. Argentine mesquite, whether pure or in any of its various hybrid forms, is a durable, large shade tree that provides light shade for an entire garden. It is tall enough to shade buildings and roofs. This

Prosopis alba (Argentine mesquite)

is also an excellent choice to hide an unfavorable view or to reduce the effect of power lines on the garden.

Prosopis chilensis

Chilean mesquite

FAMILY: Fabaceae.

DISTRIBUTION: Peru, Bolivia, central Chile, and northwestern Argentina.

Prosopis chilensis (Chilean mesquite)

MATURE SIZE: Tall, upright tree 20 to 30 ft. (6.1 to 9.1 m) tall and spreading as wide.

BLOOMING PERIOD: April to June.

EXPOSURE: Full sun in all areas.

HARDINESS: Hardy to 18°F (−7.8°C).

Chilean mesquite is a semideciduous, tall tree with a loose, spreading crown. The bark is dark, rough, and scaly and turns black with age. The branches have a pair of stout spines that are up to 2 in. (5.1 cm) long and held in pairs at the leaf nodes. Spines fall off the branches as the bark ages; older stems are virtually thorn free.

The dark green leaves are bipinnately compound with a pair of pinnae, each of which has 10 to 30 leaflets per pinna. Leaflets are linear, up to 0.5 in. (1.3 cm) apart, and up to 2 in. (5.1 cm) long but are extremely narrow, almost needles.

The flowers are held in tight, hanging spikes; there are two to four spikes clustered at a node. Flowers are yellow or pale yellow-green. The tan pods are slightly curved or straight, 5 to 7 in. (12.7 to 17.8 cm) long, and are also held in clusters at the nodes.

This species has been in horticulture in the region for many years but there has been overwhelming confusion over its taxonomy. There has been a long history of seeking more or less thornless forms for use in the area, and unfortunately it became common to consider any South American mesquite with no or minimal thorns as this species. Sometimes that is the case, but usually the plants in the trade are complex hybrids. Any species of mesquite has a wide natural variation in the size and number of thorns, and any species may have thornless individuals.

All South American species of mesquite in

their pure form are difficult to find. Virtually all the ones that are offered are hybrids. Pure Chilean mesquite is gorgeous with its fine, narrow leaves, giving the effect of shattered glass when you gaze up through the branches. But all the various forms and hybrids of the species are equally lovely trees and outstanding choices for high, light shade.

Chilean mesquite, like all the South American species and their hybrids, has an upright growth habit and a wide, spreading crown. This tree has immense heat tolerance and excellent drought tolerance. It will grow in most areas in any well-drained soil.

When plants are young, provide regular and ample water. After they have been in the ground for three or so years, taper off watering frequency so that ultimately the plants are growing on intermittent deep soaks only during extended, hot, dry spells. Otherwise they grow too fast, become top heavy, and are prone to heaving out of the ground during the fierce thunderstorms of the late summer.

Chilean mesquite is a good choice for high, filtered shade for all or a significant portion of the garden. It is tall enough to shade a roof or mask an undesirable view.

Prosopis glandulosa
Honey mesquite

FAMILY: Fabaceae.

DISTRIBUTION: In the United States in southern California and western Arizona, particularly near the Colorado River, then disjunct but widely distributed in western, southern, and central Texas, and ranges into parts of Oklahoma and Kansas. In Mexico in Sonora, Sinaloa, Chihuahua, Coahuila, Nuevo León, and Tamaulipas. It has naturalized in parts of southern Africa and is considered a pest species there.

MATURE SIZE: Multitrunked, spreading tree 20 to 30 ft. (6.1 to 9.1 m) tall and spreading 20 to 40 ft. (6.1 to 9.1 m) wide.

BLOOMING PERIOD: March to September.

EXPOSURE: Full sun in all areas.

HARDINESS: Hardy to 5°F (−17.8°C).

Honey mesquite is a deciduous tree with an open, spreading crown and low-growing branches that often curve or twist from the main trunk. The bark is rough and reddish brown and deeply furrowed with age. There are usually small thorns on new growth but they quickly fall as the bark ages.

The alternate, bipinnately compound leaves are up to 6 to 10 in. (15.2 to 25.4 cm) long and are composed of two pairs of pinnae, each with 12 to 20 pairs of leaflets. The leaflets are 1 to 2 in. (2.5 to 5.1 cm) long, linear, and smooth and five times longer than they are wide. The leaves are bright chartreuse when they first emerge and become deep green with age.

The creamy white flowers are 2 to 3 in. (5.1 to 7.6 cm) long and held in congested, hanging spikes. They are lightly fragrant and are renowned for the honey made from them.

The pods are more or less flat, straight or slightly curved, and constricted between the seeds. They are 4 to 8 in. (10.2 to 20.3 cm) long with a sweet flavor. Pods were historically ground into a meal or fermented.

Honey mesquite grows in any well-drained soil and does best with deeper soils. Water twice a month or less in the summer in the hottest deserts, but in its natural range the plant will grow entirely on natural rainfall. Prune in the late winter while still dormant

Prosopis glandulosa (honey mesquite)

to remove dead wood, crossing branches, or unruly branches.

Like most mesquites, when the plant is cut to the ground, latent crown buds are energized and begin to sprout vigorously. This creates a strong set of juvenile branches. This many-branched shrub may be difficult to remove by merely cutting it down; the roots must be cut out as well.

Honey mesquite is widely used as an ornamental within its range and has recently become popular in other parts of the region. It is an excellent choice for a deciduous tree to provide light shade in the summer. While it provides ample light shade, it is often not

an erect or upright plant but one that spreads around the space. The summer leaves of trees planted against west- or south-facing windows offer protection from the sun, and then the bare branches of winter allow in the winter sun.

Honey mesquite blends well into a large shrub planting at the edges and borders of the garden, or can be the anchor and provide shade for a perennial planting. It makes a good addition to a naturalistic garden and helps attract a wide array of wildlife. Old ones have great character, with their oddly curved branches, and make a fine focal or accent in a large garden.

Prosopis pubescens
Screwbean mesquite

FAMILY: Fabaceae.

DISTRIBUTION: In the United States from southeastern California, southern Nevada, and southwestern Utah into southern Arizona, southern New Mexico, and far west Texas from sea level to 3500 ft. (1067 m). In Mexico in Baja California, Sonora, and Chihuahua from sea level to 800 ft. (244 m).

MATURE SIZE: Upright, erratically branched tree 6 to 15 ft. (1.8 to 4.6 m) tall, occasionally to 30 ft. (9.1 m), spreading 4 to 8 ft. (1.2 to 2.4 m) wide.

BLOOMING PERIOD: April to September.

EXPOSURE: Full sun in all areas.

HARDINESS: Hardy to 0°F (−17.8°C).

Prosopis pubescens (screwbean mesquite)

Screwbean mesquite is a deciduous, straggly shrub or small tree. Stems, especially younger ones, have a pair of slender, white spines that are up to 0.75 in. (2 cm) long at the nodes. Older plants become erect and treelike, often with a graceful spreading form. Bark on young stems is smooth and gray, and on old plants peels off in long, thin, stringy flakes.

The leaves are 1 to 2.5 in. (3.8 to 6.4 cm) long, bipinnately compound, with one, occasionally two, pairs of pinnae, each of which has five to nine pairs of leaflets. Leaves are up to 2 in. (5.1 cm) long and the leaflets are sparsely hairy and gray-green.

The flowers are held in congested, hanging spikes that are 1 to 2 in. (2.5 to 5.1 cm) long. The flowers are bright yellow and are by far the most attractive flowers of all mesquites.

The pale tan to brown pod from which the species gets its common name is distinctive

and attractive. Pods are held in clusters of up to 20 pods on the stem. Each one is tightly coiled like a flat, brown spring and is 1.5 to 3 in. (3.8 to 7.6 cm) long. Pods are sweet and were valued for food, both raw and cooked, by Native Americans in their range.

Screwbean mesquite grows well in any well-drained soil, including rocky, native ones or deeper, more enriched ones. It is extremely drought tolerant and grows on natural rainfall even in the hottest deserts. In the garden, though, it is best to provide water every three to four weeks during the summer in hottest deserts for best growth and vigor.

This lovely, small tree is much underutilized

in the region. Smaller than the other mesquites, it is the best choice of all mesquites for small gardens. It makes an excellent shade tree, especially in a naturalistic or native garden. Left unpruned to grow as a shrub, it is a good addition to a hedge, barrier planting, or boundary planting. The bright flowers and delightful pods also make it a good choice for a focal or accent plant highlighting those features.

Prosopis velutina
Velvet mesquite

FAMILY: Fabaceae.

DISTRIBUTION: In the United States in southern California, central and southern Arizona, and far southern New Mexico at 1000 to 4000 ft. (305 to 1219 m). In Mexico in Baja California and north and central Sonora.

MATURE SIZE: Multitrunked, spreading tree 15 to 40 ft. (4.6 to 12.2 m) tall and spreading 20 to 30 ft. (6.1 to 9.1 m) wide.

BLOOMING PERIOD: March to May, reblooming in late summer with summer rains.

EXPOSURE: Full sun in all areas.

HARDINESS: Hardy to 5°F (–15.0°C); drops its leaves around 25°F (–3.9°C).

Prosopis velutina (velvet mesquite)

Velvet mesquite is a sprawling, multitrunked tree with dark brown to black deeply, furrowed bark. Trees are cold deciduous, but in mild winters retain their leaves until the new ones push them out. There are small spines at the axils of the leaves, especially on new branches.

The leaves are 3 to 4 in. (7.6 to 102 cm) long and are bipinnately compound with one or two pinnae per leaf. They hold 9 to 30 pairs of gray-green, linear leaflets 0.5 in. (1.25 cm) long and are 3.5 to 4 times as long as they are broad. Leaflets are coated with fine hairs, giving them the soft surface of the common name.

The flowers are congested into hanging catkins that are 2 to 3 in. (5.1 to 7.6 cm) long and are yellow to creamy white. Flowering is prolific and plants in bloom seem to turn yellow overnight.

The more or less straight pods have short beaks and rarely open while on the plant. They range in size from 4 to 9 in. (10.2 to 22.9 cm) long. Meal ground from the pods is extremely sweet; it was used as a basic food by Native American peoples in the region and is still offered by specialty growers. The common name is presumed to come from the Nahuatl word *misquitl*, which was corrupted by their Spanish-speaking conquerors into mesquite. This plant was immensely important to Native Americans within its range not only for food but also for lumber, shelter, medicine, pottery sealant, and black dye. This is truly the tree of life in the Sonoran Desert.

When cut to the ground, plants easily resprout from latent buds in the crown, a trait that is common to many species of mesquite. To remove a plant, it is necessary to rout out the roots.

Velvet mesquite grows entirely on natural rainfall once established, even in the hottest deserts. Plants grow quickly with ample water, which is desirable when young, but if prolonged, the plants become enormous and often poorly rooted. It is best to water them with a long, deep, monthly soak during the summer to establish a better root system and have a longer-lived tree.

Velvet mesquite is an outstanding shade tree for the region, with its wide, spreading crown and the height to shade a large area. It grows in any alkaline, well-drained soil.

In natural settings velvet mesquite grows most abundantly adjacent to waterways. But these great woodlands, chiefly known by their Spanish name *bosque*, are increasingly rare in the region. In a large garden a re-creation of such a bosque is wonderful. Individually, velvet mesquite offers light, spreading shade. Almost any of the wide array of succulents used in the region grow beautifully under such shade. These plants are also important to wildlife for food, shelter, and nest sites. Old ones become hotels for the birds and other wildlife of the garden.

Psorothamnus spinosus
Smoke tree

FAMILY: Fabaceae.

DISTRIBUTION: In the United States in the deserts of southern California, far southern Nevada, and western Arizona below 1500 ft. (457 m). In Mexico in Baja California, Sonora, and Sinaloa at similar elevations.

MATURE SIZE: Shrubby tree 10 to 18 ft. (3 to 5.5 m) tall and 10 to 15 ft. (3 to 4.6 m) wide.

BLOOMING PERIOD: May to July.

EXPOSURE: Full sun in all areas.

HARDINESS: Hardy to 20°F (–17.8°C).

Smoketree is an intricately branched tree that looks more like an overgrown shrub. It has smooth, gray to white bark. The branches twist, turn, and cross erratically and are stiff and forked. The stems are covered with pale, gray to white hairs, which gives the plant a ghostly, insubstantial appearance and is the source of the common name.

Psorothamnus spinosus (smoke tree)
Photo by Judy Mielke

The trees are leafless most of the year, and leaves are present for only a few weeks in the early summer. When present the gray-green leaves are thick, nearly succulent, less than 0.25 in. (0.6 cm) long, lanceolate. Leaves and stems are dotted with small, orange glands that emit a sharp, pungent aroma.

The flowers are held on short racemes that are 0.5 in. (1.3 cm) long. They are a stunning deep purple that transforms the shrub when in bloom. The pods are ovate and do not open on the plant.

Smoketree is found mainly in the gravelly washes of some of the driest parts of North America. It is notoriously temperamental about living outside its native range. To grow it successfully, it is best to grow it in soils with generous amounts of loose gravel or sand; it grows particularly well in sand.

Like many species from the Mojave Desert or other deserts of western Arizona and eastern California, smoketree is touchy about summer watering. Infrequent deep soaks are more than sufficient, and monthly watering in the winter is more than adequate for plants to thrive. When conditions are ideal, plants grow quickly under cultivation.

The exquisite ghostly look is unrivaled and makes a splendid complement to a desert garden, a succulent planting, or in an area of the garden that does not get regular irrigation.

Punica granatum
Pomegranate

FAMILY: Punicaceae.
DISTRIBUTION: Pomegranate is thought to be from Iran or other parts of southern Asia east to the base of the Himalayas. It has been cultivated for centuries and is naturalized throughout this region, making its exact origins murky.
MATURE SIZE: Clumping, multibranched shrub 6 to 20 ft. (1.8 to 6.1 m) tall and up to 10 ft. (3 m) wide.
BLOOMING PERIOD: April to May.
EXPOSURE: Full sun in all areas, although it grows equally well in filtered shade in the hottest deserts.
HARDINESS: Hardy to 15°F (−9.4°C), but late cold ruins new foliage.

Pomegranate is a deciduous shrub with numerous, fine branches that cascade and fall over. Plants that are rarely pruned become a thick shrub with a graceful, weeping appearance, pomegranate may also be pruned to a single-trunked tree.

The glossy green leaves are 1 to 3 in. (2.5 to 7.6 cm) long and lanceolate to oblong. They may be alternate, opposite, or attached in whorls, often on the same plant. They turn a clear, bright yellow before they drop in the fall.

The flowers are held in short axillary or terminal racemes with one to five flowers in the cluster. Individual flowers are up to 2 in. (5.1 cm) across and range from pure, bright red to red-orange, pink, or yellow. There are also double forms. The corolla lobes are sturdy, more or less trumpet shaped with ruffled tips. The flowers are showy and prolific on the plant.

The fruit is a round berry to which the calyx remains attached. Fruits range from 3 to 4 in. (7.6 to 10.2 cm) around and are widely regarded as the model for the so-called squash blossom necklace design of Southwest Native American jewelry makers. Fruit is initially green with reddish tinges and finishes in the fall a bright, burnished red. The juicy pulp and the seeds are edible, and dried fruit lasts for months off the tree.

Pomegranate grows best in areas with hot summers and mild winters, although it thrives in cold climates if protected. Provide a well-drained soil; deep, lightly amended soils make for more reliable fruiting. Water weekly in the hottest desert to keep the plant fit and the fruit in good shape, but the plant will grow on less-frequent watering if you aren't interested in the fruit. Plants are immune to the heat, and in my area they do well in light shade.

There are a number of named varieties, chiefly based on fruit characteristics. 'Wonderful' is the most commonly grown, with double, red-orange flowers and large, red fruit. 'Fleishman' is reported to have the sweetest fruits. 'Chico' and 'Nana' are compact, growing only to 3 ft. (0.9 m) and without palatable fruit. There are also forms that are have pink and yellow flowers, neither of which has remarkable fruit but they are lovely ornamentals.

Pomegranate is a long-lived shrub, known to survive for 75 years or more. It is a good choice in containers and takes to almost any kind of shaping and pruning. Prune in the winter when it is dormant to remove large branches or to shape the plant. Light pruning in early summer is effective in enhancing fruit production.

The Spanish brought pomegranate to the New World early in their conquest history. Relicts of these old plantings are found around the missions they left behind.

The fruit was featured in Egyptian mythology and art, in the Old Testament of the Bible, and in the Babylonian Talmud. It was carried by desert caravans for the sake of its thirst-quenching juice. It is said that Moses promised the Israelites there would be pomegranate in the Promised Land and that this helped induce them to go. Pomegranate became known in central and southern India in approximately the first century A.D. and was reported growing in Indonesia as early as 1416.

Punica granatum (pomegranate)

Quercus buckleyi

Spanish oak, Buckley's oak, Texas oak

FAMILY: Fagaceae.

DISTRIBUTION: In central Texas west through the Edwards Plateau, and in the limestone areas of Oklahoma.

MATURE SIZE: Upright, often multitrunked tree 15 to 30 ft. (4.6 to 9.1 m) tall, occasionally to 50 ft. (15.2 m), spreading to 20 to 30 ft. (6.1 9.1 m) wide.

BLOOMING PERIOD: March to April.

EXPOSURE: Full sun in all areas.

HARDINESS: Hardy to at least 15°F (−9.4°C) and probably lower.

Spanish oak is an upright, deciduous tree with a rounded crown at maturity. The bark is dark brown to gray and deeply fissured, although there are individuals with smooth, gray bark.

The leaves have a reddish cast when they first emerge but turn a deep, rich green as they age. Leaves have three to seven lobes that end in sharp points and are glossy, dark green above and paler on the underside. The entire leaf is more or less circular and 2 to 4.5 in. (5.1 to 11.4 cm) long. Leaves turn a bright red in the autumn before they fall.

The staminate inflorescence is up to 3.25 in. (8.3 cm) long. The pistillate inflorescence is less than 0.25 in. (0.6 cm) long with only one to three minute flowers.

The fruit is an oval acorn is 0.5 to 1 in. (1.5 to 2.5 cm) long, rich reddish brown, and from a quarter to half of it is covered by a saucer-shaped cup. Acorns may occur singly or in pairs. The acorns were traditionally used as food by both Native Americans and the later Anglo settlers.

Spanish oak grows well in any well-drained soil. Although it endures the desert heat well, it needs to be grown in deep, well-drained soils for best results in desert areas. However, in areas with more regular rainfall, it grows well in lean, rocky, alkaline soils.

Water deeply once a week in the summer in the hottest deserts. Be sure that it receives watering once or twice a month in the winter. Within their natural range, established trees grow on natural rainfall unless there is a prolonged dry spell.

There has been a flurry of taxonomic confusion about this species and the closely related and similar *Quercus texana* and *Q. shumardii*. From a gardener's perspective, they are so similar that they are virtually indistinguishable, with the chief taxonomic differences being leaf length and width and acorn size and shape. Plants from the more western edge of the distribution, variously known as *Q. shumardii* var. *texana*, *Q. shumardii*, or *Q. texana*, are more drought tol-

Quercus buckleyi (Spanish oak)

erant and tend to grow better in rocky, dry soils. I subscribe to the conclusion of the Texas horticulturist Benny Simpson, that most of what is known by these names is a vast, hybrid swarm extending from the Rio Grande north to Dallas, south to San Antonio, and east into north central Texas and that the entire group is best known as *Q. buckleyi*.

This lovely, moderate-sized oak is a fine shade tree in smaller gardens. Its colorful fall leaves are an extra bonus.

The larger-leaved chinkapin oak (*Quercus muehlenbergii*), while not commonly grown in the drier parts of the region, does remarkably well particularly when plants are grown from populations in the western end of its huge range. This oak grows as a round-crowned tree 40 to 80 ft. (12.2 to 24 m) tall with a crown spread of 20 to 40 ft. (6.1 to 12.2 m) wide. It is hardy to 0°F (–17.8°C) and northern populations are hardy to –20°F (–28.9°C). A deciduous tree, chinkapin oak has dark green leaves that are 4 to 7 in. (10.2 to 17.8 cm) long, leathery, with deeply serrated margins, making it unmistakable compared with other oaks commonly offered in most of the region. Leaves turn yellow-brown to red in the fall. While chinkapin oak has excellent heat tolerance, it needs to be watered weekly in the summer in the hottest deserts and monthly in less severe areas.

Quercus suber
Cork oak

FAMILY: Fagaceae.
DISTRIBUTION: Throughout the Mediterranean region.
MATURE SIZE: Wide, spreading tree 30 to 65 ft. (9.1 to 20 m) tall and 30 to 40 ft. (9.1 to 12.2 m) wide.
BLOOMING PERIOD: March to April.
EXPOSURE: Full sun in all areas.
HARDINESS: Hardy to 5°F (–15.2°C).

Cork oak is a low, spreading tree when mature. Young plants are upright with a dense, rounded crown. The bark is reddish brown when young but ages to a thick, deeply

Quercus suber (cork oak)

fissured light gray with reddish furrows. The extremely thick bark is the source of commercial cork.

The alternate leaves are evergreen, leathery, ovate to elliptical, and 1 to 4 in. (2.5 to 10.2 cm) long. The margins are either entire or more often have wavy edges. The leaves are cupped, dark green above, and fuzzy and pale below.

Plants, like all members of the genus, are monoecious. Staminate inflorescences are slender, yellow-green, and 2 to 3 in. (5.1 to 7.6 cm) long. Pistillate inflorescences are much smaller and in clusters of two to four in the axil of the leaf.

The acorn is narrowly oblong and 1 to 1.5 in. (2.5 to 3.8 cm) long. The scaly cap covers about half the nut. The acorns may be held singly or in clusters of two to five.

Cork oak has enjoyed on-again off-again interest in the desert parts of the region. It is still possible to see large, old trees in the Phoenix area but young ones are rarely encountered. These trees grow well in any deep, well-drained soil with watering two or three times a month in the summer. This is a lovely, heat-tolerant, evergreen tree. The remarkable, distinctive bark has been used for centuries to make stoppers for containers as well as various building materials.

The old bark forms a thick, dead mass on the plant, and once the plant is roughly 40 years old, it is possible to remove that inert mass, leaving the glossy, reddish living bark beneath. These are long-lived trees, and even those under commercial cultivation are known to live up to 150 years.

Quercus turbinella
Scrub oak

FAMILY: Fagaceae.

DISTRIBUTION: In the United States from southern California, southern and central Arizona, far southern Utah and Nevada, southwest New Mexico, and far western Texas at 3500 to 8000 ft. (1067 to 2438 m). In Mexico in Baja California, Sonora, and possibly northern Chihuahua.

MATURE SIZE: Multibranched, shrubby tree 6 to 15 ft. (1.8 to 4.6 m) tall and as wide.

BLOOMING PERIOD: April to June.

EXPOSURE: Full sun outside the hottest deserts; light or filtered shade in the hottest deserts.

HARDINESS: Hardy to at least 10°F (−12.2°C).

Scrub oak is an evergreen species that is more a rounded, intricately branched shrub than a tree. The mature bark is pale gray and scaly.

The hollylike leaves are stiff, thick, and leathery, and elliptic or ovate. They are 1.5 in. (3.8 cm) long with a sharp tip and three to five coarse teeth along the margin. They are a dull, dusky gray-green to blue-green above, and the underside is densely covered with gray hairs.

The staminate inflorescence is a dense, clublike structure, much less than 0.5 in. (1.3 cm) long, and crowded along the stems. The pistillate inflorescence is as small and is a bright yellow.

Acorns are 0.5 in. (1.3 cm) long or less and may be single or in clusters of two or three. They are almost round or short oblong, light brown, and covered for a quarter to a half of their length by the cup.

Quercus turbinella (scrub oak)

Scrub oak is an extremely drought-tolerant species. Even in the hottest deserts it requires minimal supplemental water except during extended dry spells. Monthly watering is sufficient.

This dense, shrubby oak is an excellent choice for a mixed border in a dry garden or to create a loose informal hedge where irrigation is not available. Wildlife is especially fond of the acorns. The prickly leaves make it a poor choice too close to walkways or other high-traffic areas. Plant it where you can enjoy it from afar.

Rhapis excelsa
Lady palm

FAMILY: Arecaceae.

DISTRIBUTION: Speculated to have originated in southern China and Taiwan, but there are no extant wild populations. It has been cultivated particularly in Japan for over 100 years.

MATURE SIZE: Multitrunked palm 2 to 6 ft. (0.6 to 1.8 m) tall and 3 to 4 ft. (0.9 to 1.2 m) wide.

BLOOMING PERIOD: Summer.

EXPOSURE: Filtered shade in all but the hottest deserts; full shade in the hottest deserts.

HARDINESS: Hardy to 20°F (–17.8°C).

Lady palm is a clustering, slow-growing palm. The thin, delicate trunks are coated with fine, dark brown to black filaments that arise from the prominent leaf bases and are long persistent on the plant. Over time the plant may have hundreds of stems.

Leaves are deep, glossy green, palmately compound, with 4 to 10 on each stem. Each leaf ranges from 12 to 30 in. (30.5 to 76.2 cm) wide and is cut into 4 to 10 segments that are deeply pleated and blunt at the tips. Each leaf is held on a slender, unarmed petiole that is 15 to 18 in. (38.1 to 45.7 cm) long.

Plants are dioecious and each pinkish inflorescence is held well within the upper leaves and is only 12 in. (30.5 cm) long. Flowers are white and the fruit is jet black.

This palm, both by its origins and its habit, seems unlikely for desert gardens but it has remarkable drought- and heat-tolerance as long as it is not exposed to direct sun. Lady palm does best in enriched, well-drained soil. It prefers either full, dense shade or only a short amount of morning sun. North-facing exposures are ideal, especially in the summer.

Because of its clustering habit, give it some room to fill in. It is an outstanding choice in an odd, dark corner, under eaves, or behind sitting areas.

In the deserts, water it weekly during the hottest part of the summer, although it will be fine with more. This species grows slowly but deliberately, and begins to grow numerous emerging stems quickly. In the deserts, it often grows only to the short end of its height range.

This palm an excellent container plant. Put it in a large pot so that the many stems may fill it out and offer a full, lush effect. It has few pests or problems of cultivation.

There are countless Japanese cultivars of this species, many of which are difficult to

Rhapis excelsa (lady palm)

find outside highly specialized palm nurseries or directly from Japan. Many are variegated forms, usually white, and some are lovely. The white variegated forms look especially arresting and light up dark areas.

Lady palm often suffers from a manganese deficiency in the alkaline soils of the region, so you may need to use a good palm fertilizer or good-quality compost applied annually in the late spring.

Lady palm was introduced to gardens in England as early as 1774 and has been a favorite ever since, especially in pots.

Rhus lancea
African sumac

FAMILY: Anacardiaceae.
DISTRIBUTION: South Africa.
MATURE SIZE: Spreading tree 15 to 30 ft. (4.6 to 9.1 m) tall and as wide.
BLOOMING PERIOD: December to March.
EXPOSURE: Full sun in all areas.
HARDINESS: Hardy to 15°F (−9.4°C), but foliage may be damaged at 20°F (−6.7°C).

African sumac is an unevenly branched tree with numerous secondary branches and upright shoots along the stems. The bark is rough, reddish brown, occasionally orange. This tree is especially fast growing. It has a flat-topped look when young but the crown becomes more dome-shaped with age.

The leaves are palmately compound and composed of three leaflets. Each leaflet is 2 to 5 in. (5.1 to 12.7 cm) long, shiny green above, and paler below.

Plants are dioecious. The greenish-white flowers are individually minute but are held in clusters up to 2 in. (5.1 cm) long. They have a delicate fragrance and blooming is profuse but not showy. On female trees, the flowers are followed by tiny, round fruit 0.25 in. (0.6 cm) or less across and ranging from cream to yellow or red. Fruit is prolific; birds are crazy about it and swarm the tree when the fruit is ripe.

African sumac has been used for decades in the hottest parts of the region for its fast growth and reliable shade. The first ones in Arizona were planted in 1929 in Tucson, and many planted in the 1940s are still growing.

Recently in Tucson and parts of southern California, African sumac has begun to grow outside a garden setting in washes and other drainages in the city limits or near housing developments. Therefore, caution is called for in using such a species. It makes copious seedlings in the garden and you are either mowing or pulling them forever. In areas deep in the urban core, this situation is merely a nuisance, but anywhere near a natural area or park or preserve, it is a recipe for future problems, so trees should not be used in these sensitive locations.

African sumac has immense heat tolerance. While it is able to withstand significant drought by shedding leaves, it is a better-looking plant with monthly watering in the summer. Plants growing in poorly drained soils become chlorotic.

Because of its erratic, free-form branching

Rhus lancea (African sumac)

it is a challenging plant to prune. Work with the emerging branches slowly over the years to turn it into an attractive tree. But trees can be easily ruined by aggressive pruning. Small branches erupt from the stem over the summer, and these may be removed anytime. More significant pruning is best done in the spring. This tree is one of the few desert-adapted ones that does best with spring planting.

Rhus microphylla

Little-leaf sumac, desert sumac

FAMILY: Anacardiaceae.
DISTRIBUTION: In the United States widespread from southern Arizona and southern New Mexico through western Texas at 1000 to 6500 ft. (335 to 1981 m). In Mexico from Baja California Sur across to Coahuila and Nuevo León and south to Zacatecas.
MATURE SIZE: Loosely branched shrub 4 to 10 ft. (1.2 to 3 m) tall and as wide.
BLOOMING PERIOD: July to August.
EXPOSURE: Full sun in all areas,
HARDINESS: Hardy to 5°F (−15.0°C).

Little-leaf sumac is a deciduous, rounded shrub that tends to branch low to the ground. Branches form small thorns at the tips.

The leaves are 1 to 2 in. (2.5 to 5.1 cm) long and are pinnately compound, with five to nine leaflets 0.5 in. (1.5 cm) long or less. Leaflets are elliptic to round with a sharp or round tip. The rachis of the leaf has small wings on each side. Leaves turn a rosy red to purplish before they fall.

The flowers are white and held in tight clusters 2 to 4 in. (5.1 to 10.2 cm) wide, usually at the axils of the leaf but sometimes at the tips of the branches. They are followed by bright red to orange-red, hairy fruit. The tree blooms before the leaves emerge.

Little-leaf sumac is a good choice to incorporate into a mixed hedge. It is so attractive to wildlife that it is easily considered for a naturalistic or wildlife garden. It is heat tolerant enough to be useful in areas of high or reflective heat.

Another exquisite deciduous member of the genus is prairie sumac (*Rhus lanceolata*), which is native from southern New Mexico through western Texas and the Edwards Plateau region of central Texas, into central Oklahoma, and scattered through Mexico in the mountains of northeastern and southern Chihuahua and eastern Coahuila, and in Nuevo León. Prairie sumac is an open-

Rhus microphylla (little-leaf sumac)

branched shrub or small tree 12 to 30 ft. (3.7 to 9.1 m) tall and 8 to 20 ft. (2.4 to 6.1 m) wide. It is hardy to −20°F (−29°C). The pinnately compound, glossy green leaves are 5 to 9 in. (12.7 to 22.9 cm) long with 9 to 21 leaflets that turn brilliant red in the fall. This stunning member of the genus makes a lovely focal point in any garden. Be sure to place it where you can enjoy the astounding fall color. Blessed with a combination of high heat tolerance and great cold tolerance, this species is easy to incorporate into gardens throughout the region. In the hottest deserts, it will need filtered shade, deeper soils, and watering once a week in the summer. In all other areas, it is more drought tolerant and will grow on leaner soils as well.

It was once considered a variety of the more eastern species, *Rhus copallina*, and they occur close together in parts of central Texas.

Rhus ovata
Sugar bush

FAMILY: Anacardiaceae.

DISTRIBUTION: In the United States from Santa Barbara, California, south into southern and central Arizona at 3000 to 5000 ft. (914 to 1524 m). In Mexico in Baja California.

MATURE SIZE: Dense, rounded shrub 5 to 12 ft. (1.5 to 3.7 m) tall and as wide.

BLOOMING PERIOD: March to May.

EXPOSURE: Full sun in all areas; tolerates filtered shade in the hottest deserts

HARDINESS: Hardy to 10°F (−12°C).

Sugar bush is a thick, round, evergreen shrub. In old plants, the bark is dark brown and quite shaggy, but otherwise is smooth.

The bright, glossy green leaves are ovate, simple, leathery, and come to a sharp point at the tip. Leaves are paler on the underside. They are 1.5 to 3 in. (3.8 to 7.6 cm) long and fold up toward the middle.

Flowers are held in short, terminal clusters of 1.25 to 2 in. (3.2 to 5.1 cm) across. The buds are surrounded by bright pink to red bracts and the flowers are white. The plant is extremely showy when in bloom.

Flowers are followed by clusters of small, hairy, red fruit. The fruit is beloved by birds and other wildlife, and when crushed and mixed with water makes a refreshing, lemon-flavored drink.

Sugar bush is a denizen of the chaparral hills of both California and Arizona but does surprisingly well in the cities in the hottest

Rhus ovata (sugar bush)

deserts. Within its range, it grows in rocky, alkaline soils. In the garden it does well in any well-drained soil. It is sensitive to both overwatering and poor drainage, quickly falling prey to lethal fungal infections. Always plant it in fall or winter. Water every two to three weeks in summer in the hottest deserts.

Within its range this species hybridizes with both lemonade bush (*Rhus trilobata*) and in California with *Rhus integrifolia*. These hybrids are occasionally brought into horticulture, particularly in southern California.

Sugar bush is a large, dense shrub that is ideal for use as a barrier or screening plant. It makes a good addition to a hedge either singly or mixed with other species. It is such a deep color that it forms a good backdrop for more colorful plantings.

The extremely rare but exquisite Kearney's sumac (*Rhus kearneyi*) also has deep green, firm leaves with prominent veins, but they are half the length of sugar bush leaves. This rounded shrub is 4 to 6 ft. (1.2 to 1.8 m) tall and as wide. It flowers from March to April but is hardy to only about 20°F (−7°C). Restricted and rare in its range, this sumac is an outstanding ornamental for the hottest deserts but can be difficult to find. It grows slowly in rocky soils, but in enriched, well-drained soils it grows more quickly. Drainage is vital; this species will develop root rot problems quickly in wet, dense, or poorly drained sites.

Rhus trilobata
Skunkbush, lemonade bush

FAMILY: Anacardiaceae.
DISTRIBUTION: In the United States through-out all the western states from Washington to North Dakota south to California, Arizona, New Mexico, and Texas at 5000 to 7500 ft. (1524 to 2286 m). In Mexico in Baja California to Durango and Coahuila.
MATURE SIZE: Mounding, rounded shrub 3 to 8 ft. (0.9 to 2.4 m) tall and spreading as wide or more.
BLOOMING PERIOD: March to June.
EXPOSURE: Full sun in all but the hottest deserts, there filtered shade is best.
HARDINESS: Hardy to 0°F (−18°C).

Skunkbush gets its name from the strong, often sickening, smell of the leaves when they are crushed. This low, spreading, deciduous plant with gray to brown stems forms large clumps over time. The branches are hairy, at least when young, but there is wide variation in this trait.

The leaves are compound, 3 in. (7.6 cm) long, with three leaflets; the terminal leaflet is up to 2 in. (2.1 cm) long. Leaves may be hairy when young but become smoother with age, another trait with great variation over the wide range of the species. Leaves are gray-green, with the lower surface paler and often with pronounced hairs. Leaves are oval to spatulate with broad tips; they turn orange to scarlet in the autumn before they fall.

The yellow flowers are held in tight terminal spikes that are up to 2.5 in. (6.4 cm) long. Plants are dioecious. Flowers emerge before the leaves in the spring. The flowers are followed by red or orange hairy fruit that often lasts through the winter. The fruit is a great favorite of wildlife and birds, and the crushed fruit mixed with water makes a lemonade-like drink.

While this species is tricky to grow in the

hottest deserts, growing it just barely beyond the desert zones is effortless. In the hottest deserts provide well-drained but moderately enriched soils, and water two to three times a month in the summer. Light shade helps keep the plants fit and able to endure extended hot spells.

Outside of the hottest deserts, skunkbush grows well in a wide array of well-drained, fertile soils. It is drought tolerant and thrives on natural rainfall outside the hottest deserts.

Plants have extensive, fibrous root systems and tend to root quickly when stem tips come into contact with the ground. This trait creates large clumps or colonies in nature and is an advantage if you want erosion control or need to stabilize a steep bank. Otherwise remove the suckers if you want a solitary plant.

Rhus trilobata (skunkbush)

Skunkbush is a fine selection for a mixed hedge or for use at the edge or boundary of the garden. It is so attractive to birds and other wildlife that it can form the background for a wildlife or native garden. In the hottest deserts, its tolerance for light shade makes it a superb understory plant to fill in a darker corner of the garden.

Rhus virens
Evergreen sumac

FAMILY: Anacardiaceae.

DISTRIBUTION: In the United States from southern Arizona through southern New Mexico, into far west Texas, to the western edge of the Edwards Plateau at 2100 to 5000 ft. (640 to 1524 m). In Mexico from Baja California Sur, Sonora, to Chihuahua and central Coahuila, south to Tamaulipas and Zacatecas, and perhaps as far as Oaxaca at similar elevations.

MATURE SIZE: Dense, rounded shrub 3 to 12 ft. (0.9 to 3.7 m) tall and spreading as wide.

BLOOMING PERIOD: July to September.

EXPOSURE: Full sun to partial shade in the hottest deserts; full sun elsewhere.

HARDINESS: Hardy to 10°F (-12°C).

Evergreen sumac is a dense, rounded, evergreen shrub. The young branches are slightly hairy and brown but they age to a smooth, rich brown.

The leaves are pinnately compound with three to nine leaflets that are slightly hairy, shiny green above, and paler beneath. Leaves are 2 to 5 in. (5.1 to 12.7 cm) long. The leaflets are oval to elliptical, 1.75 to 2 in. (3.8 to 5.1 cm) long, and come to a sharp point at the tip.

Clusters of white flowers up to 4 in. (10.2

cm) long occur in axils of the leaves. They are followed by clusters of red fruit.

Evergreen sumac is a glossy green, evergreen shrub that makes an excellent background for colorful plantings. It grows best in moderately enriched, well-drained soils and tolerates soils with high alkalinity well. Water at least weekly in the hottest deserts in the summer.

The fruit is welcome by all kinds of wildlife, particularly birds, and has long been renowned as a tart, acidic, refreshing drink when crushed and mixed with water.

Rhus virens var. *choriophylla* occupies the western end of the range. It has longer, narrower, smooth, paler green leaves that are up to 2 to 5 in. (5.1 to 12.7 cm) long. This form does best in the hottest deserts and is still erroneously offered as *R. choriophylla*.

Evergreen sumac, the smaller member of the genus, has the heat tolerance to work well around pools, seating areas, or other hot areas. It is a good choice for an evergreen screen or hedge in smaller yards.

Sabal mexicana
Mexican palmetto, Texas palmetto

FAMILY: Arecaceae.

DISTRIBUTION: In the United States in isolated populations in southern Texas especially along the southernmost reach of the Rio Grande. Throughout Mexico into Central America at least as far as Honduras from sea level to 165 ft. (50 m).

MATURE SIZE: Single-trunked palm 40 to 50 ft. (12.2 to 15.2 m) tall.

BLOOMING PERIOD: March and April.

EXPOSURE: Full sun in all areas.

HARDINESS: Hardy to at least 10°F (−12°C).

Mexican palmetto has a solitary stem with a large, cabbagelike head so typical of the genus. The grayish to brown trunk is marked with faint rings for most of its length and usually has some crisscross, persistent leaf bases near the top.

There are between 10 and 25 leaves per head and they are prominently costapalmate. There are up to 100 or more rigid leaflets that often have threads flowing from the margins. Leaves are 6 to 8 ft. (1.8 to 2.4 m) long, two thirds of which is the unarmed petiole.

The inflorescence is 7 to 8 ft. (2.1 to 2.4 m) long and branched into three parts. The white flowers are lightly fragrant. The round fruit is 0.75 to 1 in. (1.8 to 2.5 cm) in diameter. Fruit is dark purple or black and is profuse on the branched stalk.

In Mexico and Central America, this palm is one of the most commonly used for a wide array of uses including thatching and hats.

Rhus virens (evergreen sumac)

The Audubon Society maintains a preserve in far south Texas, the Audubon Sabal Palm Grove Sanctuary, to protect one of the last wild stands of Mexican palmetto in the United States. The species is widely cultivated and has been used as far north as Dallas. Although that group was wiped out in a vicious, lengthy freeze in 1983, the species is usually reliable as far north as Austin.

Sabal mexicana (Mexican palmetto)

Unlike most palms, Mexican palmetto is reported to have an extensive root system, making larger plants difficult to move. So begin with a young, smaller individual and put it where you want it to stay. It takes up to 20 years to mature, but the big, graceful head is lovely in the meantime.

Easy to grow, beautiful, and tolerant of a wide array of soils as long as they well drained, this palm is a great choice for gardeners who find the immense height of California fan palm (*Washingtonia filifera*) to be too daunting or out of scale.

Water every two or three weeks in the summer in the hottest deserts. In all other areas, provide ample water when the tree is young to get it established. This palm is ultimately able to grow more or less on its own when mature.

Mexican palmetto is an outstanding choice around pools or other areas of intense heat. Groups or groves of the palm provide excellent shade. It is a dramatic plant to line a walkway or driveway or to provide an accent or focal point in the garden.

Sabal uresana
Sonoran palmetto

FAMILY: Arecaceae.

DISTRIBUTION: In Mexico from central and southern Sonora to northern Sinaloa and southwest Chihuahua from sea level to 4000 ft. (1219 m).

MATURE SIZE: Single-trunked palm 40 to 50 ft. (12.2 to 15.2 m) tall with a crown spread of at least 20 ft. (6.1 m).

BLOOMING PERIOD: Summer.

EXPOSURE: Full sun in all areas.

HARDINESS: Hardy to 20°F (7°C).

Sonoran palmetto is a tall, solitary palm with a big, rounded head of leaves. The trunk is marked with rings and is gray to brown in maturity. The trunk is often obscured entirely by the large, hanging leaves.

There are between 15 and 35 leaves in a head, each of which is up to 8 ft. (2.4 m) long and 3 to 4 ft. (0.9 to 1.2 m) wide. The long petiole is unarmed. Leaves are coated with fine hairs, making them gray-green to nearly blue. They are prominently costapalmate and have up to 75 rigid, ascending leaflets without filaments.

The branched flowering stalk is 6 to 8 ft. (1.8 to 2.4 m) long and holds numerous, minute, bisexual white flowers. The flowers are followed by large clusters of black to dark brown fruit that is 0.75 to 1 in. (1.8 to 2.5 cm) in diameter.

Sonoran palmetto grows deep roots, and therefore it is tricky to grow in containers for a long time. In the ground, however, it is an outstanding choice for hot, dry areas. It tolerates a wide range of soils from sandy to rocky; deeper soils are best for growing the large and often deep root system.

This species is highly drought tolerant. Once established it grows well when watered once or twice a month in the summer in the hottest deserts. But young plants need to be watered at twice that frequency to become well established.

The beautiful, bluish heads of leaves are lush and interesting in a garden. Like most palms, the full head of the plant is developed before the stem begins to rise to its mature height. This may take a number of years and it is necessary to provide ample room for the expanding head of leaves.

Sonoran palmetto is a good choice in hot areas and around pools or patios where reflective heat is intense. Use it in groups to form a grove that will provide even more shade in the garden.

Sabal uresana (Sonoran palmetto)

Salvia ballotiflora
Shrubby blue sage

ALSO KNOWN AS *Salvia ballotaeflora*.

FAMILY: Lamiaceae.

DISTRIBUTION: In the United States in Texas from the western end of the Edwards Plateau south to the Gulf Coast and along the Rio Grande at 1200 to 2400 ft. (366 to 732 m). In Mexico from Coahuila, Durango, Nuevo León, and Zacatecas south to Hidalgo at 1000 to 7200 ft. (305 to 2195 m).

MATURE SIZE: Intricately branched shrub 4 to 6 ft. (1.2 to 1.8 m) tall and half as wide.

BLOOMING PERIOD: April to October.

EXPOSURE: Full sun in all but the hottest deserts; filtered shade in the hottest deserts.

HARDINESS: Hardy to 15°F (−9°C).

Shrubby blue sage is a deciduous shrub with a complex array of thin, fine branches. The oldest wood is gray and flaky but rarely peels off entirely.

The leaves are 0.5 to 1.5 in. (1.5 to 3.8 cm) long, ovate, with wavy margins or with widely spaced teeth along the margins. Leaves are extremely rough to the touch and have a pungent, somewhat rank smell.

Flowers are held in short racemes of one to three flowers in the axils of the outermost leaves. Individual flowers are less than 0.5 in. (1.3 cm) long but are profuse. Flowers range from light blue to deep blue or purple.

This unusual member of the genus grows well on any fast-draining soil, including rocky ones. It prefers alkaline soils. Water in the hottest deserts once a week, more when temperatures are severe, to prevent the plant from dropping its leaves as a response to dry conditions.

Without the flowers, the plant looks like a bee brush (*Aloysia gratissima*), with the crinkled, pinking-shearlike leaves and strong aroma, but without the delicious fragrance of bee bush.

Salvia ballotiflora (shrubby blue sage)

Prune when dormant or just as the leaves emerge in the spring, to take out small twigs that died over the winter or to reinvigorate the plant and make it bushier.

Shrubby blue sage offers a good color to blend into a perennial or mixed-shrub planting. It is a good choice as a background shrub for colorful plantings or to use in a dry bed. In the hottest deserts it is best in light shade but in all other areas it is tolerant of full sun.

Sambucus nigra subsp. *canadensis*
Common elderberry, Mexican elderberry

SYNONYM: *Sambucus mexicana*.
FAMILY: Caprifoliaceae.
DISTRIBUTION: In the United States throughout most of California, in Arizona

Sambucus nigra subsp. *canadensis*
(common elderberry)

throughout the state except for the far southwestern part at 1000 to 4000 ft. (305 to 1219 m), in southwestern New Mexico at 4000 to 5000 ft. (1219 to 1524 m), and rare in Texas along the Rio Grande in the Chisos and Davis Mountains of far west Texas.
MATURE SIZE: Multibranched shrub growing 10 to 20 ft. (3 to 6.1 m) tall, occasionally to 35 ft. (10.7 m), and 8 to 20 ft. (2.4 to 6.1 m) wide.
BLOOMING PERIOD: April to October.
EXPOSURE: Full sun or light shade in all but the hottest deserts, where filtered shade is required.
HARDINESS: Hardy to at least 10°F (–12°C), perhaps lower.

Common elderberry is a deciduous, many-branched shrub with brittle, dark gray stems that are numerous from the base.

The leaves are pinnately compound with three to five elliptic to oval leaflets. Leaflets are 1.5 to 3 in. (3.8 to 7.6 cm) long, serrate, with a sharp tip. Leaflets are pale green.

The flowers are tiny and white but held in wide, flattened heads 4 to 8 in. (10.2 to 20.3 cm) across. Flowering heads hold hundreds of flowers and are numerous on the plant and showy. Flowers are followed by large heads of dark, blue-black fruit that is delicious to both humans and wildlife.

Plants are evergreen or deciduous. In the deserts they often lose their leaves in the hottest part of the summer.

Common elderberry is fast growing. Prune it hard every couple of years to keep it bushy and under control. Pruning also promotes better bloom and fruit formation, since this species blooms on new wood.

Common elderberry grows best in deep,

fertile soils. In dry or rocky soils, it may be difficult to keep it watered enough. This species needs deep water every two weeks in the summer, and more frequent watering if the heat is severe.

This species is found in northern Mexico, but there is some question as to whether this is its natural distribution or one that is the result of long cultivation. Other varieties or species of the genus occur throughout Mexico and Central America and there is vast confusion over the taxonomic status of them all.

Common elderberry makes a delicate background shrub or component in a wildlife garden. Place it where the showy flowering can be enjoyed. It is shade tolerant enough in the hottest deserts to form a dense understory in the garden.

Sapindus saponaria var. drummondii

Western soapberry

SYNONYM: *Sapindus drummondii.*
FAMILY. Sapindaceae.
DISTRIBUTION: In the United States in central and southern Arizona, southern New Mexico, and western Texas north and east to Kansas, Oklahoma, Missouri, and Louisiana at 2500 to 5000 ft. (762 to 1524 m). In Mexico in northern Sonora, eastern Chihuahua, south to Coahuila and Tamaulipas at 3500 to 5000 ft. (1067 to 1524 m).
MATURE SIZE: Multibranched, large shrub or tree 15 to 30 ft. (4.6 to 9.1 m) tall and 10 to 20 ft. (3 to 6.1 m) wide.
BLOOMING PERIOD: May and July.
EXPOSURE: Full sun or filtered shade in all zones.
HARDINESS: Hardy to 0°F (−18°C).

Western soapberry is a deciduous plant with a broad, round, dense crown. When young it has many suckers and much branching, which can be retained if you want a large, multistemmed shrub, or the plant can be pruned to create a tree. This tendency to form continuous, low branches stops as the plant matures. The gray to light brown-red bark is rough and flakes to reveal the yellowish trunk beneath. This feature is most evident in winter when the plant is deciduous.

The pinnately compound, alternate leaves are 5 to 8 in. (12.7 to 20.3 cm) long with between 13 and 19 leaflets. Leaflets are lanceolate and taper to a fine tip. Leaves turn yellow or gold in the fall.

The creamy white flowers are held in panicles 5 to 10 in. (12.7 to 25.4 cm) long and up

Sapindus saponaria var. *drummondii* (western soapberry)

to 6 in. (15.2 cm) wide. Plants are dioecious; male flowers are larger and showier.

Fruit is round and fleshy. When immature it is translucent but it darkens to yellow. The fruit is persistent, often remaining on the plant for a year.

Western soapberry is not often seen in gardens, although it is used more widely within its natural range. It is a fine choice for deserts gardens, because it tolerates both the heat and alkaline soils as long as they are well drained

Water the plant in the hottest regions at least twice a month in the summer, and much less frequently in other parts of the region. This species also tolerates reflective heat, which makes it useful along hot walls or to cover exposed windows.

Sapindus saponaria ranges into South America as far as Argentina, but is restricted to the Gulf Coast states in the United States. The type has somewhat larger leaves that tend to be less acutely tipped and more often have an even number of leaflets that are somewhat larger than those of *S. saponaria* var. *drummondii*.

Western soapberry was used historically as soap, but care needs to be taken because it causes dermatitis in sensitive people. The interesting fruit, good blooming, fall color, and striking bark all add up to one of the best woody shrubs in the region.

Sebastiana bilocularis

Jumping bean, Mexican jumping bean

SYNONYM: *Sapium biloculare.*
FAMILY: Euphorbiaceae.
DISTRIBUTION: In the United States only in far southwestern Arizona. In Mexico in Baja California and Sonora at 800 to 2500 ft. (244 to 762 m).
MATURE SIZE: Rounded, multibranched shrub 6 to 12 ft. (1.8 to 3.7 m) tall and up to 10 ft. (3 m) wide.
BLOOMING PERIOD: March to November.
EXPOSURE: Full sun in all areas.
HARDINESS: Hardy to 25°F (−4°C).

Jumping bean is a modest-sized, rounded shrub with dense, flexible, smooth, tan to grayish branches. The sap of the shrub is toxic and will cause severe dermatitis and injury to eyes, nose, and mouth mucous membrane. As with all members of the family, even the smoke from burning the branches is toxic, so avoid inhaling it.

Sebastiana bilocularis (jumping bean)
Photo by Judy Mielke

The leaves are linear and are held in fascicles or whorls on the branches. Leaves have fine teeth along the edge. They are dark, glossy green and turn a deep, burnished red in the winter.

Plants are monoecious. The male flowers are minute and in spikes 0.5 to 1.5 in. (1.3 to 3.8 cm) long, with one or two female flowers at the base of the spike. Flowers are lightly fragrant. Flowering spikes elongate through the season, making a succession of bloom.

Fruit is a capsule that is often host to various moth larvae. These larvae eat out the seed and have the odd habit of jumping around in the pod, hence both the common name and the trait for which these plants are renowned. There are numerous species in this genus, all of which have this association and habit; the one of commerce is most often the fruit of *Sebastiana pavoniana*.

This plant is an unusual, arresting member of the huge family Euphorbiaceae. It ought to be used more than it is, but unfortunately it is not widely available, except at specialty nurseries or those growing a selection of native plants.

Jumping bean grows best in well-drained, fertile soils, but it does extremely well in the rocky, dry soils of the region. Although able to grow on natural rainfall even in the hottest deserts, plants are more vigorous and grow more quickly if given water once or twice a month in the summer.

Jumping bean is a fine choice for a hot wall or where there is reflective heat. It is nearly impossible for the temperature to be too hot for this species. Use it mixed with other desert shrubs or as a solitary specimen plant. I recall vividly coming back from Rocky Point,

Mexico, around Thanksgiving and seeing a hillside full of this species. You hardly notice it any other time, but when the dry hills are punctuated by these flaming red shrubs it is a magnificent site. It reminds me of the burning bush of the Bible.

Senna artemisioides
Feathery cassia

SYNONYM: *Cassia artemisioides.*
FAMILY: Fabaceae.
DISTRIBUTION: In Australia in the interior, arid portions of all states but Victoria.
MATURE SIZE: Round, full-branched shrub 3 to 5 ft. (0.9 to 1.5 m) tall and as wide.
BLOOMING PERIOD: January to April.
EXPOSURE: Full sun in all areas.
HARDINESS: Hardy from 28°F to 15°F (–2°C to –9°C), depending on the variety.

Feathery cassia is an intricately branched shrub that forms a tight ball of a plant. Plants are evergreen but in the hottest deserts they may lose over half their leaves during extended dry spells.

The leaves are coated with fine, gray hairs that give the plant a silvery sheen. Leaves are pinnately compound and formed of three to six pairs of leaflets that are up to 1 in. (2.5 cm) long and much narrower.

Flowers are held in dense, short inflorescences with three to eight flowers each. The flowers are 1 in. (2.5 cm) wide and have five open corolla lobes that are bright golden-yellow. They are prolific on the plant, often obscuring the foliage.

Flowers are followed by flat, greenish pods 2 to 3 in. (5.1 to 7.6 cm) long. Pods fade to a dark brown as they age and open long after they are mature.

Feathery cassia (*Senna artemisioides* subsp. *artemisioides*) grows in almost any well-drained, alkaline soil. It is important to provide good drainage; plants tend to be short lived and poor performers in soggy or wet conditions. Periodic deep waterings are best, but this species is capable of growing on natural rainfall in even the hottest deserts. It is the least cold hardy of the three subspecies described here.

In Australia the taxon is considered to have some 11 subspecies, leading to considerable confusion. Over its large range, many of these forms coexist and there are numerous hybrids and local endemic forms. In horticulture in the United States, the situation is not quite as muddled, but there may be considerable variation in plants, depending on the source of the seed for the plants offered.

Desert cassia (*Senna artemisioides* subsp. *filifolia*, formerly *Senna nemophila*) has one to four pairs of thin, needlelike, bright green leaves. It is the most cold hardy of the three described here. Like all of them, it is incredibly sturdy in the heat and is easy to use along a roadside, in areas with intermittent irrigation, or against walls with reflective heat. This bright, evergreen shrub is outstanding near patios or a pool where they can take the heat but appear cool.

The other subspecies, also called desert cassia (*Senna artemisioides* subsp. *petiolaris*, formerly *S. sturtii*), has leaves each with one to eight pairs of linear to elliptical leaflets. The gray-green leaflets are about 1 in. (2.5 cm) long and flat, compared to the two mentioned above. There are countless intermediary forms. This subspecies is hardy to 22°F (−6°C), and dies to the ground at 18°F (−8°C), but it recovers quickly.

Culture is much the same for all three varieties: excellent drainage but long intervals between deep waterings. All of these subspecies are more or less dormant in the summer, and in dry conditions they drop up to half their leaves. They recover well when given a deep soak or when it rains. So it is unwise to prune them in the summer. If pruning is required, do so in late winter or right after bloom is complete.

Feathery cassia is extremely well adapted to the deserts of Arizona, particularly around Phoenix, and lives on natural rainfall. It will reseed without the benefit of cultivation, so care should be taken not to use feathery cassia if your garden is adjacent to a park, natural areas, or a preserve.

Senna artemisioides (feathery cassia)

When I moved into my house, one of my neighbors was a renowned botanist who considered this plant beautiful, which it is. He had a few, and he gave them to all his neighbors, as we frequently do. They are now spread throughout our neighborhood and grow entirely on their own. They only behave themselves when they are not watered on purpose, but are excellent and free reseeders. I took out all the plants about 13 years ago and still find seedlings every spring. Be warned, and use this variety only in the dense urban core. The other two subspecies do not seem to reseed as aggressively.

Senna phyllodinea
Silverleaf cassia

FAMILY: Fabaceae.

DISTRIBUTION: In Australia through the arid portions of New Territory, South Australia, New South Wales, and Queensland.

MATURE SIZE: Open, rounded shrub 3 to 6 ft. (0.9 to 1.8 m) tall and as wide.

BLOOMING PERIOD: November to April.

EXPOSURE: Full sun in all areas.

HARDINESS: Hardy to 20°F (−7°C).

Silverleaf cassia is a fast-growing, openly branched, evergreen shrub.

The leaves are pinnately compound and composed of flat, sickle-shaped leaflets. These unusual, curving leaflets are about 1 in. (2.5 cm) long and help distinguish this species from the somewhat similar desert cassia, *Senna artemisioides* subsp. *petiolaris*, with which it is occasionally but erroneously considered synonymous.

Culture is the same as for the other Australian cassia: good drainage with intermittent deep soaks. Pruning is rarely required, but if necessary it should be done in the fall or directly after bloom.

As for all of the tribe, overwatering makes the plants chlorotic. Intense and prolonged drought may kill out portions of the plant, but this situation is easily corrected by clearing out the dead wood in the early fall but long before blooming.

The stunning silvery foliage make silverleaf cassia a good choice for a hedge or boundary planting, particularly in full-sun locations. It is useful in smaller gardens and is a good choice for a moonlit garden. It is heat tolerant enough to be useful around pools or other areas with high reflective heat. It does not reseed as aggressively as its close relative feathery cassia (*Senna artemisioides* subsp. *artemisioides*).

Senna phyllodinea (silverleaf cassia)

Senna purpusii
Baja senna

FAMILY: Fabaceae.
DISTRIBUTION: Found only in Baja California, Mexico.
MATURE SIZE: Dense, many-branched shrub
4 to 5 ft. (1.2 to 1.5 m) tall and as wide.
BLOOMING PERIOD: November to April.
EXPOSURE: Full sun in all areas, although
does well in filtered shade in the hottest
deserts.
HARDINESS: Hardy to 28°F (–2°C), severe
damage at 23°F (–5°C) but recovers quickly.

This unusual and exquisite senna grows as
a dense, rounded shrub with a complicated,
often intricate branching pattern. The bark is
dark gray or black and somewhat scaly.

Leaves are pinnately compound and 1 to 1.5
in. (2.5 to 3.8 cm) long. They are a dark dusky-
gray rimmed with purple. Leaves each have two
to four pairs of leaflets that are broadly oval.

Senna purpusii (Baja senna)

Flowers are held in a terminal panicle of
two to six flowers. The bright yellow flowers
are 0.5 to 1 in. (1.3 to 2.5 cm) wide and last
throughout the long blooming season. Fruit
is a round pod that is dark brown.

I have been a cheerleader for this excellent
senna for a long time, but for some reason it
has never quite caught on. It tolerates almost
any kind of well-drained soil, but does best in
slightly enriched, alkaline soils. In the hottest
deserts, it tolerates full or even reflected sun
but grows and blooms equally well in high,
filtered shade.

Water needs are modest. Weekly watering
in the summer keeps the plant in full leaf and
vigorous, but it can tolerate considerably less-
frequent watering.

Although cold-tender, older plants recover
quickly from the loss of as much as a third of
the plant.

The combination of the dusky-gray, purple-
tinged foliage and the brilliant yellow flowers
is exciting in any garden. Use Baja senna in
a mixed hedge or other mixed planting with
other desert shrubs or perennials. Give it a
prominent place to take advantage of its winter flowering that is both prolific and long
lasting.

Senna wizlizenii
Shrubby senna

FAMILY: Fabaceae.
DISTRIBUTION: In the United States from
southern Arizona and southern New
Mexico to far west Texas at 3000 to 4000 ft.
(914 to 1219 m). In Mexico in Sonora, Chihuahua, southwest Coahuila, and barely
in Nuevo León, southwest Tamaulipas,
Durango, northeast Zacatecas through San

Luis Potosí to northern Querétaro at 3000
to 7000 ft. (914 to 2134 m).

MATURE SIZE: Intricately branched shrub 4
to 8 ft. (1.2 to 2.4 m) tall and as wide.

BLOOMING PERIOD: June to October.

EXPOSURE: Full sun in all areas; tolerates
filtered shade in the hottest deserts.

HARDINESS: Hardy to 10°F (−12°C).

Shrubby senna is a gangly, much-branched
shrub whose dark branches are short, rigid,
and often thorny. Winter deciduous, it
may also drop its leaves during prolonged
drought. The bark is rough and dark brown
to nearly black. It is one of the latest of all
shrubs to leaf out in the spring.

The pinnately compound leaves are
arranged in spirals or fascicles around the
stem. They are composed of three to seven
pairs of elliptic leaflets and are 1 to 1.5 in. (2.5
to 3.8 cm) long. The leaflets are deep green,
thick, and firm but not succulent.

The bright yellow flowers are cup shaped
and are held in loose, terminal clusters up to
6 in. (15.2 cm) long. Individual flowers are 1
in. (2.5 cm) wide.

The pods are 6 in. (15.2 cm) long, flat, and
tend to hang from the branches. The dark
black to brown pods are only slightly constricted between the seeds and remain closed
on the plant.

Shrubby senna grows in most well-drained
soils, those that are somewhat acidic and
alkaline as well as moderately saline. It has
high heat tolerance and its great cold tolerance makes it useful over the entire region.

Even in the hottest deserts, watering needs
to be done at long intervals. Deep soaks once
a month are more than sufficient. This species is highly intolerant of wet soils or those
that drain poorly, but it is always best to allow
soils to dry out significantly between waterings. In areas like central Texas, where wet
soils in the summer are common in some
years, this species may be difficult to grow
well, owing to its strong intolerance of wet
soils.

Desert senna provides a beautiful contrast between the prolific, large flowers and
the small, dark green leaves and dark bark.
It provides a good deep green backdrop for
more colorful plantings and is heat tolerant enough to be useful against hot walls or

Senna wizlizenii (shrubby senna)

around a pool. Use desert senna in wild or naturalistic plantings or against reflected surfaces like walls, buildings, or pool fencing.

Velvet-leaf senna (*Senna lindheimeriana*) is a smaller shrub that grows 3 to 6 ft. (0.9 to 1.8 m) tall and up to 2 to 4 ft. (0.6 to 1.2 m) wide. It flowers from August to October, with a branched, flowering stalk that holds up to 25 light yellow flowers. The stems and pinnately compound leaves are 2.5 to 6 in. (6.4 to 15.2 cm) long and are covered with fine, dense hairs. Leaves have four to eight pairs of pinnae each, and the oval leaflets are dark green. Velvet-leaf senna is hardy to 20°F (–7°C) and grows well in any well-drained soil. Although this plant does well with monthly watering in the hottest deserts, it grows quickly and more vigorously with watering two or three times a month. In other areas, watering every three to four weeks is sufficient. Its late-season flowering extends the blooming season in a mixed planting. The plant is a good choice to blend with other desert shrubs of its size.

Twin-flowered senna (*Senna pallida*, syn. *Cassia biflora*) is another less common member of this exuberant, flowering genus. It is native to Sonora, Baja California, and parts of Chihuahua south into South America and the West Indies, and is hardy to 20°F (–7°C). Twin-flowered senna is an open branched shrub or small tree 10 to 15 ft. (3 to 4.6 m) tall and 8 to 10 ft. (2.4 to 3 m) wide that is evergreen or occasionally deciduous. The pinnately compound leaves hold 4 to 10 pairs of deep green, narrow leaflets that are up to 0.75 in. (2 cm) long with a rounded or blunt tip. While the bright yellow flowers are only 0.5 in. (1.5 cm) wide, they bloom in pairs throughout the summer and are prolific on the plant. This charming summer-blooming shrub offers a light, airy look around seating areas or patios. It is heat tolerant enough to work well around pools or other areas of intense heat. Its smaller stature makes it an ideal choice for summer color in a smaller garden, either singly or in groups for an enhanced effect.

Simmondsia chinensis
Jojoba

FAMILY: Buxaceae.

DISTRIBUTION: In the United States from the arid portions of southern California, east into central and southern Arizona from 1500 to 5000 ft. (457 to 1524 m). In Mexico in Sonora and Baja California at similar elevations.

MATURE SIZE: Dense shrub 6 to 8 ft. (1.8 to 2.4 m) tall and as wide.

BLOOMING PERIOD: April to June.

EXPOSURE: Full sun in all areas.

HARDINESS: Hardy to 20°F (–7°C).

Jojoba is a rounded, evergreen shrub with rigid branches that rebranch freely. The dark gray bark is usually obscured by the branches.

The opposite leaves are dark blue-green, elliptic, end in a sharp tip, and are 1 to 2 in. (2.5 to 5.1 cm) long. They are thick and leathery with smooth margins. They often close in toward the stem during extreme heat or drought.

Plants are dioecious. Both staminate and pistillate flowers are small, creamy white, and innocuous. They are followed on the female plants by a large, brown, hard nut that is less than 1 in. (2.5 cm) long and holds the small seed.

Simmondsia chinensis (jojoba)

This seed has been a source of food for Native Americans. It also made a grim coffee substitute for Anglo settlers and in more recent times has enjoyed minor commercial value as a liquid wax.

Jojoba grows well on any well-drained, alkaline soil, even rocky, unamended ones. It is sensitive to overwatering or being grown in a spot with poor drainage; then it will become soft and floppy, chlorotic, and have a short life.

Watering, even in the hottest deserts, is best when provided as deep soaks every three to four weeks in the summer, although plants will survive on much less water. Young plants may be watered more often to encourage faster growth, but in that case the drainage must be excellent.

This evergreen shrub has an attractive, tight, natural form. Pruning, if needed at all, should be done in the early spring when plants are just starting to grow, but must never be done in the summer. I have seen jojoba sheared or made into topiary: they take it well but it ruins their wonderful character.

Use as a background plant, in areas that are not regularly irrigated, to hide or screen unsightly areas, or to define a space. It makes an excellent hedge by itself or mixed with other desert woody plants.

Jojoba resembles mangle dulce (*Maytenus phyllanthoides*) but is easily distinguished by its opposite, bluish-gray leaves with a sharp tip. The hard, brown nut of this species also distinguishes it from mangle dulce, which has bright red fruit in season.

Sophora arizonica
Arizona sophora

SYNONYM: *Sophora formosa.*

FAMILY: Fabaceae.

DISTRIBUTION: In the United States known mainly in western Arizona especially south of Kingman and in a disjunct range in far southeastern Arizona, as well as in scattered and isolated populations in southern New Mexico and far west Texas at 2000 to 4000 ft. (610 to 1219 m).

MATURE SIZE: Dense shrub 3 to 10 ft. (0.9 to 3 m) tall and as wide.

BLOOMING PERIOD: March.

EXPOSURE: Full sun in all areas.

HARDINESS: Hardy to at least 15°F (−9°C), but hardiness is not well documented.

Arizona sophora is a heavily branched, evergreen shrub of the western deserts of Arizona. Leaves are pinnately compound, with broad, rounded leaflets less than 0.5 in. (1.5 cm) wide. There are five to ten leaflets per leaf that are coated with fine hairs, giving them a gray-green or silvery-white cast.

Flowers are held in loose panicles with each about 1 in. (2.5 cm) long. They are pealike and light lavender to dark purple. Flowers are followed by flat pods that contain a few bright red seeds.

Arizona sophora is a highly heat-tolerant species and may be used with success in dry, rocky, alkaline soils. It grows best in full sun,

even in the hottest deserts. But I have known plants to grow well in high, filtered shade although they don't bloom as prolifically.

Although drought tolerant, the plant is more vigorous when watered monthly in the hottest deserts. Good drainage is essential, especially when watering more frequently. The plant's roots easily rot when overwatered or when growing in a spot with poor drainage.

Arizona sophora is good choice for a small garden or near a seating area or patio. Its immense heat tolerance makes it a good choice near a pool or other areas of high, reflective heat. Use it to form a hedge either

Sophora arizonica (Arizona sophora)
Photo by Elaine Wilson

by itself or mixed with similarly sized shrubs. It also serves as a good focal plant or accent plant.

Sophora secundiflora
Texas mountain laurel, mescal bean

FAMILY: Fabaceae.

DISTRIBUTION: In the United states from far southern New Mexico into west and central Texas through the Edwards Plateau below 5000 ft. (1524 m). In Mexico from eastern Chihuahua to Coahuila, Nuevo León, south to Zacatecas, San Luis Potosí, Tamaulipas, Querétaro, Hidalgo, and Puebla above 4200 ft. (1280 m).

MATURE SIZE: Upright shrub 8 to 15 ft. (2.4 to 4.6 m) tall and up to 6 to 10 ft. (1.8 to 3 m) wide.

BLOOMING PERIOD: March.

EXPOSURE: Full sun or filtered shade in all areas.

HARDINESS: Hardy to 15°F (−9°C) and possibly lower.

Texas mountain laurel is a densely branched, round, evergreen shrub with dark gray to black bark. As the bark ages it forms shallow fissures, ridges, and scales.

The alternate leaves are 4 to 6 in. (10.2 to 15.2 cm) long and pinnately compound with seven to nine leaflets per leaf. The thick leaflets are glossy, dark green, elliptic with rounded tips, and are 1 to 2 in. (2.5 to 5.1 cm) long. Some forms have fine hairs, giving the leaves a gray color; in the trade they often go by the name 'Silver Peso'.

The flowers are held in congested, hanging clusters 3 to 7 in. (7.6 to 17.8 cm) long. They are lavender to purple and have a strong, grape soda smell. Most people find the scent appealing; it is strong enough to be detected long before you see the plant.

Flowers are followed by pods that are fat, gray, felty, and 1 to 7 in. (2.5 to 17.8 cm) long; they hold shiny, red seeds. Pods do not open on the plant and are so tough they are a chore to open. The pod is deeply constricted between the seeds. Seeds are poisonous if eaten but are often made into jewelry, particularly in Mexico.

The plant is plagued by the tenting larvae of the genista moth. This can be an annoying cosmetic problem even in young plants. The

Sophora secundiflora (Texas mountain laurel)

best remedies are to prune the tip or pull the insects off to get the numbers down.

Texas mountain laurel grows well in dry, alkaline soils. But it grows more quickly and vigorously in moderately enriched, deep soils with excellent drainage. It may develop chlorosis in response to overwatering or poorly drained soils.

Renowned as a slow-growing species, it is mainly slow to start. It may take two to three years for a plant to begin to grow significantly after planting, but after that the growth rate increases.

Texas mountain laurel makes a fine, large, evergreen hedge. It is also a great addition to a mixed planting of large shrubs. Its immense heat tolerance makes it useful around pools or other areas of high, reflective heat. If you miss wisteria or find it hard to grow, this plant is a good substitute although it doesn't bloom as long.

Tabebuia chrysantha

Yellow amapa, golden trumpet tree

FAMILY: Bignoniaceae.

DISTRIBUTION: In Mexico from central and southeastern Sonora and Chihuahua south into northern South America.

MATURE SIZE: Tree 30 to 50 ft. (9.1 to 15.2 m) tall with a crown spread of about 30 ft. (9.1 m). In the tropical parts of its natural range, it grows up to 100 ft. (30 m) tall.

BLOOMING PERIOD: February and March.

EXPOSURE: Full sun in all areas.

HARDINESS: Hardy only to about 28°F (−2°C), particularly when young.

Yellow amapa is an upright tree with a rounded crown and dark brown to light gray, rough, flaking bark. Plants are cool-season deciduous. Flowers occur before the leaves emerge.

The soft, olive-green leaves are palmately compound, covered with fine hairs, and are 4 to 7 in. (10.2 to 17.8 cm) long. Leaflets are ovate to obovate and 0.5 to 1 in. (1.5 to 2.5 cm) long.

Flowers are up to 2.5 to 3 in. (6.4 to 7.6 cm) wide and bright yellow. Flowers are held in crowded clusters at the ends of the branches. In nature and in tropical zones, there are two blooming cycles, but in this region that is rarely the case. Flowers have a long, deep tube with a wide, flaring mouth. The ends of the corolla lobes are flattened. The lobes are free at the ends and are papery thin and ruffled along the edges, but because of the size of the tree you may not see these features clearly. Dark pink to purple nectar guides mark the throat. Flowers are held in large clusters and appear to smother the entire barren tree

Tabebuia chrysantha (yellow amapa)

when in full bloom. Fruit is a long, pendulous pod that is velvety green when young but eventually turns yellow to tan.

Yellow amapa grows best in deep, moderately fertile soils. Although drought resistant, the plant grows better when given supplemental water every week or two in the summer in the hottest deserts. This species is highly tolerant of the heat of the hottest deserts, and may be planted in areas that receive full and even reflected sun.

The bloom is stunning, so place the tree where you can see the late winter or early spring flowering. Plants bloom even when they are small.

Tabebuia impetiginosa
Pink amapa

FAMILY: Bignoniaceae.

DISTRIBUTION: In Mexico in eastern and southern Sonora and Chihuahua from sea level to 3500 ft. (1067 m), and continuing south into Central America and northern Argentina.

MATURE SIZE: Spreading tree from 15 to 60 ft. (4.6 to 18 m) tall, although in our region rarely over 30 ft. (9.1 m) tall, and spreads about half as wide.

BLOOMING PERIOD: January to March.

EXPOSURE: Full sun in all areas.

HARDINESS: Hardy to about 25°F (−4°C), although individuals have survived 18°F (−8°C) with minimal damage.

Pink amapa is a wide-spreading, deciduous tree. The bark is dark brown to gray and smooth. Leaves are palmately compound with five leaflets. Leaflets are elliptic to ovate, smooth, and dark green with small serrations along the margin. The leaflets are 4.5 to 8 in. (11.4 to 20.3 cm) long.

Flowers are held in large, showy clusters at the tips of the branches. Each flower has a long, spreading tube and the corolla lobes flare at the ends. They range in color from deep pink to light lavender and are 2.5 to 3.25 in. (6.4 to 8.3 cm) long. When you view the flowers up close, you can see that the tube is lined with bright yellow and the edges of the lobes are ruffled.

Tabebuia impetiginosa (pink amapa)

The fruit is a thin pod 1 to 1.5 in. (2.5 to 3.8 cm) long.

Pink amapa grows best in deep, moderately fertile soils but tolerates xeric soils better than yellow amapa (*Tabebouia chrysantha*) does.

Water every two to three weeks in the summer in the hottest deserts, and less often in the winter when the plant is leafless.

Plants are deciduous. The flowers emerge before the new leaves. This species is routinely reported to take a few years to begin blooming but it is well worth the wait. It is spectacular when planted as a focal or accent plant or where its astounding bloom may be fully enjoyed. It mixes well with other drought-tolerant trees in a large garden, and provides an unexpected pop of color during its bloom.

Tecoma capensis
Cape honeysuckle

SYNONYM: *Tecomaria capensis.*
FAMILY: Bignoniaceae.
DISTRIBUTION: Widely distributed in South Africa and Mozambique.
MATURE SIZE: Rounded shrub 5 to 8 ft. (1.5 to 2.4 m) tall, occasionally up to 12 ft. (3.7 m) tall, and as wide.
BLOOMING PERIOD: Intermittent throughout the year but heaviest from March to June and October to December.
EXPOSURE: Full sun in all areas; also appreciates filtered shade in the hottest deserts.
HARDINESS: Hardy to 28°F (–2°C); serious damage at 23°F (–5°C) but recovers quickly.

Cape honeysuckle is a rapidly growing shrub that is occasionally regarded as a shrubby vine. It is more or less evergreen although late

cold snaps may turn the leaves black. The pale tan bark is completely concealed by the dense branching and lush leaves.

The leaves are opposite, pinnately compound, and are up to 6 in. (15.2 cm) long with 5 to 11 leaflets. The leaflets are ovate to oblong, 0.5 to 1.5 in. (1.5 to 3.8 cm) long, and glossy deep green, and are strongly serrate.

The thin, tubular, bright orange flowers are 2 in. (5.1 cm) long. A variety with flowers of a paler color called 'Aurea' is available from time to time.

Cape honeysuckle grows best in deep, moderately fertile soil that is well drained. It also tolerates either acidic or alkaline soils and some salt spray. This species is an old standby in older neighborhoods of the region, particularly in the Phoenix area. Some of these plants are now quite large and make a brilliant show when in bloom.

Cape honeysuckle needs weekly irrigation in the summer in the hottest deserts, and regular water for most of the year. It is more drought tolerant where temperatures are cooler or rainfall is more reliable than is usually the case in the hottest deserts.

There is no heat too strong for this lovely member of the wide-ranging genus. Use it to soften a hot or heat-reflecting wall, to provide a deep green look around pools or seating areas, as a background shrub for more colorful plantings, and for its lovely orange flowers throughout the late spring and summer. Hummingbirds feast on the flowers.

When left entirely unpruned, it grows more like a vine than a shrub, with branches reaching over 30 ft. (9.1 m) long. Much like bougainvillea, it may need support to grow as a vine. You also might want to allow it to just cascade and fill up a large spot. Cape honey-

Tecoma capensis (Cape honeysuckle)

suckle roots along the ground so it is a good erosion-control species for some areas.

This plant has escaped cultivation and has naturalized in parts of central Florida and Hawaii, but it does not appear to have naturalized within this region. Prune in the spring to keep it tidy or to maintain a specific size or shape.

Another orange-flowered member of the genus, Argentine tecoma (*Tecoma garrocha*), is offered from time to time. It is an upright, dense shrub 6 to 10 ft. (1.8 to 3 m) tall and 5 to 6 ft. (1.5 to 1.8 m) wide. The light green, pinnately compound leaves are made up of 7 to 11 leaflets that are 0.5 to 2 in. (1.5 to 5.1 cm) long.

Argentine tecoma is hardy to 20°F (–7°C) and is root hardy to even lower temperatures. The tubular flowers occur from March to August in shades from salmon to orange-red and are held in terminal racemes that are 6 in. (15.2 cm) long. Argentine tecoma grows best in well-drained, moderately fertile soils with weekly watering in the summer, particularly in the hottest deserts. This plant can be easily confused with both *Tecoma alata* and *T.* 'Orange Jubilee', but this species is a small, open-branched shrub rather than the large, woody shrub to tree of the other two, and has smaller leaves with fewer leaflets.

Tecoma 'Orange Jubilee'
Orange jubilee

FAMILY: Bignoniaceae.
DISTRIBUTION: A hybrid of *Tecoma alata* and *Tecoma stans*.
MATURE SIZE: Multistemmed shrub 6 to 12 ft. (1.8 to 3.7 m) tall and 4 to 6 ft. (1.2 to 1.8 m) wide.
BLOOMING PERIOD: March to November.
EXPOSURE: Full sun in all areas.
HARDINESS: Hardy to 10°F (−12°C), and even when frozen to the ground recovers quickly.

Tecoma 'Orange Jubilee' is a hybrid, made by Dr. Ying Doon Moy working with the San Antonio Botanic Garden, between yellowbells (*Tecoma stans*) and its Argentine relative *T. alata*. It is an exuberant shrub that grows fast and quickly makes a good screening plant.

The long stems are thin and begin tan but age to light brown. Older stems often die out after a few years, and may be pruned away in the summer to allow newer ones to grow.

The flowers are held in clusters near the tips of the branches. Individual flowers are narrowly tubular and end in a strongly recurved tip; they are 3 to 4 in. (7.6 to 10.2 cm) long. There is some variation in flower color but all are mainly orange. In some the orange is mainly on the back of the lobes and the tip is yellow, whereas in others the lobes are entirely orange. Fruit is a tan pod that is typical of the genus.

This hybrid was also backcrossed with yellowbells to create another selection, 'Burnt Out', which has deeper orange flowers and a more compact, shrubby habit.

Tecoma 'Orange Jubilee'

In much of the region, plants sold as 'Orange Jubilee' are actually *Tecoma alata*. While the differences are fine, *T. alata* has shorter leaves, 1 in. (2.5 cm) long versus 2 in. (5.1 cm) long for 'Orange Jubilee'. In addition, the flowers of *T. alata* are a slender tube that is inflated only at the tip, while those of 'Orange Jubilee' are inflated for their entire length. *Tecoma alata* is a narrow, long-limbed shrub with a vertical habit, while 'Orange Jubilee' is a compact, shrubby plant. Both are outstanding plants for summer color in a hot spot.

Tecoma stans

Yellowbells, esperanza

FAMILY: Bignoniaceae.

DISTRIBUTION: In the United States from southern Arizona, southern New Mexico, and south Texas, and a disjunct population in southern Florida. Throughout Mexico into Central America and the Caribbean, and south to Argentina at 2000 to 5000 ft. (610 to 1524 m).

MATURE SIZE: Lanky shrub to small tree 6 to 15 ft. (1.8 to 4.6 m) tall and usually about half as wide.

BLOOMING PERIOD: March to October.

EXPOSURE: Full sun in all areas.

HARDINESS: Root hardy to 25°F (−4°C).

Yellowbells is a loose-branched shrub or small tree with dark brownish bark that becomes dark brown and fissured as it ages. Plants are deciduous or semideciduous and often lose their leaves only when new leaves emerge in the spring.

The leaves are 4 to 8 in. (10.2 to 20.3 cm) long, opposite, pinnately compound, and

Tecoma stans (yellowbells)

made up to 5 to 13 leaflets. Leaflets are linear to lanceolate and come to a sharp tip. Leaflets are light green to olive-green and serrate.

Flowers are showy, bright yellow and held in terminal clusters that are 3 to 5 in. (7.6 to 12.7 cm) long and comprised of 3 to 17 individuals. Each flower is 1 to 2 in. (2.5 to 5.1 cm) long with a wide, tubular corolla that strongly flares at the end.

The fruit is a long capsule that looks more like a pod and is 4 to 8 in. (10.2 to 20.3 cm) long. The empty pod remains on the tree for a long time after it has opened and released the winged seed.

There are two distinct forms of *Tecoma stans*. The one formerly known as var. *angustata* (a varietal name that is no longer recognized) has slender stems and thin, deeply serrate, light green leaves. Its flowers are on the small end of the range. The other, formerly called var. *stans*, is a large, treelike form that grows up to 20 ft. (6.1 m) tall, with larger flowers and large, darker green leaves.

Yellowbells grows in a wide array of soils, from rocky, dry alkaline soils to deeper, more enriched ones. In all cases, it is best to provide good drainage.

Water requirements vary widely depending on the temperatures and soils. Yellowbells is highly drought tolerant and survives on minimal watering throughout the area. But in the hottest deserts, it retains better form and bloom when watered two or three times a month in the summer.

There is no heat that is too much for this species. It is excellent against a hot wall or window, to shade the western edge of a seating area, or around the cool deck of a pool.

Many selections and hybrids are offered in the region at this time. 'Gold Star' is a selection from Texas horticulturist Greg Grant. It is extremely heat tolerant, highly floriferous, and blooms much earlier than most other yellowbells. *Tecoma* ×*smithii* is a hybrid between *Tecoma mollis* and cape honeysuckle (*Tecoma capensis*) with 8-in. (20.3-cm) sprays of 2-in. (5.1-cm) flowers that are yellow tinged with orange. It is not often seen in the region and is probably more than worth a try.

Thevetia peruviana
Lucky nut

FAMILY: Apocynaceae.

DISTRIBUTION: Throughout central and southern Mexico south to Central America, the Caribbean, and most of tropical South America. Widely cultivated, and perhaps naturalized, in southern Africa and often erroneously described as native there.

MATURE SIZE: Large shrub or small tree 10 to 20 ft. (3 to 6.1 m) tall and 6 to 12 ft. (1.8 to 3.7 m) wide.

BLOOMING PERIOD: April to October.

EXPOSURE: Full sun or filtered shade in all areas.

HARDINESS: Fully hardy to 28°F (–2°C), and while damaged at 23°F (–5°C), recovers quickly.

Lucky nut is an evergreen shrub that is frequently pruned into a single or multi-trunked small tree. The bark is a light tan and when older turns dark brown and slightly furrowed.

The alternate, narrow leaves are 4 to 6 in. (10.2 to 15.2 cm) long. They are glossy green with smooth margins and prominent veins that give them a dimpled look.

The flowers are more or less triangular with

a tubular corolla that is twisted at the end so it resembles an origami pinwheel. Flowers are 2 in. (5.1 cm) long and held in loose, terminal clusters. Flowers are slightly fragrant, and blooming is both prolific and lengthy. Flowers are bright, clear yellow; there are light peach-colored selections as well as pure white ones.

The fruit, which is the source of the common name, is a green, triangular pod 1 in. (2.5 cm) long. It looks like a bishop's miter and begins bright green but fades to dull yellow.

The sap of lucky nut is poisonous if ingested and care must be taken to protect your eyes and other sensitive areas when pruning the tree. Lucky nut is tolerant of a wide range of soils but grows best in well-drained, lightly enriched ones. It often becomes chlorotic on rocky sites or areas with poor drainage.

Thevetia peruviana (lucky nut)

Lucky nut is highly heat tolerant and is able to be grown well in the hottest deserts in locations that have strong or reflective heat. The long, graceful leaves provide a soft look around pools or seating areas. The summer color is most welcome as well.

I have grown the white-flowering form of lucky nut for a long time. I find it the most lovely of the group, but I am partial to white-blooming plants in the summer. My tree took a big hit in the January 2007 freeze, which in my yard was around 23°F (−5°C), setting it back by about a third. But recovery has been swift and by the end of the summer no damage was obvious.

Water weekly in the hottest deserts and less often in areas with regular summer rainfall or when temperatures moderate.

The closely related giant thevetia (*Thevetia thevetioides*) is a larger species with similar leaves that are 2.5 to 5 in. (6.4 to 12.7 cm) long with a wavy margin. The flowers are up to 4 in. (10.2 cm) long and held in spectacular terminal clusters. This species is more tender than lucky nut, but if damaged it recovers quickly. It is from Mexico from Michoacán to Tamaulipas, Vera Cruz, and Oaxaca and south into Central America.

Trachycarpus fortunei
Windmill palm

FAMILY: Arecaceae.

DISTRIBUTION: Temperate and subtropical mountainous areas of southeastern China, Taiwan, and the Zhoushan Islands.

MATURE SIZE: Solitary palm 10 to 40 ft. (3 to 12.2 m) tall; in the deserts it is rarely over 25 ft. (7.6 m) tall.

BLOOMING PERIOD: Summer.

EXPOSURE: Full sun or filtered shade in the hottest deserts; full sun in all other areas.
HARDINESS: Hardy to 12°F (–11°C).

Windmill palm is a slow-growing solitary palm with its slender stem covered by dark brown, coarse fibers that age to gray. The fibers arise in the leaf scars and are thick and unruly.

The leaves are palmately compound on a thin, flat petiole that is 2 to 3 ft. (0.6 to 0.9 m) long. The leaves are 2 to 3 ft. (0.6 to 0.9 m) wide and nearly round, with from 30 to 36 segments split about half way up their length.

Trachycarpus fortunei (windmill palm)

There are up to 30 leaves on each plant, which form a highly symmetrical, rounded crown. The rigid leaves are deep green above and grayish below.

Plants are dioecious. Both male and female inflorescences are densely packed and nearly concealed by the huge hood of the woody bract before they are released as branched stalks. The flowering stalk is 1.5 to 2.5 ft. (0.5 to 0.8 m) long with yellow flowers. Flowers are followed by glossy, blue fruit that is 0.5 in. (1.3 cm) long.

This slow-growing species is more adaptable to desert conditions than its origins might suggest. It has moderate salt tolerance and will grow in almost any well-drained soils, but does best in deep, enriched soils that are well drained.

The plant is moderately drought tolerant, especially once established, and needs to be watered once or twice a month in the summer in the hottest deserts. It is moderately susceptible to chlorosis and lethal yellowing in the hottest areas, but this is not a severe problem for this species.

Ungnadia speciosa
Mexican buckeye

FAMILY: Sapindaceae.
DISTRIBUTION: In the United States from southern New Mexico into the Trans-Pecos and the Edwards Plateau of Texas at 1000 to 6000 ft. (305 to 1829 m), and in the southern coastal plains of Texas. In Mexico in northeastern Chihuahua through central Coahuila down to Nuevo León and Tamaulipas at 4500 to 6600 ft. (1372 to 2012 m).
MATURE SIZE: Shrub 8 to 12 ft. (2.4 to 3.7 m) tall and 5 to 6 ft. (1.5 to 1.8 m) wide.

BLOOMING PERIOD: March to April.

EXPOSURE: Full sun or filtered shade in all areas.

HARDINESS: Hardy to at least 5°F (–15°C), possibly lower.

Mexican buckeye is a tidy, densely branched, deciduous shrub. Plants have thin, brown bark that is smooth when young but ages to gray with ridges and shallow furrows.

The alternate leaves are pinnately compound with five to seven leaflets and an overall length of up to 12 in. (30.5 cm). The oval leaflets are 3 to 5 in. (7.6 to 12.7 cm) long, are shiny, dark green above and paler beneath, and turn yellow in the fall.

The numerous flowers are 0.5 in. (1.3 cm) long. They emerge in the spring before the leaves and range from pale pastel pink to deep rose-red. They are followed by a three-lobed, woody capsule that is up to 2 in. (5.1 cm) wide with glossy black seeds. The seeds are toxic if eaten.

Mexican buckeye is widely adapted to a range of well-drained soils including dry, rocky ones and highly alkaline ones. It grows faster, however, in deeper, more fertile soils.

Water Mexican buckeye once a month in the summer in the hottest deserts, but much less frequently in the other areas. In most of Texas, it grows entirely on natural rainfall.

I have known this species for a long time. It grew untended behind the fence of my parents' house in Austin, Texas. It was always gorgeous, full of pink flowers and lush, deep green leaves in the spring, punctuated by the fanciful seedpods, then bright yellow in the fall. I grew plants from that tree for a while at the Desert Botanical Garden, and some individuals on the grounds came from that plant.

Ungnadia speciosa (Mexican buckeye)

It grows there on extremely rocky sites and is a short shrub, but in less rugged conditions it is larger, even in the deserts.

Mexican buckeye is resistant to cotton root rot. Plants in the western part of the range are often smaller in stature and they have smaller leaves. Plants from these populations also tend to have darker flowers.

Vallesia laciniata
Vallesia

SYNONYM: *Vallesia baileyana*.

FAMILY: Apocynaceae.

DISTRIBUTION: In Mexico in western and central Sonora from sea level to 425 ft. (0 to 130 m), and in Baja California Sur.

MATURE SIZE: Upright shrub or small tree 8 to 12 ft. (2.4 to 3.7 m) tall and 5 to 7 ft. (1.5 to 2.1 m) wide.

BLOOMING PERIOD: March to May.

EXPOSURE: Full sun in all areas; and in filtered shade in the hottest deserts.

HARDINESS: Hardy to 24°F (−4°C) with
minor damage.

Vallesia is a thick, upright, tightly branched,
evergreen shrub. It is highly symmetrical,
nearly oval, when mature.

The deep yellow-green, glossy leaves are
oblong to lanceolate and 2 to 4.5 in. (5.1 to
11.4 cm) long. They are alternate and leathery
with smooth, entire margins.

The white flowers are 0.5 in. (1.25 cm) wide.
They are held in terminal clusters that are 1 to
1.5 in. (2.5 to 3.8 cm) wide and are comprised
of 10 to 25 flowers. Individual flowers are star
shaped and exude a heady fragrance much
like jasmine or gardenia. The fruit is a white,
translucent berry that remains on the plant
for months.

Vallesia is a sadly underused, extremely
durable, evergreen shrub for parts of the
region that do not have regular, hard freezes.
The dark green foliage and upright, full habit
make it a terrific choice as a hedge, to fill in
a hot, dry corner, or to go against a wall. The
fragrant flowers are splendid: plant it where
the fragrance may be fully enjoyed. Plants
bloom heavily in the spring, and rebloom
repeatedly over the summer in response to
rain or deep irrigation.

Vallesia grows moderately fast and is tolerant of any well-drained soil. Established
plants show great drought tolerance. But in
the hottest deserts in the summer, water it
once or twice a month to keep it tidy and
vigorous.

The similar *Vallesia glabra* has a much
larger range in Mexico, occurring as far south
as Argentina and in the Caribbean. Although
the two species look similar, the flowers are
less than 0.25 in. (0.6 cm) wide in this species.
It flowers over the winter as opposed to the
spring blooming of *Vallesia laciniata*.

Vallesia laciniata (vallesia)

Vauquelinia californica
Arizona rosewood

FAMILY: Rosaceae.

DISTRIBUTION: In the United States from
southern Arizona to southwestern New
Mexico at 2500 to 5000 ft. (762 to 1524 m).
In Mexico in central and southern Baja
California, Sonora, Chihuahua, central
Coahuila, and eastern Durango at 4500 to
7500 ft. (1372 to 2286 m).

MATURE SIZE: Large shrub 6 to 15 ft. (1.8 to
4.6 m) tall and as wide.

BLOOMING PERIOD: June to August.
EXPOSURE: Full sun in all areas.
HARDINESS: Hardy to 15°F (−9°C).

Arizona rosewood is a densely branched, evergreen shrub or small tree. Young stems have a sparse or dense coating of fine hairs and become smooth with age.

The leaves are lanceolate to linear, 1.5 to 3 in. (3.8 to 7.6 cm) long, and about 0.5 in. (1.3 cm) wide. They are a deep green, firm, and have fine teeth along the edges. Leaves are markedly bicolored: the upper leaf is deep green and the underside is pale gray.

The tiny, white flowers are held in dense, congested, rounded heads at the ends of the branches. The blooming heads are 4 to 6 in. (10.2 to 15.2 cm) wide. Flowers have a slight musklike fragrance.

The fruit is an oval capsule that becomes woody and is surrounded by the old bracts. The fruit, including the dry, brown bracts, remains on the plant for months.

Arizona rosewood is an attractive, symmetrical, evergreen shrub. It is tolerant of a wide range of alkaline soils as long as they are well drained. In deeper or richer soils, it grows faster but thrives in rocky, dry soils as well.

This species is a highly drought tolerant. Outside the hottest deserts it lives on natural rainfall. In the hottest deserts, water once a

Vauquelinia californica (Arizona rosewood)

month in summer to keep the plants fit and healthy. Young plants may be watered more often to bring them up to size quickly.

Arizona rosewood, with its dense, evergreen form, is one of the best choices in the hottest deserts for an evergreen shrub that can serve as a screen or hedge. It may be mixed with other shrubs to complement its deep green color and finer leaves, or used as a striking specimen plant.

Vauquelinia corymbosa

Chisos rosewood, slim-leaf vauquelinia

FAMILY: Rosaceae.

DISTRIBUTION: In the United States in far west Texas at approximately 6500 ft. (1981 m). In Mexico in eastern Chihuahua, south central Coahuila, Nuevo León, Tamaulipas, and San Luis Potosí at 3500 to 5000 ft. (1067 to 1524 m).

MATURE SIZE: Large shrub or small tree 9 to 15 ft. (2.7 to 4.6 m) tall and as wide.

BLOOMING PERIOD: May to August.

EXPOSURE: Full sun in all areas.

HARDINESS: Hardy to at least 10°F (−12°C).

Chisos rosewood is a large, multibranched shrub or small tree. The bark is reddish brown and is largely obscured by the dense foliage.

The leaves are 1.5 to 4 in. (3.8 to 10.2 cm) long and less than 0.5 in. (1.3 cm) wide. They are deep green on the top, and grayish-white on the underside. Leaves are stiff and leathery with fine teeth along the margin. They are often drooping or cascading from a long petiole.

The tiny white flowers are held in flattened, terminal heads 4 to 6 in. (10.2 to 15.2 cm) wide. The flowers have a light, musklike fragrance. Flowers are followed by small, tan, woody capsules that remain on the plants for months.

Vaquelinia corymbosa subsp. *angustifolia*, often offered as *Vauquelinia angustifolia*, is similar but the leaves are upright rather than hanging down and extremely thin, 2.5 to 5 in. (6.4 to 12.7 cm) long, and 0.25 to 0.5 in. (0.6 to 1.3 cm) wide. The blooming heads are also smaller, 3 to 4 in. (7.6 to 10.2 cm) wide.

Chisos rosewood is tolerant of almost any well-drained soils and is one of the best choices for sites with dry, rocky soils. Water once a month in the summer in the hottest deserts, although the plant can to grow on less water.

This species is an excellent choice where a

Vauquelinia corymbosa (Chisos rosewood)

large screening plant is useful. Chisos rosewood makes a fine, evergreen hedge either alone or mixed with other large shrubs. The lovely blooming heads make it an excellent choice as a focal or accent plant in gardens with enough room for this shrub.

Vitex agnus-castus
Chaste tree, monk's chaste tree

FAMILY: Verbenaceae.

DISTRIBUTION: Southern Europe and western Asia; naturalized in the southern United States as well as in northeast and central Texas.

MATURE SIZE: Wide, spreading tree 10 to 25 ft. (3 to 7.6 m) tall and spreading as wide.

BLOOMING PERIOD: May to September.

EXPOSURE: Full sun in all areas.

HARDINESS: Hardy to 0°F (−18°C).

Chaste tree is a deciduous tree that grows to a low-spreading form. The bark is rough, fissured, and gray.

The leaves are palmately compound with five to seven leaflets that are 1.5 to 5 in. (3.8 to 12.7 cm) long; the middle leaflet is largest at 3 to 4 in. (7.6 to 10.2 cm) in length. They are dusky dark green above and grayish to white below. The leaflets are lanceolate and come to sharp point at the tip. They are strongly aromatic, with a pungent, sharp aroma. In some parts of the world the leaves have culinary use.

Flowers are held in dense, terminal spikes that are 4 to 12 in. (10.2 to 30.5 cm) tall, rising well above the foliage. Flower color ranges from pale pastel blue to a deep blue that is almost purple. There are also pink- and white-flowering forms as well as selections with larger flowers.

The fruit is brown to black and is small and round. The fruits are long persistent on the tree and are used for both culinary and medicinal purposes.

Chaste tree grows best in deep, moderately fertile, alkaline soils. Water two or three times a month in the summer in the hottest deserts to keep plants fit and vigorous. In milder and wetter areas, plants grow on natural rainfall. In fact under these conditions it may become naturalized.

This plant is a good choice for shade in smaller gardens or patios. The blue-flowered examples are the most striking to me; the ones with pink and white flowers tend to fade and look insipid, although a bright, pure white-flowering selection would be a good find. There is great variation in the intensity

Vitex agnus-castus (chaste tree)

of the flower color, so choose one when it is blooming.

This species has been cultivated for centuries and enjoys great popularity as an ornamental all over the world. In the region, especially the hottest deserts, it is a good choice as a small tree or for added spring color.

The name var. *latifolia* has no botanical standing but is often used for a shorter form with broader leaves and larger inflorescence. It is widely regarded as a vigorous grower that is more cold hardy than the type.

There are also a number of named selections, not all of which are commonly sold in the region but are available in other areas or by mail order. These include 'Colonial Blue', which has tiny, fragrant, blue flowers appearing in loose panicles to 12 in. (30.5 cm) long; 'LeCompte', a dense, fully flowered form that is purple; 'Montrose Purple', which has flowers with a vibrant, deep color; 'Salinas Pink', with flowering spikes 8 to 12 inches (20.3 to 30.5 cm) long; 'Shoal Creek', a vase-shaped, deciduous shrub to 15 ft. (4.6 m) tall with fragrant, lilac flowers; and 'Silver Spire', which is white flowered.

Vitex rotundifolia
Beach vitex

SYNONYM: *Vitex ovata* and *V. trifolia* var. *simplicifolia*.
FAMILY: Verbenaceae.
DISTRIBUTION: In Australia in Queensland and New Territory, and also in Southeast Asia, and in Hawaii and other Pacific islands.
MATURE SIZE: Low or upright shrub 3 to 4 ft. (0.9 to 1.2 m) tall and 6 to 8 ft. (1.8 to 2.4 m) wide.
BLOOMING PERIOD: May to July.
EXPOSURE: Full sun or filtered shade in the hottest deserts; full sun in other areas.
HARDINESS: Hardy to at least to 23°F (–5°C) and probably lower.

Beach vitex is a deciduous shrub that grows low, crawling along the ground, or upright and intricately branched. It is particularly prone to low growth in the face of strong and consistent wind or salt spray. But in inland conditions, it is more often a short, upright shrub.

The leaves are ovate to entirely round and up to 1.5 in. (3.8 cm) long. They are gray or dusky green on the upper side with silvery gray hairs on the underside. The leaves have a spicy, eucalyptuslike fragrance and turn a burnished copper-red in the fall.

The flowers are held in racemes 1 to 2 in. (2.5 to 5.1 cm) long above the leaves. The flowers range from sky blue to darker blue and also white. The fruits are small, round, and are held on the spent spikes for months. The red-tinged husk of the fruit eventually splits open, revealing the black seeds within.

The shrub is invasive along the beaches of North and South Carolina. Serious efforts are under way to eradicate it from these areas. It is better behaved in the arid parts of the country.

In this region, beach vitex grows in both rocky and more enriched soils, but drainage is crucial. As might be expected, it also grows well in sandy soils or near salt spray, although its invasive properties must be kept in mind in those situations. It grows in any well-drained soils including alkaline ones. Water beach vitex every two to three weeks in the summer in the hottest deserts. It

Vitex rotundifolia (beach vitex)

thrives on natural rainfall in milder, wetter regions.

Beach vitex is a charming, small shrub that blends well with mixed beds of perennials, bulbs, or other smaller shrubs. It is also useful for creating a low hedge when planted generously, and it makes a good choice for a hot, dry corner of the garden.

Vitex trifolia
Simple-leaf chaste tree

FAMILY: Verbenaceae.

DISTRIBUTION: In Australia in coastal areas of Queensland, northern New South Wales, and New Territory, and in eastern India, and in many Pacific islands but not Hawaii.

MATURE SIZE: Upright, densely branched 10 to 20 ft. (3 to 6.1 m) tall and spreading 10 to 15 ft. (3 to 4.6 m) wide.

BLOOMING PERIOD: April to June.

EXPOSURE: Full sun or filtered shade in the hottest deserts; full sun elsewhere.

HARDINESS: Hardy to at least 23°F (–5°C).

This plant is a moderate-sized, dense, deciduous shrub. The bark is dark gray when mature and is rough and flaky.

The leaves are opposite and palmately compound with one to three leaflets that are up to 3 in. (7.6 cm) long. The leaflets are elliptical or lanceolate with a sharp tip.

The flowers are blue to purple in long terminal clusters that are 6 to 9 in. (15.2 to 22.9 cm) long. They are followed by rounded fruit that is barely noticeable.

Simple-leaf chaste tree grows well in either full sun or filtered shade in the hottest deserts. It produces voluminous numbers of tiny secondary branches, especially in the early spring. Although a tedious chore, it is best to remove these during the late winter while the plant is dormant to clean up the stems and accentuate its interesting form.

Simple-leaf chaste tree grows in any well-drained soil, but does not do well on dry, rocky sites. Water this excellent vitex species weekly in the summer in the hottest deserts but much less frequently in all other areas.

There are two variegated forms of this species. One has white slashes throughout the leaves and short flowering stalks of sky blue flowers. I have grown this selection for a long time and find it a wonderful choice for filtered shade. The white accents are soothing in darker areas of the garden, and it doesn't seem to mind the ever-increasing shade of the large South American mesquite nearby. The other variegated form has dusky gray leaves tinged with purple on the upper side and darker purple underneath. Like the white variegated form, it maintains this stunning leaf color best in filtered shade.

Slender-leaf chaste tree is a fine moderate-sized shrub either alone or blended with other species. It is also a good choice for smaller gardens as a background planting or as a focal point.

Washingtonia filifera
California fan palm

FAMILY: Arecaceae.

DISTRIBUTION: In the United States in isolated locales in southern California, particularly in the Coachella Valley and its environs, and in Arizona in localized populations in western and south-central parts of the state. In Mexico in Baja California.

MATURE SIZE: Solitary palm 40 to 60 ft. (12.2 to 18 m) tall.

BLOOMING PERIOD: August to September.

EXPOSURE: Full sun in all areas.

HARDINESS: Hardy to 18°F (−8°C), severe damage at 12°F (−11°C).

California fan palm is a large, solitary palm that retains the spent leaves for many years before finally shedding them. Some individuals, if left unpruned, never shed the spent leaves and the result is a skirt of the long,

Vitex trifolia (simple-leaf chaste tree)

fibrous leaves. The stem is thick, and where there are no leaf bases it is clean, dark gray to brown, with light rings.

The fan-shaped leaves are palmately compound and nearly round. They are 6 to 8 ft. (1.8 to 2.4 m) long and up to 6 ft. (1.8 m) wide on a petiole of the same length. The petiole has sharp, hooked teeth. Each leaf is split for about 2 ft. (0.6 m) of the length, creating about 70 segments, each graced with thin filaments. Leaves are light green with a slight grayish cast.

The flowers are perfect, minute, and numerous on a flowering stalk 8 to 10 ft. (2.4 to 3 m) long. The flowering stalks reach far beyond the leaves, beginning parallel with the ground and then hanging straight down. Flowers are followed by clusters of black, round fruit.

This species has moderately deep roots, particularly in fine, sandy soils, which are common were it occurs in nature. In other soils, it is not so deep rooted.

California fan palm is one of the most commonly grown ornamental palms in the world. It graces the streets of almost all major cities in warm, dry regions. It is the most common palm in southern California and Arizona in both residential and public plantings.

California fan palm grows in almost any well-drained soil. Although in nature it grows in the seeps and standing water adjacent to fault lines, in cultivation it needs watering only every one to three weeks in the summer in the hottest deserts.

California fan palm is tolerant of almost any level of heat, but the leaves turn yellow when subjected simultaneously to extreme heat and water stress. It is important to plant or transplant palms when soils are warm, even hot. The roots are sensitive to temperature and virtually cease functioning when soil temperatures are 65°F (18°C) or less.

Native American people ate the berries, buds, and heart of this palm and considered it a reliable indicator of the presence of water, which is true in the arid regions where it is native.

Some groves in the region are ancient and appear to have been planted, probably before the Spanish conquest. Others may have occurred naturally, probably by birds spreading the seeds. There are reports of groves in far southern Nevada that may or may not

Washingtonia filifera (California fan palm)

be part of the natural range. It is difficult to establish the exact extent of this species' natural range before the intervention of preconquest people and postconquest settlers.

A young plant is difficult to distinguish from its near relative, Mexican fan palm (*Washingtonia robusta*). A mature California fan palm has a sturdier, thicker trunk, a big, rounded head, and duskier gray leaves. They have both been grown together for so long that there is a vast amount of integration, and hybrids between the two species have resulted in countless individuals used throughout the region that have characteristics halfway between the two.

Most plants grown ornamentally begin to self-prune after the trunk is about 15 ft. (4.6 m) tall. This puzzling characteristic is rarely the case in natural populations, where the gorgeous skirts hang fully to the ground.

Although this palm is large for most small urban lots, California fan palm is lovely when planted in larger gardens or where you can establish a grove. One of the most beautiful planting schemes is to put them downslope, so you can look directly into the thick head of leaves.

Washingtonia robusta
Mexican fan palm, skyduster

FAMILY: Arecaceae.

DISTRIBUTION: In Mexico in canyons and dry waterways of central and southern Baja California and southern Sonora at 100 to 450 ft. (30 to 137 m).

MATURE SIZE: Solitary palm 40 to 100 ft. (12.2 to 30 m) tall.

BLOOMING PERIOD: Summer.

EXPOSURE: Full sun in all areas.

HARDINESS: Hardy to 20°F (–7°C).

Mexican fan palm is widely cultivated in the warm parts of the world, and is a common ornamental in Arizona and southern California. The palm has a solitary, slender trunk that leans and twists with age. This palm sheds its dead leaves quickly, leaving prominent boots only at the base of the head. The trunk is clean, dark gray, and lightly ringed from the leaf scars.

The leaves are palmately compound, 6 to 7 ft. (1.8 to 2.1 m) long, up to 6 ft. (1.8 m) wide, and are more or less circular. There are 50 to 70 segments in the leaf, each of which is split for up to 3 ft. (0.9 m) of the length. The bright green, glossy leaves are rimmed with fine, white filaments. The petiole is 3 to 4 ft. (0.9 to 1.2 m) long and tinged with orange.

The branched flowering stalk is 8 to 12 ft. (2.4 to 3.7 m) long. Flowers are creamy white to pale yellow and are followed by huge amounts of black, round seeds.

Like its close relative California fan palm (*Washingtonia filifera*), Mexican fan palm is a fast-growing palm that is immune to heat. It has moderate salt tolerance, a bit less than California fan palm, but otherwise grows in any well-drained soils as well as in rocky, dry soils.

This species has great drought tolerance once established. It grows on nearly natural rainfall in the hottest deserts. It is best to water once or twice a month in the summer, to keep the plants vigorous and growing well. Like most palms, but especially the desert species, roots are virtually dormant when soil temperatures are 65°F (18°C) or lower, so plant or transplant them when soils are warm or hot.

The fanciful name skyduster describes these tall plants well. In some parts of southern California, you can still see lines of these tall palms indicating the roads and accessways of previous groves and farm areas. Now old, they tower up to 100 ft. (30 m) tall and create a memorable outline on the horizon. Old plants often sway and bend slightly, giving them even more character.

This species and the closely related California fan palm have both been in horticulture a long time and hybrids are common. Pure strains of this species are distinguished from California fan palm by the slender, often bending trunk and the dark green, glossy leaves that are held in a tight, rough crown.

Less cold hardy than California fan palm, Mexican fan palm is most useful in areas with warm, nearly frost-free, winters. Tall and slender, this palm is appropriate for the outer edges of a large garden or along a street. It makes light shade when planted in a grove or groups. Like many tall palms, if there is sufficient relief at the garden, plant it downhill so that you can enjoy viewing the vivid green heads.

Washingtonia robusta (Mexican fan palm)

Zizyphus obtusifolia
Graythorn

FAMILY: Rhamnaceae.

DISTRIBUTION: In the United States in the deserts of southern California, southern Nevada, far southwestern Utah, central and southern Arizona, into southern New Mexico at 3500 to 5000 ft. (1067 to 1524 m), and in far west, south, and central Texas and Oklahoma at 1000 to 5500 ft. (305 to 1676 m). In Mexico in Baja California and Sonora southeast to Tamaulipas, northern Vera Cruz, and Puebla to 5000 ft. (1524 m).

MATURE SIZE: Dense shrub 6 to 10 ft. (1.8 to 3 m) tall and as wide.

BLOOMING PERIOD: March to September.

EXPOSURE: Full sun in all areas.

HARDINESS: Hardy to 15°F (−9°C).

Graythorn is a deciduous shrub with intricate branching. Young stems are coated with fine hairs, giving the gray-green stems a white to silver cast. These hairs turn waxy as the plant ages but keep their soft color. The branches end in sharp thorns and are lined with long spurs that are thorny as well. These features make the plant look like a puzzle of thorny branches grasping each other in a tight, upright form.

The leaves are narrowly elliptical, oblong, to ovate, and are up to 1 in. (2.5 cm) long. Various populations show a lot of variation in the size, shape, and color of the leaves. They range from grayish-green to yellow-green.

Most blades tend to be cupped, and all are ephemeral, falling quickly when the weather warms in spring.

The flowers are minute and held in short, congested umbels that are 0.5 to 1 in. (1.25 to 2.5 cm) wide and comprised of up to six flowers. They are creamy white to yellowish. While not showy, they are prolific on the plant.

Fruit is a dark black drupe. It is completely beloved by birds, which feast on it. A plant can be stripped of fruit in a day if there are enough thrashers, wrens, and mockingbirds in the vicinity.

Zizyphus obtusifolia (graythorn)

A rugged shrub for dry areas, graythorn grows well on natural rainfall even in the hottest deserts. It is tolerant of any well-drained soil, even rocky, alkaline ones. If you wish to water it, do so only monthly in the summer.

Birds favor this plant over all you will put in your garden. Besides loving the fruit, they like the complex, intricate branches for their nests. The shrub is a beast to prune, so put it where you may leave it undisturbed and appreciate its intricate natural form. My own plant was in my garden when we moved in and is too close to a well-used path. So unfortunately, I have to prune it regularly. Pruning this species requires being covered in leather up to your eyeballs, and even then blood will be spilled. It is best pruned in the late summer to remove dead or unruly branches.

Graythorn makes a nearly impenetrable hedge, and is useful as boundary plant or as part of a hedge along the edge of the garden. It is heat- and drought-tolerant enough to be placed where watering is intermittent or irregular. It is an excellent choice for a wildlife or native garden. Its gray, jungle-gym look is intriguing from a distance.

Bibliography

References

Arizona Municipal Water Users Association (AMWUA). 2001. *Landscape Watering by the Numbers: A Guide for the Arizona Desert*. Phoenix: AMWUA.

Benson, Lyman, and Robert A. Darrow. 1981. *Trees and Shrubs of the Southwestern Deserts*. Tucson: University of Arizona Press.

Blombery, Alec, and Tony Rodd. 1982. *Palms*. Sydney, Australia: Angus & Robertson Publishers.

Bornstein, Carol, David Fross, and Bart O'Brien. 2005. *California Native Plants for the Garden*. Los Olivos, California: Cachuma Press.

Busco, Janice, and Nancy R. Morin. 2003. *Native Plants for High-Elevation Western Gardens*. Golden, Colorado: Fulcrum Publishing.

Carter, Jack L. 1997. *Trees and Shrubs of New Mexico*. Silver City, New Mexico: Mimbres Publishing.

Correll, Donovan Stewart, and Marshall Conring Johnston. 1979. *Manual of the Vascular Plants of Texas*. Richardson: University of Texas at Dallas.

Cox, Paul W., and Patty Leslie. 1988. *Texas Trees: A Friendly Guide*. San Antonio, Texas: Corona Publishing.

Duffield, Mary Rose, and Warren Jones. 2001. *Plants for Dry Climates: How to Select, Grow and Enjoy*. Cambridge, Massachusetts: Perseus Publishing.

Ellison, Don, and Anthony Ellison. 2001. *Betrock's Cultivated Palms of the World*. Hollywood, Florida: Betrock Information Systems.

Everitt, James H., D. Lynn Draw, and Robert I. Lonard. 2002. *Trees, Shrubs and Cacti of South Texas*. Lubbock: Texas Tech University Press.

Felger, Richard Stephen. 2000. *Flora of the Gran Desierto and Rio Colorado of Northwestern Mexico*. Tucson: University of Arizona Press.

Felger, Richard Stephen, Matthew Brian Johnson, and Michael Francis Wilson. 2001. *The Trees of Sonora, Mexico*. New York: Oxford University Press.

Fleming, Gary. 1975. *A Guide to Plants of Central Texas with Edible, Medicinal and Ecological Value* (unpublished manuscript).

Haislet, John A., ed. 1970. *Famous Trees of Texas*. College Station: Texas Forest Service.

Haislet, John A., ed. 1971. *Forest Trees of Texas: How to Know Them.* 8th ed. College Station: Texas Forest Service.

Henderson, Andrew, Gloria Galeano, and Rodrigo Bernal. 1995. *Field Guide to the Palms of the Americas.* Princeton, New Jersey: Princeton University Press.

Henrickson, James, and Marshall C. Johnston. 1997. "Flora of the Chihuahuan Desert" (unpublished manuscript).

Hickman, James C., ed. 1993. *The Jepson Manual: Higher Plants of California.* Berkeley: University of California Press.

Johnson, Eric A., David Harbison, and Dennis C. Mahr. 2001. *Lush and Efficient: Gardening in the Coachella Valley.* Coachella, California: Coachella Valley Water District.

Johnson, Matthew B., and Kenneth Coppola. 2007. The January 2007 freeze: Effects of cold on plants in DELEP's fields. *Aridus* 19: 1, 1–7.

Jones, Fred B. 1975. *Flora of the Texas Coastal Bend.* Sinton, Texas: Rob and Bessie Welder Wildlife Foundation.

Jones, Warren, and Charles Sacamano. 2000. *Landscape Plants for Dry Regions.* Tucson, Arizona: Fisher Books.

Kearney, Thomas H., and Robert H. Peebles 1960. *Arizona Flora.* Berkeley: University of California Press.

Lamb, Samuel H. 1971. *Woody Plants of New Mexico and Their Value to Wildlife.* Bulletin 14, New Mexico Department of Game and Fish.

Lau, Carol P. Y., Lawrence Ramsden, and Richard M. K. Saunders. 2005. Hybrid origin of *Bauhinia blakeana* inferred using morphological, reproductive and molecu- lar data. *American Journal of Botany* 92: 525–533.

Lenz, Lee W., and John Dourley. 1981. *California Native Trees and Shrubs.* Claremont, California: Rancho Santa Ana Botanic Garden.

Lonard, Robert I., James H. Everitt, and Frank W. Judd. 1991. *Woody Plants of the Lower Rio Grande Valley, Texas.* Miscel- laneous Publication of the Texas Memorial Museum, No. 7. Austin: University of Texas Press.

Lord, Ernest E. 1970. *Shrubs and Trees for Australian Gardens.* Sydney, Australia: Lothian Publishing.

Lynch, Brother Daniel. 1981. *Native and Naturalized Woody Plants of Austin and the Hill Country.* Austin, Texas: Acorn Press.

McCurrach, James C. 1960. *Palms of the World.* New York: Harper & Brothers.

Meerow, Alan W. 2005. *Betrock's Cold Hardy Palms.* Hollywood, Florida: Betrock's Information Systems.

Mielke, Judy. 1993. *Native Plants for South- western Landscapes.* Austin: University of Texas Press.

Miller, George O. 1991. *Landscaping with Native Plants of Texas and the Southwest.* Stillwater, Minnesota: Voyageur Press.

Mills, Linn, and Dick Post. 2005. *Nevada Gardener's Guide.* Nashville, Tennessee: Cool Springs Press.

Morrow, Baker H. 1994. *Best Plants for New Mexico Gardens and Landscapes.* Albu- querque: University of New Mexico Press.

Munz, Philip, and David D. Keck. 1968. *A California Flora.* Berkeley: University of California Press.

Nelson, Kim. 2001. *A Desert Gardener's*

Companion. Tucson, Arizona: Rio Nuevo
Press.

Nokes, Jill. 2001. *How to Grow Native Plants
of Texas and the Southwest.* Austin: University of Texas Press.

Oakman, Harry. 1979. *Garden and Landscape
Trees in Australia.* Sydney, Australia: Rigby.

Osborne, Barry, Trish Reynoso, and Geoff
Stein, compilers. 2000. *Palms for Southern
California: A Quick Reference Guide to
Palms.* Thousand Oaks: Palm Society of
Southern California.

Padilla, Victoria. 1961. *Southern California
Gardens: An Illustrated History.* Santa
Barbara, California: Allen A. Knoll.

Palgrave, Keith Coates. 1977. *Trees of
Southern Africa.* Johannesburgh, South
Africa: C. Struik Publishers.

Peattie, Donald Culross. 1953. *A Natural
History of Western Trees.* New York:
Bonanza Books.

Perry, Bob. 1989. *Trees and Shrubs for
Dry California Landscapes.* Claremont,
California: Land Design Publishing.

Perry, Bob. 1992. *Landscape Plants for
Western Regions: An Illustrated Guide to
Plants for Water Conservation.* Claremont,
California: Land Design Publishing.

Phillips, Judith. 1995. *Natural by Design:
Beauty and Balance in Southwest Gardens.*
Santa Fe: Museum of New Mexico Press.

Phillips, Judith. 1995. *Plants for Natural
Gardens: Southwestern Native and Adaptive Trees, Shrubs, Wildflowers and Grasses.*
Santa Fe: Museum of New Mexico Press.

Phillips, Judith. 2005. *New Mexico Gardener's
Guide.* Nashville, Tennessee: Cool Springs
Press.

Powell, A. Michael. 1988. *Trees and Shrubs

of Trans-Pecos Texas.* Big Bend National
Park, Texas: Big Bend Natural History
Association.

Preston, Richard J. 1961. *North American
Trees.* Ames: Iowa State University Press.

Shreve, Forrest, and Ira L. Wiggins. 1964.
Vegetation and Flora of the Sonoran Desert.
Stanford, California: Stanford University
Press.

Simpson, Benny J. 1988. *A Field Guide
to Texas Trees.* Houston, Texas: Gulf
Publishing Company.

Stevenson, George B. 1974. *Palms of South
Florida.* Miami, Florida: International
Palm Society.

Taylor, Richard B., Jimmy Rutledge, and Joe
G. Herrera. 1999. *A Field Guide to Common
South Texas Shrubs.* Austin: Texas Parks
and Wildlife Press.

Turner, B. L. 1959. *The Legumes of Texas.*
Austin: University of Texas Press.

Turner, Raymond M., Janice E. Bowers, and
Tony L. Burgess. 1995. *Sonoran Desert
Plants: An Ecological Atlas.* Tucson:
University of Arizona Press.

Vines, Robert A. 1984. *Trees of Central Texas.*
Austin: University of Texas Press.

Waldon, H. B. 1998. Sonoran desert rhizobia
found to nodulate *Acacia constricta. Desert
Plants* 8 (3): 106–110.

Walters, James E., and Balbir Backhaus. 1992.
*Shade and Color with Water-Conserving
Plants.* Portland, Oregon: Timber Press.

Wasowski, Sally. 1985. *Landscaping with Native
Texas Plants.* Austin: Texas Monthly Press.

Wasowski, Sally, with Andy Wasowski. 1988.
*Native Texas Plants: Landscaping Region
by Region.* Austin: Texas Monthly Press.

Waterfall, Patricia H. 2004. *Harvesting

Rainwater for Landscape Use. Tucson: University of Arizona Cooperative Extension Service.

Wrigley, John W., and Murray Fagg. 1996. *Australian Native Plants.* Australia: Reed Books.

Electronic Sources

While there are countless sites and resources on the Internet, it is daunting to try to find ones that are reliable and useful. These sites are but a few of those I consulted, but I found all useful and reliable. These sites also have numerous links that provide a wider reach.

http://aggie-horticulture.tamu.edu. Principal site for ornamental agriculture from the Texas A&M University Extension Service and its associated research site.

http://www.anbg.gov.au/index.html. Australian Government's Department of the Environment and Water Resources site that serves as a clearinghouse site for numerous databases about Australian native plants and its associated site for Western Australia http://florabase.calm.wa.gov.au.

http://www.calflora.net/botanicalnames/index2.html. A portal to a host of useful sites on California native plants, including the Jepson Herbarium at the University of California at Berkeley and the California Native Plant Society.

http://www.desertmuseum.org. Site for the Arizona Sonora Desert Museum in Tucson, Arizona, and an excellent resource for selected Sonoran Desert species and related research.

http://www.desert-tropicals.com. Covering much more than tropical plants, a good general resource for plants for the Phoenix area.

http://www.efloras.org. A collection of floras, including many from Asia and the flora of North America.

http://www.floridata.com. An online plant encyclopedia site useful as a reference for a wide array of plants.

http://www.ildis.org. International Legume Database and Information Services site with reports, links, and database on the taxonomy, uses, and distribution of the legume family.

http://www.kew.org/epic. Site from Royal Botanic Garden at Kew that is attempting to document the plants of the world, particularly useful for European and some African species.

http://wc.pima.edu/~bfiero/tucsonecology. Useful site for plants in and around Tucson, Arizona.

http://plants.usda.gov. The principal plant-related site of the United States Department of Agriculture; reflects the work of the Biota of North America project in its taxonomy and distributions.

http://www.plantzafrica.com. Useful site for information and links for plants of southern Africa.

http://wildflower.utexas.edu. Site of the Lady Bird Johnson Wildflower Research Center; an excellent resource for many species, particularly those native to Texas.

Index

Bold-faced numbers indicate main entry pages. *Italic* numbers indicate photo pages.